Terrorism and
the Constitution

Terrorism and the Constitution

The Post-9/11 Cases

H. L. Pohlman

ROWMAN & LITTLEFIELD PUBLISHERS, INC.
Lanham • Boulder • New York • Toronto • Plymouth, UK

ROWMAN & LITTLEFIELD PUBLISHERS, INC.

Published in the United States of America
by Rowman & Littlefield Publishers, Inc.
A wholly owned subsidiary of The Rowman & Littlefield Publishing Group, Inc.
4501 Forbes Boulevard, Suite 200, Lanham, Maryland 20706
www.rowmanlittlefield.com

Estover Road
Plymouth PL6 7PY
United Kingdom

British Library Cataloguing in Publication Information Available

Library of Congress Cataloging-in-Publication Data:

Pohlman, H. L., 1952–
   Terrorism and the constitution : the post-9/11 cases / H.L. Pohlman.
     p. cm.
   Includes index.
   ISBN-13: 978-0-7425-6040-6 (cloth : alk. paper)
   ISBN-10: 0-7425-6040-6 (cloth : alk. paper)
   ISBN-13: 978-0-7425-6041-3 (pbk. : alk. paper)
   ISBN-10: 0-7425-6041-4 (pbk. : alk. paper)
    1. War on Terrorism, 2001—Law and legislation—United States. 2. Civil rights—
United States. 3. Terrorism—United States—Prevention. 4. Intelligence service—Law
and legislation—United States. 5. Detention of persons—United States. 6. Combatants
and noncombatants—Legal status, laws, etc.—United States. 7. Terrorists—Legal
status, laws, etc.—United States. 8. Military courts—United States. 9. Internal
security—United States. I. Title.
   KF9430.P64 2008
   345.73'02—dc22   2007023943

Printed in the United States of America

⊗™ The paper used in this publication meets the minimum requirements of American
National Standard for Information Sciences—Permanence of Paper for Printed Library
Materials, ANSI/NISO Z39.48-1992.

Contents

Introduction

The war on terrorism is arguably unlike any other war in American history. It is a real war, unlike the rhetorical wars on poverty and drugs, but it is being waged against a nonstate actor and an ideology, not a political nation or a state. The enemy is al Qaeda, all related terrorist groups, independent and quasi-independent *jihadist* cells that have arisen in western countries, and the ideas and values that have inspired all these groups.[1] The weapons of choice of this new enemy are those of mass destruction (WMD) and their targets are often innocent civilians. This conjunction of Islamic fundamentalism, WMD, and terrorism has set the stage for a new form of warfare and ushered in a period of national reflection and debate about the proper balance between national security and the rights of the individual. As of today, more than five years after the September 11, 2001, attacks that triggered the war, the outcome of this debate is still uncertain, but there is little doubt that the war on terrorism has marked an important turning point in the history of American constitutional law. Many important constitutional questions involving civil liberties in the war on terrorism remain unanswered, but several major cases have been decided. Some of these cases appear to expand presidential power and contract individual rights, while others are ambiguous or ambivalent in their meaning and significance. In the middle of this transition period, the situation is confused and uncertain, but the stakes for the future of the American constitutional system are enormous.

This book contributes to the ongoing national debate on civil liberties during the war on terrorism by providing easy access to relevant documents from major post-9/11 cases. The book's goal is to give students an opportunity to consider two fundamental questions (and other issues related to these two). First, is the war on terrorism a type of war that requires a shift in the balance between national security and individual rights? If so, what is that new balance? Should traditional civil liberties be narrowed because al Qaeda's tactics rely on surprise, stealth, and deception, or should traditional civil liberties remain unaffected by the war since it is impossible for al Qaeda to defeat the United States militarily? Second, following the 9/11 attacks, are the three branches of the federal government functioning properly? What is the proper role of the president, the Congress, and the federal judiciary during this new kind of war? Should the courts defer to the political branches as the judiciary did in conventional wars of the past or does the war on terrorism demand a different orientation, perhaps because the war on terrorism has no definite military front or end point? Is the system of checks and balances broken or is it possible that the system is obsolete in a world in which suicidal terrorists are actively seeking access to weapons of mass destruction?

By providing access to materials from major post-9/11 cases, this book encourages a vigorous examination of these contentious issues from an adversarial perspective. Each of the five chapters examines one major post-9/11 case and begins with a brief description of the political context of the litigation. Crucial documents relevant to the case are set in boxes. Excerpts from the legal briefs filed in the case are included in each chapter, as well as excerpts from the transcript of the case's oral argument, with additional commentary interwoven between the excerpts. The adversarial character of the briefs and the oral argument contribute to a thoroughgoing review of what both sides of the litigation thought were the best arguments for their conflicting positions. Each chapter also includes excerpts from the court's decision, including any dissents. Most of the chapters have a postscript that discusses what has transpired since the court handed down its decision. The book is therefore a roadmap of the major constitutional cases involving the war on terrorism that have occurred over the last five years. It will provoke discussion concerning where we should go in the future, but, like a roadmap, not itself point in any particular direction.

The format of the book necessitated limiting it to five chapters. Three of the five slots were relatively easy to fill because the Supreme Court has addressed three specific questions arising out of the war on terrorism: first, *Hamdi v. Rumsfeld* (2004) and *Padilla v. Bush* (2004) raised the question whether President Bush had the legal authority to detain American citizens as enemy combatants during the war on terrorism and what procedures had to be followed to determine whether a particular citizen was an enemy combatant; second, in *Rasul v. Bush* (2004) the Court considered whether the federal courts had jurisdiction to entertain petitions for writs of habeas corpus from foreign detainees held at Guantanamo Bay Naval Base (GBNB); and, third, in *Hamdan v. Rumsfeld* (2006) the Court reviewed whether President Bush had the legal authority to establish military commissions to try enemy combatants for war crimes and whether the procedures he established for such commissions violated the rights of the defendants. Obviously, the issues that are the focus of these four Supreme Court decisions are directly related to the fundamental questions this book is intended to explore.

The decision as to the other two slots was more difficult. Since 9/11, the lower federal judiciary has considered numerous issues regarding civil liberties and the war on terrorism. Most, if not all, of these cases deserve consideration, but choices had to be made. The Foreign Intelligence Surveillance Court of Review's decision in *In re Sealed Case* (2002) was selected as the topic of chapter 1. This case addressed the issue of whether surveillance under the Foreign Intelligence Surveillance Act (FISA) was consistent with the Fourth Amendment if the "primary" purpose of the surveillance was law enforcement or if law enforcement personnel directed and controlled the surveillance. The question is an important one because it is generally easier for law enforcement personnel to obtain authorization for surveillance under FISA than under the rules controlling surveillance for criminal law enforcement purposes. Also, it is unlikely that the Supreme Court will review this question for many years, leaving the FISA Court of Review's decision in force. The federal government would have to prosecute a criminal defendant with evidence obtained directly or indirectly under a FISA order and the defendant would have to establish that the "primary purpose" of the surveillance had been for law enforcement purposes. The defendant would then have to raise objections to the admissibility of such evidence at the trial and appeal the decision to the Court of Appeals before the issue could ever reach the Supreme Court. Accordingly, any possibility that the Supreme Court will overrule *In re Sealed Case* is years in the future, by which time the American legal system might become so habituated to the result in *In re Sealed Case* that it would be a constitutional fait accompli.

The fifth post-9/11 case that will be considered is the 4th Circuit's decision in *United States v. Moussaoui* (2004). The question considered in this litigation concerns the Sixth Amendment and the Due Process Clause: if the defendant is given the option of reading to the jury relevant excerpts from the summaries of the interrogations of al Qaeda detainees who could provide exculpatory evidence on his behalf, can the government refuse to provide direct or indirect access to the al Qaeda detainees, yet at the same time prosecute him and seek the death penalty? Although this case is complicated by the fact that Moussaoui eventually pleaded guilty and implicated himself under oath in the 9/11 attacks, the underlying question has lost none of its significance. Can the government execute a convicted terrorist if he has not been given the opportunity to call witnesses who have relevant and admissible testimony? The Sixth Amendment gives ordinary defendants the right to use compulsory judicial process to compel the attendance of witnesses and the Fifth Amendment permits the federal government to deprive a person of life, liberty, or property only if it is done in accordance with due process. The 4th Circuit's *Moussaoui* decision permitting such a prosecution to go forward is likely to be the controlling precedent in any future civilian prosecution of a terrorist of Moussaoui's stature simply because it is unlikely that the government will prosecute such a person in a civilian court outside the 4th Circuit. Lastly, the civilian prosecution of Moussaoui would provide a good basis for comparison regarding the procedures of the military commissions considered in chapter 5. The two chapters together will pose the important question as to whether high profile terrorists are better tried in civilian courts or military commissions.

The specific issues raised in these post-9/11 cases are the basis for evaluating the proper balance between national security and individual rights during the war on terrorism and the respective roles of the three branches of the federal government. Regarding the first question, there are a number of underlying assumptions that will strongly influence how the balance is struck. On one side of the spectrum, some commentators deny that the war on terrorism is a real war because it is not a conflict between states. Of course, if there is no war, then the federal government cannot rely on its war power to justify intrusions into civil liberties. Congress can authorize the use of military force, as it did in response to the 9/11 attacks on September 14, 2001,[2] and the president can act on that authorization, as President Bush did by invading Afghanistan, destroying the Taliban regime, and dispersing al Qaeda, but such a military action can constitute a war only if it is directed against a state. Although the Taliban perhaps could have been characterized in late 2001 as the government of Afghanistan, al Qaeda is not now and never has been a state. Accordingly, using force against this terrorist group cannot qualify as a war and therefore the federal government's war power cannot justify any limitation on traditional American civil liberties. The government's only recourse is to proceed against members of al Qaeda and other related groups as common criminals. This view of the proper balance between national security and individual rights during the war on terrorism can be referred to as the "criminal process model." According to it, no sacrifice of civil liberties during the war on terrorism is necessary or justified.

A slightly different assumption is that, even if a state of war exists, that fact should have no effect on civil liberties. The Constitution is one and the same, whether the country is at war or not. Justice David Davis articulated this point of view in a famous passage from his majority opinion in *Ex Parte Milligan* (1866), a Supreme Court decision holding that military trials of civilians were unconstitutional during wartime if civilian courts were open and functioning. In support of this conclusion, Davis wrote the following:

The Constitution of the United States is a law for rulers and people, equally in war and in peace, and covers with the shield of its protection all classes of men, at all times, and under all circumstances. No doctrine, involving more pernicious consequences, was ever invented by the wit of man than that any of its provisions can be suspended during any of the great exigencies of government. Such a doctrine leads directly to anarchy or despotism, but the theory of necessity on which it is based is false; for the government, within the Constitution, has all the powers granted to it, which are necessary to preserve its existence; as has been happily proved by the result of the great effort to throw off its just authority.[3]

According to Davis, the federal government had all the authority it needed to overcome any wartime exigency without invading constitutional rights and liberties. Davis's opinion in *Milligan* has been praised as a "landmark decision" in the defense of "individual rights" as well as attacked as overly rigid and inflexible.[4] It is a model of civil liberties during wartime that refuses to engage in any balancing. Accordingly, for all intents and purposes, it is equivalent in substance to the criminal process model.

A different approach denies that the conflict with terrorism is a war, but endorses a "constitutional state of emergency" as the proper response to the 9/11 attacks. The meaning of this shift in terminology is unclear, however, since it is largely unknown whether the limits of the federal government's war power are greater or lesser than what the government's powers would be if Congress declared a constitutional state of emergency. Bruce Ackerman, a professor of law and political science at Yale University and a prominent advocate of the "emergency constitution," provides a short list of the powers he thinks a government should have in a constitutional emergency in addition to the basic one of detaining suspected terrorists:

Curfews, evacuations, compulsory medical treatment, border controls, authority to search and seize suspicious materials and to engage in intensive surveillance and data compilation; freezing financial assets and closing otherwise lawful businesses; increasing federal control over state governments, expanding the domestic role of the military, and imposing special limitations on the right to bear arms—*to name only some of the hot-button issues* (emphasis added).[5]

If all this can be done in the context of a constitutional emergency, then it is at least arguable that little is denied the government by refusing to recognize the war on terrorism as a real war.

Moreover, Ackerman's account does not explain how Congress could declare a constitutional state of emergency that could suspend constitutional rights. A fundamental principle of American constitutionalism since the Supreme Court proclaimed the doctrine of judicial review in *Marbury v. Madison* (1803) is that a statute, even if it is called a "framework statute," cannot violate the Constitution. To his credit, Ackerman tries to ensure that constitutional emergencies would be limited in time by incorporating into the framework emergency statute a "supermajoritarian escalator" under which emergency powers would lapse unless Congress would vote every two or three months to reauthorize the emergency by ever larger majorities up to the top limit of 80 percent. However, it would always be the case that Congress could simply rescind the supermajoritarian escalator by majority vote, which would mean that a simple majority in Congress could make the emergency constitution permanent, a conclusion contrary to basic features of American constitutionalism.[6] Ackerman argues that the federal courts should protect the sanctity of the escalator,[7] but it is not easy to see how they could do so given the statutory basis of the escalator. In the end, Ackerman's approach, though interesting and certainly imaginative, may be unworkable because he is trying to create an emergency constitution by ordinary legislation without amending the Constitution.

Although Ackerman's "emergency Constitution model" is not a part of the American constitutional tradition, the concept of emergency has fundamentally shaped the approach to civil liberties that assumes that the Constitution must temporarily adapt, adjust, or accommodate itself to crises, including those crises associated with war. In *Wilson v. New* (1917), a wartime case involving the constitutionality of a federal law that arguably violated the liberty of contract by compelling railroad employees to work no more than eight hours per day, Chief Justice Edward D. White wrote that "Although an emergency may not call into life a power which has never lived, nevertheless *emergency may afford a reason for the exertion of a living power* already enjoyed" (emphasis added).[8] In a similar vein, Justice Oliver Wendell Holmes wrote in a free speech case during World War I that he did not

> doubt for a moment that by the same reasoning that would justify punishing persuasion to murder, the United States constitutionally may punish speech that produces or is intended to produce a clear and imminent danger that it will bring about forthwith certain substantive evils that the United States constitutionally may seek to prevent. *The power undoubtedly is greater in time of war than in time of peace because war opens dangers that do not exist at other times. But as against dangers peculiar to war, as against others, the principle of the right to free speech is always the same* (emphasis added).[9]

During the crisis of the Great Depression, Chief Justice Charles Evans Hughes returned to this theme in a case dealing with the constitutionality of a law that established a moratorium on foreclosures. "While emergency does not create power," he wrote, "emergency may *furnish the occasion for the exercise of power*" (emphasis added).[10] Each of these passages suggests that the Constitution must be flexible enough to respond temporarily to the crises and emergencies of war, including the war on terrorism. In times of war, constitutional rights and liberties are not suspended or abolished, but they can be adapted and adjusted to accommodate the needs of the moment. Of course, once the emergency is over, the Constitution is expected to revert back to its normal pre-crisis condition.

A primary concern about this "accommodation model" is that legal precedents supporting the legality of the extreme steps taken during an emergency could eventually erode the civil rights and liberties of the peacetime Constitution. In his famous dissent in *Korematsu v. United States* (1944), the case in which the Supreme Court upheld the legality of the forced evacuation of the Japanese from the west coast during World War II, Justice Robert Jackson addressed this problem in his typical forceful manner. He conceded that the military during wartime operations would not always conform its conduct to "conventional tests of constitutionality," but he argued it was a mistake for a court to "distort the Constitution to approve all that the military may deem expedient." It was a mistake to do so because the precedent would lie about "like a loaded weapon ready for the hand of any authority that can bring forward a plausible claim of an urgent need," while an unconstitutional military order was "not apt to last longer than the military emergency."[11] Jackson therefore thought that unconstitutional actions should be expected during wartime emergencies, but courts should decline to uphold their legality.

Justice Jackson did not say whether the military officers who violated the constitutional rights of individuals could later be held legally or politically accountable for their conduct, but later proponents of this approach to emergency power have suggested that possibility. Advocating what he calls "the Extra-Legal Measures model" of emergency powers, Oren Gross has recently claimed that public officials who act outside the legal order during an emergency must openly "acknowledge" their actions, after which the "people" must decide whether the officials should "resign," whether they should "face criminal charges or civil suits," whether they should be impeached and removed from office, or whether they should not be reelected to office.[12] Gross argues that his Extra-Legal Measures model to emergency powers avoids both the "rigidity" of Justice Davis's criminal process model and the "innate susceptibility to manipulation" and the dangerous "slippery slope toward excessive governmental infringement on individual rights" that is inherent to all "models of accommodation."[13]

Unconstitutional actions may be appropriate and reasonable during an emergency, according to Gross, but the above sanctions will discourage public officials from acting outside the legal order except "for truly extraordinary occasions."[14] Gross, however, implies that the ongoing war against terrorism poses such an "extraordinary occasion." For example, he claims that his model will help maintain the "integrity" of the American legal system during this ongoing struggle. Relying on an interesting metaphor, he alleges that "under the Extra-Legal Measures model, while government and its agents sink lower in their fight against terrorism, the legal system remains afloat above the muddy water's surface."[15] Although it is not clear how the American legal system can remain afloat if the government is under the muddy water, the metaphor seems to imply that members of the Bush administration are engaging in unconstitutional actions and the American people have the responsibility of deciding whether and how to hold them accountable.

Gross's Extra-Legal Measures model shares with all the different forms of the accommodation model the assumption that the Constitution should revert back to its traditional peacetime balance between national security and individual rights as soon as the emergency is over. This feature of both models does not fit very well with the indefinite character of the war on terrorism. Since the war on terrorism stretches so far out into the future, it might not be sensible to understand the proper balance between national security and civil liberties through any sort of model that assumes only a temporary accommodation or what Gross refers to as a "truly extraordinary occasion." Even if the war on terrorism is not a total war comparable to the American Civil War or World War II, both of which were threats to our national existence, neither is it a short-term crisis. So, even if it is true, as it is often said, that nothing is the same as it was prior to 9/11, things have not changed that much, even if the changes that have occurred seem relatively enduring in character.

It is, of course, possible that a specific terrorist attack could be so serious that it would trigger short-term emergency powers, but that leaves unanswered the question whether the war on terrorism itself, apart from any particularly horrific attack, justifies recalibrating the constitutional balance of national security and individual rights on a more permanent basis. The goal of the recalibration would not be to ensure that no terrorist attack could ever be successful, which is an impossible goal. It would rather be to make such attacks less likely and less lethal by making long-term readjustments to individual rights. This "evolutionary model" of the proper balance between national security and individual rights during the war on terrorism assumes that long-term problems require long-term solutions, but it rejects any radical alternation because there is no ongoing emergency or extraordinary occasion. The Constitution has to evolve, as it has always done in the past, so that the government can confront and overcome the challenges of the present and the foreseeable future. In confronting the challenge of terrorists potentially armed with weapons of mass destruction, the Evolutionary model weighs the gains to national security that can be achieved through modest but relatively long-term revisions of individual rights.

A recent book that reflects the assumptions of the Evolutionary model is Philip B. Heymann and Juliette N. Kayyem's *Protecting Liberty in an Age of*

Terror,[16] which is a distillation of the views of the Board of Advisors of the Long-Term Legal Strategy Project for Preserving Security and Democratic Freedom in the War on Terrorism.[17] Although in their introduction the authors say that the "passage of time could show that the United States can safely return to tradition" and that "new executive powers should not be allowed to survive any longer than the extraordinary danger that justifies them," the clear focus of their book and the project's mission is on the long-term. This point of view is the proper one, the authors insist, because the war on terrorism "is limitless in duration and place" and "has no clear end point."[18] Accordingly, Heymann and Kayyem try to achieve a balance between civil liberties and national security that will endure for decades—a period of time longer than an emergency or a truly extraordinary occasion. Moreover, the balance that they strike does not require a major adjustment to civil liberties:

> We agree that U.S. practices at home and abroad had to, and have to, change to reflect the threats of far more dangerous terrorism than previously seen. We reject, however, the notion that those dangers warrant a major shift in the country's historical balance among legislative authority, judicial powers, individual rights and executive authority. It is not possible to have minimal risk from terrorism and absolutely maximally protected freedoms, but it is possible to preserve 90 percent of what concerns each camp.[19]

Heymann and Kayyem are properly characterized as adherents to an evolutionary model because of the long-term character of their suggested proposals and their assumption that radical alterations of civil liberties are not necessary to provide sufficient protection for national security in an age of terrorism. A modest recalibration is required, but the recalibration for all intents and purposes is permanent, at least for the foreseeable future.

One last model for understanding the balance of national security and individual rights during wartime, one that is at the opposite end of the spectrum from Justice Davis's criminal process model, is based on an old Roman adage: *Inter arma silent leges* (In times of war, the law is silent). While Davis's model assumes that the Constitution is the same and fully enforceable in peace or war, the Roman adage implies the exact opposite: during war the Constitution is suspended. The policies that should be pursued during war are those that insure a quick victory, regardless of their impact on traditional civil rights and liberties. This "suspension model" is different from Gross's Extra-Legal Measures model because the law is suspended and without effect. Public officials acting in good faith could therefore violate civil liberties during wartime with impunity.

During the Roman Republic, when almost every war was a struggle for the city's survival and defeat meant death or slavery for most Roman citizens, *Inter arma silent leges* may have had a great deal of validity. Today, however, it might have less given the variety of wars in the contemporary world. They come in many different shapes and sizes, shades and colors, and some clearly pose no threat to our national existence. Since the war on terrorism is arguably a conflict of this type, the suspension model is a theoretical option, but perhaps not a politically viable one. In his book *All the Laws But One* (1998), Chief Justice William Rehnquist warmly cites the old Roman adage, yet at the same time he modifies it in terms of the American legal experience. On the one hand, Rehnquist states that it is "neither desirable nor is it remotely likely that civil liberty will occupy as favored a position in wartime as it does in peacetime." On the other hand, after referring to a "historic trend" in opposition to previous violations of civil liberties during wartime, such as the internment of Japanese citizens during World War II, he predicts that this trend "will continue in the future" and observes that it is "both desirable and likely that more careful attention will be paid by the courts to the basis for the government's claims of necessity as a basis for curtailing civil liberty."[20] Accordingly, Rehnquist advocates an important role for courts during wartime. Their job is to carefully review whether the specific type of violation of civil liberties that the government is proposing is in fact necessary for the war effort. He sums up his approach by saying that the "laws will thus not be silent in time of war, but they will speak with a somewhat different voice."[21] The upshot is that Rehnquist in fact only endorses the Roman adage in a rhetorical sense. He in fact follows an accommodation model, one that reserves an important role for the federal judiciary yet contemplates the likelihood of significant intrusions on civil liberties during wartime.

Justice William Brennan Jr. partially agrees with Chief Justice Rehnquist, but he argues that historically, courts have not been as aggressive as they should have been in assessing the government's national security claims. For that reason, after each crisis, "the United States has remorsefully realized that the abrogation of civil liberties was unnecessary."[22] Unfortunately, according to Brennan, despite these remorseful realizations, the country "has proven unable to prevent itself from repeating the error when the next crisis comes along."[23] Geoffrey Stone, a professor of law at the University of Chicago, has provided detailed historical support for Brennan's thesis in his book *Perilous Times: Free Speech in Wartime* (2004). Stone argues that American history proves that most, if not all, violations of civil liberties during wartime were "overreactions" based on "excessive" and "ill-formed fear." He recounts six episodes from our past in which freedom of speech was unnecessarily sacrificed on the altar of national security during wartime. There was, at these times, Stone claims, "not too much judicial enforcement of the First Amendment in wartime, but too *little*."[24] He agrees that national security is as important as liberty, but generally denies that a curtailment of freedom of speech, or any other civil liberty for that matter, is necessary or even related to security needs. The government should take dangers to national security "seriously," but the "right way to do that" is "not by stifling free speech or otherwise restricting civil liberties."[25]

Since there is this "repeated *pattern* of excessive restriction of civil liberties in wartime," Stone continues, "the goal is not only to recognize this pathology when it occurs, . . . but to create *safeguards* that will make it less likely to happen in the future."[26] The Supreme Court during peacetime "must define clear constitutional rules that are not easily circumvented or manipulated by prosecutors, jurors, presidents, or even future Supreme Court justices"[27] during wartime. Stone questions many, though not all, of the actions taken by the Bush administration during the ongoing war on terrorism and is unsure if current Supreme Court justices will have the courage to preserve liberty in these "perilous times." He ends his book with an ambivalent, "And, so, we shall see."[28]

Mark Tushnet, a law professor at Georgetown University Law Center, in an article titled "Defending *Korematsu*? Reflections on Civil Liberties During Wartime," also argues that citizens today should take a "stance of watchful skepticism about claims from executive officials that the actions of the officials are in fact justified by, and are sensible policy responses to, threats to national security."[29] Public officials working in bureaucracies have a built-in tendency to "exaggerate uncertain threats" and to "avoid disclosure of mistakes."[30] Tushnet adds that skepticism is even more appropriate if officials claim that the nature of the threat requires secrecy as to why civil liberties must be violated during wartime. However, Tushnet's skepticism about such claims does not rise to the level of Stone's. In his article, he writes that "to the extent that we are concerned with developing a law that will guide policymakers, we should be careful not to constrain them because of our hindsight wisdom."[31] In the past, wartime policy makers all too often have shouted, "The sky is falling! The sky is falling!" when in fact it was not, but that does not mean that in some present or future wartime emergency, the sky won't in fact fall. In that situation, Tushnet concludes, we will want policy makers able and willing to respond to the situation effectively and efficiently.

The various models of balancing national security and liberty during wartime discussed above will permit the examination of the major post-9/11 cases from multiple perspectives. The various models can be evaluated in terms of the legal arguments and judicial decisions of these cases and the judicial rulings themselves in terms of the advantages and disadvantages of the various models. The goal is to develop a more mature and coherent perspective on how civil liberties and national security should be balanced during wartime. A similar evaluative approach is also appropriate for the second fundamental question this textbook explores: what are the respective roles of the three branches of the federal government during the war on terrorism? In grappling with the substance of this question and its implications, it is useful to begin with Justice Robert Jackson's analysis of presidential power in *Youngstown Sheet and Tube Company v. Sawyer* (1952), a Supreme Court decision that denied President Harry Truman the authority to seize the property of the steel companies to resolve a labor dispute during the Korean War. Jackson recognized three types of presidential power: those that Congress authorized; those that it explicitly denied; and those that it was silent about. According to Jackson, presidential power was at its zenith if it were of the first type, at its lowest ebb if it were of the second, and somewhere in between if it were of the third. Jackson referred to the third type of power as a "zone of twilight" in which congressional "inertia, indifference, or quiescence" could "invite" an executive assertion of power. The "test of power" for presidential actions that occurred in the "zone of twilight," Jackson observed, was "likely to depend on the imperatives of events and contemporary imponderables rather than on abstract theories of law."[32]

In *Youngstown*, President Truman relied on three textual provisions of Article II of the Constitution to support his claim that he did have the authority to seize the steel mills: "The executive Power shall be vested in a president . . . "; the president "shall take Care that the Laws be faithfully executed"; and the president "shall be Commander in Chief of the Army and Navy of the United States." Justice Jackson claimed that he was willing to give these powers "the scope and elasticity afforded by what seem to be reasonable, practical implications,"[33] but he, along with a majority of the justices, declined to interpret them so broadly that an authority to seize private property during a wartime emergency was within their scope. In coming to this conclusion, Jackson noted that claims of presidential power in opposition to Congress's will "must be scrutinized with caution, for what is at stake is the equilibrium established by our constitutional system."[34] On similar grounds, Jackson rejected the view that "inherent" or "emergency" powers should be vested in the executive branch. Pointing to the experience of twentieth-century European governments, Jackson argued that such powers were "consistent with free government only when their control is lodged elsewhere than in the executive who exercises them."[35] Accordingly, although the president has constitutional powers that Congress cannot take away, the scope and substance of these powers must be understood, according to Jackson, in a way that preserves the "equilibrium" of our constitutional system and the "balanced power structure of our Republic."[36]

In a recent article titled "Between Civil Libertarianism and Executive Unilateralism," Samuel Issacharoff and Richard H. Pildes have defended a position that is somewhat reminiscent of Justice Jackson's opinion in *Youngstown*. In their judgment, Congress should play a pivotal role in balancing civil liberty and national security during wartime. They argue that courts have generally agreed with this proposition and that courts would be well served if they would continue to do so in the ongoing war on terrorism. The most important advantage of this approach, according to the two commentators, is that it assigns responsibility for deciding controversial issues involving the relationship of national security and individual rights during wartime to the politically accountable bodies.[37] If there is no consensus between the political branches that a certain policy impinging upon civil liberties is necessary for national security during wartime, then courts should side with Congress by opposing "the institutional tendency to concentrate power in the hands of the executive and its military."[38] Accordingly, Congress is the branch of the federal government that makes the crucial decision regarding the balance of civil liberties and national security during wartime. If Congress agrees with the president, courts should defer; if it disagrees, the courts should rule against the president's unilateral use of power.

Proponents of presidential power during the war on terrorism are relatively unconcerned about "the institutional tendency to concentrate power in the hands of the executive and its military." In his recently published book titled *The Powers of War and Peace* (2005), John Yoo, a former deputy assistant attorney general in the Justice Department's Office of Legal Counsel (OLC), writes that it "seems obvious that the presidency best meets the requirements for taking rational action on behalf of the nation in the modern world."[39] He quotes extensively from *The Federalist* Nos. 70 and 74, both written by Alexander Hamilton, to support his position that the president has complete operational control of the military, even if Congress has not declared war or authorized the use of military force.[40] Congress can check the president's use of military force, Yoo suggests, only by refusing to appropriate funds or to raise armies. Similar cumbersome restraints are placed on Congress's ability to control the president's exclusive control over foreign policy. In contrast to the approach defended by Issacharoff and Pildes, Yoo advocates a strict separation of powers and a delegation of all operational control over war and foreign affairs to the executive branch.

One major concern with leaving the issue of balancing civil liberties and national security during wartime to one of the two political branches of the federal government, or to both of them together, is that they are subject to shifts of public opinion, including the hysteria that all too often accompanies wartime crises and emergencies. For that reason, both the president and Congress are arguably less well suited for performing this responsibility than the unelected federal judiciary. As they are somewhat insulated from political pressures and events, federal judges with life tenure, according to this view, should make the final call on how national security and individual rights should be balanced during the war on terrorism. In the end, it is their detachment and impartiality that qualify federal judges for this important responsibility. Of course, having judges make these determinations does not necessarily mean that civil liberties will be protected. Having judges balance civil liberties and national security during wartime does not necessarily dictate any particular result, but it does mean that judges should not be deferential during wartime; they should be at the forefront of deciding if the war on terrorism is a war, if it is a type of war that has triggered a "constitutional emergency" or a "suspension" of the Constitution, or if it is a war that requires either an "accommodation" of civil liberties or a more or less permanent "modification" of them.

Although analytically distinct, the two fundamental questions that this book explores are, to some degree, related. The first question focuses on the merits: what is the proper balance between national security and individual rights during the war on terrorism? The second focuses on the allocation of authority: who decides the proper balance? Obviously, those who think the president should decide the balance will lean in the direction of sacrificing civil liberties during the war on terrorism because the executive branch will largely have operational control over the war on terrorism. The president, Congress, or the courts can set limits and parameters regarding the war, but it is the president and his subordinates who will fight the war within those limits and parameters. Obviously, if the president is doing the fighting, he will have a built-in incentive to give himself as much flexibility as he can so that he can achieve victory as quickly as possible. A proponent of presidential power, such as Yoo, grants the president wide latitude in part because he does not think this policy will endanger core American values or fundamentally change the American way of life.

Whether it is wise to give the president this kind of power and discretion during wartime depends to some extent on the seriousness of the threat. How much should we fear radical Islamic fundamentalists who might now or someday soon have access to weapons of mass distruction? Is the threat real? What is its size? What is its proximity? Although more than five years have passed since the 9/11 attacks, there are no clear and definite answers to these questions. The war on terrorism, if it is a war, is one with unique qualities and unprecedented characteristics. We should therefore not expect quick and definitive resolutions of the issues this book explores. It will take time for the country to think through what is at stake and what is the proper way to respond to the tragic conjunction of radical Islamic fundamentalists, WMD, and terrorism. However, the following materials from the major post-9/11 cases are a good place to begin the process of thinking through these issues. Every citizen has a right, and perhaps a duty, to join the ongoing national debate concerning the proper balance between national security and the rights of the individual during the war on terrorism and the respective roles of the three branches of the federal government.

NOTES

1. Of course, as the bombing of the Murrah Federal Building in Oklahoma City by Timothy McVeigh and Terry Nichols in 1995 demonstrates, there is no necessary linkage between Islam and terrorism. The historical reality is that the current war on terrorism is focused on radical Islamic fundamentalists, but it is certainly possible that in the future other religious, political, social, or economic groups could adopt terrorist tactics, both at the national and the international level. Whether the war against terrorism would be broadened to include such groups would largely depend on the size and lethality of any attacks they sponsor or inspire. If any group successfully uses WMD to kill large numbers of innocent civilians, it is likely that the war would be expanded accordingly. The war on terrorism is therefore not a war against a particular religion, but rather a war against those who try to achieve their political objectives, whatever their ideology, by mass murder and comparable threats of violence.

2. See Public Law 107-40; 115 Stat. 224 (2001).

3. 71 U.S. (4 Wall.) 2, 120–21 (1866).

4. For positive and negative reference to Justice Davis's approach to civil liberties in wartime, see Oren Gross, "Chaos and Rules: Should Responses to Violent Crises Always be Constitutional," 112 *Yale L. J.* 1011, 1053–58.

5. Bruce Ackerman, *Before the Next Attack: Preserving Civil Liberties in an Age of Terrorism* (New Haven, CT: Yale University Press, 2006), p. 96.

6. A declaration of war would more than likely trigger powers that would be equal to or greater than those recognized by Ackerman's "emergency Constitution." Accordingly, if judges protected the sanctity of the "escalator," a majority in Congress could proceed on that basis without seeking the support of a supermajority.

7. Ibid., pp. 136–140.

8. 243 U.S. 332, 348 (1917).

9. *Abrams v. United States*, 250 U.S. 616, 627–28 (1919) (Holmes dissenting).

10. *Home Building & Loan Ass'n v. Blaisdell*, 290 U.S. 398, 425–26 (1934).

11. 323 U.S. 214, 244–46 (1944).

12. Oren Gross, "Chaos and Rules: Should Responses to Violent Crisis Always Be Constitutional?" 112 *Yale Law Journal* 1011, 1099 (2003).

13. Ibid., pp. 1021–22.

14. Ibid., p. 1134.

15. Ibid., p. 1132–33.

16. Cambridge, MA: MIT Press, 2005.

17. See www.mipt.org/Long-Term-Legal-Strategy.asp. The Long-Term Legal Strategy Project issued its report in 2004. Although Heymann and Kayyem's book includes updates and significant editorial changes, it is similar to the report that can be found at the above website.

18. *Protecting Liberty in an Age of Terror*, pp. 7, 8, and 9.

19. Ibid., p. 4.

20. Rehnquist, *All the Laws But One: Civil Liberties in Wartime* (New York: Knopf, 1998), pp. 216–17.

21. Ibid. For Rehnquist's views of the internment of Japanese citizens, see pp. 208–9.

22. William J. Brennan Jr., "The Quest to Develop a Jurisprudence of Civil Liberties in Times of Security Crises," *Israel Yearbook on Human Rights* (1988), pp. 16–17.

23. Ibid.

24. *Perilous Times: Free Speech in Wartime: From the Sedition Act of 1798 to the War on Terrorism* (New York: Norton, 2004), p. 545.

25. Ibid., p. 547.

26. Ibid.

27. Ibid., pp. 548–49.

28. Ibid., pp. 550–57, 557. A number of prominent academics concur with Brennan and Stone that a cycle of excessive deference to national security claims followed by a remorseful realization that the violation of civil liberties was unnecessary has repeated itself a number of times in American history. For a representative collection of articles, see David Cole and James X. Dempsey, eds., *Terrorism and the Constitution: Sacrificing Civil Liberties in the Name of National Security* (New York: The New Press, 2002); Cynthia Brown, ed., *Lost Liberties: Ashcroft and the Assault on Personal Freedom* (New York: New Press, 2003); Richard Leone and Greg Anrig Jr., eds., *The War on Our Freedoms: Civil Liberties in an Age of Terrorism* (New York: Public Affairs, 2003).

29. "Defending *Korematsu?*" in *The Constitution in Wartime: Beyond Alarmism and Complacency*, ed. Mark Tushnet (Durham, NC: Duke University Press, 2005), p. 136.

30. Ibid., pp. 131–32.

31. Ibid., p. 128.

32. 343 U.S. 579, 635-638 (1952).

33. Id. at 640.

34. Id. at 638.

35. Id. at 652.

36. Id. at 634.

37. See Issacharoff and Pildes, "Between Civil Libertarianism and Executive Unilateralism," in *The Constitution in Wartime*, ed. Mark Tushnet (Dunham, NC: Duke University Press, 2005), p. 171.

38. Ibid., p. 177.

39. Yoo, *The Powers of War and Peace: The Constitution and Foreign Affairs After 9/11* (Chicago: Chicago University Press, 2005), p. 20. Also see Yoo, *War by Other Means: An Insiders Account of the War on Terror* (New York: Atlantic Monthly Press, 2006).

40. Ibid., p. 21.

Chapter 1

Foreign Intelligence Surveillance

In re Sealed Case

310 F.3d 717 (FISA Court of Review 2002)

The USA PATRIOT Act, enacted six weeks after the 9/11 attacks, amended the Foreign Intelligence Surveillance Act (FISA) of 1978 in two ways that arguably violated the Fourth Amendment's protection against unreasonable searches. First, while FISA required that any surveillance authorized under its provisions be for "the purpose" of obtaining "foreign intelligence information," the Patriot Act permitted such surveillance if only a "significant purpose" was to obtain information of this type. Second, the Patriot Act added a provision that allowed foreign intelligence (FI) and foreign counterintelligence (FCI) officers to "consult with Federal law enforcement officers to coordinate efforts to investigate or protect against" actual or potential attacks, sabotage, international terrorism, or clandestine intelligence activities by foreign powers.[1] Relying on these two amendments, Attorney General John Ashcroft on March 6, 2002 issued new regulations allowing significantly more consultation and coordination between law enforcement and FI/FCI personnel. On May 17, 2002, the FISA court (FISC)—a special court of Article III judges that approves all FISA searches—held that Ashcroft's new procedures violated a provision of FISA that governed the retention and dissemination of FISA information. The government appealed the FISA court's ruling to the FISA Court of Review, a special appellate court of Article III judges constituted under FISA that had never convened before. At the Court of Review, a fascinating debate occurred concerning the meaning of the original FISA statute, the purpose and substance of the Patriot Act amendments, and the constitutionality of FISA searches conducted primarily for law enforcement purposes.

On November 18, 2002, the FISA Court of Review handed down its decision. It held that, although FISA searches for law enforcement purposes in the investigation and prosecution of foreign intelligence crimes had been legal under the initial FISA statute, the USA PATRIOT Act had narrowed the scope of FISA by requiring that "a significant purpose" of a FISA search be for the purpose of obtaining foreign intelligence. Accordingly, in the post-9/11 world, FISA searches could not be authorized, even in cases of foreign intelligence crimes, unless "a significant purpose" of the search was to obtain foreign intelligence information. Second, regarding the constitutional question, the Court of Review decided that FISA searches whose "primary purpose" was law enforcement did not violate the Fourth Amendment's protection against unreasonable searches so long as "a significant purpose" of the search was to prevent acts of terrorism or espionage. The court considered the prevention of such acts to be a "special need" of the government distinct from ordinary law enforcement. This "special need" rendered the search "reasonable" and therefore constitutional.

I. BACKGROUND

The Fourth Amendment of the U.S. Constitution protects against unreasonable searches and prohibits warrants that are not supported by probable cause. The language is as follows:

> The right of the people to be secure in their persons, houses, papers, and effects, against unreasonable searches and seizures, shall not be violated, and no Warrants shall issue, but upon probable cause, supported by Oath or affirmation, and particularly describing the place to be searched, and the persons or things to be seized.

The two clauses of the amendment are usually linked together, requiring law enforcement officials to obtain a warrant from "a neutral and detached" magistrate prior to a search. However, there are several exceptions to the warrant requirement: a warrant is not required for a search subsequent to an arrest; a stop and frisk of a suspicious individual; or a search conducted either in hot pursuit to prevent destruction of evidence or in a foreign country.[2] A warrantless search is therefore not necessarily unconstitutional. It could be constitutional if the circumstances made the search reasonable.

Although warrantless searches were not necessarily unconstitutional, the Supreme Court ruled in *Katz v. United States* (1967) that a wiretap of a phone booth required a warrant from "a neutral and detached" magistrate.[3] Following this landmark decision, warrantless electronic surveillance of American citizens by the government was presumptively unconstitutional, although the executive branch continued to use warrantless wiretaps for the purpose of protecting national security. In 1968, in response to reports that the government had engaged in widespread use of unlawful electronic surveillance, Congress enacted the Omnibus Crime and Control and Safe Streets Act. Title III of this statute regulated the conditions under which electronic surveillance could be used in criminal investigations of designated federal offenses.[4] It required that, before a "neutral and detached" magistrate could issue a warrant, he or she must find the following: first, that there is probable cause for believing that an individual "is committing, has committed, or is about to commit" a particular offense; second, that there is probable cause to believe that "particular communications" concerning the particular offense will be obtained through the electronic surveillance; and, third, that "normal investigative procedures" have failed and are not likely to be successful. In addition, Title III limited the surveillance to thirty days, imposed strict guidelines so that communications outside the warrant were not collected, required that all tape recordings of intercepted communications be sealed upon the expiration of the warrant, and mandated that the government inform the target of the surveillance when it expired. Finally, a defendant moving to suppress evidence collected under a Title III warrant was normally permitted to examine all the application materials for the warrant.

In 1972, the Supreme Court addressed the issue of the lawfulness of warrantless electronic surveillance for the purpose of protecting national security from domestic threats in *United States v. United States District Court (Keith)*. The question was whether the government could use evidence obtained by a wiretap that was authorized, not by a judge or magistrate, but by the attorney general. The three defendants, none of whom were agents of foreign powers, were charged with conspiring to bomb a Michigan office of the Central Intelligence Agency. The government argued that the surveillance was lawful, and the evidence was therefore admissible, because the purpose of the wiretap was "to protect the nation from attempts of domestic organizations to attack and subvert the existing structure of the Government." The Supreme Court disagreed, holding that in domestic security cases there was no exception to the Fourth Amendment requirement of a judicial warrant. Such cases might pose a greater danger to the public, the Court conceded, but at the same time domestic security cases reflected "a convergence of First and Fourth Amendment values not present in cases of 'ordinary' crime." Accordingly, though "the investigative duty of the executive may be stronger in such cases, so also is there greater jeopardy to constitutionally protected speech."[5]

Though the Court in *Keith* refused to recognize an exception to the warrant requirement in domestic security cases, it hinted that Title III's standards and procedures were not required in such cases because "domestic security surveillance may involve different policy and practical considerations from the surveillance of 'ordinary crime.'" The gathering of domestic security intelligence, for example, was often "long range," the Court observed, and involved "the interrelation of various sources and types of information," often making it more difficult to identify the targets of surveillance in domestic security cases than in typical criminal investigations. In addition, the goal in domestic intelligence gathering was the "prevention of unlawful activity" or the "enhancement of the Government's preparedness," which might mean that the focus of surveillance may be "less precise" than if it were directed at conventional crimes. For these reasons, the Court suggested that Congress might want to consider standards and procedures for domestic security surveillance that would be different from those of Title III. "Different standards may be compatible with the Fourth Amendment," the Court concluded, "if they are reasonable both in relation to the legitimate need of Government for intelligence information and the protected rights of our citizens."[6]

The Court in *Keith* also indicated that it was not limiting the president's power to engage in warrantless wiretaps for foreign intelligence purposes. At two separate occasions in its opinion, the Court denied that it was addressing in any way whether the executive branch could constitutionally engage in warrantless surveillance of agents of foreign powers.[7] Despite the Court's reluctance to address this constitutional question, lower federal courts upheld the constitutionality of such surveillance throughout the 1970s. The trend was generally uniform, although some of these decisions insisted that the surveillance was lawful only if its primary purpose was to gather foreign intelligence information. Evidence from such warrantless surveillance could still be used to convict an agent of a foreign power of a crime, but only if the primary purpose of the surveillance had been to obtain foreign intelligence information, not a criminal conviction.[8]

Although the Supreme Court had invited Congress to enact a statute comparable to Title III that would have regulated warrants in domestic intelligence cases, Congress instead passed the Foreign Intelligence Surveillance Act (FISA) in 1978. Congress enacted this legislation largely because, two years earlier, the Senate Select Committee to Study Governmental Operations with Respect to Intelligence Activities ("the Church Committee") had concluded that the FBI, the CIA, and other governmental intelligence agencies had consistently abused their powers by engaging in warrantless national security surveillance. FISA established a special court of seven Article III judges appointed by the chief justice, which the Patriot Act later expanded to eleven. Each of these FISA judges could issue orders authorizing foreign intelligence surveillance. Initially, FISA orders could only authorize electronic surveillance, but Congress expanded the scope of the statute to include physical searches in 1995.

In the FISA, Congress adopted a definition of probable cause very different from the one used in Title III warrants. Instead of finding that there was probable cause to believe that a particular "individual is committing, has committed, or is about to commit a particular offense," a FISA judge had decided whether there was probable cause to believe that the target was a foreign power or an agent of a foreign power. FISA defined "a foreign power" to include a "component" of a foreign government, an "entity" that was "directed and controlled" by foreign governments, a "group" engaged in international terrorism, and certain "political organizations" that were foreign-based. An "agent of a foreign power" could be either a "U.S. person" (which included all citizens and permanent residents) or a "non-U.S. person." Non-U.S. persons qualified as agents of foreign powers if they were "officers" or "employees" of a foreign power or if they "acted" on behalf of a foreign power that was engaged in clandestine intelligence activities in the United States. They did not have to be linked in any way to criminal activity before FISA surveillance could be authorized. In contrast, U.S. persons could qualify as agents of a foreign power only if they (1) knowingly engaged in clandestine intelligence gathering activities on behalf of a foreign power that "involve or may involve" criminal activity; (2) knowingly engaged in sabotage or international terrorism or acts in preparation thereof; (3) entered the United States under a false identity on behalf of a foreign power or assumed such an identity after his or her arrival; or (4) knowingly aided, abetted, or conspired with persons engaged in espionage, sabotage, or international terrorism.[9]

Based on these definitions, U.S. persons could not be subjected to FISA surveillance unless the executive branch could link them to certain types of crimes: espionage, sabotage, terrorism, fraud, or conspiracy. However, the link between the target and crime did not have to meet the relatively high standards of Title III. In the case of espionage, the target could be subjected to FISA surveillance if he or she was engaged in clandestine intelligence activities that "may involve" criminal activity. Probable cause of a "possibility" of criminal activity was a significantly lower threshold than probable cause of criminal activity itself. Also, the executive branch did not have to show that the target was "committing, has committed, or is about to commit" espionage or terrorism. FISA surveillance was permissible if the government only had evidence that the target had engaged in "acts in preparation," which could conceivably be significantly removed in time and place from any substantive offense.

Although FISA lowered the threshold of probable cause in these two significant ways, it also said that the probable cause finding in cases involving U.S. persons could not rest "solely upon the basis of activities protected by the first amendment."[10] Accordingly, if the target of FISA surveillance was a U.S. person, the government had to produce some evidence of criminal activity

apart from the target's speech or associational activity, but it did not have to
show that there was probable cause to believe that the target had committed,
was committing, or was about to commit a specific criminal offense. It only
had to show probable cause of a "possibility" of criminal activity or of acts of
preparation for future criminal activity.

Before issuing a warrant, Title III also required a judge to find "probable
cause" to believe that the wiretap would produce particular communications
concerning a specific criminal offense. FISA required no such finding by the
judge. The judge simply confirmed that a proper executive official had certified that the purpose of the wiretap was to gather "foreign intelligence information" to protect the United States from an "actual or potential attack" or
other "grave hostile acts" of a foreign power. When the target of the FISA surveillance was a non-U.S. person, the judge simply confirmed the certification.
If the target was a U.S. person, the judge could reject the certification, but
only if it was "clearly erroneous," a very difficult standard to meet since the
target had already been identified as an agent of a foreign power. Accordingly,
while judges took a relatively active role in assessing whether a particular Title III wiretap would produce communications regarding a specific crime,
they were much more deferential in assessing whether a FISA wiretap would
produce foreign intelligence information.

Title III also required a judge to find "probable cause" to believe that the
place about to be wiretapped was a place that was to be used in connection
with the specific criminal offense or was "leased, listed in the name of, or
commonly used by" the person suspected of the specific offense. FISA did
not require this link between the place of the wiretap and either the alleged
offense or the alleged criminal. Before issuing an order, a FISA judge only
had to find probable cause to believe that the place of the wiretap was being
used or was about to be used by "a foreign power or an agent of a foreign
power." The place of the wiretap did not have to be linked to any criminal activity, much less a specific offense, and it did not have to be "leased to" or
"commonly used by" the target. For a FISA order, it was sufficient if the target was "using" or "about to use" the place of the wiretap.

Another major difference between FISA and Title III regarded the government's obligation to inform the target of the surveillance or search. When the
government relied on a Title III warrant, it had to inform the target of the surveillance after it had expired, at which time the judge could provide the target with "portions of the intercepted communications, applications and orders." In contrast, a FISA target was given notice only if the government
intended to use the evidence obtained from the surveillance in a legal proceeding, such as a criminal trial. Moreover, if the evidence collected under a
Title III warrant was used in a prosecution, the target was entitled to see all

the applications materials if there was a motion to suppress the evidence in question. A target of FISA surveillance did not have this right if the attorney general filed an affidavit under oath "that disclosure or an adversary hearing would harm the national security of the United States." Accordingly, if a FISA target was prosecuted, the trial judge could review in camera and *ex parte* the application materials to decide if the surveillance was lawfully authorized, but the defendant would have no such opportunity unless the judge thought it was necessary to determine the lawfulness of the surveillance. In making the latter determination, the trial judge applied the same standards that the FISA judge had initially applied when the government requested the FISA order.

FISA also established time limits very different from those of Title III. While authorization orders under Title III can be issued for periods of up to 30 days, FISA (after the USA PATRIOT Act) permitted periods of surveillance up to 90 days for U.S. persons and 120 days for non-U.S. persons (with the possibility of renewals for up to one year). The result was that there were fewer opportunities for judicial review of FISA orders than there were of Title III warrants. In sum, compared to Title III, FISA permitted surveillance under lower standards of probable cause, with greater secrecy, for longer periods of time. For these reasons, law enforcement officials often found FISA orders to be an attractive alternative to Title III warrants.

During the 1980s, federal circuit courts upheld the constitutionality of FISA orders if the primary purpose of the surveillance had been to collect foreign intelligence information.[11] If the primary purpose of the surveillance had been to collect evidence to prosecute someone, then it violated the Fourth Amendment and could not be used in a criminal trial. To insure that the primary purpose of FISA orders was to gather foreign intelligence information, Attorney General Janet Reno in 1995 instituted a set of guidelines that sharply limited the degree to which the Justice Department's Criminal Division could control or influence how FBI intelligence officers were using FISA surveillance. Although the guidelines permitted the Criminal Division to give guidance to the FBI that was "aimed at preserving the option of a criminal prosecution," they directed both the Criminal Division and the FBI to take whatever steps were necessary to ensure that such advice did not "inadvertently result in either the fact *or the appearance*" (emphasis added) of the Criminal Division's directing or controlling FISA surveillance. The only sure way not to inadvertently create the appearance of control was to reduce and monitor the flow of information from the Criminal Division to the FI/FCI officers in the FBI. The 1995 guidelines gave this responsibility to the Justice Department's Office of Intelligence Policy and Review (OIPR). Representatives of this office monitored all contacts between the FI/FCI officers and the federal prosecutors/criminal investigators, thereby insuring that the primary purpose of FISA orders was to collect foreign intelligence information, not to prosecute crimes.

The practical result of the 1995 procedures was that a metaphorical wall arose between FI/FCI officers of the FBI and all law enforcement personnel, including FBI criminal agents, the Justice Department's Criminal Division, and the prosecutors working in U.S. Attorneys' offices around the country. The wall's potential for producing disastrous results became evident during the FBI's investigation of Wen Ho Lee, an American citizen suspected of selling or giving America's most sensitive nuclear weapons secrets to China. Partly to take advantage of FISA surveillance, the investigation of Lee began in September 1995 as a counterintelligence operation, but all the FI/FCI officers involved knew that an espionage prosecution was a definite possibility, if not a likely outcome. Nevertheless, these officers never informed the Criminal Division of what might have been the worst case of espionage in the country's history. The Criminal Division learned about the case from a story in the *Wall Street Journal* on January 7, 1999.

One reason why the FI/FCI officers did not inform the Criminal Division of the Lee investigation was that it did not want to risk the smallest chance that it might lose the option of FISA surveillance in such an important case. However, the downside of keeping the Criminal Division out of the loop was that the FBI could not rely on the expertise of the Computer Crime Section to determine if the FBI could legally search Lee's computer in the Los Alamos National Laboratory. Although Lee had no reasonable expectation of privacy regarding this computer, the FBI did not search it from 1995 until 1998, during which time Lee moved classified files regarding nuclear weapons data to an unprotected computer and downloaded many of them in 1997. In addition, the Criminal Division would have been able to provide advice on how the investigation should have been conducted to increase the likelihood of conviction. Lastly, since flight was a real possibility, the FBI's refusal to inform the Criminal Division risked whether there would ever be a prosecution. If a quick arrest became necessary, it would be difficult for the prosecutors to justify it since they knew nothing about the case. In such circumstances, a judge might order Lee's release, enabling him to get on a plane and fly to China![12]

Lee eventually pleaded guilty to one count of misusing a government computer and was sentenced to time served: 277 days.[13] It is possible that the resolution of this case might have been very different if the Criminal Division had been actively involved throughout the investigation. The case showed that the lack of coordination between FI/FCI officers and law enforcement personnel reduced the amount of shared information, which in turn could endanger national security. Compounding the problem was the widespread perception in the FBI during the late 1990s that unauthorized contact between

FI/FCI officers and a prosecutor in the Criminal Division was a "career stopper."[14] FI/FCI officers accordingly became increasingly cautious, even to the point of refusing to share information *not* collected under FISA with criminal investigators.

Regarding information collected under FISA, the all-important underlying constitutional issue was how much coordination between FI/FCI officers and law enforcement personnel was compatible with the Fourth Amendment. During the late 1990s, the FISA court routinely approved "information screening walls" to ensure that FISA surveillance was not being used for the purpose of criminal prosecution. In cases involving overlapping intelligence and criminal investigations, the court would not permit criminal investigators and prosecutors to examine all the raw FISA intercepts or seized material. Instead, the chief counsel in an FBI field office, or an assistant U.S. attorney not involved in the criminal investigation, the OIPR in the Justice Department, or the FISA court itself would "screen" the raw material and pass on to the criminal investigators and prosecutors only "evidence" that was "relevant" to the criminal case. The FISA court took on this role in major cases during the late 1990s, including the cases involving the bombings of the U.S. embassies in Africa and the investigations of a possible millennium terrorist attack.[15]

Following the September 11, 2001, attacks, the Bush administration repeatedly insisted that better coordination between intelligence agencies and law enforcement was necessary to prevent future terrorist attacks. In a press conference on October 18, 2001, Attorney General Ashcroft noted that the FISA provisions of the USA PATRIOT Act would make the utilization of wiretaps against terrorists "much more workable" and would "facilitate greater coordination between law enforcement and the intelligence side of our investigative resources" and claimed that such coordination was "at the heart of our ability to prevent future attacks."[16] On January 23, 2002, terrorists kidnapped Daniel Pearl, a reporter for the *Wall Street Journal*, in Karachi, Pakistan. A videotape of his brutal beheading appeared on February 20. On March 6, 2002, Attorney General Ashcroft promulgated a new set of secret Justice Department procedures governing the sharing of information between law enforcement and FI/FCI personnel, setting aside those of 1995. The new procedures allowed "FISA to be used *primarily* for a law enforcement purpose, as long as a significant foreign intelligence purpose remains." Second, they made it clear that the wall between FI/FCI officers and law enforcement personnel was completely down.

Consultations may include the exchange of advice and recommendations on all issues necessary to the ability of the United States to investigate or protect against foreign attack, sabotage, terrorism, and clandestine intelligence activities, including protection against the foregoing through criminal investigation and prosecution. . . . Relevant issues include, but are not limited to, the strategy and goals for the investigation; the law enforcement and intelligence methods to be used in conducting the investigation; the interaction between intelligence and law enforcement components as part of the investigation; and the initiation, cooperation, continuation, or expansion of FISA searches or surveillance. Such consultations are necessary to the ability of the United Sates to coordinate efforts to investigate and protect against foreign threats to national security.[17]

Accordingly, even if the primary purpose of FISA surveillance or searches was criminal prosecution, law enforcement personnel were authorized to advise and make recommendations concerning "the initiation, cooperation, continuation, or expansion" of the surveillance. The bottom line after March 2002 was that law enforcement personnel would not have to satisfy the requirements of a Title III surveillance warrant if a significant purpose of the investigation was to collect foreign intelligence information.

On the day following the promulgation of the new intelligence sharing procedures, the government filed a secret motion with the FISA court to vacate the "wall procedures" that the Court had ordered for all FISA investigations in November 2001, procedures that resembled the ones Reno had promulgated in 1995. The secret *ex parte* character of this litigation was typical of the way the FISA court operated since FISA targets could not be given any notice that they were under surveillance. In fact, relevant policy makers and the American public knew very little about the activities of the FISA court. All FISA orders were classified and any memorandum opinions issued by FISA judges were not publicly released, even if they were unclassified.[18] The FISA statute only required the attorney general to send a yearly report to Congress indicating the number of applications that had been filed with the FISA court and the number that the court had approved (see box 1.1).[19] These yearly reports showed that during its twenty-three years of operation the FISA court had issued over 14,000 FISA orders and that it had never turned down any of the government's applications. What this remarkable record implied was unclear. Did it mean that the FISA court was functioning as a rubber stamp for a system of governmental surveillance or did it mean that the FISA court was an "active enforcer" of the Fourth Amendment that used the OIPR in the Justice Department as its enforcement arm, both to probe beforehand the validity of the government's applications for FISA orders and to enforce the court's "wall procedures?"[20]

On May 17, 2002, in a unanimous decision signed by all seven judges, the FISA court secretly granted the government's motion and vacated the existing wall procedures, but nonetheless held that Ashcroft's 2002 procedures had to be significantly modified. First, although the court allowed complete consultation and coordination between FI/FCI officers and law enforcement per-

Box 1.1. ELECTRONIC PRIVACY INFORMATION CENTER (EPIC)

Foreign Intelligence Surveillance Act Orders, 1979–2001

Year	Number of FISA Applications Presented	Number of FISA Applications Approved	Number of FISA Applications Rejected	Year	Number of FISA Applications Presented	Number of FISA Applications Approved	Number of FISA Applications Rejected
1979	199	207	0	1991	593	593	0
1980	319	322	0	1992	484	484	0
1981	431	433	0	1993	509	509	0
1982	473	475	0	1994	576	576	0
1983	549	549	0	1995	697	697	0
1984	635	635	0	1996	839	839	0
1985	587	587	0	1997	749	748	0
1986	573	573	0	1998	796	796	0
1987	512	512	0	1999	886	880	0
1988	534	534	0	2000	1005	1012	0
1989	546	546	0	2001	932	934	0
1990	595	595	0				

The above chart can be found at EPIC's website (www.epic.org/privacy/wiretap/stats/fisa_stats.html). It is reprinted here with EPIC's permission.

sonnel, it required that a representative of the OIPR either be present at such meetings or be fully informed of the substance of the meetings in writing (the so-called "chaperone" requirement). In turn, it was OIPR's responsibility to inform the FISA court at the earliest opportunity about the degree and the nature of the coordination. Second, although the two types of officials could consult with one another, "law enforcement officials shall not make recommendations to intelligence officials concerning the initiation, operation, continuation or expansion of FISA searches or surveillances," nor shall any "advice intended to preserve the option of a criminal prosecution" inadvertently result in "the Criminal Division's directing or controlling the investigation using FISA searches and surveillances toward law enforcement objectives."[21] Lastly, the FISA court adopted a new administrative rule (Rule 11) to monitor compliance with its May 17 order. The rule required that all future FISA applications include a "description of any ongoing criminal investigations of FISA targets, as well as any consultations between FBI and criminal prosecutors at the Department of Justice or a United States Attorney's Office."[22]

While the 1995 procedures had required law enforcement officers to do whatever was necessary to avoid the appearance that they were directing or controlling FISA surveillance, the secret May 17 FISA court's opinion relaxed this condition somewhat. Prosecutors and criminal investigators could advise FI/FCI personnel on what they should do to preserve the option of a criminal prosecution, but they could not give such advice if it "inadvertently" resulted in the "actual" control of FISA surveillance or searches by law enforcement officers, not simply "the appearance" of control. As mentioned earlier, the FISA court's rationale for modifying Ashcroft's 2002 "intelligence sharing" procedures was based, not on the Fourth Amendment, but rather on the "minimization procedures" provision of the original FISA. This provision required the attorney general "to minimize the acquisition and retention, and prohibit the dissemination, of nonpublicly available information concerning unconsenting U.S. persons consistent with the need of the United States to obtain, produce, and disseminate foreign intelligence information."[23] Although a different FISA provision clearly indicated that information obtained under a FISA order could be retained and disseminated for law enforcement purposes,[24] the FISA court argued that allowing law enforcement personnel and prosecutors to make recommendations concerning FISA surveillance, or, even more troublesome, to permit them to direct and control such surveillance, violated the minimization requirement because, in the FISA context, such input from prosecutors and law enforcement personnel was designed "to enhance the acquisition, retention and dissemination of *evidence for law enforcement purposes*" (emphasis added). Such input violated FISA because it was not "consistent with the need of the United States to 'obtain, produce, and disseminate foreign intelligence information.'" In fact, the FISA court concluded, Ashcroft's new procedures appeared to be "designed to amend the law and substitute the FISA for Title III electronic surveillances."[25] Since the attorney general had no authority to amend FISA, the March procedures had to be modified as indicated above. Law enforcement personnel could not direct and control FISA surveillance and OIPR had to monitor the consultation and coordination that did occur to ensure that any advice intended to preserve, not enhance, the option of criminal prosecution did not inadvertently produce such direction or control. In coming to this conclusion, the FISA court relied on a statutory provision that restricted the way information was retained and disseminated after it was collected as the basis for restricting the way law enforcement personnel could participate in the collection of information.

II. BRIEF OF THE UNITED STATES

At first, neither the Congress nor the public had any knowledge of either the new procedures regarding the sharing of information that the attorney general had issued on March 6, 2002 or the May 17 ruling by the FISA court, but news of these developments leaked out during the summer of 2002 in a hearing before the Senate Judiciary Committee. In reaction to the disclosure, Senator Patrick J. Leahy (D-VT), chairman of the committee, along with Senators Charles E. Grassley (R-IO) and Arlen Specter (R-PA), on July 31, 2002 sent a letter to the presiding judge of the FISA court, Judge Colleen Kollar-Kotelly expressing concern that the FISA court's May 17 ruling might have conflicted with relevant provisions of the USA PATRIOT Act. So that the committee could properly perform its oversight responsibilities, the letter asked Judge Kollar-Kotelly to provide the committee with copies of the attorney general's March 2002 procedures, any memorandum opinions by the FISA court that explained why the procedures were revised, and any legal memoranda submitted by the government to the FISA court.[26] On the same day the letter was sent, a bomb at Jerusalem's Hebrew University killed nine persons and wounded eighty-seven others. Five of the dead and four of the wounded were U.S. citizens.

Judge Kollar-Kotelly complied with the Senate Judiciary Committee's request on August 20.[27] For the first time, members of Congress and the public had access to documents that revealed what the FISA court was doing and why. To the surprise and consternation of many, these documents showed that in November 2001, just weeks after the Congress had enacted the USA PATRIOT Act's provisions expanding the scope of FISA surveillance and the degree of permissible coordination between FI/FCI officers and law enforcement personnel, the FISA court had, in large part, incorporated the 1995 procedures controlling the sharing of information into all future FISA orders. By incorporating the 1995 procedures into all future FISA orders, it seemed as if the FISA court had secretly and preemptively blocked the implementation of provisions of the USA PATRIOT Act that were central to the Bush administration's efforts to prevent another terrorist attack.

In its May 17 opinion, the FISA court indirectly explained why it had decided to block these provisions of the USA PATRIOT Act by pointing to a number of "misstatements and omissions of material facts" that had appeared in recent FISA applications. In reaction to this apparent pattern of disobedience of its orders, the FISA court took a number of actions, including barring one FBI agent from ever appearing before it again. The FISA court did not explicitly say that the pattern of disobedience was part of an effort to hide or disguise the degree to which law enforcement personnel had been influencing, directing, or controlling FISA surveillance in 2000 and 2001, but that was one possible interpretation (see box 1.2).

The public release of the May 17 opinion in August 2002 added a new layer of controversy regarding the general question of the lawfulness of certain kinds of FISA surveillance. The legacy of the Wen Ho Lee case profiled the reluctance

---

Box 1.2. EXCERPTS FROM FISA COURT'S MAY 17 DECISION*

In September 2000, the government came forward to confess error in some seventy-five FISA applications related to major terrorist attacks directed against the United States. The errors related to misstatements and omissions of material facts, including:

- an erroneous statement in the FBI director's FISA certification that the target of the FISA was not under criminal investigation;
- erroneous statements in the FISA affidavits of FBI agents concerning the separation of the overlapping intelligence and criminal investigations, and the unauthorized sharing of FISA information with FBI criminal investigators and assistant U.S. attorneys;
- omissions of material facts from FBI FISA affidavits relating to a prior relationship between the FBI and a FISA target, and the interview of a FISA target by an assistant U.S. attorney.

In November of 2000, the Court held a special meeting to consider the troubling number of inaccurate FBI affidavits in so many FISA applications. After receiving a more detailed explanation from the Department of Justice about what went wrong, *but not why*, the court decided not to accept inaccurate affidavits from FBI agents whether or not intentionally false. One FBI agent was barred from appearing before the court as a FISA affiant. The court decided to await the results of the investigation by the Justice Department's Office of Professional Responsibility before taking further action.

In March of 2001, the government reported similar misstatements in another series of FISA applications in which there was supposedly a "wall" between separate intelligence and criminal squads in FBI field offices to screen FISA intercepts, when in fact all of the FBI agents were on the same squad and all of the screening was done by the one supervisor overseeing both investigations. . . .

In virtually every instance, the government's misstatements and omissions in FISA applications and violations of the court's orders involved information sharing and unauthorized disseminations to criminal investigators and prosecutors. These incidents have been under investigation by the FBI's and the Justice Department's Offices of Professional Responsibility for more than one year to determine how the violations occurred in the field offices, and how the misinformation found its way into the FISA applications and remained uncorrected for more than one year despite procedures to verify the accuracy of FISA pleadings. As of this date, no report has been published, and how these misrepresentations occurred remains unexplained to the court. . . .

Given this history in FISA information sharing, the court now turns to the revised 2002 minimization procedures. We recite this history to make clear that the court has long approved, under controlled circumstances, the sharing of FISA information with criminal prosecutors, as well as consultations between intelligence and criminal investigations where FISA surveillance and searches are being conducted. However, the proposed 2002 minimization procedures eliminate the bright line in the 1995 procedures prohibiting direction and control by prosecutors on which the court has relied to moderate the broad acquisition, retention, and dissemination of FISA information in overlapping intelligence and criminal investigations. . . .

* *In re All Matters Submitted to the Foreign Intelligence Surveillance Court,* 218 F. Supp. 2d 611, 621–22 (May 17, 2002).

of FI/FCI intelligence officers to consult with law enforcement personnel because they did not want to risk ongoing FISA surveillance in high-profile national security cases. The 9/11 attacks highlighted the dangers of not sharing all types of foreign intelligence information, not just information obtained through FISA, with domestic law enforcement authorities. The publication of the FISA court's May 17 opinion revealed a fairly extensive pattern of inaccuracies in FISA applications, a pattern that was possibly designed to hide the degree to which law enforcement personnel were involved in the direction and control of FISA surveillance. It was against this background that the Bush administration decided to appeal the FISA court's May 17 decision to the FISA Court of Review, the first time this tribunal had ever been convened to hear a case.[28]

The government's brief to the FISA Court of Review made the unprecedented claim that FISA surveillance was permissible in certain types of criminal cases even if prosecution was the *sole* purpose of the surveillance. Since FISA defined "foreign intelligence information" as any information that was related to the ability of the United States to protect itself against "actual or potential attack," "sabotage or international terrorism," or "clandestine intelligence activities," or that was necessary to "the national defense or the security of the United States" or "the conduct of the foreign affairs of the United States," the government argued that any prosecution designed to protect the United States in these ways could rely on a FISA order to collect the evidence against the defendant.

However, the brief went on, if the FISA Court of Review did not accept this new argument, the government had an alternative or fallback argument: the USA PATRIOT Act permitted a FISA order if there was a "significant purpose" of collecting "foreign intelligence information." Even if the primary purpose of the FISA order was to prosecute the target, the order was valid if the government had a significant purpose of obtaining foreign intelligence information. So long as the request for the FISA order was for the proper purpose, it simply did not matter, according to the government, that law enforcement personnel had advised or directed the FISA surveillance. Lastly, the government claimed that FISA surveillance for the sole or primary purpose of criminal prosecution was constitutional. The Supreme Court in its *Keith* decision had recognized the need for flexibility in domestic security cases. If flexibility was reasonable in domestic security cases, it was, the government argued, even more reasonable, and therefore constitutional, in the context of foreign threats to national security.

EXCERPTS FROM THE BRIEF OF THE UNITED STATES

[[1. Crimes of Espionage and Terrorism.]] . . . [[According to FISA,]] information is foreign intelligence information only if it is relevant or necessary to help the United States protect against certain specified threats, including attack, sabotage, terrorism, and espionage committed by foreign powers or their agents. Thus, information concerning purely *domestic* threats to the United States—e.g., information concerning Timothy McVeigh's plan to bomb the Oklahoma City Federal Building—is not foreign intelligence information. Correspondingly, information concerning foreign activities that do not threaten *national security*—e.g., an international fraud scheme—is also not foreign intelligence information. However, information about an al Qaeda conspiracy to bomb New York is foreign intelligence information because it concerns international terrorism committed by a foreign power and is needed to protect against that threat.

Although "foreign intelligence information" must be relevant or necessary to "protect" against the specified threats, the statutory definition does not limit *how* the government may use the information to achieve that protection. In other words, the definition does not discriminate between protection through diplomatic, economic, military, or law enforcement efforts, other than to require that those efforts be "lawful." Thus, for example, where information is relevant or necessary to recruit a foreign spy or terrorist as a double agent, that information is "foreign intelligence information" if the recruitment effort will "protect against" espionage or terrorism. Similarly, where information is relevant or necessary to prosecute a foreign spy or terrorist, that information is also "foreign intelligence information" if the prosecution will "protect against" espionage or terrorism.

Prosecution is often a most effective means of protecting national security. For example, the recent prosecution of Ahmed Ressam, who was charged with attempting to destroy Los Angeles International Airport, protected the United States by incapacitating Ressam himself from committing further attacks, and by deterring others who might have contemplated similar action. Moreover, as a result of his conviction and sentence, Ressam agreed to cooperate with the government and provided information about the training that he received at an al Qaeda camp overseas. That kind of prosecution thus protects the United States directly, by neutralizing a threat, and indirectly, by generating additional foreign intelligence information. The same is true of the recent prosecution of Robert Hanssen: By far the best source of intelligence on Hanssen's espionage activities is Hanssen himself; and the government gained access to Hanssen only as a result of his capture, prosecution, and plea agreement.

In sum, information is "foreign intelligence information" if it is relevant or necessary to the ability of the United States to protect against threats posed by foreign spies and terrorists. Such protection may be achieved in several ways, including by prosecuting the spy or terrorist. Information therefore may be "foreign intelligence information" solely by virtue of its importance to such a prosecution. Where the government conducts a search or surveillance for the purpose of obtaining information for use in such a prosecution, it satisfies FISA's standards. . . .

The USA PATRIOT Act confirms this understanding of FISA by incorporating the definition of "foreign intelligence information" into new provisions of the statute that authorize consultations and coordination between federal law enforcement officers and intelligence officers who conduct FISA searches and surveillances. . . .

[[These new provisions define]] . . . the scope of authorized coordination by incorporating verbatim the foreign threats to national security that are specified in the definition of "foreign intelligence information"—attack, sabotage, terrorism, and espionage committed by foreign powers or their agents. The amendment authorizes consultation to coordinate the government's various "efforts to investigate or protect" against such threats. Thus, consultations concerning purely *domestic* threats to national security (Timothy McVeigh), or foreign activities that do not threaten national security (international fraud schemes), are not within the scope of the coordination amendment. Consultations concerning an al Qaeda conspiracy to bomb New York, however, are within the scope of the provision, for the same reason that information concerning such a conspiracy is "foreign intelligence information.". . .

[[2. A Significant Non-law Enforcement Purpose.]] . . . [[T]]he USA PA-
TRIOT Act eliminated the "primary purpose" standard by enacting a "significant purpose" standard . . . .

By requiring only a "significant" purpose to obtain foreign intelligence information, Congress allowed for other purposes, including a purpose to obtain evidence for use in a prosecution, to be the "primary" reason for conducting a search or surveillance. Members of Congress who voted for and
against the USA PATRIOT Act discussed and understood that the "significant
purpose" amendment would allow the government to use FISA *primarily* to
collect evidence for use in a criminal prosecution.

The "significant purpose" standard also differs from the "primary purpose"
standard because it eliminates the need for courts routinely to compare and
weigh competing purposes for using FISA. Unlike "primary," the adjective
"significant" is not an inherently relative or comparative term. A purpose may
be "significant," in the sense of having "influence or effect," regardless of
whether there are other purposes present. Thus, to determine whether a "significant" purpose for using FISA is to obtain foreign intelligence information,
courts need not examine the extent of any purpose to obtain evidence for a
prosecution. . . .

Two of the FISC's requirements have particularly stifled coordination in
this case. First, there is the FISC's warning that prosecutors may not advise
intelligence officials in a way that results in "direction or control" of the intelligence investigation. This has chilled the substance of consultations between intelligence and law enforcement officials. Second, there is the rule
that prosecutors may not even meet or discuss the case with intelligence
agents without first inviting OIPR to participate, and the related requirement
that OIPR cannot allow the meeting to occur without its participation unless
it is "unable" to do so. This "chaperone" requirement has made it difficult for
any consultations to occur at all. . . .

In sum, the FISC has misinterpreted FISA, and has done so in a way that
inhibits necessary coordination. The USA PATRIOT Act, which the FISC effectively ignored, expressly authorizes coordination between intelligence and
law enforcement officials. The Act reflects Congress' recognition that the
country and its people can no longer afford a fragmented, blinkered, com-
partmentalized response to international terrorism and espionage. The FISC
has refused to give effect to the Act and the changes it made. This Court
should not allow that refusal to stand. . . .

[[3. Constitutionality of USA PATRIOT Act.]] Today, as in 1978 the *Keith*
case remains the leading decision of the Supreme Court in this area. In *Keith*,
the Court addressed the "delicate question of the President's power, acting
through the Attorney General, to authorize electronic surveillance in internal

security matters without prior judicial approval." The defendants in *Keith* were domestic terrorists, and the Court therefore did not address "the scope of the President's surveillance power with respect to the activities of foreign powers, within or without this country." Nor did *Keith* involve "any question or doubt as to the necessity of obtaining a warrant in the surveillance of crimes unrelated to the national security interest" under Title III. Thus, *Keith* addressed the validity of warrantless electronic surveillance for the purpose of protecting against domestic threats to national security (e.g., Timothy McVeigh).

The Court in *Keith* held that a warrant is required for domestic security surveillance, but that more flexible standards could apply to the issuance of such a warrant. The Court explained the reasons for its conclusion:

> We recognize that domestic security surveillance may involve different policy and practical considerations from the surveillance of "ordinary crime." The gathering of security intelligence is often long range and involves the interrelation of various sources and types of information. The exact targets of such surveillance may be more difficult to identify than in surveillance operations against many types of crimes specified in Title III. Often, too, the emphasis of domestic intelligence gathering is on the prevention of unlawful activity or the enhancement of the Government's preparedness for some possible future crisis or emergency. Thus, the focus of domestic surveillance may be less precise than that directed against more conventional types of crime.

In light of these "potential distinctions between Title III criminal surveillances and those involving the domestic security," the Court suggested that "Congress may wish to consider protective standards for the latter which differ from those already prescribed for specified crimes in Title III."

Keith's emphasis on the need for flexibility applies with even greater force to surveillance (or searches) directed at *foreign* threats to national security. As the Senate Intelligence Committee Report on FISA explained, quoting from *Keith*, "[f]ar more than in domestic security matters, foreign counterintelligence investigations are 'long range' and involve 'the interrelation of various sources and types of information.'" Surveillance directed at foreign threats also requires deferential standards of judicial review because it involves an area in which the President, as "Commander-in-Chief and as the Nation's organ for foreign affairs," exercises "very delicate, plenary and exclusive power," and in which judicial intervention "is rarely proper."

These concerns, which justify the use of FISA's different standards, do not recede merely because the government intends to protect national security through law enforcement rather than nonlaw-enforcement efforts. On the contrary, *Keith* makes clear that it is the nature of the *threat*, not the nature of the government's response to the threat, that determines the constitutionality of national security surveillance. Whether the government intends to prosecute a foreign spy or recruit him as a double agent (or use the threat of the former to accomplish the latter), the investigation will often be long range, involve the interrelation of various sources and types of information, and present unusual difficulties because of the special training and support available to foreign enemies of this country. . . .

Nothing in *Keith* suggests that the availability of more relaxed constitutional standards for a search or surveillance depends on the absence of a law enforcement purpose. . . .

JOHN ASHCROFT,
Attorney General

III. ORAL ARGUMENT

The FISA Court of Review heard oral argument on September 9, two days before the first anniversary of the 9/11 attacks. Solicitor General Theodore Olson presented the government's case, although there were at least eleven other attorneys representing the government in the courtroom. The judges on the Court of Review were Ralph B. Guy from the Sixth Circuit, Edward Leavy from the Ninth, and Laurence H. Silberman from the D.C. Circuit. Of the three judges, Silberman had the most foreign-policy experience. He was a deputy attorney general in 1974, ambassador to Yugoslavia in 1975, and a presidential special envoy in 1976. Ronald Reagan appointed him to the D.C. Circuit in 1985, where he served full-time until he assumed senior status in 2000. Chief Justice Rehnquist appointed Silberman to the FISA Court of Review in the mid-1990s. On February 6, 2004, more than a year after the FISA litigation was completed, President George W. Bush appointed Silberman cochair of the Commission on the Intelligence Capabilities of the United States Regarding Weapons of Mass Destruction. The commission's purpose was to explain why U.S. intelligence agencies mistakenly believed that Iraq had weapons of mass destruction prior to the American invasion in March 2003. At the time, critics charged that Silberman was a poor choice for this position because of his "partisanship" and commitment to "right-wing orthodoxy."[29]

Perhaps because of Judge Silberman's expertise in foreign policy and intelligence gathering, he was the most active and inquisitive of the three judges at the session of oral argument on September 9. He focused particularly on the government's claim that it could use FISA surveillance for the *sole purpose* of convicting an agent of a foreign power of any criminal act. The government could use FISA to protect national security in such a situation, Olson argued, whether the crime in question was an "ordinary crime," such as spouse abuse, child pornography, or tax fraud, or a crime related to espionage or international terrorism. Olson's argument, not clearly articulated in the government's brief, stepped beyond using FISA to prosecute national security crimes, such as espionage or international terrorism. The government's new position was that FISA could be used for any type of crime if the purpose of the prosecution was to protect national security.

A skeptical Silberman underlined the unprecedented nature of the government's argument and wondered about the meaning of the Patriot Act's requirement that a "significant purpose" of the surveillance must be to collect "foreign intelligence information" if the government could use FISA surveillance for the sole purpose of convicting an agent of a foreign power. The underlying problem that Silberman had uncovered was that a premise of the government's main argument was in tension with a premise of the government's "alternative" or "fallback" argument. If collecting evidence to prosecute "an agent of a foreign power" of any type of criminal activity was equivalent to collecting "foreign intelligence information," which was a premise of the government's main argument, then what did the requirement of a "significant purpose" mean in the government's fallback argument? Since Olson refused to recognize the bifurcation between gathering "foreign intelligence information" and prosecuting "agents of foreign powers" in the main argument, he could not avoid the appearance of inconsistency when he recognized and applied the distinction in the "alternative" one. In the end, all that Olson could say was that a FISA judge could not preclude the possibility that FISA surveillance would not uncover some thing that in the future was important "in a purely intelligence context." If that were true, Olson seemed to be suggesting, the certification that a "significant purpose" of the surveillance was to collect "foreign intelligence information" would be valid. Silberman seemed to worry that Olson's argument deflated the requirement of a "significant purpose" to the point of meaninglessness. In response to Silberman's request, Olson agreed to submit a supplemental brief on the issue whether it was constitutional for the government to use a FISA order to collect evidence if the government's *sole* or *primary* purpose was to convict an agent of a foreign power of a crime.

An implication of the government's argument was that the original FISA statute had expanded the government's power to use warrantless surveillance in criminal cases, while the Patriot Act had contracted it. This paradoxical conclusion did not escape Silberman's attention. Olson insisted that the "primary purpose" test, which the courts had enforced throughout the 1980s and 1990s, had been a mistake. In his view, the government's primary purpose did not have to be the collection of foreign intelligence information because there was no bifurcation between collecting such information and protecting national security through criminal prosecutions. However, if Olson was right, then the USA PATRIOT Act, which had clearly been enacted to broaden the government's authority to engage in FISA surveillance, had in fact narrowed it because it required that a significant purpose of the surveillance be for the purpose of collecting foreign intelligence information, which the statute seemed to imply was distinct from law enforcement. Sensitive to these paradoxes, Silberman forced Olson to admit that, when the USA PATRIOT Act was enacted, Congress thought that FISA required the "primary purpose" test and accepted the bifurcation between intelligence gathering and law enforcement. If that were true, then it was possible that, even in criminal cases involving agents of foreign power, FISA surveillance after the enactment of the Patriot Act could no longer be authorized unless there was a significant purpose of gathering foreign intelligence information.

The September 9 oral argument had a number of important themes woven around the substantive arguments concerning the lawfulness of FISA surveillance. First, the tragedy of the 9/11 attacks pervaded the session, partly because the anniversary was just a couple of days away, but even more so because Olson lost his wife in the crash of American Airlines Flight 77 into the Pentagon. Secondly, the judges more than once underlined the strange *ex parte* character of the proceedings and speculated on how it was affecting the oral argument. Lastly, certain remarks by Olson highlighted the extremely urgent and important character of the litigation. In one passage, Olson called the FISA application that was under appeal a "potential matter of life or death." Moreover, although Olson was unwilling to say that the lack of coordination and consultation between FI/FCI officers and law enforcement personnel "caused" the 9/11 attacks or "failed to prevent" them, he did argue that the way to "go about" not detecting or preventing another September 11 type of attack was to uphold the FISA court's May 17 decision. Olson's challenge to the judges on the FISA Court of Review was fairly explicit. If they upheld the May 17 decision, they were making it significantly more difficult for the executive branch to protect the American people from another terrorist attack.

EXCERPTS FROM THE TRANSCRIPT
OF THE ORAL ARGUMENT

JUDGE GUY. Good morning, everyone, and welcome to the first ever meeting of the Foreign Intelligence Surveillance Court of Review. . . . Mr. Olson, are you going to be the lead speaker for this group?

SOLICITOR GENERAL OLSON: I am, Your Honor. Thank you very much. . . . [[W]]e're here today because the Foreign Intelligence Surveillance Court's May 17th Order . . . has perpetuated a serious and increasingly destructive barrier which has hamstrung the President and his subordinates in utilizing the Foreign Intelligence Surveillance Act to accomplish the vital and central purpose for which it was created; that is to say, the protection of the United States and its citizens from attack and from international terrorism.

Unfortunately and sadly, two days from now the entire nation will pause to reflect on how bad things can be if our Government is not prepared with every lawful tool available to protect our country and our people from the immeasurable toll that international terrorism can inflict, and to remember the 3,000 lives that were taken from us that day because the resources that we have been given to protect us from such acts either did not work or were not being used effectively.

To prevent this sort of thing from happening again, which is why FISA was enacted in the first place, our intelligence agencies and law enforcement personnel, the President's principal agencies in the war against terrorism, must be able to work together efficiently and effectively and cooperatively. Sadly, that is not the condition in which they operate today.

And the Foreign Intelligence Surveillance Court's Order of May 17th is the most formidable, the most inexplicable and the most easily removable obstacle to achieving the goal for effective and efficient gathering of intelligence to protect the people of this country and this country itself from international terrorism. . . .

JUDGE SILBERMAN: . . . Wait a minute. Stop for a second. Remember this is a strange situation where we don't have an adversary. If we thought the . . . FISA court was in error, . . . wouldn't it be necessary for us to consider the question whether the Patriot Act amendments were constitutional? . . .

SOLICITOR GENERAL OLSON: I understand that if I were on that side of the table I would feel that it would be appropriate to consider the constitutionality of what I was being asked to do. I don't think that it's a close case at all. Because of the reasons that have been articulated by the Supreme Court, for example, in the Keith case, . . . because of the degree of the threat, because of the nature of . . . foreign powers, their ability to work in secret, their ability to frustrate normal law enforcement mechanisms— . . .

JUDGE SILBERMAN: Is it your view . . . [[that]] the Government's motivation, the degree of interest in the Government seeking criminal prosecution, is wholly irrelevant in constitutional terms?

SOLICITOR GENERAL OLSON: Well, I hate—whenever I'm faced with that kind of a question, wholly irrelevant, I hate to say so because I don't know how we can conceive—

JUDGE SILBERMAN: Excuse me, Mr. Olson, your brief actually says that motivation is irrelevant.

SOLICITOR GENERAL OLSON: And I believe that that is the case. Whether one could come up with a conceivable concept in which someone is out to get someone, or something like that, I don't know, but I believe that with respect to FISA the motivation needs to be to collect information to protect the public and to protect the Republic. That's what the definition of foreign intelligence is.

JUDGE SILBERMAN: I'm talking constitutional.

SOLICITOR GENERAL OLSON: I understand that and I agree with what is said in the brief and I can't conceive of a situation in which, especially in this context— . . .

JUDGE SILBERMAN: . . . I for one would like a brief on the constitutionality question. I don't see any way to avoid grappling with that issue.

SOLICITOR GENERAL OLSON: We have no problem whatsoever in providing that brief. We would want a few days to put it together but . . . it's something that we'd be happy to address. . . .

JUDGE SILBERMAN: . . . [[Y]]our brief argues the original FISA statutes never adopted the bifurcation between primary purpose and a criminal law purpose. However, it is fair to say, is it not, that the first time the Justice Department presents that argument it is before this Court. It never was presented before.

SOLICITOR GENERAL OLSON: That's correct.

JUDGE SILBERMAN: And indeed the Justice Department went along with the bifurcation for many years. Not only went along but endorsed it in the letter to Congress asking for modifications of the FISA statute and the Patriot Act.

SOLICITOR GENERAL OLSON: It endorsed it as a reality that the Department was dealing with. Whatever the words that were used, Judge Silberman. And I'm here to say that we do not—we do believe today and after having studied this as intensely as I could possibly have done, I believe that it is correct that that bifurcation based upon purpose is inconsistent with FISA and it was accepted as a matter of accommodation by the Justice Department over the years. . . .

JUDGE SILBERMAN: I'm just trying to figure out what is that significant purpose. . . .

SOLICITOR GENERAL OLSON: . . . [[T]]he Department was attempting to be free from the shackles of having to quantify what it was motivated by or who was interested in what information. . . . That it wouldn't have to say that that was 80 percent of the reasons or 60 percent of the reasons or 49 percent of the reasons and 2 percent this and 5 percent of this. It was intended to make it easier for the Justice Department if it said not a primary purpose but a [[significant]] purpose. . . .

JUDGE SILBERMAN: Suppose the FISA court had before it a case in which the application makes clear that the only methodology that the Justice Department contemplates is criminal prosecution, they wish to get this target and criminally prosecute him, not to prevent something happening in the future because of something he or she did in the past. And they are adamant on that. Would the FISA court be authorized to say since the only purpose suggested or indicated in the documents before us is criminal prosecution, . . . we deny it?

SOLICITOR GENERAL OLSON: Well, I think that that would be still a legitimate application [[for a FISA order]] because we cannot go away from the definition [[of "foreign intelligence information]] in the statute. . . .

JUDGE SILBERMAN: You would [[then]] have us give no meaning to [["significant purpose." It]] . . . means nothing?

SOLICITOR GENERAL OLSON: No, I do believe that it does, provided that the certification by the appropriate officials . . . must be accepted and that the FISA court does not have to start quantifying what the purpose is. You see, . . . whatever the motivation of . . . the Attorney General might be at the time the application is submitted to the Court, that motivation may change later on. The Attorney General has to decide later whether or not that information once acquired will be used for a prosecution. And it seems inconceivable—you posit something that's theoretically possible but in the real world I do not think it's possible. I do not think it is possible that once this information is obtained if it has to do with terrorists and it has to do with agents of foreign powers who are deemed under the definitions of the statute to be violating or could be violating or might be violating the criminal laws of the United States, that that information would then be put in a box someplace that could only and exclusively and invariably be used for a criminal prosecution. The Attorney General might decide [[not]] to go forward with that prosecution, but would that information be discarded? I don't think so. I think that information would still be a part of the information that is acquired with respect to a threat from people that want to violate the criminal laws who are agents of a foreign Government.

In other words, I still don't buy the dichotomy, however persuasive it might be packaged in terms of, well, if you have only this in mind and only this and you can only do that, I don't think that's realistic. . . .

JUDGE SILBERMAN: Is it not fair to say that Congress was certainly under the impression that the primary purpose test stemmed from FISA, which is one of the reasons they amended it. . . . Congress thought it stemmed from FISA, whether or not it's true. . . .

SOLICITOR GENERAL OLSON: Yes, . . . the Justice Department regrettably, in my opinion, went along with where the FISA court was taking [[it]], . . . but the outcome was wrong. . . .

At one point I was talking about—in preparation for this argument, and I talked about the concept of a surgeon and the anesthesiologist not communicating with one another except through the hospital administrator about the condition on a moment-to-moment basis of a patient who is on the operating table. And someone said you've got it a lot more easy than it is, if that operation is taking place in Los Angeles and the person that has to be consulted and scheduled for a consultation is in Washington and there are only certain times during the week when that can happen. Instead of a manic exchange of information when people who are attempting to accomplish a result have in the way of communication, we have made it virtually impossible. . . .

As I said earlier in order to be able to connect the dots someone has got to have knowledge of those various different dots. We can't say that the constraints under which we're operating now caused what happened or failed to prevent what happened or what happened on September 11th could have been prevented had we done this the right way, but we do know, I have no doubt whatsoever, if one would want to make it difficult for us to detect and prevent another September 11th, this is the way I'd go about doing it. I would allow people that have intelligence from here not to talk with people who are experienced here. I would allow people that gather intelligence not talk to people who have the resources of a grand jury or immunity who can obtain other information. I would not allow knowledge with respect to a terrorist ring be brought to the attention of someone who can put legal pressure on someone to come over to the other side. . . .

JUDGE SILBERMAN: . . . Do you have a view what we should do with amicus briefs?

SOLICITOR GENERAL OLSON: Our position is we have no objection to the Court receiving amicus briefs. In fact, I think it's probably good that the Court receives amicus briefs.

JUDGE SILBERMAN: That sets a precedent for this process which worries me a little bit.

SOLICITOR GENERAL OLSON: I understand that. . . . I don't think a Court deciding in a particular case to accept or not accept an amicus brief has ever been done as requiring the Court to always do that or invariably do that, but because this is a special issue and it is important and for the very reasons that you imply when you say that it might be good to address and resolve the constitutional questions, I think it's good for the process.

We would like, again with the constraints that . . . this is one of those cases where we can say it's a potential matter of life or death and so, therefore, we want to get it done, we want to make sure we get to you everything we can as quickly as we can, but I would like to once we saw those amicus briefs have an option within two days or so, again we'll go as fast as we can, to respond to those. . . .

JUDGE SILBERMAN: Mr. Olson, we'd like you to answer a question that assumes arguendo that which you do not wish to assume, that is to say, that you're reduced to your second alternative argument, that the amendment to the statute caused by the Patriot Act relaxed the primary purpose test to a significant purpose test. But that therefore implies that the other purpose would be criminal. If that's the reading of the statute and that's your second alternative argument, that's the appropriate reading of the statute, how does one go about—how does the Court go about determining as part of the review that we've just been describing whether there is a significant purpose or not? You have made the argument that it is no longer a comparative question, but how does the Court go about determining whether this is significant purpose of seeking foreign intelligence information as opposed to criminal prosecution? . . .

SOLICITOR GENERAL OLSON: The problem I have with the premise is that—I have to say that I think that the problem that we have with the premise informs the answer to that question because the range of information . . . that relates to the conduct, activity, behavior of a person who engages in a conspiracy to bomb a building, the Capitol or something like that . . . might relate to a criminal prosecution, might also at the same time have very valuable significance aside from the prosecution.

JUDGE SILBERMAN: I understand. Help me out. Give me an example of one that would fall outside of the significant purpose, assuming Congress meant—

SOLICITOR GENERAL OLSON: Well, I have trouble with that, Judge Silberman—

JUDGE SILBERMAN: So do I. That's why I'm asking. . . .

SOLICITOR GENERAL OLSON: . . . [[I]]t's difficult for me to come up with an illustration that accepts the premise which I think is such an unworkable premise, especially if one considers what the statute meant in the first instance, what the language of the statute clearly means, and the desire of Congress to make it easier, certainly not more difficult, for the President to do the job which is the fundamental job, that is to say, to protect against the terrorists.

JUDGE SILBERMAN: You can't think of any hypothetical? . . . [[Suppose]] the face of the application indicated a desire to use foreign surveillance to determine strictly a domestic crime, that would be—but then you wouldn't have an agent [[of a foreign power]], you wouldn't have an agent. You must have some substantive requirement here if significant purpose is given its literal meaning, you must have some logic to the interpretation of that section which falls outside of the interpretation of an agent of a foreign power.

SOLICITOR GENERAL OLSON: And I suppose if the application itself revealed that there was a purpose to take personal advantage of someone who might be the subject of an investigation, to blackmail that person, or if that person had a domestic relationship and that person was seeing another person's spouse or something like that, if that would be the test on the face of things.

In other words, I'm suggesting that the standard is relatively high for the very reason that it's difficult for the judiciary to evaluate and second guess what a high level executive branch person attempting to fight terrorism is attempting to do. . . .

JUDGE SILBERMAN: I'll try one more time and I'll give up. What other purpose is contemplated besides the purpose of obtaining foreign intelligence information? By stating significant purpose must be to obtain foreign intelligence information necessarily implies there's another kind of purpose.

SOLICITOR GENERAL OLSON: It could be revenge, it could be extortion. It could be vindictiveness.

JUDGE SILBERMAN: Under your alternative argument—your alternative argument is you can have a primary purpose of seeking criminal prosecution. That's your alternative argument in the brief. Nonetheless, a significant purpose is to obtain foreign intelligence information. That's the alternative argument in the brief in which you accept the bifurcation.

SOLICITOR GENERAL OLSON: For the purposes of dealing with it.

JUDGE SILBERMAN: Exactly. That's my problem. So that if you had then a total purpose of criminal prosecution, does that mean you violate . . . [[the "significant purpose" provision]]?

SOLICITOR. GENERAL OLSON: I don't think so, Judge Silberman, for the reason that I explained before.

JUDGE SILBERMAN: We're going around in circles.

SOLICITOR GENERAL OLSON: We're going around in circles but we're going around in circles because the real world, the use of that information even if it is used for a prosecution, it's impossible as I sit here for me in good faith to imagine a situation and I think it would be irresponsible for me to do so, imagine a situation where that might not also be useful in something that comes out in another FISA situation that might have come out six months ago, given that we're dealing with an agent of a foreign Government, to preclude that, that's something that won't have importance to the President in a purely intelligence context? . . .

JUDGE GUY: Then let me close. . . . This is a strange proceeding because it is not adversarial. It is *ex parte*. And if one were to just read the transcript of this hearing today one might think that the adversary, if there was one, is what the insiders refer to as the FISC, the lower body in this matter. And I want to say, first of all, that to the degree that our questions have contributed to that, they're intended for the purpose of gathering information and that's all. . . .

IV. *AMICI CURIAE* BRIEFS AND THE GOVERNMENT'S SUPPLEMENTAL BRIEF

On September 10, the day after the Court of Review heard oral argument and the day before the first anniversary of the 9/11 attacks, the Senate Judiciary Committee held a public hearing that focused on the May 17 decision of the FISA court and the other documents concerning FISA that had become public in August 2002. The title of the hearing was "The USA PATRIOT Act in Practice: Shedding Light on the FISA Process." In his opening statement, Chairman Patrick J. Leahy (D-VT) lamented the secrecy of the FISA process, noting that the oversight committees of Congress had not found out about the "misstatements" and "omissions" in FISA applications in 2000 and 2001 until the disclosure of the FISA court's secret May 17 decision in the summer of 2002. He also expressed his dissatisfaction with the Justice Department's "sweeping claim" in its brief to the Court of Review that FISA surveillance could be used in a case even if the "sole and exclusive purpose" of the investigation was criminal prosecution. He was particularly incensed that the administration had quoted him in support of the argument that prosecutors could "initiate and direct" FISA surveillance. In response, Senator Orrin G. Hatch (R- UT), the ranking Republican member on the committee, argued that the USA PATRIOT Act clearly allowed "greater use of FISA for criminal purposes" and increased "the sharing of intelligence information and coordination of investigations between intelligence and law enforcement officers." Hatch conceded that "the line" between intelligence gathering and criminal investigations was yet unclear and that courts would have to decide whether prosecutors could give "advice and direction" in FISA investigations. In resolving these questions, Hatch added, courts had to appreciate the fact that terrorism in 2002 was far more decentralized and deadly than it was in 1978, the year FISA was enacted. Hatch urged the committee to be "forward looking" and not exaggerate past "missteps and miscues," presumably a reference to the number of "misstatements and omissions" contained in FISA applications in 2000 and 2001 (see box 1.3).

Box 1.3. "SHEDDING LIGHT ON THE FISA PROCESS"*

CHAIRMAN PATRICK J. LEAHY (D-VT):

. . . Over the last two decades, the FISA process has occurred largely in secret. Clearly, specific investigations must be kept secret, but even the basic facts about the FISA process have been resistant to sunlight. The law interpreting FISA has been developed largely behind closed doors. The Justice Department and FBI personnel who prepare the FISA applications work behind closed doors. When the FISA process hits snags, such as during the year immediately before the September 11 attacks, and adversely affects the processing of FISA surveillance applications and orders, the oversight Committees of the Congress should find out a lot sooner than the summer after the September 11 attacks. Even the most general information on FISA surveillance, including how often FISA surveillance targets American citizens, or how often FISA surveillance is used in a criminal case, is unknown to the public.

In matters of national security, we must give the Executive Branch the power it needs to do its job. But we must also have public oversight of its performance. When the Founding Fathers said "if men were all angels, we would need no laws,'" they did not mean secret laws.

. . . The Department of Justice brief makes a sweeping claim regarding the USA PATRIOT Act amendments. The Department asserts that the longstanding "purpose" analysis adopted by numerous courts for more than 20 years is simply wrong. Specifically, the Department claims that using FISA for the sole and exclusive purpose of pursuing a criminal prosecution, as opposed to collecting intelligence, is allowed.

. . . They claim that criminal prosecutors can now initiate and direct secret FISA wiretaps, without normal probable cause requirements and discovery protections, as another tool in criminal investigations, even though they know that the strictures of Title III of the Fourth Amendment cannot be met. In short, the Department is arguing that the normal rules for Title III and criminal search warrants no longer apply in terrorism or espionage cases, even for U.S. persons.

I was surprised to learn that, as the "drafter of the coordination amendment" in the USA PATRIOT Act, the Department cites my statement to support its arguments that there is no longer a distinction between using FISA for a criminal prosecution and using it to collect foreign intelligence. Well, had the Department of Justice taken the time to pick up a phone and call me, I would have told them that was not and is not my belief. . . . .

SENATOR ORRIN G. HATCH (R-UT):

. . . The timing of this hearing—one day before the first-year anniversary of the attack on our country—could not be more telling. Our joint session last Friday in New York City helped to emphasize to everyone the horrible tragedy that our country suffered on September 11th. It reminded us of our continuing need to be vigilant in protecting our country from further terrorist attacks. . . .

Based on the . . . [[relevant provisions of the Patriot Act]], it is clear that Congress intended to allow greater use of FISA for criminal purposes, and to increase the sharing of intelligence information and coordination of investigations between intelligence and law enforcement officers.

At issue now is a very difficult but critical issue, and that is, where to draw the line between intelligence gathering and criminal investigations to ensure that our intelligence community and law enforcement agencies are fully capable of detecting and preventing future terrorist attacks while at the same time ensuring that Americans' civil liberties are preserved. . . .

In reviewing the FISA process, we need to consider the fact that there has been a dramatic change in the terrorist landscape since 1978 when FISA was enacted. There is no question that in response to our country's efforts to fight terrorism worldwide, terrorists are increasingly operating in a more decentralized manner, far different from the terrorist threat that existed in 1978. The threat posed by a small group—even a lone terrorist—may be very real and may involve devastating consequences, even beyond those suffered by our country on September 11th.

(Continued)

Box 1.3. "SHEDDING LIGHT ON THE FISA PROCESS"* (Continued)

Given this increasing threat, we have to ensure that intelligence and law enforcement agencies have sufficient tools to meet this new—and even more dangerous—challenge. . . . This Committee's inquiry should be forward-looking and done without exaggeration of past missteps and miscues which have since been corrected. The stakes are simply too high for anyone to inject politics into an area which requires careful and studied deliberation. . . .

* See "USA PATRIOT Act in Practice: Shedding Light on the FISA Process," hearings before Senate Judiciary Committee, 107th Congress, 2nd Session, September 10, 2002, available at http://www.fas.org/irp/congress/2002_hr/091002 transcript.html.

While senators debated the meaning of the Patriot Act's revisions of FISA, the American Civil Liberties Union, the Center for Democracy and Technology, the Center for National Security Studies, the Electronic Privacy Information Center, the Electronic Frontier Foundation, and the Open Society Institute filed one *amicus curiae* brief (hereafter the "ACLU brief") to the FISA Court of Review, while the National Association of Criminal Defense Lawyers (NACDL) filed a second. The ACLU brief took the position that the FISA provisions of the USA PATRIOT Act could be interpreted in a way consistent with the Fourth Amendment. FISA surveillance was constitutional if the significant purpose of gathering foreign intelligence information was interpreted to preclude criminal prosecution as the primary purpose of the investigation, though it could be a subordinate, secondary, or incidental goal. In contrast, the NACDL argued that there was no viable way to inject significant purpose with enough substance so as to insure, as a matter of statutory construction, that criminal prosecution was not the primary purpose of an investigation. Accordingly, in its view, the provision was inherently constitutionally flawed. It could not be saved through statutory construction.

Despite this difference in whether the "significant purpose" provision was constitutionally salvageable, both *amici* briefs agreed on where to draw the constitutional line. If the sole or primary purpose of an investigation was criminal prosecution, then it was a violation of the Fourth Amendment to permit FISA surveillance. Secondly, FI/FCI officers could share information with law enforcement personnel and they could consult with each other and coordinate their activities to some extent, but what was constitutionally impermissible was for law enforcement to advise or direct how FISA surveillance should be conducted. Accordingly, Ashcroft's March 2002 information-sharing procedures were unconstitutional to the extent that they permitted prosecutors and law enforcement personnel to engage in the "initiation, operation, continuation, or expansion of FISA searches or surveillance."

The following excerpts from the *amici* briefs and the government's supplemental brief focus on the above constitutional question. All three briefs address the Supreme Court's "special needs" cases involving warrantless searches without probable cause in "special circumstances": one of these cases considered whether a public hospital could test pregnant patients for drug use; the other, whether the police could establish vehicle checkpoints for the purpose of interdicting illegal drugs. The Court invalidated both programs because they served a law enforcement purpose. The ACLU's brief highlighted the fact that the Court had not recognized an exception, despite the "seriousness" of the problem of illicit drug use. The NACDL's brief emphasized that the vehicle checkpoint program was not upheld even though it had two lawful secondary purposes: removing impaired drivers from the road and verifying licenses. Based on these cases, the *amici* briefs argued that the government's goal of protecting national security could not justify an exception to the Fourth Amendment. The ACLU brief also argued that the March 2002 information-sharing procedures violated a number of "constitutionally protected interests" other than the Fourth Amendment, while the NACDL's brief explained why existing FISA procedures provided insufficient protections for Fourth Amendment values.

The government's supplemental brief began by endorsing the conclusion that the president has inherent constitutional authority to conduct warrantless surveillance if its purpose in "any degree" was the collection of foreign intelligence information. Accordingly, the FISA framework established a set of procedures clearly higher than the minimum required by the Fourth Amendment. If the target was a U.S. person, Article III judges issued a FISA order only if there was probable cause that the target was an agent of a foreign power. When compared to other types of warrantless searches approved by the Supreme Court, such as checkpoints placed near borders to stem the flow of illegal immigrants, FISA surveillance that satisfied the "significant purpose" test was clearly constitutional. Lastly, the government's brief argued that the FISA court's May 17 order was an unconstitutional judicial intrusion into the executive branch. Judges had no authority to order the OIPR to chaperone all meetings between FI/FCI officers and law enforcement personnel or to enforce Rule 11. Under the cover of reviewing FISA applications, the FISA court was unconstitutionally exercising "the Executive Branch's core national security and foreign policy functions."

EXCERPTS FROM THE ACLU'S *AMICUS CURIAE* BRIEF

. . . [[1. National Security Crimes.]] The government boldly argues that the USA PATRIOT Act authorizes a waiver of the Fourth Amendment's usual requirements whenever the government engages in criminal investigations related to "national security." The government should not be permitted to turn the quest for foreign intelligence into a "pro forma justification for any degree of intrusion into zones of privacy guaranteed by the Fourth Amendment." Indeed, "the whole point of Fourth Amendment protection in this area is to avoid . . . executive abuses through judicial review.". . .

The government's central contention is that FISA "does not discriminate between law enforcement and nonlaw-enforcement protective methods"—that FISA is available even for investigations that are purely criminal, so long as the ultimate purpose of the investigation is to protect against foreign threats to national security. The government vaguely suggests that its ability to protect the nation will be compromised if it cannot rely on FISA for investigations whose primary or exclusive purpose is to gather evidence of criminal conduct. *Amici* of course do not dispute that the government should be able to prosecute spies and terrorists. The government simply misses the constitutional point, however, when it argues that this need justifies use of FISA even for investigations that are purely criminal. . . . [[T]]he raison d'etre of FISA is the collection of foreign intelligence information, and the legitimacy of its departures from the Fourth Amendment's normal requirements rests entirely on the fact that FISA searches and surveillance are directed primarily to the collection of foreign intelligence. If the Government's primary or exclusive purpose in an investigation is the enforcement of criminal law, it must proceed according to the normal strictures of the Fourth Amendment. . . .

The Supreme Court has recognized limited exceptions to the probable cause requirement in a line of cases involving "special needs." Under these cases, Justice Scalia has explained, "[a] search unsupported by probable cause can be constitutional . . . when special needs, *beyond the normal need for law enforcement*, make the warrant and probable-cause requirement impracticable." The "special needs" doctrine simply has no application to searches whose primary purpose is law enforcement. Indeed, the Supreme Court clearly reiterated this well-settled rule only last term.

Ferguson [[*v. City of Charleston* (2001)]] involved a public hospital's policy of testing pregnant patients for drug use and employing the threat of criminal prosecution as a means of coercing patients into substance-abuse treatment. The Court invalidated the policy. "In other special needs cases," the Court wrote, "we . . . tolerated suspension of the Fourth Amendment's warrant or probable cause requirement in part because there was no law enforcement purpose behind the searches in those cases, and there was little, if any, entanglement with law enforcement." In *Ferguson*, however, "the central and indispensable feature of the policy from its inception was the use of law enforcement."

The government concedes that a general interest in crime control cannot constitute a "special need" sufficient to dispense with the probable cause requirement, but it contends, relying on *City of Indianapolis v. Edmond* (2002), that "a 'special interest' concerning a particular type of crime" may suffice. In fact, *Edmond* only reinforces the rule that any search whose primary or exclusive purpose is law enforcement may proceed only on the basis of probable cause. *Edmond* involved vehicle checkpoints instituted in an effort to interdict illegal drugs. The government asserted that the drug crimes were a "severe and intractable" problem, and the Court agreed that "traffic in illegal narcotics creates social harms of the first magnitude." The Court also noted that "[t]he law enforcement problems that the drug trade creates likewise remain daunting and complex, particularly in light of the myriad forms of spin-off crime that it spawns." Notwithstanding the seriousness of the law-enforcement interest with respect to the particular crimes at issue, however, the Court invalidated the checkpoint policy. "[T]he gravity of the threat alone," Justice O'Connor wrote, "cannot be dispositive of questions concerning what means law enforcement officers may employ to pursue a given purpose." The dispositive fact, the Court held, was that the checkpoint policy was instituted "primarily for the ordinary enterprise of investigating crimes." Where the government's "primary purpose . . . is to detect evidence of ordinary criminal wrongdoing," the Fourth Amendment forecloses the government from conducting searches except based on probable cause.

The "special needs" cases reflect that the Fourth Amendment is particularly concerned with intrusions whose purpose is to gather evidence of crime. There is no support, however, for the position—implied by the government's argument—that the Fourth Amendment recognizes a hierarchy amongst crimes. The Fourth Amendment applies to all criminal investigations, not merely those that are concerned with minor crimes. . . .

The Supreme Court's "special needs" cases clearly reaffirm that any search whose primary or exclusive purpose is criminal investigation may proceed only on the basis of probable cause. This basic constitutional protection is not suspended for investigation of crimes that are particularly serious, or for investigations whose ultimate purpose is to protect against threats to national security. Any investigation whose primary or exclusive purpose is to collect evidence of criminal conduct must adhere to the ordinary requirements of the Fourth Amendment.

[[2. Ordinary Crimes.]] . . . While the government refers to espionage and international terrorism as crimes that are entitled to special constitutional status, it repeatedly asserts the arrant principle that FISA is available to purely criminal investigations so long as the government believes that the prosecution of the crime will protect national security. The suggestion appears to be that the government could bypass the ordinary requirements of the Fourth Amendment not just in espionage and international terrorism investigation— a disturbing proposition on its own—but that the government could bypass the Fourth Amendment in *any* criminal investigation, however minor the crime being investigated, so long as the government believes that the prosecution is designed to protect national security threats.

The notion that a search or surveillance may be justified simply because the government invokes the rubric of "national security" flies in the face of the most basic principles of American constitutional democracy. The government's theory would effectively allow the executive branch unilaterally to suspend the ordinary requirements of the Fourth Amendment simply by claiming that a prosecution is designed to address a threat to national security. This Court should not sanction the government's attempt to exploit the rubric of "national security" as a means of avoiding the basic Constitutional requirement that the government stay clear of constitutionally protected areas until it has probable cause to believe that a crime has been committed.

[[3. Other Constitutionally Protected Interests.]] The government's brief urges this Court to dissolve the constitutional borders that separate intelligence investigations from criminal ones and thereby dramatically to extend FISA's reach. As discussed above, any such extension would effectively institutionalize an end-run around the Fourth Amendment's usual requirements. Given the secrecy that cloaks FISA proceedings, any such extension would also jeopardize a host of other constitutionally protected interests. . . .

While some degree of secrecy may be intrinsic to the very nature of foreign intelligence surveillance, as a general matter such secrecy stands in profound tension with basic democratic values. In a democracy, public scrutiny is the principal check on government misconduct. More fundamentally, citizens cannot be said to have chosen their government in any meaningful sense if they are foreclosed from learning what the government's policies are. Even accepting for the moment the necessity of the heavy veil of secrecy that has cloaked FISA proceedings over the past two decades, it must be acknowledged that if secrecy serves the nation, it does so at the expense of democracy. . . .

FISA's failure to require that surveillance targets eventually be notified that their privacy was compromised raises related Due Process concerns because it denies individuals whose communications were inappropriately intercepted any opportunity to challenge the government's actions. Innocent people whose communications are intercepted will probably never find out about the intercept, and those who somehow find out have no way of holding the government to account. . . .

Expanding the circumstances in which the government may invade the individual's protected sphere without probable cause also presents the danger that the government's surveillance power will chill dissent, and indeed that the government may wield its power with the specific intent of chilling dissent. Traditionally, the warrant and probable cause requirements have served as important safeguards of First Amendment interests by precluding the government from intruding into an individual's protected sphere merely because of that individual's exercise of First Amendment rights. . . . Any expansion of the government's authority to conduct electronic surveillance under FISA could easily chill protected speech and implicate serious First Amendment concerns. . . .

Respectfully submitted,

ANN BEESON,
JAMEEL JAFFER,
STEVEN R. SHAPIRO, ACLU

JAMES X. DEMPSEY,
Center for Democracy
    and Technology

KATE MARTIN,
Center for National Security Studies

LEE TIEN,
Electronic Frontier Foundation

DAVID L. SOBEL,
Electronic Privacy Information Center

EXCERPTS FROM THE NATIONAL ASSOCIATION OF CRIMINAL DEFENSE LAWYER'S BRIEF

[[1. "Significant Purpose" Unconstitutional.]] . . . [[E]]ven as Congress rushed to pass the USA PATRIOT Act in October 2001, a number of Members expressed reservations about the constitutionality of the "significant purpose" amendment to FISA in light of the settled "primary purpose" requirement rooted in the Fourth Amendment.

The Supreme Court's "special needs" cases—on which the DOJ inexplicably purports to rely—underscore the principle that searches and seizures that have law enforcement as their primary purpose must satisfy the traditional warrant and probable cause requirements. In *City of Indianapolis v. Edmond* (2000), for example, the Court found unconstitutional a checkpoint program that involved warrantless and suspicionless stops of motorists for "the primary purpose of interdicting illegal narcotics." The Court noted that "[w]e have never approved a checkpoint program whose primary purpose was to detect evidence of ordinary criminal wrongdoing."

The *Edmond* Court rejected two arguments that parallel the DOJ's arguments here. First, the Court dismissed the claim that "the severe and intractable nature of the drug problem" justified the checkpoint program. . . . Similarly here, terrorism-related crimes undoubtedly inflict "social harms of the first magnitude," but the "gravity of the threat alone" cannot justify abandoning the traditional protections of the Fourth Amendment. In a variety of other contexts as well the Supreme Court has refused to recognize Fourth Amendment exceptions based on the seriousness of the crime under investigation.

Second, *Edmond* rejected the argument that the checkpoint program "is justified by its lawful secondary purposes of keeping impaired motorists off the road and verifying licenses and registrations"—an argument that parallels the DOJ's contention here that it may proceed under FISA as long as it has the "lawful secondary purpose" of collecting foreign intelligence information. *Edmond* noted that if such "lawful secondary purposes" sufficed to exempt a search or seizure from the usual Fourth Amendment requirements, "law enforcement authorities would be able to establish checkpoints for virtually any purpose so long as they also included a license or sobriety check." The Court concluded: "For this reason, we examine the available evidence to determine the primary purpose of the checkpoint program. While we recognize the challenges inherent in a purpose inquiry, courts routinely engage in this enterprise in many areas of constitutional jurisprudence as a means of sifting abusive governmental conduct from that which is lawful." Similarly here, if it were enough to avoid the Fourth Amendment warrant and probable cause requirements that an electronic surveillance or physical search had some connection to foreign intelligence that was more than "trivial," "incidental," or "pretextual," federal criminal investigators could use those highly intrusive techniques for "virtually any purpose," as long as a DOJ official could certify to such a foreign intelligence connection and the other requirements of FISA were satisfied.

The Supreme Court reinforced the holding of Edmond in *Ferguson v. City of Charleston* (2001). *Ferguson* involved a state hospital's performance of nonconsensual, warrantless drug screens on pregnant women, the results of which were turned over to law enforcement officers. The Court concluded that the screens violated the Fourth Amendment because the "primary purpose" of the program was to "generate evidence for law enforcement purposes." Just as the DOJ argues here that its proposed use of FISA for law enforcement purposes would serve broader foreign intelligence or national security goals, the City of Charleston argued in *Ferguson* that its drug screening program served the broader goal of "get[ting] the women in question into substance abuse treatment and off of drugs." The Court squarely rejected this contention. . . . *Ferguson*—which the DOJ dismisses in a footnote—leaves no doubt that the government's attempt to use the relaxed FISA standards for surveillance and searches that have the primary purpose of law enforcement violates the Fourth Amendment. . . .

[[2. Inadequacy of FISA Procedures.]] At the outset, the DOJ's emphasis on the "added protections afforded by FISA" seems odd, in light of the disclosure in the May 17, 2002 FISC decision that the executive branch, by its own admission, made "misstatements" and omitted material facts in more than seventy-five FISA applications. These are the misstatements and omissions that the government has chosen to disclose; it is impossible for anyone outside the executive branch to know how many additional falsehoods and errors have gone unreported. That so many "misstatements" could have occurred without detection by the FISC casts significant doubt on the value of FISA's purported "protections."

Nor should the revelation that the executive branch has systematically misled the FISC come as a surprise. The substance and factual aspects of FISA proceedings occur entirely *ex parte* and in secret, not only before the FISC, but even in United States District Court when a criminal defendant seeks to suppress the fruits of FISA surveillance. When a defendant contests the legality of FISA evidence, the Attorney General may file an affidavit in the district court that "disclosure or an adversary hearing would harm the national security of the United States." Upon the filing of such an affidavit, the district court must review the government's application to the FISC, the FISC order authorizing electronic surveillance or a physical search, and other such materials in camera and *ex parte*, unless disclosure of the FISA materials to the defense is "necessary to make an accurate determination of the legality of the surveillance."

In practice, . . . [[the above procedure]] has completely barred defense counsel from access to the application and other materials underlying FISA orders issued by the FISC. To our knowledge, the Attorney General has filed an affidavit in every case where a defendant has sought access to the government's FISA application and related materials; no district court has ever found . . . that disclosure to the defense was "necessary to make an accurate determination of the legality of the surveillance"; and no court of appeals has ever reversed a district court's decision to deny defense access to FISA materials. . . . It is surely no coincidence that "misstatements" have flourished in a regime where the defense never obtains access to the underlying materials and all significant proceedings occur *in camera* and *ex parte*.

The use of *ex parte* procedures to decide the merits of FISA issues represents an extraordinary departure from the normal judicial process in this country. The District of Columbia Circuit has declared that "[o]nly in the most extraordinary circumstances does our precedent countenance court reliance upon *ex parte* evidence to decide the merits of a dispute." Courts enforce this principle because "[i]t is a hallmark of our adversary system that we safeguard party access to the evidence tendered in support of a requested court judgment. The openness of judicial proceedings serves to preserve both the appearance and the reality of fairness in the adjudications of United States courts. It is therefore the firmly held main rule that a court may not dispose of the merits of a case on the basis of *ex parte, in camera* submissions."

Courts generally bar the use of secret evidence and *ex parte* proceedings outside the FISA context because of the grave risk of error that such procedures entail. The Supreme Court has declared that "'[f]airness can rarely be obtained by secret, one-sided determination of facts decisive of rights. . . . No better instrument has been devised for arriving at truth than to give a person in jeopardy of serious loss notice of the case against him and opportunity to meet it.'" . . .

> Respectfully submitted,
> JOHN D. CLINE,
> ZACHARY A. IVES,
> JOSHUA DRATEL,
> NACDL

EXCERPTS FROM THE U.S.'S SUPPLEMENTAL BRIEF

[[1. Inherent Presidential Authority.]] . . . In considering the constitutionality of the amended FISA, it is important to understand that FISA is not required by the Constitution. Rather, the Constitution vests in the President inherent authority to conduct warrantless intelligence surveillance (electronic or otherwise) of foreign powers or their agents, and Congress cannot by statute extinguish that constitutional authority. Both before and after the enactment of FISA, courts have recognized the President's inherent authority to conduct foreign intelligence surveillance. In general, these courts have arrived at the "primary purpose" test as a result of balancing the President's inherent authority against the privacy interests that are affected by warrantless searches.

Given the enormous—and unique—importance of the President's constitutional obligation to protect national security from foreign threats, there is a strong argument that the "primary purpose" test is too strict even for electronic surveillance conducted without prior judicial approval. The government in *Truong* argued that such surveillance is constitutional whenever there is "any degree" of foreign intelligence purpose. . . .

The factors favoring warrantless foreign intelligence searches have become substantially more compelling in the wake of the attacks of September 11. The government's interest has shifted to defense of the Nation from violent attack. "It is more obvious and unarguable that no governmental interest is more compelling than the security of the Nation." While the magnitude of the current threat alone justifies expanding the warrant exception to searches with a significant foreign intelligence purpose, the nature of the threat is also an important consideration. Combating international terrorism is inescapably both a foreign affairs and a law enforcement function. In this context, separation-of-powers concerns require a relaxation of that standard.

[[2. Reasonableness of FISA Surveillance.]] This Court need not decide whether the "primary purpose" test would govern unilateral Executive Branch surveillance conducted today, because the surveillance at issue here is governed by FISA's extensive procedural protections. As mentioned above, FISA orders are issued pursuant to individualized suspicion by an Article III judge. The statute requires certifications from high-ranking Executive Branch officials. It provides for intricate minimization procedures and extensive congressional oversight. And it requires a finding of probable cause—albeit not always the same probable cause that is required in ordinary criminal cases. . . .

. . . [[E]]ven if FISA orders are not warrants in the constitutional sense, the pivotal question for Fourth Amendment purposes is whether FISA-authorized surveillance is reasonable. The Supreme Court has upheld the use of administrative search warrants issued without a traditional showing of probable cause. In *Camara*, for example, the Court held that routine inspections for violations of a city's housing code required a "warrant procedure." However, the Court went on to hold, in this "administrative warrant" context, that the probable cause standard should be "reasonableness." The Court specifically rejected the contention that such "warrants should issue only when the inspector possesses probable cause to believe that a particular dwelling" was in violation of the code, let alone when there is probable cause of a crime.

Indeed, the Supreme Court has also upheld warrantless and suspicionless searches undertaken for reasons other than ordinary, general law enforcement. The Court has recognized that special law enforcement needs—in particular, needs related to foreign affairs and national security—can justify such warrantless and suspicionless searches. See, for instance, *United States v. Martinez-Fuerte* (1976) (upholding permanent immigration checkpoints, in part, due to the "formidable law enforcement problems" inherent in stemming the flow of illegal immigration); *City of Indianapolis v. Edmond* (2000) (characterizing

Martinez-Fuerte as reflecting the "longstanding concern for the protection of the integrity of the border"); see also *Illinois v. McArthur* (2001) ("When faced with *special law enforcement needs*, diminished expectations of privacy, minimal intrusions, or the like, the Court has found that certain general, or individual, circumstances may render a warrantless search or seizure reasonable" (emphasis added; citations omitted).

Whether or not FISA establishes a "warrant" procedure, it clearly imposes procedural protections far beyond those associated with unilateral Executive Branch surveillance of the sort at issue in *Truong*. Thus, FISA surveillance is distinguishable from unilateral surveillance, if not under the Warrant Clause of the Fourth Amendment, then at least under the Reasonableness Clause. As the Supreme Court recognized in the *Keith* case, "security surveillance may involve different policy and practical considerations from the surveillance of 'ordinary crime,'" and may therefore support standards "which differ from those already prescribed for specified crimes in Title III." These different standards, the Court explained in *Keith*, are "compatible with the Fourth Amendment if they are reasonable both in relation to the legitimate need of Government for intelligence information and the protected rights of our citizens." At issue in *Keith* was protection against domestic threats to national security. This case, of course, involves protection of the country from foreign threats, and therefore implicates even more important government interests, and the core of the President's Article II powers.

[[3. Separation of Powers.]] Apart from any constitutional defense of the Patriot Act as interpreted by the government, there are significant constitutional questions raised by the FISC's May 17 order—particularly the "chaperone" requirement and the reporting requirements of its new Rule 11. No Supreme Court opinion has ever recognized the authority of a federal court to impose such structural requirements on the Executive, let alone with respect to such core executive functions. The reasons for this are clear: Article III simply does not grant federal courts any power to order the *internal* workings of the Executive Branch, particularly in the area of foreign intelligence. But even if federal courts had some power to micromanage the Executive Branch, separation of powers prohibits the use of that power to the extent it interferes with core functions of the Executive.

First, nothing in the text of Article III even hints that federal courts have authority to micromanage the Executive Branch. By its plain terms, Article III makes clear that the judicial power is limited to cases and controversies. This limitation "defines the role of the judiciary in a tripartite allocation of power to assure that the federal courts will not intrude into areas committed to other branches of government." Federal courts must "carefully abstain from exercising any power that is not strictly judicial in its character, and which is not clearly confided in [them] by the Constitution." Here, the FISC went beyond the mere decision of an Article III case or controversy by attempting to impose rules for the operation of the Executive Branch and structure the functions of different units with the Executive Branch. . . .

Concern about the appropriate role of the Article III judiciary is especially pronounced where, as here, the case involves the functions of the Executive Branch in the area of national security. The Supreme Court has explained that "no government interest is more compelling than the security of the Nation." The text, structure, and history of the Constitution demonstrate that the primary responsibility to protect this interest is vested in the President. Article II, section 2 states that he "shall be Commander in Chief of the Army and Navy of the United States." The Constitution also vests in the President all of the executive power and imposes on him a duty to execute the laws. These powers give the President broad constitutional authority to respond to threats to the national security. Further, as the courts have repeatedly recognized, the President possesses *exclusive* power over the conduct of foreign affairs. The conduct of foreign counterintelligence investigations is a necessary correlate to these executive powers. In order to successfully defend the Nation from threats to its security, the President must have the ability to gather and disseminate foreign intelligence information that will allow him and his assistants to develop and execute the most appropriate policies. This is an area where Article III intervention is particularly unsuited, in light of the structural advantages of the Executive to act with speed, secrecy, and unity of energy and the relative incompetence of the federal judiciary in such matters. . . .

> JOHN ASHCROFT,
> Attorney General

V. THE DECISION

While the FISA Court of Review considered the briefs filed by the government and the ACLU and the NACDL during September and October of 2002, the Senate–House joint inquiry into the activities of the U.S. intelligence community regarding the 9/11 attacks held a number of public hearings. Constituted in February, the joint inquiry was charged in part with conducting "a factual review" of what the intelligence community "knew or should have known" prior to September 11, 2001, and identifying and examining any systemic problems that "may have impeded" the intelligence community in "learning of or preventing" the 9/11 attacks. At the hearings, Eleanor Hill, staff director of the joint inquiry, recounted what the investigation had uncovered. On September 20, she explained that the CIA knew that two members of al-Qaeda, Khalid al-Mihdhar and Nawaf al-Hazmi, had met in Kuala Lumpur, Malaysia, in December 1999, but did not add either individual to any watchlist denying entry into the United States. Nor did the CIA tell the FBI that Mihdhar had a U.S. multiple-entry visa. In March 2000 the CIA learned that Hazmi had entered the United States through the Los Angeles International Airport, but the CIA did nothing with this information, nor did it make any attempt to discover if Mihdhar had arrived with him. Following the attack on the USS *Cole* in October 2000, the CIA determined that one of the planners of the attack, Tawfiq Mahomed Aleh Atash, had also attended the 1999 meeting in Malaysia. In June 2001, FBI agents handling the criminal investigation of the *Cole* attack requested more information on Mihdhar, but the CIA declined to provide any.[30]

On August 21, 2001 an FBI analyst assigned to the CIA's Counter Terrorism Center discovered that Mihdhar had entered the United States with Hazmi in March 2000, that he had left in June, and that he had just returned in July 2001 through New York. Both Mihdhar and Hazmi were watchlisted and a routine intelligence investigation was opened concerning Mihdhar's whereabouts. On August 29, a New York FBI agent working the *Cole* criminal case asked headquarters by e-mail to open a full criminal investigation to find Mihdhar, but headquarters declined to do so because the only evidence connecting Mihdhar to the *Cole* attack was gathered on the foreign intelligence side of the "wall." Headquarters advised the law-enforcement agent that he could not be present at any future interview of Mihdhar. The agent complained bitterly in a follow-up e-mail, "Whatever has happened to this—someday someone will die—wall or not—the public will not understand why we were not more effective and throwing every resource we had at certain 'problems.' Let's hope the [[FBI's]] National Security Law Unit will stand behind their decisions then, especially since the biggest threat to us now, UBL [[Osama bin Laden]], is getting the most 'protection.'" The intelligence investigation did not locate either Mihdhar or Hazmi prior to the 9/11 attacks.[31] Both were on American Airlines Flight 77 that crashed into the Pentagon.

Four days later, on September 24, 2002, Hill summarized the so-called "Phoenix memo" that FBI Special Agent Kenneth Williams had circulated inside the FBI during July 2001. The memo noted that an "inordinate" number of individuals with links to al-Qaeda were pursuing aviation-related training and speculated that such training might be related to some future terrorist attack. Although Williams sent the memo to counterterrorism units at FBI Headquarters and to several agents on the International Terrorism squad in the New York Field Office, it was generally ignored. Even after the Minneapolis Field Office opened an international terrorism investigation of Zacarias Moussaoui in August 2001, the memo received little to no attention. Moussaoui had raised suspicions because he wanted to train on a Boeing 747 Model 400 aircraft simulator at a flight school in Minneapolis, even though he lacked the typical qualifications for such training: he did not have a pilot's license, was not employed by an airline, and had only fifty hours of flight training in light civil aircraft.[32]

The Immigration and Naturalization Service took Moussaoui into custody because his visa had expired, but lawyers at FBI headquarters refused to seek a FISA order authorizing a search of his computer because they mistakenly thought that there was insufficient evidence that he was an agent of a foreign power. A Minneapolis FBI supervisor objected, pointing to the possibility that Moussaoui might "take control of a plane and fly it into the World Trade Center." Despite the supervisor's concerns, Headquarters advised the Minneapolis Office not to seek a standard criminal search warrant for the computer because any such effort might undermine a later FISA application. The result was that Moussaoui's computer was not searched prior to 9/11, although a later search confirmed that it contained information that might have enabled the FBI to prevent the attacks.[33]

The media's coverage of the joint inquiry's public hearings was comprehensive and intense. Accordingly, the nation's attention was focused on the failures of the intelligence community as the FISA Court of Review deliberated on the constitutionality of the Patriot Act's revisions of FISA. Finally, on November 18, the three judges unanimously reversed the May 17 decision of the FISA court and invalidated the so-called minimization procedures that had limited the degree to which prosecutors could initiate and control FISA surveillance. In doing so, the Court of Review accepted the government's argument that FISA had never precluded the use of foreign intelligence information in criminal prosecutions. Since gathering this sort of information almost invariably led to the accumulation of evidence of criminal activity, Congress never intended for FISA to bar its use in any prosecution of national security crimes. The Court of Review, however, conceded that the Patriot Act had "muddied the landscape" by requiring that a "significant purpose" of FISA surveillance must be to collect foreign intelligence information. Congress had made this change without altering the definition of "foreign intelligence information." The result was what the Court of Review called an "analytic conundrum." If gathering evidence of foreign intelligence crimes fit the definition of gathering foreign intelligence information, then why could the government not use FISA if its sole purpose was to investigate and prosecute a crime of this sort? In the end, the Court of Review concluded that the "better reading" of the statute was that the "significant purpose" requirement precluded the use of FISA if the government's sole purpose was prosecution. At a minimum, if FISA surveillance was to be authorized, the government had to have a significant purpose of gathering foreign intelligence information separate and distinct from criminal prosecution.

What was remarkable about the Court of Review's position was that a statute that had been intended to broaden the president's power to use FISA surveillance had in fact narrowed it. The requirement of a significant purpose allowed FISA surveillance if the primary purpose of the surveillance was criminal prosecution, but not if the government's sole and exclusive purpose was to prosecute crimes implicating national security. In practical terms, the court noted, this implication would make no difference so long as the government retained a realistic option of dealing with the target in some way other than by criminal prosecution. In addition, the Court of Review held that the government could not use FISA surveillance if an agent of a foreign power was involved in criminal activity wholly unrelated to espionage or terrorism. In such a case, even if the government's purpose was to protect national security, its only recourse was to meet the probable cause standards of a Title III warrant.

As to constitutional issues, the Court of Review assumed that the president did have inherent authority to conduct warrantless searches for the purpose of collecting foreign intelligence information. The real question was whether FISA "amplified" presidential power by providing a "mechanism" by which FISA surveillance became "reasonable" and therefore compatible with the Fourth Amendment. The court ruled that, so long as there was "a significant purpose" of collecting foreign intelligence information, the surveillance was compatible with the Fourth Amendment and therefore any evidence collected could be used in a criminal trial. The court rejected the argument that the government's foreign policy interests "recede" if and when criminal prosecution becomes the "primary purpose." Halting acts of terrorism and espionage through criminal prosecutions was one form of pursuing counterintelligence initiatives. In such cases, the government's purpose was not, as it was in cases of ordinary crime, to punish the wrongdoer or deter other people from engaging in comparable conduct; rather, it was "to stop or frustrate the immediate criminal activity" because punishment of a terrorist was "often a moot point." The Court of Review claimed that the line drawn between ordinary crime and foreign intelligence crimes was a reasonable one since preventing the latter type of crime served a special need apart from ordinary law enforcement, a type of need that the Supreme Court had said could justify warrantless and even suspicionless searches in other contexts, such as apprehending drunk drivers or securing a national border. Lastly, the FISA court's chaperone requirement and Rule 11, according to the Court of Review, constituted an unconstitutional intrusion of the judicial branch into the internal operations of the executive.

EXCERPTS FROM THE FISA COURT OF REVIEW'S DECISION

[[1. The Original FISA.]] . . . The origin of what the government refers to as the false dichotomy between foreign intelligence information that is evidence of foreign intelligence crimes and that which is not appears to have been a Fourth Circuit case [[*United States v. Truong Dinh Hung*]] decided in 1980. That case, however, involved an electronic surveillance carried out prior to the passage of FISA and predicated on the President's executive power. In approving the district court's exclusion of evidence obtained through a warrantless surveillance subsequent to the point in time when the government's investigation became "primarily" driven by law enforcement objectives, the court held that the Executive Branch should be excused from securing a warrant only when "the object of the search or the surveillance is a foreign power, its agents or collaborators," and "the surveillance is conducted 'primarily' for foreign intelligence reasons." Targets must "receive the protection of the warrant requirement if the government is primarily attempting to put together a criminal prosecution." Although the *Truong* court acknowledged that "almost all foreign intelligence investigations are in part criminal" ones, it rejected the government's assertion that "if surveillance is to any degree directed at gathering foreign intelligence, the executive may ignore the warrant requirement of the Fourth Amendment."

Several circuits have followed *Truong* in applying similar versions of the "primary purpose" test, despite the fact that *Truong* was not a FISA decision. . . .

[[These circuit courts never explained why they]] . . . apparently read foreign intelligence information to exclude evidence of crimes—endorsing the district court's implied dichotomy—when the statute's definitions of foreign intelligence and foreign agent are actually cast in terms of criminal conduct. . . .

[[It is almost as if these courts have assumed]] . . . that the government seeks foreign intelligence information (counterintelligence) for its own sake—to expand its pool of knowledge—because there is no discussion of how the government would use that information outside criminal prosecutions. That is not to say that the government could have no other use for that information. The government's overriding concern is to stop or frustrate the agent's or the foreign power's activity by any means, but if one considers the actual ways in which the government would foil espionage or terrorism it becomes apparent that criminal prosecution analytically cannot be placed easily in a separate response category. . . .

In sum, we think that the FISA as passed by Congress in 1978 clearly did *not* preclude or limit the government's use or proposed use of foreign intelligence information, which included evidence of certain kinds of criminal activity, in a criminal prosecution. [[However,]] . . . some time in the 1980s—the exact moment is shrouded in historical mist—the [[Justice]] Department applied the *Truong* analysis to an interpretation of the FISA statute. What is clear is that in 1995 the Attorney General adopted "Procedures for Contacts Between the FBI and the Criminal Division Concerning Foreign Intelligence and Foreign Counterintelligence Investigations."

Apparently to avoid running afoul of the primary purpose test used by some courts, the 1995 Procedures limited contacts between the FBI and the Criminal Division in cases where FISA surveillance or searches were being conducted by the FBI for foreign intelligence (FI) or foreign counterintelligence (FCI) purposes. The procedures state that "the FBI and Criminal Division should ensure that advice intended to preserve the option of a criminal prosecution does not inadvertently result in either the fact or the appearance of the Criminal Division's *directing or controlling* the FI or FCI investigation toward law enforcement objectives. Although these procedures provided for significant information sharing and coordination between criminal and FI or FCI investigations, based at least in part on the "directing or controlling" language, they eventually came to be narrowly interpreted within the Department of Justice, and most particularly by OIPR, as requiring OIPR to act as a "wall" to prevent the FBI intelligence officials from communicating with the Criminal Division regarding ongoing FI and FCI investigations. Thus, the focus became the nature of the underlying investigation, rather than the general purpose of the surveillance. Once prosecution of the target was being considered, the procedures, as interpreted by OIPR in light of the case law, prevented the Criminal Division from providing any meaningful advice to the FBI. . . .

[[2. The Impact of the Patriot Act.]] The passage of the Patriot Act altered and to some degree muddied the landscape. In October 2001, Congress amended FISA to change "the purpose" language . . . to "a significant purpose." It also added a provision allowing "Federal officers who conduct electronic surveillance to acquire foreign intelligence information" to "consult with Federal law enforcement officers to coordinate efforts to investigate or protect against" attack or other grave hostile acts, sabotage or international terrorism, or clandestine intelligence activities, by foreign powers or their agents. . . .

[[These]] . . . Patriot Act amendments clearly disapprove the primary purpose test. And as a matter of straightforward logic, if a FISA application can be granted even if "foreign intelligence" is only a significant—not a primary—purpose, another purpose can be primary. One other legitimate purpose that could exist is to prosecute a target for a foreign intelligence crime. We therefore believe the Patriot Act amply supports the government's alternative argument but, paradoxically, the Patriot Act would seem to conflict with the government's first argument because by using the term "significant purpose," the Act now implies that another purpose is to be distinguished from a foreign intelligence purpose.

. . . In short, even though we agree that the original FISA did not contemplate the "false dichotomy," the Patriot Act actually did—which makes it no longer false. The addition of the word "significant". . . imposed a requirement that the government have a measurable foreign intelligence purpose, other than just criminal prosecution of even foreign intelligence crimes. [[Therefore,]] . . . the significant purpose amendment . . . must be interpreted as giving the FISA court the authority to review the government's purpose in seeking the information.

That leaves us with something of an analytic conundrum. On the one hand, Congress did not amend the definition of foreign intelligence information which, we have explained, includes evidence of foreign intelligence crimes. On the other hand, Congress accepted the dichotomy between foreign intelligence and law enforcement by adopting the significant purpose test. Nevertheless, it is our task to do our best to read the statute to honor congressional intent. The better reading, it seems to us, excludes from the purpose of gaining foreign intelligence information a sole objective of criminal prosecution. We therefore reject the government's argument to the contrary. Yet this may not make much practical difference. Because, as the government points out, when it commences an electronic surveillance of a foreign agent, typically it will not have decided whether to prosecute the agent (whatever may be the subjective intent of the investigators or lawyers who initiate an investigation). So long as the government entertains a realistic option of dealing with the agent other than through criminal prosecution, it satisfies the significant purpose test.

The important point is—and here we agree with the government—the Patriot Act amendment, by using the word "significant," eliminated any justification for the FISA court to balance the relative weight the government places on criminal prosecution as compared to other counterintelligence responses. If the certification of the application's purpose articulates a broader objective than criminal prosecution—such as stopping an ongoing conspiracy—and includes other potential nonprosecutorial responses, the government meets the statutory test. Of course, if the court concluded that the government's sole objective was merely to gain evidence of past criminal conduct—even foreign intelligence crimes—to punish the agent rather than halt ongoing espionage or terrorist activity, the application should be denied.

The government claims that even prosecutions of *non*foreign intelligence crimes are consistent with a purpose of gaining foreign intelligence information so long as the government's objective is to stop espionage or terrorism by putting an agent of a foreign power in prison. That interpretation transgresses the original FISA. It will be recalled that Congress intended [[FISA]] . . . to prevent the government from targeting a foreign agent when its "true purpose" was to gain nonforeign intelligence information—such as evidence of ordinary crimes or scandals. It can be argued, however, that by providing that an application is to be granted if the government has only a "significant purpose" of gaining foreign intelligence information, the Patriot Act allows the government to have a primary objective of prosecuting an agent for a nonforeign intelligence crime. Yet we think that would be an anomalous reading of the amendment. For we see not the slightest indication that Congress meant to give that power to the Executive Branch. Accordingly, the manifestation of such a purpose, it seems to us, would continue to disqualify an application. That is not to deny that ordinary crimes might be inextricably intertwined with foreign intelligence crimes. For example, if a group of international terrorists were to engage in bank robberies in order to finance the manufacture of a bomb, evidence of the bank robbery should be treated just as evidence of the terrorist act itself. But the FISA process cannot be used as a device to investigate wholly unrelated ordinary crimes. . . .

[[3. Fourth Amendment.]] Having determined that FISA, as amended, does not oblige the government to demonstrate to the FISA court that its primary purpose in conducting electronic surveillance is *not* criminal prosecution, we are obliged to consider whether the statute as amended is consistent with the Fourth Amendment. . . .

Ultimately, the question becomes whether FISA, as amended by the Patriot Act, is a reasonable response based on a balance of the legitimate need of the government for foreign intelligence information to protect against national security threats with the protected rights of citizens. To answer that question . . ., it is necessary to consider carefully the underlying rationale of the primary purpose test.

It will be recalled that the case that set forth the primary purpose test as *constitutionally required* was *Truong*. The Fourth Circuit thought that *Keith*'s balancing standard implied the adoption of the primary purpose test. We reiterate that *Truong* dealt with a pre-FISA surveillance based on the President's constitutional responsibility to conduct the foreign affairs of the United States. Although *Truong* suggested the line it drew was a constitutional minimum that would apply to a FISA surveillance, it had no occasion to consider the application of the statute carefully. The *Truong* court, as did all the other courts to have decided the issue, held that the President did have inherent authority to conduct warrantless searches to obtain foreign intelligence information. It was incumbent upon the court, therefore, to determine the boundaries of that constitutional authority in the case before it. We take for granted that the President does have that authority and, assuming that is so, FISA could not encroach on the President's constitutional power. The question before us is the reverse, does FISA amplify the President's power by providing a mechanism that at least approaches a classic warrant and which therefore supports the government's contention that FISA searches are constitutionally reasonable.

The district court in the *Truong* case had excluded evidence obtained from electronic surveillance after the government's investigation—the court found—had converted from one conducted for foreign intelligence reasons to one conducted primarily as a criminal investigation. (The defendants were convicted based in part on surveillance evidence gathered before that point.) The district judge had focused on the date that the Criminal Division had taken a central role in the investigation. The court of appeals endorsed that approach stating:

> We think that the district court adopted the proper test, because once surveillance becomes primarily a criminal investigation, the courts are entirely competent to make the usual probable cause determination, and because, importantly, individual privacy interests come to the fore *and government foreign policy concerns recede* when the government is primarily attempting to form the basis of a criminal prosecution.

That analysis, in our view, rested on a false premise and the line the court sought to draw was inherently unstable, unrealistic, and confusing. The false premise was the assertion that once the government moves to criminal prosecution, its "foreign policy concerns" recede. As we have discussed in the first part of the opinion, that is simply not true as it relates to counterintelligence. In that field the government's primary purpose is to halt the espionage or terrorism efforts, and criminal prosecutions can be, and usually are, interrelated with other techniques used to frustrate a foreign power's efforts. Indeed, the Fourth Circuit itself, rejecting defendants' arguments that it should adopt a "solely foreign intelligence purpose test," acknowledged that "almost all foreign intelligence investigations are in part criminal investigations."

The method the court endorsed for determining when an investigation became primarily criminal was based on the organizational structure of the Justice Department. The court determined an investigation became primarily criminal when the Criminal Division played a lead role. This approach has led, over time, to the quite intrusive organizational and personnel tasking the FISA court adopted. Putting aside the impropriety of an Article III court imposing such organizational strictures . . . , the line the Truong court adopted—subsequently referred to as a "wall"—was unstable because it generates dangerous confusion and creates perverse organizational incentives. That is so because counterintelligence brings to bear both classic criminal investigation techniques as well as less focused intelligence gathering. Indeed, effective counterintelligence, we have learned, requires the wholehearted cooperation of all the government's personnel who can be brought to the task. A standard which punishes such cooperation could well be thought dangerous to national security. Moreover, by focusing on the subjective motivation of those who initiate investigations, the *Truong* standard, as administered by the FISA court, could be thought to discourage desirable initiatives.

Recent testimony before the Joint Intelligence Committee amply demonstrates that the *Truong* line is a very difficult one to administer. Indeed, it was suggested that the FISA court requirements based on *Truong* may well have contributed, whether correctly understood or not, to the FBI missing opportunities to anticipate the September 11, 2001 attacks.

The Fourth Circuit recognized that the Supreme Court had never considered the constitutionality of warrantless government searches for foreign intelligence reasons, but concluded the analytic framework the Supreme Court adopted in *Keith*—in the case of domestic intelligence surveillance—pointed the way to the line the Fourth Circuit drew. The Court in *Keith* had, indeed, balanced the government's interest against individual privacy interests, which is undoubtedly the key to this issue as well; but we think the *Truong* court misconceived the government's interest and, moreover, did not draw a more appropriate distinction that Keith at least suggested. That is the line drawn in the original FISA statute itself between ordinary crimes and foreign intelligence crimes. . . .

The main purpose of ordinary criminal law is twofold: to punish the wrongdoer and to deter other persons in society from embarking on the same course. The government's concern with respect to foreign intelligence crimes, on the other hand, is overwhelmingly to stop or frustrate the immediate criminal activity. As we discussed in the first section of this opinion, the criminal process is often used as part of an integrated effort to counter the malign efforts of a foreign power. Punishment of the terrorist or espionage agent is really a secondary objective; indeed, punishment of a terrorist is often a moot point.

The distinction between ordinary criminal prosecutions and extraordinary situations underlies the Supreme Court's approval of entirely warrantless and even suspicionless searches that are designed to serve the government's "special needs, beyond the normal need for law enforcement." Apprehending drunk drivers and securing the border constitute such unique interests beyond ordinary, general law enforcement.

A recent case, *City of Indianapolis v. Edmond* (2000), is relied on by both the government and *amici*. In that case, the Court held that a highway checkpoint designed to catch drug dealers did not fit within its special needs exception because the government's "primary purpose" was merely "to uncover evidence of ordinary criminal wrongdoing." The Court rejected the government's argument that the "severe and intractable nature of the drug problem" was sufficient justification for such a dragnet seizure lacking any individualized suspicion. *Amici* particularly rely on the Court's statement that "the gravity of the threat alone cannot be dispositive of questions concerning what means law enforcement officers may employ to pursue a given purpose."

But by "purpose" the Court makes clear it was referring not to a subjective intent, which is not relevant in ordinary Fourth Amendment probable cause analysis, but rather to a programmatic purpose. The Court distinguished the prior checkpoint cases *Martinez-Fuerte* (involving checkpoints less than 100 miles from the Mexican border) and *Sitz* (checkpoints to detect intoxicated motorists) on the ground that the former involved the government's "longstanding concern for the protection of the integrity of the border," and the latter was "aimed at reducing the immediate hazard posed by the presence of drunk drivers on the highways." The Court emphasized that it was decidedly not drawing a distinction between suspicionless seizures with a "nonlaw-enforcement primary purpose" and those designed for law enforcement. Rather, the Court distinguished general crime control programs and those that have another particular purpose, such as protection of citizens against special hazards or protection of our borders. The Court specifically acknowledged that an appropriately tailored roadblock could be used "to thwart an imminent terrorist attack." The nature of the "emergency," which is simply another word for threat, takes the matter out of the realm of ordinary crime control.

[[5. Conclusion.]] FISA's general programmatic purpose, to protect the nation against terrorists and espionage threats directed by foreign powers, has from its outset been distinguishable from "ordinary crime control." After the events of September 11, 2001, though, it is hard to imagine greater emergencies facing Americans than those experienced on that date.

We acknowledge, however, that the constitutional question presented by this case—whether Congress's disapproval of the primary purpose test is consistent with the Fourth Amendment—has no definitive jurisprudential answer. The Supreme Court's special needs cases involve random stops (seizures) not electronic searches. In one sense, they can be thought of as a greater encroachment into personal privacy because they are not based on any particular suspicion. On the other hand, wiretapping is a good deal more intrusive than an automobile stop accompanied by questioning.

Although the Court in *City of Indianapolis* cautioned that the threat to society is not dispositive in determining whether a search or seizure is reasonable, it certainly remains a crucial factor. Our case may well involve the most serious threat our country faces. Even without taking into account the President's inherent constitutional authority to conduct warrantless foreign intelligence surveillance, we think the procedures and government showings required under FISA, if they do not meet the minimum Fourth Amendment warrant standards, certainly come close. We, therefore, believe firmly, applying the balancing test drawn from *Keith*, that FISA as amended is constitutional because the surveillances it authorizes are reasonable.

Accordingly, we reverse the FISA court's orders in this case to the extent they imposed conditions on the grant of the government's applications, vacate the FISA court's Rule 11, and remand with instructions to grant the applications as submitted and proceed henceforth in accordance with this opinion.

VI. POSTSCRIPT

The ACLU asked the Supreme Court to review the FISA Court of Review's decision, but its petition was turned down, perhaps because the ACLU was not a true party to the case, but only an *amicus curiae*, a "friend of the court." The government could have appealed the decision, but it had no interest in doing so because it had largely prevailed at the Court of Review. Perhaps the person who was the target of the FISA surveillance that was litigated before the Court of Review could have appealed, but that person obviously did not because he or she did not know about the surveillance. The upshot of the denial of the ACLU's petition is that the Supreme Court will not consider the Court of Review's decision until someone is convicted of a crime based on evidence collected under the March 2002 procedures regarding FISA surveillance. If and when that happens, a defendant will be able to argue that the FISA surveillance was unconstitutional because the government's primary purpose had been to gain a criminal conviction, not to gather foreign intelligence information, and because criminal prosecutors had initiated and controlled the FISA surveillance, not FI/FCI personnel. How long it will take for such a case to reach the Supreme Court is anyone's guess, but there is no question that it will take years. Moreover, although the "significant purpose" provision of the USA PATRIOT Act was scheduled to sunset on December 31, 2005, Congress, after a series of extensions, reauthorized the Patriot Act in March 2006 without imposing any sunset provisions on the changes to FISA. The upshot is that the FISA Court of Review's decision will remain the law of the land for the foreseeable future. For that very reason, the reasoning contained in it deserves to be studied and scrutinized.

Following the 9/11 attacks, the number of FISA orders approved by the FISA court has gone up significantly. While 934 applications were approved in 2001, 1,228 of 1,228 applications were approved in 2002, followed by

1,724 of 1,727 in 2003, and 1,754 of 1,758 in 2004. In both 2003 and 2004, the eleven judges on the FISA court issued more FISA orders than the total number of Title III warrants issued by all federal judges. Although the FISA court modified a significant number of FISA applications during this time frame, it only denied four requests (all in 2003), two of which were subsequently approved by the court. The government withdrew three of its applications in 2004, but one of these was approved after it was resubmitted.[34] What these statistics suggest is that FISA surveillance is playing an important role on the war on terrorism and that federal criminal investigators and prosecutors are relying heavily on FISA to gather evidence to prosecute international terrorists. On the other hand, there are indications that the pattern of abuses of FISA surveillance outlined in the FISA court's May 17 decision has not been rectified. In 2002, the Electronic Privacy Information Center obtained through an FOIA lawsuit a revealing FBI memo. It described a disturbing picture of FBI agents illegally videotaping suspects, intercepting e-mails without any court approval, recording phone conversations not authorized by any FISA order, and continuing surveillance past legal deadlines.[35]

In 2004, Congress expanded FISA's definition of an agent of a foreign power. The so-called "lone wolf" provision of the Intelligence Reform and Terrorism Prevention Act authorized FISA surveillance for those who "engage in international terrorism" or "activities in preparation" for such acts of terrorism.[36] Accordingly, even if a terrorist acted independently of all foreign governments or other foreign entities, he or she was nonetheless, somewhat paradoxically, identified as an agent of a foreign power. In deciding whether to authorize FISA surveillance of such a non-U.S. person, a FISA judge would not have to find probable cause that there was any connection between that person and any kind of foreign entity. All that was required was that there was probable cause to believe that the person in question was involved in international terrorism or preparing to become so involved. It was not at all clear how individuals involved in international terrorism were to be distinguished from those who were only domestic terrorists.

Lastly, in August 2007, Congress enacted the "Protect America Act," which exempted international phone calls and e-mails from FISA requirements even if the origin or destination of the communication was from someone in the United States. The only substantive restriction was that the surveillance had to be "directed at a person reasonably believed to be located outside of the United States." The FISA Court's role was limited to reviewing the "reasonableness" of the procedures that the director of national Intelligence and the attorney general adopted to insure this result.[37] It had no role in approving individual instances of surveillance on a case-by-case basis. The upshot was that evidence against a resident of the United States could be obtained through surveillance initiated completely by executive officials, so long as it was "directed" at someone outside the United States. In turn, the government could use this evidence to obtain a FISA order that would authorize surveillance of the resident's domestic communications, which in turn could produce additional evidence that could be used in a criminal prosecution of the resident. Whether such a scenario is consistent with the Fourth Amendment is a debatable question, but it is unlikely that the Supreme Court will be able to rule on this controversial issue in the foreseeable future.

NOTES

1. The USA PATRIOT Act also amended FISA in other important ways that are not discussed in this chapter. For example, see Sections 206, 214, and 215 of the USA PATRIOT Act, available at www.epic.org/privacy/terrorism/hr3162.html.

2. *Chimel v. California*, 395 U.S. 752 (1969); *Terry v. Ohio*, 392 U.S. 1 (1968); *United States v. Santana*, 427 U.S. 38 (1976); *United States v. Verdugo-Urquidez*, 494 U.S. 259 (1990).

3. 389 U.S. 347 (1967). Also see *Berger v. New York*, 388 U.S. 41 (1967).

4. Public Law 90-351, 82 Stat. 211, adding 18 U.S.C. Section 2510 et seq.

5. 407 U.S. 297, 301, 313 (1972).

6. Id. at 322-323.

7. Id. at 308 and 322.

8. See *United States v. Brown*, 484 F.2d 418 (5th Cir. 1973); *United States v. Butenko*, 494 F.2d 593 (3rd Cir. 1974); *United States v. Buck*, 548 F.2d 871 (9th Cir. 1977); and *United States v. Truong Dinh Hung*, 629 F.2d 908 (4th Cir. 1980). *Butenko* and *Truong*, in particular, insisted that the primary purpose of the warrantless search had to be for the collection of foreign intelligence information. Against this trend of cases in favor of the constitutionality of warrantless surveillance in cases involving foreign intelligence gathering, the D.C. Circuit held that it violated the Fourth Amendment in *Zweibon v. Mitchell*, 516 F.2d 594 (D.C. Cir. 1975).

9. 50 U.S.C. 1801 (a) and (b).

10. 50 U.S.C. 1805(a)(3)(A).

11. See *United States v. Duggan*, 743 F.2d 59 (2d Cir. 1984); *United States v. Pelton*, 835 F.2d 1067 (4th Cir. 1987); *United States v. Radia*, 827 F.2d 1458 (11th Cir. 1987); *United States v. Johnson*, 952 F.2d 565 (1st Cir. 1992). The 9th Circuit raised doubts concerning the practicality of the "primary purpose" test in *United States v. Sarkissian*, 841 F.2d 959 (9th Cir. 1988), but the trend of circuit court decisions supported this standard.

12. *Final Report of the Attorney General's Review Team on the Handling of the Los Alamos National Laboratory Investigation* (*Bellows Report*), especially chapter 19; and General Accounting Office, *FBI Intelligence Investigations: Coordination with Justice on Counterintelligence Criminal Matters is Limited* (July 2001) (GAO-01-780).

13. Dan Stober and Ian Hoffman, *The Convenient Spy: Wen Ho Lee and the Politics of Nuclear Espionage* (New York: Simon and Shuster, 2001), p. 328.

14. *Bellows Report*, p. 714.

15. See *In re all Matters Submitted to the Foreign Intelligence Surveillance Court*, 218 F. Supp. 2d 611, 620 (2002).

16. See Attorney General Ashcroft's Press Conference, October 18, 2001, available at www.usdoj.gov/archive/ag/speeches/2001/index.html.

17. Memorandum from Attorney General on "Intelligence Sharing Procedures for Foreign Intelligence and Foreign Counterintelligence Investigations Conducted by the FBI," March 6, 2002, available at www.fas.prg/irp/agency/doj/fisa/ag03602.html.

18. During the early 1980s, the presiding judge of the FISA court published a memorandum opinion explaining that the FISA court had no authority to issue orders authorizing physical searches. See letter from FISA Presiding Judge Colleen Kollar-Kotelly to Senators Patrick J. Leahy, Arlen Specter, and Charles E. Grasley, August 20, 2002 (hereafter the Kollar-Kotelly letter), available at www.epic.org/privacy/terrorism/fisa/fisc_ltr_08_2002.html. Congress granted the FISA court the authority to issue orders for physical searches in intelligence investigations by statute in the mid-1990s.

19. See 50 U.S.C. 1807

20. For the suggestion that government's perfect FISA record meant that OIPR was applying a higher standard than probable cause, see *Bellows Report*, pp. 492–93.

21. *In Re All Matters Submitted to the Foreign Intelligence Surveillance Court*, 218 F. Supp. 2d. 611, 625 (May 17, 2002) (hereafter *In re All Matters*).

22. See the Order (as amended) that the FISA court issued with *In re All Matters* at 627.

23. 50 U.S.C. 1801(h)(1). Also see Section 1821(4).

24. 50 U.S.C. 1801(h)(3).

25. *In re All Matters* at 623.

26. Letter from Senators Patrick Leahy, Charles E. Grassley, and Arlen Spectre to the Honorable Colleen Kollar-Kotelly, July 31, 2002 (hereafter the Leahy letter), available at www.epic.org/privacy/terrorism/fisa/letter_07_31_02.

27. See Kollar-Kotelly letter.

28. In fact, the government did not appeal the May 17 decision because that decision related to the government's motion to vacate the 1995 procedures for all future FISA orders. It was therefore not linked to any specific FISA order. Following this decision, the FISA court approved a FISA order that the government requested, but modified the order in accordance with the May 17 decision. The government then appealed this modification to the FISA Court of Review.

29. See sources cited by Source Watch at www.sourcewatch.org/index.php?title=Laurence_Silberman.

30. Statement of Eleanor Hill before the joint inquiry, "The Intelligence Community's Knowledge of the September 11 Hijackers Prior to September 11, 2001," September 20, 2002, available at www.fas.org/irp/congress/2002_hr/092002hill.html.

31. Ibid.

32. Statement of Eleanor Hill before the joint inquiry, "The FBI's Handling of the Phoenix Electronic Communication and Investigation of Zacarias Moussaoui Prior to

September 11, 2001," September 24, 2002 [as supplemented October 17, 2002], available at www.fas.org/irp/congress/2002_hr/092402hill.html.

33.Ibid.

34. See Electronic Privacy Information Center's statistics page on FISA surveillance, available at www.epic.org/privacy/wiretap/stats/fisa_stats.html.

35. See FBI memo, "Caution on FISA Issues," available at www.epic.org/privacy/terrorism/fisa/FISA-mistakes.pdf

36. 50 U.S.C. Section 1801 (b) (1) (C).

37. See Section 2 of the statute. Text of the "Protect America Act of 2007" is available at http://thomas.loc.gov/cgi-bin/query/D?c110:3:./temp/~c1103OSGnK::.

Chapter 2

Detention of Citizen Enemy Combatants

Hamdi v. Rumsfeld, 542 U.S. 507 (2004)
Rumsfeld v. Padilla, 542 U.S. 426 (2004)

In response to the September 11 attacks on the World Trade Center and the Pentagon, Congress enacted the Authorization for the Use of Military Force (the AUMF), which gave President George W. Bush authority to "use all necessary and appropriate force against those nations, organizations, or persons *he determines* planned, authorized, committed, or aided the terrorist attacks." In addition, the resolution recognized that the president had the constitutional authority "to take action *to deter and prevent* acts of international terrorism against the United States" (emphasis added).[1] Based on this statutory grant of authority and on his constitutional authority as commander in chief, President Bush in October 2001 sent U.S. armed forces into Afghanistan to destroy Al Qaeda and the Taliban regime that supported it. Though the Taliban regime collapsed in a matter of weeks, members of both groups, including Taliban leader Mullah Omar and Al Qaeda chief Osama bin Laden, fled into the region's vast mountainous countryside. Others left the area to form new terrorist cells or join existing ones already operating in countries around the world. Determined to rout out this decentralized worldwide network, the Bush administration set up multiple fronts in its war on terrorism, from direct military operations to financial restrictions and criminal prosecutions. One of the more controversial tactics pursued by President Bush was to place two American citizens—Yaser Esam Hamdi and Jose Padilla—in military detention as enemy combatants.[2] The purpose of the detention was, first, to prevent Hamdi and Padilla from rejoining the terrorists and, second, to interrogate them about al Qaeda, the Taliban, and related terrorist groups. For the sake of increasing the effectiveness of the interrogations, neither detainee was allowed to communicate with his family or an attorney. They were detained incommunicado in a military brig. No criminal charges were filed against them.

I. BACKGROUND

Yaser Esam Hamdi, a Saudi national, arrived in Afghanistan in July or August of 2001, where he allegedly received weapons training from a Taliban military unit. Following the American attack in October, Hamdi surrendered to the Northern Alliance, a local anti-Taliban group allied with the United States. At the time of his surrender, Hamdi was purportedly armed with a Kalishnikov assault rifle. He was quickly transferred to U.S. custody and American military authorities transported him to the Guantanamo Bay Naval Base (GBNB) in Cuba in January 2002, where it was confirmed that he had been born in Baton Rouge, Louisiana, on September 26, 1980 and that he was therefore a U.S. citizen. The son of a Saudi chemical engineer, Hamdi had moved back to Saudi Arabia with his family when he was three years old. In April 2002, military authorities brought Hamdi to the naval brig in Norfolk, Virginia, where he was detained without any contact with family or legal counsel. No military tribunal met to decide whether Hamdi was an unlawful enemy combatant, a prisoner of war, or a civilian. His status depended solely on a presidential determination that all the GBNB detainees captured in Afghanistan were "unlawful enemy combatants." On May 10, 2002, Frank W. Dunham Jr., federal public defender for the Eastern District of Virginia, filed a petition for writ of habeas corpus on Hamdi's behalf with District Judge Robert G. Doumar.

José Padilla was born in New York and convicted of murder in Chicago in 1983 and of a gun charge in Florida in 1991. He moved to Egypt in 1998 and subsequently traveled to Pakistan and Saudi Arabia. In 2001, he allegedly met al Qaeda lieutenant Abu Zubaydah in Afghanistan and discussed with him the possibility of conducting terrorist operations in the United States. Zubaydah arranged to have Padilla receive explosives training from al Qaeda operatives in Pakistan as part of a plan to build and detonate a radioactive device—a so-called "dirty bomb"—in the United States, possibly in Washington, D.C. In 2002, Padilla met with other senior al Qaeda operatives in Pakistan to discuss the "dirty bomb" plot and other operations, including setting off explosions in hotel rooms and gas stations. Presumably to carry out reconnaissance and/or attacks of the above sort, Padilla returned to the United States on May 8, 2002 on a flight from Pakistan to Chicago via Switzerland. On his arrival, authorities arrested him at O'Hare Airport in Chicago as a material witness in a grand jury investigation and transferred him to New York City. On about May 15, Chief Judge Michael B. Mukasey appointed Donna R. Newman to be Padilla's counsel. Over the next few weeks, Newman regularly consulted with Padilla at the Metropolitan Correctional Center, but her visits ended when President Bush issued an executive order on June 9 specifically designating

Padilla an "enemy combatant." Based on this order, the Defense Department took custody of Padilla and placed him in detention in a naval brig in Charleston, South Carolina. Padilla's conditions of confinement were the same as Hamdi's: no access to family or counsel. Newman filed a habeas petition on Padilla's behalf with Judge Mukasey on June 11, 2002.

In common law countries, the writ of habeas corpus ("you have the body") is the time-honored way to contest the lawfulness of detention. Dating back to the Magna Carta, this writ, often referred to as the "Great Writ," orders the person who has control of a prisoner or detainee to produce that person for a hearing, at which time evidence would be taken so that a judge could determine if the deprivation of liberty was justified or not. The Supreme Court has characterized the writ of habeas corpus as "the fundamental instrument for safeguarding individual freedom against arbitrary and lawless state action." Because it is such a "fundamental instrument," the Court continued, the writ must be "administered with the initiative and flexibility essential to insure that miscarriages of justice within its reach are surfaced and corrected."[3] In regard to the detention of both Hamdi and Padilla, the Bush administration argued that the petitions should be denied on the basis of sworn written declarations submitted by Michael H. Mobbs, special adviser to the under secretary of defense for policy. Mobbs had reviewed all relevant records and reports concerning Hamdi's capture (see box 2.1) and Padilla's links to high-level al Qaeda operatives (see box 2.2) and he could be prosecuted for perjury if anything in his declarations proved false.[4] Since these declarations were sufficient, in the government's view, to dismiss the petitions, there was no reason to hold additional evidentiary hearings or provide either detainee with counsel.

After a number of appeals regarding standing, attorney access, and appointment of counsel, the 4th Circuit on July 12, 2002 instructed Doumar to "consider the sufficiency of the Mobbs Declaration as an independent matter before proceeding further" with Hamdi's habeas petition. Following these instructions, Judge Doumar on August 14, 2002 ruled against the government, holding that the Mobbs Declaration was an inadequate basis for detaining Hamdi because, among other things, it failed to indicate what authority Mobbs had regarding classification decisions of enemy combatants; did not provide enough information to determine whether the screening criteria and the transfer decisions violated Hamdi's due process rights; included no definition of what "affiliated" meant in the claim that Hamdi was affiliated with a Taliban military unit; provided no explanation of how the Northern Alliance came to the conclusion that Hamdi was an enemy combatant; and did not delineate the criteria used by screening teams to confirm this determination. In conclusion, Doumar said that if he were to accept the Mobbs Declaration as a sufficient justification for Hamdi's detention, then he would simply be functioning as "a

---

Box 2.1.

Declaration of Michael H. Mobbs
Special Advisor to the Under Secretary of Defense for Policy

Pursuant to 28 U.S.C. § 1746, I, Michael H. Mobbs, Special Advisor to the Under Secretary of Defense for Policy, hereby declare that, to the best of my knowledge, information and belief, and under the penalty of perjury, the following is true and correct.

1. I am a Special Advisor to the Under Secretary of Defense for Policy. In this position, I have been substantially involved with matters related to the detention of enemy combatants in the current war against the al Qaeda terrorists and those who support and harbor them (including the Taliban). I have been involved with detainee operations since mid-February 2002, and currently head the Under Secretary of Defense for Policy's Detainee Policy Group.

2. I am familiar with Department of Defense, U.S. Central Command and U.S. land forces commander policies and procedures applicable to the detention, control and transfer of al Qaeda or Taliban personnel in Afghanistan during the relevant period. Based upon my review of relevant records and reports, I am also familiar with the facts and circumstances related to the capture of Yaser Esam Hamdi and his detention by U.S. military forces.

3. Yaser Esam Hamdi traveled to Afghanistan in approximately July or August of 2001. He affiliated with a Taliban military unit and received weapons training. Hamdi remained with his Taliban unit following the attacks of September 11 and after the United States began military operations against the al Qaeda and Taliban on October 7, 2001.

4. In late 2001, Northern Alliance forces were engaged in battle with the Taliban. During this time, Hamdi's Taliban unit surrendered to Northern Alliance forces and he was transported with his unit from Konduz, Afghanistan to the prison in Mazar-e-Sharif, Afghanistan which was under the control of the Northern Alliance forces. Hamdi was directed to surrender his Kalishnikov assault rifle to Northern Alliance forces en route to Mazar-e-Sharif and did so. After a prison uprising, the Northern Alliance transferred Hamdi to a prison at Sheberghan, Afghanistan, which was also under the control of Northern Alliance forces.

5. While in the Northern Alliance prison at Sheberghan, Hamdi was interviewed by a U.S. interrogation team. He identified himself as a Saudi citizen who had been born in the United States and who entered Afghanistan the previous summer to train with and, if necessary, fight for the Taliban. Hamdi spoke English.

Box 2.1. (Continued)

6. Al Qaeda and Taliban were and are hostile forces engaged in armed conflict with the armed forces of the United States and its Coalition partners. Accordingly, individuals associated with al Qaeda or Taliban were and continue to be enemy combatants. Based upon his interviews and in light of this association with the Taliban, Hamdi was considered by military forces to be an enemy combatant.

7. At the Sheberghan prison, Hamdi was determined by the U.S. military screening team to meet the criteria for enemy combatants over whom the United States was taking control. Based on an order of the U.S. land forces commander, a group of detainees, including Hamdi, was transferred from the Northern Alliance-controlled Sheberghan prison to the U.S. short-term detention facility in Kandahar. Hamdi was in-processed and screened by U.S. forces at the Kandahar facility.

8. In January 2002, a Detainee Review and Screening Team established by Commander, U.S. Central Command reviewed Hamdi's record and determined he met the criteria established by the Secretary of Defense for individuals over whom U.S. forces should take control and transfer to Guantanamo Bay.

9. A subsequent interview of Hamdi has confirmed the fact that he surrendered and gave his firearm to Northern Alliance forces which supports his classification as an enemy combatant.

MICHAEL H. MOBBS
Special Advisor to the Under Secretary of
Defense for Policy

Dated: _24_ July 2002

Box 2.2.

Declaration of Michael H. Mobbs
Special Advisor to the Under Secretary of Defense for Policy

Pursuant to 28 U.S.C. § 1746, I, Michael H. Mobbs, Special Advisor to the
Under Secretary of Defense for Policy, hereby declare that, to the best of my
knowledge, information and belief, and under the penalty of perjury, the following
is true and correct:

1. I am a government employee (GS-15) of the U.S. Department of Defense and
    serve as a Special Advisor to the Under Secretary of Defense for Policy. The
    Under Secretary of Defense for Policy is appointed by the President and
    confirmed by the Senate. He is the principal staff assistant and advisor to the
    Secretary and Deputy Secretary of Defense for all matters concerning the
    formulation of national security and defense policy and the integration and
    oversight of DoD policy and plans to achieve national security objectives.
    The Under Secretary of Defense for Policy has directed me to head his
    Detainee Policy Group. Since mid-February 2002, I have been substantially
    involved with matters related to the detention of enemy combatants in the
    current war against the Al Qaeda terrorists and those who support and harbor
    them (including the Taliban).

2. As part of my official duties, I have reviewed government records and reports
    about Jose Padilla (also known as "Abdullah al Muhajir" and "Ibrahim Padilla")
    relevant to the President's June 9, 2002 determination that Padilla is an
    enemy combatant and the President's order that Padilla be detained by U.S.
    military forces as an enemy combatant.

3. The following information about Padilla's activities with the Al Qaeda terrorist
    network was provided to the President in connection with his June 9, 2002
    determination. This information is derived from multiple intelligence sources,
    including reports of interviews with several confidential sources, two of whom
    were detained at locations outside of the United States.[1] The confidential

Box 2.2. (Continued)

sources have direct connections with the Al Qaeda terrorist network and claim to have knowledge of the events described. Certain aspects of these reports were also corroborated by other intelligence information when available.

4. Padilla was born in New York. He was convicted of murder in Chicago in approximately 1983 and incarcerated until his eighteenth birthday. In Florida in 1991, he was convicted of a handgun charge and sent to prison. After his release from prison, Padilla began referring to himself as Ibrahim Padilla.[2] In 1998, he moved to Egypt and was subsequently known as Abdullah Al Muhajir. In 1999 or 2000 Padilla traveled to Pakistan. He also traveled to Saudi Arabia and Afghanistan.

5. During his time in the Middle East and Southwest Asia, Padilla has been closely associated with known members and leaders of the Al Qaeda terrorist network.

6. While in Afghanistan in 2001, Padilla met with senior Usama Bin Laden lieutenant Abu Zubaydah. Padilla and an associate approached Zubaydah with their proposal to conduct terrorist operations within the United States. Zubaydah directed Padilla and his associate to travel to Pakistan for training from Al Qaeda operatives in wiring explosives.

---

[1] Based on the information developed by U.S. intelligence and law enforcement agencies, it is believed that the two detained confidential sources have been involved with the Al Qaeda terrorist network. One of the sources has been involved with Al Qaeda for several years and is believed to have been involved in the terrorist activities of Al Qaeda. The other source is also believed to have been involved in planning and preparing for terrorist activities of Al Qaeda. It is believed that these confidential sources have not been completely candid about their association with Al Qaeda and their terrorist activities. Much of the information from these sources has, however, been corroborated and proven accurate and reliable. Some information provided by the sources remains uncorroborated and may be part of an effort to mislead or confuse U.S. officials. One of the sources, for example, in a subsequent interview with a U.S. law enforcement official recanted some of the information that he had provided, but most of this information has been independently corroborated by other sources. In addition, at the time of being interviewed by U.S. officials, one of the sources was being treated with various types of drugs to treat medical conditions.

[2] Padilla's use of the name "Ibrahim Padilla" was not included in the information provided to the President on June 9, 2002.

Box 2.2. (Continued)

7. Padilla and his associate conducted research in the construction of a "uranium-enhanced" explosive device. In particular, they engaged in research on this topic at one of the Al Qaeda safehouses in Lahore, Pakistan.

8. Padilla's discussions with Zubaydah specifically included the plan of Padilla and his associate to build and detonate a "radiological dispersal device" (also known as a "dirty bomb") within the United States, possibly in Washington, DC. The plan included stealing radioactive material for the bomb within the United States. The "dirty bomb" plan of Padilla and his associate allegedly was still in the initial planning stages, and there was no specific time set for the operation to occur.

9. In 2002, at Zubaydah's direction, Padilla traveled to Karachi, Pakistan to meet with senior Al Qaeda operatives to discuss Padilla's involvement and participation in terrorist operations targeting the United States. These discussions included the noted "dirty bomb" plan and other operations including the detonation of explosives in hotel rooms and gas stations.[3] The Al Qaeda officials held several meetings with Padilla. It is believed that Al Qaeda members directed Padilla to return to the United States to conduct reconnaissance and/or other attacks on behalf of Al Qaeda.

10. Although one confidential source stated that he did not believe that Padilla was a "member" of Al Qaeda, Padilla has had significant and extended contacts with senior Al Qaeda members and operatives. As noted, he acted under the direction of Zubaydah and other senior Al Qaeda operatives, received training from Al Qaeda operatives in furtherance of terrorist

[3] These attacks were to involve multiple, simultaneous attacks on such targets, and also included train stations. The additional facts in this footnote were not included in the information provided to the President on June 9, 2002.

Box 2.2. (Continued)

activities, and was sent to the United States to conduct reconnaissance and/or other attacks on their behalf.

11. Padilla traveled from Pakistan to Chicago via Switzerland and was apprehended by federal officials on May 8, 2002, upon arrival in the United States. Pursuant to court order, Padilla was held by the U.S. Marshals Service as a material witness in a grand jury investigation.

12. On June 9, 2002, George W. Bush, as President of the United States and Commander in Chief of the U.S. armed forces, determined that Jose Padilla is, and was at the time he entered the United States in May 2002, an enemy combatant in the ongoing war against international terrorism, including the Al Qaeda international terrorist organization. A redacted version of the President's determination is attached at Tab 1.

13. The President specifically determined that Padilla engaged in conduct that constituted hostile and war-like acts, including conduct in preparation for acts of international terrorism that had the aim to cause injury to or adverse effects on the United States.

14. The President further determined that Padilla posed a continuing, present and grave danger to the national security of the United States, and that detention of Padilla as an enemy combatant was necessary to prevent him from aiding Al Qaeda in its efforts to attack the United States or its armed forces, other governmental personnel, or citizens.

15. On June 9, 2002, the President directed the Secretary of Defense to detain Padilla as an enemy combatant.

Box 2.2. (Continued)

---

16. On June 9, 2002, acting on the President's direction, the Secretary of
Defense ordered the U.S. armed forces to take control of Padilla as an enemy
combatant and to hold him at the Naval Consolidated Brig, Charleston, South
Carolina.

MICHAEL H. MOBBS
Special Advisor to the
Under Secretary of Defense for Policy

---

rubber stamp," which would be incompatible with the kind of "meaningful judicial review" required in a habeas proceeding.

Since Doumar found the Mobbs Declaration to be an insufficient basis to assess the lawfulness of Hamdi's detention, he ordered the government to produce, "solely for in camera review by the Court," the following items: (1) copies of all of Hamdi's statements and notes of his interviews; (2) a list of the names of all Hamdi's interrogators; (3) copies of relevant statements by members of the Northern Alliance; (4) date of Hamdi's capture and dates and locations of his subsequent detention; (5) names and titles of the U.S. officials who determined that Hamdi was an illegal enemy combatant and who decided to move him to the Norfolk Naval Station; and (6) the screening criteria used to decide Hamdi's status.[5] Judge Doumar gave the government one week to produce the above information.

The government quickly appealed to the 4th Circuit, claiming that Judge Doumar applied "distrust," rather than the proper "deference" that the judiciary owed the executive branch during wartime. To substantiate this claim, the government quoted from a transcript of a hearing where Doumar had said that, if he was to rely on the Mobbs Declaration, then he must "challenge everything" in it and "pick it apart."[6] While the 4th Circuit considered the government's appeal in *Hamdi*, Judge Mukasey in New York on December 4, 2002 ruled that detention of enemy combatants was lawful, but that the government would have to provide Padilla with access to counsel to contest his classification as an enemy combatant. In his decision, Mukasey argued that both the Constitution and the AUMF authorized the president to detain enemy combatants, like Padilla, who were arrested far from a battlefield. In his view, such detainees must be given a lawyer and an opportunity to contest their designations, but detention was lawful so long as the government had "some evidence" that the persons detained were "enemy combatants." In other words, according to Mukasey, Padilla had a right to an attorney, but the standard that the government had to meet to justify his detention was not very high.

On January 8, 2003, a little over a month after Judge Mukasey had handed down his initial ruling in *Padilla*, a three-judge panel of the 4th Circuit unanimously held that the petition for a writ of habeas corpus that Dunham had filed on behalf of Hamdi should be dismissed. In his accompanying opinion, Chief Judge J. Harvie Wilkinson balanced Hamdi's right to "meaningful judicial review" of his habeas petition against the "great deference" the judiciary owed the executive branch during wartime. Dismissal of the petition was the correct result, he claimed, because both the Mobbs Declaration and Hamdi's petition agreed (1) that Hamdi was captured in Afghanistan during a period of active military operations and (2) that the government had named him an enemy combatant. Since these two facts were undisputed by the parties, no further litigation was required to justify Hamdi's detention. Since President Bush had lawful authority under his Article II war powers to detain battlefield detainees as enemy combatants and since Hamdi conceded that he was a battlefield detainee, he had no right to challenge the validity of what was contained in the Mobbs Declaration. Nor, by implication, did he have any right to counsel.[7]

On January 9, the day after the 4th Circuit's panel decision in *Hamdi*, the government requested Judge Mukasey to reconsider his ruling granting Padilla access to counsel. In support of its request, the government submitted, besides a copy of the 4th Circuit decision in *Hamdi*, an additional declaration (including a sealed supplement) by Vice Admiral Lowell E. Jacoby, director of the Defense Intelligence Agency (DIA), an agency of 7,000 civilian and military employees that advises the president and the secretaries of defense and state. The Jacoby Declaration underlined the importance of interrogation as a tactic in the war on terrorism, the intelligence value of Padilla, and the negative impact that access to counsel would have on Padilla's interrogation specifically and on national security generally. The Declaration concluded that providing "Padilla access to counsel risks the loss of a critical intelligence resource, and could affect our ability to detain other high value terrorist targets and to disrupt and prevent additional terrorist attacks."[8]

On March 11, Judge Mukasey declined the government's request. He explained that the Jacoby Declaration had not convinced him to change his mind in part because of its "lack of concreteness." It was, for example, "silent" on "the particulars of Padilla's actual interrogation thus far, and what they suggest about the prospect of obtaining additional information from him." Also, the Declaration had not indicated "when, if at all, intelligence personnel have ever experienced effects of an interruption in interrogation like the effects" it predicted. Lastly, Mukasey dismissed as "speculative" Jacoby's claims as to how Padilla would react to an interruption of his interrogation. An interruption, the judge suggested, might in fact lead to Padilla's cooperation if access to counsel produced a relatively quick dismissal of his habeas petition on the basis of the "some evidence" standard. If Padilla lost on the merits, "the assured hopelessness of his situation would quickly become apparent to him." In any case, Mukasey concluded, even if "the predictions in the Jacoby Declaration were reliably more certain than they in fact are," the law left him no choice but to grant Padilla access to counsel. Only by providing Padilla with an attorney and giving him an opportunity to contest his designation as an enemy combatant could Mukasey determine whether he was being arbitrarily detained in violation of the Fifth Amendment.[9]

About the time Mukasey issued this ruling, Frank Dunham requested a 4th Circuit *en banc* rehearing in *Hamdi*. In his request, he criticized the three-judge panel for rejecting the petition on the basis of "undisputed facts" when Hamdi's "next-friend" petition had been filed without any input from Hamdi himself. In addition, he claimed that the petition had only conceded that Hamdi had "resided in Afghanistan" when he was seized, not that he had been seized on a battlefield or that all of Afghanistan was a battlefield. While the 4th Circuit debated the merits of Dunham's objections, a truck bomb attack in Saudi Arabia killed thirty-four people, including nine U.S. citizens. Saudi authorities arrested eleven al Qaeda suspects on May 28. Seven weeks later, on July 9, 2003, the 4th Circuit denied Dunham's request for an *en banc* hearing. Though eight judges supported the three-judge panel's approach to justifying the dismissal of Hamdi's petition on the basis of "undisputed facts," four dissented. Judges J. Michael Luttig and Diana Gribbon Motz wrote dissenting opinions that sharply attacked both the majority's reasoning and the reasoning of each other.

Luttig described the majority's approach, which relied heavily on the language of Hamdi's petition, as "unpersuasive," if only because the detainee had never been allowed to speak for himself or through counsel. The three-judge panel that had denied the petition, in Luttig's view, had neither provided Hamdi with "meaningful judicial review" nor practiced the degree of deference the judiciary owed to the executive branch during wartime. A rule that barred judicial review of a presidential designation of an enemy combatant only if the detainee "gratuitously or foolishly" conceded that he had been seized in a foreign zone of combat was in reality not a rule of deference at all. At most it was what Luttig called "a Pyrrhic victory." The government may have won the battle of detaining Hamdi, but at the risk of losing the war of detaining future enemy combatants because their next friends would not make similar concessions regarding the place of seizure. What the 4th Circuit should have done, according to Luttig, was to confront the difficult question: What was the proper standard for judges to use in reviewing presidential designations of enemy combatants? Although in his dissent Luttig reserved ultimate judgment on this underlying issue, he did express his belief that "at most" judges should merely confirm that there is "a factual basis" supporting the military's determination that a detainee is indeed an enemy combatant.[10]

Judge Motz agreed with Luttig that the panel's approach to deciding the case based on an "innocuous" statement in a document filed by the petitioner's next friend, "without access or consultation with" the petitioner himself, was unsound. She called it "a thin reed on which to rest abrogation of constitutional rights and one that collapses completely upon examination." At this point, however, Motz sharply diverged from Luttig. In her view, the Mobbs Declaration could not justify Hamdi's indefinite detention, even if he was seized on a battlefield. She suggested two alternatives: a judge could regard Hamdi's battlefield capture as a rebuttable presumption and give him a chance, with the aid of counsel, to prove that he was a noncombatant; or a judge could demand from the executive branch "all relevant records and reports" for an *ex parte* and *in camera* review as to whether the designation was proper or not. Motz was not clear whether the second alternative would include an opportunity for Hamdi to contest the allegations against him in court or to consult with counsel. More likely than not, however, she would have supported these elements of due process because, in her view, courts have "no higher duty than the protection of the individual freedom guaranteed by our Constitution," especially "in time of war."[11]

In the *Padilla* litigation, both the government and Donna Newman, Padilla's attorney, appealed Judge Mukasey's decision to the Second Circuit. The government was unhappy with Mukasey's decision because it gave Padilla access to an attorney and Newman objected to Mukasey's holding that Padilla's detention was legal if the government had "some evidence" that he was an "enemy combatant." On December 18, 2003, in a 2-1 decision, the Second Circuit Court of Appeals reversed Judge Mukasey's decision, ruling that President Bush did not have either constitutional or statutory authority to detain "citizens on American soil outside a zone of combat." A huge win for Newman, the decision implied that Padilla should be released, unless he was charged with a crime, at which point he would have a right to an attorney. The key to the decision was the Second Circuit's insistence that the Non-Detention Act of 1971 (8 U.S.C 4001(a))—"No citizen shall be imprisoned or otherwise detained by the United States except pursuant to an Act of Congress"—prohibited any form of detention not explicitly authorized by Congress, including military detention during a time of war. Since the AUMF did not mention detention, there was simply no way for it to function, in the view of the Second Circuit, as a statutory basis for the Bush administration's policy of detaining citizen enemy combatants.[12]

All of the lower court decisions discussed above were handed down over a period of a year-and-a-half, from mid-2002 until late 2003. The various stances taken by the lower court judges on whether President Bush had the authority to detain American citizens as enemy combatants in the war on terrorism reflect the complex and fundamental character of the question. On one side of the spectrum, Judge Doumar advocated that judges should pursue fairly aggressive reviews of any detentions of American citizens, while on the other Judge Luttig endorsed a deferential approach, upholding the principle that the executive branch could detain an American citizen so long as it had some evidence that the person in question was an enemy combatant. Judge Mukasey agreed with Judge Luttig that the government only needed some evidence to justify designating someone an enemy combatant, but insisted that the detainee had to be given legal representation and an opportunity to contest the evidence. Judge Wilkinson refused to supply Hamdi with either legal representation or an opportunity to contest the evidence, but that was because, unlike Padilla, Hamdi was presumed to be a battlefield detainee. Judge Motz insisted that even battlefield detainees deserved counsel and a hearing, but she criticized Judge Dounmar's production order as too demanding. Which of these judges strikes the appropriate balance between national security and individual liberty during the war on terrorism?

II. BRIEFS FILED IN *HAMDI* AND *PADILLA*

While the 2nd and 4th Circuit Courts of Appeal struggled with the issues of *Padilla* and *Hamdi*, the war on terrorism entered a new and more difficult phase. On March 19, 2003, President Bush, along with a number of allied countries, invaded Iraq to destroy the weapons of mass destruction that Saddam Hussein presumably had and dismantle his tyrannical regime. American forces encircled Baghdad by April 6. Though President Bush announced that the military phase of Operation Iraqi Freedom was over on May 1, a low-level insurgency ebbed and flowed in the months that followed. Since no weapons of mass destruction were ever found, doubts about the justification for the war and the effectiveness of the Bush administration's plan for stabilizing Iraq grew in tandem. By August 26, 2003 more American soldiers had died in the postwar insurgency than in the actual war itself. Though Hussein's sons, Uday and Qusay, were killed in an American raid in July and though Saddam himself was finally captured on December 14, 2003, prospects for real peace and stability in Iraq appeared dim, at least in the short term. Popular support for the Iraq war waned, from a high of 75 percent when Baghdad was taken in April 2003 to about 45 percent sixteen months later.[13]

The Supreme Court agreed to hear *Hamdi* on January 9, 2004 and *Padilla* six weeks later on February 20, setting the stage for an unprecedented debate on the proper balance between presidential war powers and individual rights at a time when popular support for a controversial war was slowly ebbing. However, on March 11, an al Qaeda-linked terrorist cell coordinated bomb attacks on commuter trains in Madrid, Spain, killing 191 people and injuring more than 1,500. Interest in the question whether the Bush administration could detain American citizens in the war on terrorism was reflected in the fact that *amici curiae* filed over thirty-five briefs in *Hamdi* and *Padilla*. The central issues of the two cases were as follows: first, did the president have constitutional authority to detain citizen enemy combatants? Second, could Congress authorize such detention without suspending the writ of habeas corpus? Third, against the background of the Non-Detention Act of 1971 (18 U.S.C. 4001(a)), did the AUMF authorize such detention? Fourth, did detention of this type violate the Geneva Convention or any other international treaty? Fifth, what kind of process should be granted to those who have been designated unlawful enemy combatants? Are they entitled to a hearing in front of a federal judge? Must they have an opportunity to contest their designation as enemy combatants? Do they have a right to an attorney? What standard should a judge use to review the lawfulness of the detention? Is the "some evidence" standard sufficient? Is a higher standard required? Lastly, who bears the burden of proof? Must the government prove that the detainee is an enemy combatant or must the detainee prove that he is not?

Several Supreme Court precedents functioned as pivotal points of contention in the debate, both in the briefs and at oral argument. In *Ex parte Milligan* (1866), the Court had ruled that neither Congress nor the president could establish military trials for civilians as long as the civilian courts were open and functioning.[14] Citing this key ruling, the *Hamdi* and *Padilla* briefs claimed that only Congress could suspend the writ of habeas corpus in cases of "Rebellion or Invasion" (see Article I, Section 9 of the Constitution) or authorize detention of enemy combatants. Since Congress had done neither, the indefinite detention of Hamdi and Padilla far from any battlefield was illegal. After all, the Court in *Youngstown Sheet and Tube Co. v. Sawyer* (1952) had ruled that President Truman did not have the power to seize steel mills to avoid a strike and a resulting shortage of munitions during the Korean War.[15] If Truman's commander-in-chief power could not justify the seizure of private property without statutory authorization, the Bush administration could not justify the seizure of American citizens during the war on terrorism.

In defense of its policy of detaining citizen enemy combatants, the Bush administration relied heavily on *Ex parte Quirin* (1942), a decision that upheld the military trial of eight German soldiers (one of whom was an American citizen) who surreptitiously entered the United States during World War II for the purpose of committing espionage. Since Congress had authorized military trials for enemy soldiers who violated the laws of war, the Court in *Quirin* did not explicitly decide whether the president could have ordered the trial on his own constitutional authority.[16] Despite this implicit reservation, the Bush administration claimed that *Quirin* provided strong support for the recognition of a presidential power to detain enemy combatants during war. If the president could try and execute violators of the law of war during World War II, the government's brief argued, he certainly had the power, after Congress passed the AUMF, to detain enemy combatants for the duration of hostilities. In cases of such detention, the judiciary had a very limited role to play in any habeas proceeding. Access to an attorney should be denied and the court should reject any petition for a writ if the government had "some evidence" that the detainee was an enemy combatant.

An interesting question is whether Hamdi and Padilla were more like the defendant in *Milligan*, a civilian who sympathized with the southern cause but who resided in the state of Indiana, or more like the defendants in *Quirin*, who were all members of the German armed forces at a time when the United States was in a declared war against Germany. Another important issue debated in the briefs was whether the Bush administration had violated international law, in particular the Geneva Convention Relative to the Treatment of Prisoners of War (GPW), an international treaty ratified by the United States. Article V of the GPW required that a detainee's status as a prisoner of war be determined by "a competent tribunal" if there was "any doubt" of his status. Since Hamdi had not been granted a hearing before such a tribunal, his brief argued that the Bush administration had violated this provision of the GPW, which was arguably binding based on the Supremacy Clause of Article VI of the Constitution. The government's brief denied this claim, arguing, first, that President Bush was constitutionally the highest "competent authority" to make determinations of prisoner-of-war status, and, second, that Bush had "conclusively" determined in a February 7, 2002 memorandum that all al Qaeda and Taliban detainees, including both Hamdi and Padilla, were unlawful enemy combatants who did not qualify for prisoner-of-war status. Moreover, the government added, even if Bush had violated the GPW, that did not mean that the grieved party could sue the United States in federal court. The GPW was not a self-executing treaty. For Hamdi or Padilla to have a specific cause of action, Congress would have had to enact implementing legislation granting him the right to sue, which it had not done.

Most of the *amici curiae* briefs filed in *Hamdi* and *Padilla*—excerpts from a few of which are included below—opposed the Bush administration's policy of detaining American citizens as unlawful enemy combatants. One of these briefs was filed by Fred Korematsu, the Japanese American who had fought the legality of Japanese evacuation and internment during World War II, but who had lost his case before the Supreme Court.[17] His brief poignantly reminded the Court that the "country's darkest episodes" have occurred when judges failed to protect civil liberties during times of war or national emergency. In a similar vein, a number of former American prisoners of war filed a brief lamenting the Bush administration's policy of detention, claiming that it violated the GPW and thereby increased the risk that American soldiers in future conflicts will be denied prisoner-of-war status. These briefs, coming from individuals who had suffered the pains of detention in earlier wars, had a powerful emotional appeal, whatever the relative merits of the legal arguments contained in them.

Hamdi and Padilla also received *amici* support from a rather unexpected quarter of the American legal community: a group of retired federal judges that included Herbert J. Stern (nominated by Richard M. Nixon), district judge for the District of New Jersey from 1973 until 1987; Abner J. Mikva (nominated by Jimmy Carter), chief judge of the District of Columbia Circuit Court of Appeals from 1991 to 1994 and White House Counsel under President Clinton from 1994 to 1995; and H. Lee Sarokin (nominated by Jimmy Carter), district judge for the District of New Jersey from 1979 to 1994 and a judge on the U.S. Court of Appeals for the Third Circuit from 1994 to 1996. That such a prominent group of American jurists would file a brief in a Supreme Court case was highly unusual, especially in such a high-profile case. The judges' brief sharply attacked the Fourth Circuit's decision to provide Hamdi with only minimal judicial review. It amounted to a surrender of judicial power, which is "the power to find the facts that are determinative of a specific dispute before the court." Accordingly, the former judges concluded, both Hamdi and Padilla were entitled to counsel and a full hearing, at which time they must have a "meaningful opportunity" to contest their designations as enemy combatants.

One group that filed an *amicus curiae* brief defending President's Bush constitutional power to detain enemy combatants was the Citizens for the Common Defense (CCD), an association that advocated a "robust Executive Branch authority to meet the national security threats that confront the nation in its war against international terrorists." The brief described its members as lawyers and law professors, "most of whom served as law clerks to federal court judges or Justices of this Court [[i.e., the Supreme Court]], and/or as executive branch officials in the current or past Administrations." In an appendix to the brief, a list of "selected members" included the names of Robert Bork, a former federal judge and unsuccessful nominee to the Supreme Court during the late 1980s; Miguel A. Estrada, a former Justice Department official and a former Bush nominee for a seat on the Court of Appeals for the District of Columbia; and John Yoo, a Berkeley law professor who had worked in the Office of Legal Counsel in Bush's Justice Department from 2001 to 2003. The CCD's brief insisted that American judges had no business second guessing the judgment of either American soldiers or the president during wartime. What was being overlooked, according to the CCD, was that the detention of enemy combatants triggered the president's authority under the Commander-in-Chief Clause, "not his power as chief domestic law enforcement officer." In such a wartime context, the judicial task under the Due Process Clause was simply to check "Executive arbitrariness." So long as the president was functioning in good faith, judges should defer and not interfere with the war effort by imposing trial-type procedures on the executive branch.

EXCERPTS FROM HAMDI'S BRIEF

[[1. Habeas Review.]] Hamdi's detention is offensive to the most basic and unimpeachable rule of due process: that no citizen may be incarcerated at the will of the Executive without recourse to a timely proceeding before an independent tribunal to determine whether the Executive's asserted justifications for the detention have a basis in fact and a warrant in law. . . .

The Fourth Circuit held that ordinary habeas procedures were not required on the ground that Hamdi is being held pursuant to "well-established laws and customs of war." Nonetheless, the Fourth Circuit refused to consider whether Respondents have actually complied with those laws in detaining Hamdi.

The government has acknowledged, and the conditions of confinement confirm, that Hamdi is not being held as an ordinary prisoner of war. On the contrary, his prolonged indefinite solitary confinement amounts to punishment as a criminal serving an indeterminate sentence without a trial or due process. Before detaining him as anything but a prisoner of war, however, Article 5 of the Geneva Convention Relative to the Treatment of Prisoners of War ("GPW"), and United States regulations designed to implement the GPW, require that Hamdi's status be "determined by a competent tribunal" if any doubt arises whether he is entitled to prisoner of war status. At a minimum, such a hearing would have permitted Hamdi to assert that he was not a combatant at all.

The Fourth Circuit held that the GPW was unenforceable because it evinces no intent to provide a right of action and therefore is not self-executing. The habeas statute itself, however, authorizes review of detention in violation of treaties. No other implementing legislation is necessary for a habeas petitioner to claim that his detention violates the GPW.

As for the military regulations designed to implement the GPW, "[s]o long as this regulation remains in force the Executive Branch is bound by it, and indeed the United States as the sovereign composed of the three branches is bound to respect and enforce it." Hamdi's indefinite detention without a hearing therefore is inconsistent with the Constitution, international law, and military regulations designed to implement international law. . . .

Driven by its interpretation of the separation of powers, the Fourth Circuit refused to permit "[a]ny evaluation of the accuracy of the executive branch's determination that a person is an enemy combatant." It thereby limited the power of Article III courts to review the factual basis for any war-time detention of a citizen by the Executive. This is a dangerous misconstruction of the division of powers among the branches of our government. Under its ruling, the Fourth Circuit ceded power to the Executive during wartime to define the conduct for which a citizen may be detained, judge whether that citizen has engaged in the proscribed conduct, and imprison that citizen indefinitely, thereby allowing the separation of powers doctrine to be used as a means to concentrate, not separate, power in a single branch. . . .

Constitutional protections against illegitimate executive detention would mean little without the opportunity to secure judicial review of the basis upon which the Executive claims the power to detain. The Great Writ, in fact, was designed to guarantee precisely this type of review.

The Fourth Circuit's refusal to permit "any inquiry" into the factual circumstances related to Hamdi's indefinite detention is flatly contrary to this historic function and effectively eviscerates habeas corpus as "the fundamental instrument for safeguarding individual freedom against arbitrary and lawless" executive detention. The lower court's ruling, in fact, guarantees a judicial rubber stamp rather than an independent check on the Executive's power to engage in unauthorized detentions, a result plainly at odds with the separation of powers. . . .

Without muscular judicial review of executive detention, the Great Writ cannot fulfill its historic common law role as a "bulwark" against the threat of arbitrary government. . . .

[[2. Presidential War Powers.]] The court of appeals found that "[b]ecause it is undisputed that Hamdi was captured in a zone of active combat in a foreign theater of conflict, . . . the [Mobbs] declaration is a sufficient basis upon which to conclude that the Commander in Chief has constitutionally detained

Hamdi pursuant to the war powers entrusted to him by the United States Constitution." The Fourth Circuit's conclusion rests on at least two mistaken premises: (1) the Commander-in-Chief Clause empowers the President to detain citizens indefinitely; and (2) this Court's opinion in *Ex parte Quirin* establishes the President's authority to detain "enemy combatants" under the law of war. These premises are inconsistent with both the Constitution and precedent.

The Constitution gives the Executive no inherent power to detain citizens indefinitely during war or peace. While the Commander-in-Chief Clause necessarily entails plenary executive authority in areas of actual fighting, the power over citizens incident to this authority is only temporary. The Executive enjoys the authority to detain citizens seized in areas of actual fighting without specific statutory authority or judicial review for only a limited period of time as required by military necessity. Once the citizen is removed from the area of actual fighting, the Constitution requires statutory authorization to hold that citizen indefinitely. . . .

To be sure, military commanders in areas of actual fighting have plenary authority in those areas. Accordingly, "in the place where actual military operations are being conducted, the ordinary rights of citizens must yield to paramount military necessity." But Hamdi's habeas petition challenges his indefinite detention as an "enemy combatant" outside of areas of actual fighting, not the Executive's authority to initially apprehend him overseas. . . .

The Fourth Circuit found no reason to distinguish between the military's authority to detain citizens in an area of combat and those detained in the United States, reasoning that courts are ill positioned to review such decisions regardless of the location of detention. Expanding the scope of military authority over citizens based solely on the location of their initial seizure, however, may result in the indefinite and unreviewable detention of innocent Americans such as journalists or humanitarian workers. "Military commanders must act to a great extent upon appearances. As a rule, they have but little time to take and consider testimony before deciding." Consequently, the military's decision under exigent circumstances overseas to seize an American citizen is an extraordinarily illegitimate predicate for the indefinite detention of that citizen in the United States.

Furthermore, the scope of the "zone of active combat" that defines the range of the executive power over citizens was committed by the Fourth Circuit to the discretion of the Executive branch. Because the Executive can exercise its extraordinary power to detain American citizens anywhere it says it can, the location of Hamdi's seizure permits merely "superficial distinguishment on fact (though not in principle) of the case in which a citizen seized on American soil is denominated an enemy combatant."

Like the temporary seizure of the nation's steel mills, the indefinite detention of citizens by the Executive "cannot properly be sustained as an exercise of the President's military power as Commander in Chief of the Armed Forces." Hamdi is far from any location approximating a battlefield, and courthouses remain open near where he is imprisoned in South Carolina. His continued detention by the military therefore is indistinguishable from the "gross usurpation of power" rejected by this Court in *Ex parte Milligan*.

[[3. Congress's Role.]] The Fourth Circuit relied upon *Ex parte Quirin* to conclude that citizens are treated no differently than anyone else alleged to "take[ ] up arms against the United States in a foreign theater of war." The court of appeals not only misconstrued the Court's language in *Quirin*, it also ignored plainly applicable statutory language requiring congressional authorization for the detention of citizens. . . .

Nothing in *Quirin*'s dictum, however, permits the indefinite detention of citizens without trial and without statutory authority. Congress had not only explicitly authorized the tribunals in *Quirin*, but the Court declined to address the President's power without this authorization. *Quirin* therefore cannot support the unilateral exercise of power by the Executive over citizens. . . .

Furthermore, *Quirin* involved the jurisdiction of military tribunals. The power to detain indefinitely without charge—particularly in the context of a war against terrorism that will never end—is different in kind from the power to subject citizens to a military tribunal for a violation of the law of war. A tribunal implies at least some protection for the innocent, and a tangible and codified basis for the imposition of a punishment certain; unreviewable indefinite detention on the word of the Executive branch does not. The power to detain Hamdi without charges, in sum, is a much broader and more dangerous power than that at issue before this Court in *Ex parte Quirin*.

Finally, *Quirin*'s dictum must be considered in light of the subsequent enactment of 18 U.S.C. § 4001(a), a statute that draws in unmistakable terms a limitation on the Executive's authority to detain citizens. Regardless of the scope of the Executive's unilateral authority with respect to enemy aliens, section 4001(a) eliminates any doubt as to the Executive's authority to indefinitely detain Hamdi without statutory authorization—it has none. For these reasons, *Quirin* does not support the Fourth Circuit's holding that the Executive branch may treat American citizens and enemy aliens without distinction. . . .

A unilateral executive power to indefinitely detain citizens has the potential to jeopardize our democratic system. The structure and text of the Constitution, legislation dating back to the founding of this country, legal precedent, and the plain language of 18 U.S.C. § 4001(a) all demonstrate that the authority to permit the prolonged detention of citizens is entirely entrusted to Congress. . . .

Passed only one week after the September 11, 2001 terrorist attacks, the AUMF grants the President the power to "use all necessary and appropriate force against those nations, organizations, or persons he determines planned, authorized, committed, or aided the terrorist attacks that occurred on September 11, 2001, or harbored such organizations or persons." The concise terms of the joint resolution say little else except that it constitutes "specific statutory authorization" as required by the War Powers Resolution.

By its terms, therefore, the AUMF constitutes no greater authorization of power to the President than if Congress had issued a declaration of war. And a "declaration of war has only the effect of placing . . . two nations in a state of hostility, of producing a state of war, of giving those rights which war confers; but not of operating, by its own force, any of those results such as a transfer of property, which are usually produced by ulterior measures of government." Indeed, the power to detain prisoners of war in the United States is not granted simply "by virtue of the declaration of war."

Moreover, the text and history of section 4001(a) weigh against a finding that the AUMF permits the indefinite detention of citizens. Section 4001(a) prohibits detention "of *any kind* absent a congressional grant of authority to detain." By virtue of this statute, Congress specifically addressed the precise authority at issue and required that citizens not be imprisoned or otherwise detained by the United States "except pursuant to an Act of Congress." The statute was partly in response to the detention of Japanese Americans in the United States during World War II. Construing section 4001(a) to allow the Executive to detain citizens based solely on a declaration of war runs directly counter to this basis for its enactment. . . .

Respectfully submitted,
FRANK W. DUNHAM JR.,
Federal Public Defender

EXCERPTS FROM GOVERNMENT'S BRIEF IN *HAMDI*

[[1. Presidential Power.]] . . . Article II, § 2, Cl. 1 of the Constitution states that "[t]he President shall be Commander in Chief of the Army and Navy of the United States." . . .

It is well-settled that the President's war powers include the authority to capture and detain enemy combatants in wartime, at least for the duration of a conflict. Indeed, the practice of capturing and detaining enemy combatants in wartime not only is deeply rooted in this Nation's history, but is as old as warfare itself.

In *Quirin*, the Court explained that the "universal agreement and practice" under "the law of war" holds that "[l]awful combatants are subject to capture and detention as prisoners of war by opposing military forces." "Unlawful combatants are likewise subject to capture and detention" for the duration of the conflict, "but *in addition* they are subject to trial and punishment by military tribunals for acts which render their belligerency unlawful." As a matter of practice, moreover, the mere detention of opposing forces as enemy combatants or prisoners of war without military punishment has been the rule, and detention and prosecution of enemy combatants for specific war crimes the exception.

The U.S. military has captured and detained enemy combatants during the course of virtually every major conflict in the Nation's history, including more recent conflicts such as the Gulf, Vietnam, and Korean wars. During World War II, the United States detained hundreds of thousands of POWs in the United States (some of whom were, or claimed to be, American citizens) without trial or counsel. During the Civil War, the United States detained hundreds of thousands of confederate combatants—who remained United States citizens. As the court of appeals recognized, the military's settled authority to detain captured enemy combatants in wartime applies squarely to the global armed conflict in which the United States is currently engaged, in which—as the September 11 attacks demonstrate—the stakes are no less grave.

The detention of captured enemy combatants serves vital military objectives. First, "detention prevents enemy combatants from rejoining the enemy and continuing to fight against America and its allies." Second, detention enables the military to gather vital intelligence from captured combatants concerning the capabilities, internal operations, and intentions of the enemy. Such intelligence gathering is especially critical in the current conflict because of the unconventional way in which the enemy operates. The detention of captured combatants during an ongoing armed conflict "'is neither a punishment nor an act of vengeance,' but rather a 'simple war measure.'"

Petitioners repeatedly characterize Hamdi's detention as "indefinite." But the detention of enemy combatants during World War II was just as "indefinite" while that war was being fought. It is true that, given its unconventional nature, the current conflict is unlikely to end with a formal cease-fire agreement, but that does not mean that Hamdi will not be released. The military has made clear that it has no intention of holding captured enemy combatants any longer than necessary in light of the interests of national security, and scores of captured enemy combatants have been released by the United States or transferred to the custody of other governments. . . .

The military's authority to detain enemy combatants in wartime is not diminished by a claim, or even a showing, of American citizenship. As this Court observed more than 50 years ago in *Quirin*, "[c]itizenship in the United

States of an enemy belligerent does not relieve him from the consequences of a belligerency which is unlawful." To be sure, the fact that a detained enemy combatant is a presumed American citizen may enable him to proceed with a habeas action that could not be brought by an alien held overseas, but—as this Court squarely held in *Quirin*—it does not affect the military's settled authority under the law of war to treat him as an enemy combatant.

Petitioners suggest that a presumed United States citizen should be relieved of the consequences of his status as an enemy combatant when it comes to *detention*, as opposed to trial and *punishment* for a war crime. That is incorrect. *Quirin* involved a challenge to the "detention and trial of petitioners." Moreover, if, as this Court held in *Quirin*, citizenship does not relieve an enemy combatant of the most severe consequences of violating the law of war—a military commission and punishment up to death—then citizenship does not relieve an enemy combatant of the normal and less drastic consequence of capture by opposing forces, *i.e.*, detention during the conflict.

The *Quirin* Court's discussion of *Ex parte Milligan* reinforces the conclusion that citizens, no less than aliens, who are "part of or associate[d] with the armed forces of the enemy" may be held accountable under the law of war for their status or actions as enemy belligerents. *Milligan* involved a citizen who was seized by the military and was convicted by a military commission on charges that he conspired against the Union in the Civil War. He challenged the military's authority to proceed against him, arguing that he was not a member of the U.S. armed forces and was not "within the limits of any State whose citizens were engaged in rebellion against the United States, at any time during the war." The Court found that Milligan was "in nowise connected with the military service," and held that he therefore was not subject to punishment under the law of war.

The presumed American in *Quirin*, Herman Haupt, argued that the law of war did not apply to him under the rationale of *Milligan*. In rejecting that claim, the *Quirin* Court emphasized that *Milligan*'s "statement as to the inapplicability of the law of war to Milligan's case" was limited to "the facts before it." In particular, the *Quirin* Court stressed, "Milligan, not being a part of or associated with the armed forces of the enemy, was a non-belligerent, not subject to the law of war." Haupt, unlike Milligan, associated with the forces of the enemy and therefore was an "enemy belligerent." As a result, the *Quirin* Court held, Haupt was fully subject to the law of war even though he was a presumed American. Hamdi, who surrendered in Afghanistan with a Taliban unit while armed with an AK-47, is, like Haupt, a prototypical enemy belligerent subject to the law of war.

Petitioners argue that "Congress alone" has the power to authorize the detention of a captured enemy combatant who is a presumed American citizen.

That is incorrect. Especially in the case of foreign attack, the President's authority to wage war is not dependent on "any special legislative authority." The Nation was viciously attacked on September 11, 2001; the President dispatched the armed forces with orders to destroy the organizations and individuals responsible for that attack; and, as Commander in Chief, the President may employ the armed forces "in the manner he may deem most effectual to harass and conquer and subdue the enemy." That includes the authority to engage in the time-honored and humanitarian practice of *detaining* enemy combatants captured in connection with the conflict, as opposed to subjecting such combatants to the more harmful consequences of war.

Petitioners acknowledge that the Executive has "plenary power" to capture and detain enemy combatants like Hamdi "in areas of actual fighting," but argue that once a "citizen is removed from the area of actual fighting," the Executive cannot detain the citizen without "statutory authorization." That argument is misguided. This Court has long recognized that the commander-in-chief power "is not limited to victories in the field and the dispersion of the insurgent forces," but "carries with it inherently the power to guard against the immediate renewal of the conflict." One of the most conventional and humane ways of protecting against the "immediate renewal" of fighting in connection with an ongoing conflict is to detain captured combatants so that they may not rejoin the enemy.

Moreover, the general practice of the U.S. military—and the practice called for by the GPW—is to evacuate captured enemy combatants from the battlefield and to a secure location for detention. That protects both U.S. soldiers and detainees. Once the military makes a determination that an individual is an enemy combatant who should be detained in connection with the conflict, the *place* where the combatant is detained in no way affects the legality of that determination, much less the circumstances that led to the determination in the first place.

[[2. Congressional Authorization.]] In any event, Congress *has* affirmed the type of classic wartime detention at issue in this case. As explained above, immediately following the September 11 attacks, Congress not only recognized by statute that "the President has authority under the Constitution to take action to deter and prevent acts of international terrorism against the United States," but explicitly backed the President's use of "all necessary and appropriate force" in connection with the current conflict. As the court of appeals explained, "capturing and detaining enemy combatants is an inherent part of warfare; the 'necessary and appropriate force' referenced in the congressional resolution necessarily includes the capture and detention of any and all hostile forces arrayed against our troops." . . .

Accordingly, far from being at odds with Congress's actions, the classic wartime detention at issue comes with the express statutory backing of

Congress. And the President's constitutional authority in these matters therefore is at its apogee. Although they did not raise the claim in their habeas petition, petitioners argue that Hamdi's detention is barred by 18 U.S.C. 4001(a). The court of appeals properly rejected that argument. . . . Section 4001 does not intrude on the authority of the Executive to capture and detain enemy combatants in wartime. To the contrary, Congress placed Section 4001 in Title 18 of the United States Code—which governs "Crimes and Criminal Procedure"—and addressed it to the control of civilian prisons and related detentions. Moreover, the legislative history of Section 4001(a) confirms that it was enacted to repeal the Emergency Detention Act of 1950, which was addressed solely to *civil* detentions. The fact that Section 4001(a) does not apply to military detentions is bolstered by subsection (b) of Section 4001, which is addressed to "control and management of Federal penal and correctional institutions," and *exempts* "military or naval institutions."

In any event, as the court of appeals explained, the military detention at issue in this case is authorized by at least two different Acts of Congress, and thus would be exempt from Section 4001(a) even if it were otherwise covered. First, as discussed, the challenged executive action in this case falls within Congress's statutory Authorization for Use of Military Force in the wake of the September 11 attacks. Second, Congress has authorized the use of appropriated funds to the Department of Defense to pay for the detention of "prisoners of war" and individuals—such as enemy combatants—"similar to prisoners of war." . . .

[[3. The Geneva Convention Relative to Prisoners of War (GPW).]] . . . [[P]]etitioners argue that Hamdi's detention is barred by Article 5 of the GPW. That is incorrect. To begin with, the GPW supplies no basis for granting habeas relief because it is not self-executing. Moreover, as the court of appeals explained, the fact that the habeas statute permits an individual to challenge his detention based on a violation of a treaty does not mean that a habeas petitioner may challenge his detention based on an alleged violation of a non-self-executing treaty like the GPW, which does not confer any privately enforceable rights.

In any event, petitioners' Article 5 claim fails for the same reason as their claim that Hamdi's detention is inconsistent with the military's regulations concerning POWs and other detainees. Both Article 5 and the military's regulations call for a military tribunal only when there is "doubt" as to an individual's "legal status" under the GPW to receive POW privileges, and not as to each and every captured combatant. In the case of Hamdi and the other al Qaeda and Taliban detainees in the current conflict, there is no such doubt. The President—the highest "competent authority" on the subject—has conclusively determined that al Qaeda and Taliban detainees, including Hamdi, do not qualify for POW privileges under the GPW.

Furthermore, neither Article 5 nor the military's regulations apply to the threshhold determination whether an individual is in fact subject to capture and detention. As explained, they apply only to the determination whether a captured combatant is entitled to POW privileges under the GPW, which in turn is based on whether the combatant is a lawful or unlawful combatant. As the court of appeals explained, for purposes of this habeas petition, that is "a distinction without a difference, since the option to detain until the cessation of hostilities belongs to the executive in either case." . . .

[[4. Judicial Deference.]] A court's review of a habeas petition filed on behalf of a captured enemy combatant in wartime is of the "most limited scope," and should focus on whether the military is authorized to detain an individual that it has determined is an enemy combatant. That is, the central question for a court is whether "the detention complained of "—here, the detention of a presumed American who the military has determined surrendered with an enemy unit in an active combat zone in a foreign land—"is within the authority of [the military]." If such a classic wartime detention is authorized (and it is, for the reasons discussed above), the courts do not inquire whether the military authorities "have made a wrong decision on disputed facts." . . .

The government also has justified Hamdi's detention under a "some evidence" standard. . . .

Under the some evidence standard, the focus is exclusively on the factual basis supplied by the Executive to support its own determination. This Court has applied the some evidence standard in evaluating habeas challenges to executive determinations in *less* constitutionally sensitive areas than the wartime detention of captured enemy combatants. . . .

While necessarily limited in scope, the some evidence standard offers a legal framework for assuring that the Executive is not detaining an individual arbitrarily. As discussed above, the sworn [[Mobbs]] declaration presented by the government in its return provides a more than ample basis for the military's determination that Hamdi is indeed an enemy combatant and thus satisfies the some evidence standard. If a court disagreed, however, the proper course would be to permit the Executive to present additional evidence concerning its enemy-combatant determination and not, as petitioners suggest, to order discovery or evidentiary proceedings.

Petitioners argue that Hamdi is entitled to more "muscular judicial review" of his wartime detention, a full-blown evidentiary proceeding, and immediate access to counsel. The court of appeals correctly rejected those arguments and held that no further proceedings or access to counsel was required to establish the lawfulness of Hamdi's detention. . . .

[[5. Right to Counsel.]] Petitioners argue that Hamdi has "a right to consult with an attorney in connection with the assertion of [his] legal rights," and that he was deprived of due process because he was not granted access to a lawyer immediately upon the filing of this habeas action. That argument should be rejected. Indeed, the notion of requiring the military to afford captured enemy combatants with an attorney to help plot a legal strategy to gain their release by a court is antithetical to the very object of war.

There is no right under the law of war for an enemy combatant to meet with counsel to contest his wartime detention. Even lawful enemy combatants who are entitled to POW privileges under the GPW—which does not include the detainees in the current conflict—are not entitled to counsel to challenge their detention. Rather, Article 105 of the GPW provides only that a POW may be afforded counsel in the event that formal *charges* are initiated against him in a prosecution, underscoring that POWs who have not been charged with specific war crimes enjoy no right to counsel to challenge their detention. . . .

The military has learned that creating a relationship of trust and dependency between a questioner and a detainee is of "paramount importance" to successful intelligence gathering. The formation of such a relationship takes time and varies from one detainee to another, but when such a relationship is formed, critical intelligence may be—and has been—gathered. The intelligence collected to date from captured enemy combatants has proven vital to the strategic military operations that are ongoing in Afghanistan (such as in learning the routes that the enemy uses to travel through difficult terrain) as well as in understanding the manner in which the enemy operates (including how it communicates, recruits members, and obtains funding).

This critical source of information would be gravely threatened if this Court held that the moment a next-friend habeas petition is filed on behalf of a captured enemy combatant, a right of access to counsel automatically attaches with respect to the detainee. . . .

> Respectfully submitted.
> THEODORE B. OLSON,
> Solicitor General

EXCERPTS FROM PADILLA'S BRIEF

[[1. *Ex parte Milligan.*]] Throughout the Nation's history, this Court has carefully policed the boundaries of military jurisdiction and has struck down incursions of martial law into civilian life. The most important of these cases grew out of the Civil War, when the very existence of our Republic was threatened and large swaths of the country became battlefields. In the context of that grave crisis, the Court nevertheless held that military jurisdiction could not extend to civilians in areas "where the courts are open and their process unobstructed." Padilla's case fits squarely within the framework of *Milligan*.

Milligan, like Padilla, was charged with conspiring with a secret society to commit hostile and warlike acts against the United States. Milligan was alleged to have joined and aided a secret paramilitary group for the purpose of overthrowing the government; to have violated the law of war; to have held communications with the enemy; and to have conspired to seize munitions, liberate prisoners of war, and commit other violent acts in an area under constant threat of invasion by the enemy. Milligan, like Padilla, was seized by the military. As in this case, the Government argued that the President's role as Commander-in-Chief placed all powers in his hand, making him simultaneously "supreme legislator, supreme judge, and supreme executive." Unlike Padilla, however, Milligan was charged with crimes and tried before a military commission, before which he was represented by counsel and allowed to present a defense.

Despite Milligan's direct participation in planning attacks on the Nation itself in a time of war, this Court firmly rejected the expansion of military jurisdiction over a civilian American citizen and held that Milligan was entitled to a civilian criminal trial and to release from military custody. The Court in *Milligan* recognized the extreme importance of the question presented—which, as here, "involves the very framework of the government and the fundamental principles of American liberty." It observed that the Constitution itself—notably the Fifth and Sixth Amendments—specifies in plain terms how citizens must be tried. And it reaffirmed that "it is the birthright of every American citizen, when charged with crime, to be tried and punished according to law." . . .

The Court recognized that the Constitution allows soldiers and sailors in the armed forces to be tried under military jurisdiction. But it refused to equate Milligan with a soldier, noting that "he was not engaged in legal acts of hostility against the government, and only such persons, when captured are prisoners of war." As the Court explained, "[i]f he cannot enjoy the immunities attaching to the character of a prisoner of war, how can he be subject to their pains and penalties."

The Court acknowledged that necessity also permits the military to exercise jurisdiction over civilians in conquered territories that are ruled by military government, as well as when martial law is lawfully imposed in the United States itself during war or invasion "within district or localities where ordinary law no longer adequately secures public safety or private rights." But outside those narrow circumstances, it made clear that "no usage of war could sanction a military trial . . . for any offence whatever of a citizen in civil life, in no wise connected with the military service."

Throughout its brief, the Government paints the limited military jurisdiction over trials of German soldiers upheld in *Ex parte Quirin* as the general rule, to which *Milligan* forms a narrow exception. But the framework is exactly backwards. *Quirin* was a narrow decision, explicitly confined to the precise facts before the Court. . . .

[[2. *Ex Parte Quirin*.]] *Quirin* . . . involved admitted soldiers in a foreign army. Each of the defendants was conceded to be a member of the German Army and wore a German uniform when landing with explosives in the United States. In short, "the petitioners in *Quirin* admitted that they were soldiers in the armed forces of a nation against whom the United States had formally declared war." In contrast, the Government merely alleges that Padilla is "associated" with, but is not believed to be a "member" of, al Qaeda.

That is a critical distinction. . . . The difference between a citizen who merely aids an enemy army and one who is a member of that army distinguished *Milligan* from *Quirin*—a fundamental distinction that has long been recognized in the law of war. Outside of zones subject to actual martial law or military government, the law of war provides for military jurisdiction only over members of our own armed forces or over "[i]ndividuals of the *enemy's army*." That fundamental distinction between soldiers and civilians informs *Quirin*'s every reference to "combatants" or "belligerents" and its further distinction between "lawful and unlawful combatants," all of which refer to members of the armed forces. . . .

Not surprisingly, then, the Government attempts to cast Padilla as the equivalent of a soldier in order to subject him to military jurisdiction. But even the Government's own declaration attempting to make that case is forced to admit that Padilla is at most "closely associated" with "known members and leaders of the Al Qaeda terrorist network," but is not himself believed to be "a 'member' of Al Qaeda." On that reasoning, however, the civilians who conspired with the members of the German military in the Wessels and Quirin plots would also have been subject to military jurisdiction, because those civilians were plainly "closely associated" with the enemy armed forces. So too would the Milligan plotters have been. But this country's unbroken practice has been to try citizen civilians—even those who, like Padilla, were accused of aiding the enemy—in Article III courts. . . .

[[3. *Youngstown*.]] The Court's most important pronouncement on the scope of the Commander-in-Chief Clause came in *Youngstown*. There, at the height of the Korean War, President Truman seized domestic steel mills in order to avert a strike, asserting his power as Commander-in-Chief and citing the "indispensability of steel as a component of substantially all weapons and other war materials." The Court firmly rejected the argument.

The Government cites to no authority remotely suggesting that the President, acting in contravention of legislation by Congress, and absent a compelling military exigency, may seize an American citizen in the United States and detain him in a military prison. The Government places principal reliance on *Quirin* and *The Prize Cases* [[1862]], but neither is on point. As discussed above, *Quirin* rested on express and specific statutory authorization of military trials. In *The Prize Cases*, the Court simply made the unremarkable observation that the President could act to suppress an internal insurrection when there was no time for Congress to meet in advance. The President then sought, and received, express congressional approval at the earliest possible juncture. In addition, the President already *had* express approval to repel insurgencies under prior acts of Congress. Nothing in *Quirin* or *The Prize Cases* even hints at the remarkable proposition the Government asserts here: that the President may ignore the will of Congress and detain American citizens in a military prison simply because he is Commander-in-Chief.

It is important to recognize the awesome nature of the unilateral authority the President claims: the inherent power under the Commander-in-Chief Clause to imprison citizens he decides are "associated" with organizations he deems to be "enemies" of the United States, indefinitely, without access to counsel, without meaningful judicial review, and without congressional authorization. And he claims the authority to exercise these extraordinary powers not simply overseas, or on the field of battle, or in situations where there is no time to go to Congress for authorization or to obtain review by the courts—but here, at home, when Congress and the courts are open and operating. These are powers fundamentally inconsistent with a democracy based on the rule of law. . . .

> Respectfully submitted,
> DONNA R. NEWMAN,
> Counsel of Record

EXCERPTS FROM THE GOVERNMENT'S BRIEF IN *PADILLA*

[[1. *Ex Parte Quirin.*]] . . . The settled authority of the military to capture and detain enemy combatants fully applies to a combatant who is an American citizen and is seized within the borders of the United States. In *Quirin*, this Court upheld the President's exercise of military jurisdiction over a group of German combatants who were seized in the United States before carrying out plans to sabotage domestic war facilities during World War II. . . .

The saboteurs sought habeas relief in this Court, contending that the President lacked authority under the Constitution and federal law to subject them to military detention and trial by commission, and that they were entitled to be detained as civilians and tried in the civilian courts. The Court denied the saboteurs' claims. Of particular significance, the Court rejected their reliance on *Ex parte Milligan*, which had held that the military lacked authority to subject to trial by military commission a citizen who was alleged to have "conspired with bad men" against the United States during the Civil War. The *Quirin* Court found *Milligan* "inapplicable" to the circumstances before it, explaining that Milligan, "not being a part of or associated with the armed forces of the enemy, was a non-belligerent, not subject to the law of war." By contrast, because the *Quirin* saboteurs not only conspired to harm the United States but did so as persons associated with the enemy's forces, they were enemy combatants subject to military jurisdiction under the laws and customs of war. . . .

Indeed, the factual parallels between *Quirin* and this case are striking. The *Quirin* combatants affiliated with German forces during World War II, received explosives training in Germany, entered the United States with plans to destroy certain of the United States's war facilities, and were seized by FBI agents in Chicago and New York. Padilla was in Afghanistan and Pakistan after the attacks of September 11, he engaged there in extended discussions with senior al Qaeda operatives about conducting terrorist operations in the United States, he researched explosive devices at an al Qaeda safehouse and received training on wiring explosives, he returned to the United States to advance the conduct of further al Qaeda attacks, and he was seized by law enforcement agents in Chicago. The Court's conclusion in *Quirin* that the saboteurs were enemy combatants subject to military detention and jurisdiction thus is equally applicable in this case. . . .

The Court's opinion in *Quirin* likewise makes clear that the military's authority to try an enemy combatant for violating the laws of war necessarily includes the lesser authority to detain him in the course of the conflict. . . .

[[2. *Youngstown*.]] The court of appeals nonetheless held that the President lacks any inherent power to decide whether Padilla should be seized and detained as an enemy combatant, reasoning that the Commander-in-Chief authority is strictly confined in the "domestic sphere." The court rested its conclusion in large part on *Youngstown Sheet & Tube Co. v. Sawyer*. There, President Truman ordered the Secretary of Commerce to seize and assume control over the Nation's steel mills based on concerns that a work stoppage could jeopardize the production of war materials for the Korean War. The government acknowledged that the President had acted without support from Congress, and argued that the President's authority "should be implied from the aggregate of his powers under the Constitution," including in part the Commander-in-Chief power because of the potential implications for the availability of war materials. This Court disagreed. With respect to the government's reliance on the Commander-in-Chief authority, the Court found that the President lacked independent "power as such to take possession of private property in order to keep labor disputes from stopping production." The Court deemed that a job for "lawmakers, not . . . military authorities."

This case involves a decidedly different question. President Truman's order to seize the steel mills was not addressed to the military. The order instead called for action in the *civilian* sector in the form of a directive to the Secretary of *Commerce* to assume control over private industry. In sharp contrast, an order directed to the military to detain an individual as an enemy combatant is a quintessentially *military* measure concerning the military's actions toward the enemy's forces. And the military's actions vis-à-vis the enemy's forces lie at the core of the Commander-in-Chief authority. Because the authority to detain enemy combatants is part and parcel of the conduct of war, the logic of the decision below would hamstring the President's authority to respond to attacks on United States soil or to take action to deter such attacks. . . .

As the September 11 attacks make manifestly clear, moreover, al Qaeda eschews conventional battlefield combat, yet inflicts damage that, if anything, is more devastating. Al Qaeda combatants assimilate into the civilian population and plot to launch large-scale attacks against civilian targets far from any traditional battlefield. Confining the President's authority to traditional combat zones thus would substantially impair the ability of the Commander in Chief to engage and defeat the enemy's forces. The President's authority under Article II should not "be made almost unworkable, as well as immutable, by refusal to indulge some latitude of interpretation for changing times," but should be given the "scope and elasticity afforded by what seem to be reasonable, practical implications instead of the rigidity dictated by a doctrinaire textualism." The Commander in Chief therefore has authority to seize and detain enemy combatants wherever found, including within the borders of the United States. . . .

[[3. AUMF.]] The court of appeals [[of the Second Circuit]] determined that the Authorization of Force "contains nothing authorizing the detention of American citizens captured on United States soil," even going so far as to conclude that the Authorization "contains no language authorizing detention." That reading is insupportable. . . .

There also is no basis for reading the broad language of Congress's Authorization to contain an unstated exception for enemy combatants captured within the United States. Congress recognized the President's authority to "take action to deter and prevent acts of international terrorism against the United States," and Congress specifically noted that it was "necessary and appropriate that the United States exercise its rights . . . to protect United States citizens both *at home* and abroad." Indeed, Congress was acting in direct response to attacks that took place on United States soil and were initiated by combatants located within the borders of the United States. Congress cannot be assumed to have intended to withhold support for the use of force against forces identically situated to those that perpetrated the September 11 attacks. To the contrary, Congress recognized that the September 11 attacks "continue to pose an unusual and extraordinary threat to the national security," and the enemy remains committed to launching further attacks within the Nation's borders. . . .

> Respectfully submitted.
> THEODORE B OLSON,
> Solicitor General

EXCERPTS FROM FRED KOREMATSU'S *AMICUS* BRIEF IN *PADILLA*

. . . Time sometimes reveals the unforgivable nature of our actions. Many of our country's darkest episodes have occurred when we have failed to protect civil liberties during exigent times of war or in the name of national security. These failures are well-illustrated by the internment of American citizens of Japanese descent on American soil during World War II. . . .

In 1980, Congress established a Commission on Wartime Relocation and Internment of Civilians to review the circumstances surrounding Executive Order No. 9066, and its impact on people of Japanese ancestry. Comprised of former Congressional members, Cabinet members, and members of the Supreme Court, the Commission unanimously condemned the decisions justifying the internment of American citizens in this country.

Later, a federal district court vacated the 1942 conviction of Fred Korematsu, one of the many excluded and interned Americans of Japanese ancestry. . . . The court found that the government had failed to inform the Court of crucial evidence during World War II, which justified correcting Mr. Fred Korematsu's conviction under the stringent standard of *coram nobis*. In so doing, the court noted that the *Korematsu* case "stands as a constant caution that in times of war or declared military necessity our institutions must be vigilant in protecting constitutional guarantees." It "stands as a caution that in times of distress the shield of military necessity and national security must not be used to protect governmental actions from close scrutiny and accountability."

On January 18, 1998, President Clinton presented Mr. Korematsu with the Presidential Medal of Freedom. In doing so, the President praised Mr. Korematsu's "extraordinary stand" and noted that "[i]n the long history of our country's constant search for justice, some names of ordinary citizens stand for millions of souls. Plessy, Brown, Parks. . . . To that distinguished list, today we add the name of Fred Korematsu."

Mr. Padilla has been indefinitely detained for almost two years without access to counsel or any communication with his family, based on the President's unilateral determination that Mr. Padilla is an "enemy combatant." No charges have been brought against him.

This detention is unwarranted and cannot be justified by the government's claims that we face a time of national crisis. No one can dispute the horror inflicted upon the nation on September 11. However, as illustrated by the Japanese American detention and the repeal of the Emergency Detention Act, it is imperative that we carefully balance our concerns for safety and security with the liberties afforded us in our Bill of Rights. As stated by the Court in *United States v. Robel*, "[i]t would indeed be ironic if, in the name of national defense, we would sanction the subversion of one of those liberties . . . which makes the defense of the Nation worthwhile." . . .

Respectfully submitted,
ARTURO J. GONZALES,
Counsel of Record

EXCERPTS FROM POW *AMICUS* BRIEF IN *HAMDI*

Reciprocity—the expectation that acting in a humanitarian manner may encourage one's enemy to do the same—remains "a powerful actual factor" in the application of international humanitarian law. Treating those captured in a war zone, such as Petitioner, in accordance with basic shared standards means that our own captured forces stand a much better chance of surviving captivity unharmed. Ignoring that reality not only contravenes the plain text of the GPW, but also places Americans around the world at grave risk of precisely the type of mistreatment the Geneva Conventions aim to prevent. . . .

The Defense Department's clear departure from its established practice in its treatment of Petitioner and others similarly situated not only lowers the bar for its own conduct, it encourages authoritarian regimes around the globe to commit abuses in the name of counterterrorism. . . .

Since September 11, 2001, these concerns have multiplied. The following regimes, among others, have acted to suppress lawful dissent and quell political opposition, all the while self-consciously invoking the very language the United States has used in justifying its treatment of individuals such as Petitioner: Egypt (where President Mubarak endorsed a diminished post-September 11 concept of the "freedom of the individual"); Liberia (where then-President Taylor ordered a critical journalist declared an "enemy combatant," jailed, and tortured); Zimbabwe (where President Mugabe, while voicing agreement with the Bush Administration's policies in the war on terror, declared foreign journalists and others critical of his regime "terrorists" and suppressed their work); Eritrea (where the governing party arrested 11 political opponents, has held them incommunicado and without charge, and defended its actions as being consistent with United States actions after September 11); and China (where the Chinese government charged a peaceful political activist with terrorism and sentenced him to life in prison; the U.S. State Department noted "with particular concern the charge of terrorism in this case, given the apparent lack of evidence [and] due process").

Regardless whether these regimes are currently at peace with the United States, the time may come when their nations become hostile ground. Americans some day may be captured or detained in these locations as a result of actions arising out of, or incident to, military operations. The Defense Department's decision to deny Petitioner access to a competent tribunal to adjudicate his case will only serve to harm the future interests of Americans in these countries and around the world. . . .

Respectfully submitted.
PHILIP ALLEN LACOVARA,
Counsel of Record

EXCERPTS FROM FEDERAL JUDGES' *AMICI* BRIEFS IN *HAMDI* AND *PADILLA*

[[1. *Hamdi*.]] . . . The Fourth Circuit decision misapplies the separation-of-powers doctrine by elevating to a preferred position the executive's military prerogatives, while surrendering a core attribute of judicial power: the power to find the facts that are determinative of a specific dispute before the court. . . .

This Court has repeatedly indicated that the judicial power does not disappear in times of war. There is no reason to believe that federal courts would unduly interfere with military operations or compromise national security by performing a role in which the courts are expert—resolving factual disputes—and numerous cases involving substantial national security concerns have been successfully processed by the courts. The Fourth Circuit's mistrust of the courts' ability to do so should be rejected.

The history and purpose of the writ of habeas corpus are also contrary to the decision below. The power to question facts alleged by the executive as support for a petitioner's detention, particularly when there have been no prior judicial or quasi-judicial findings, is essential if the writ is to fulfill its purpose as a bulwark against unlawful executive detention. To hold, as the court below did, that the habeas court is powerless to look behind the government's representations of fact would have the same effect as suspending the writ, which can properly be done only by Congress. . . .

[[2. *Padilla*.]] The long-term deprivation of Mr. Padilla's liberty cannot constitutionally be accomplished without affording Mr. Padilla the essentials of due process: notice of the grounds for his detention and a meaningful opportunity to be heard to contest those grounds, both legally and factually. While notice and a hearing may be deferred to a point in time after the initial detention where it would be impossible or improvident to grant a predeprivation hearing, due process must be afforded promptly thereafter, as determined by the courts.

In order to effectuate Mr. Padilla's due process rights, he must be afforded meaningful access to and assistance of counsel as of right. Doing so will not interfere with legitimate national security concerns.

In order to effectuate Mr. Padilla's due process rights, and to maintain the independence of the judiciary as the cornerstone of the separation of powers, the burden and standard of proof must be allocated properly. Once a habeas petition is filed that *prima facie* demonstrates that the petitioner has been deprived of a liberty interest protected by the Due Process Clause and that no prior constitutionally adequate proceedings have occurred to establish the basis for the detention, the burden lies with the Executive to justify the detention. It must do so by at least clear and convincing evidence, because the habeas court is sitting not in collateral review of a prior adjudication but by default as the initial forum. The "some evidence" standard is not sufficient where there has been no prior judicial or quasi-judicial process whatsoever. . . . .

> Respectfully submitted,
> ROBERT P. LOBUE,
> Counsel of Record

EXCERPTS FROM CITIZENS FOR THE COMMON DEFENSE'S *AMICUS* BRIEF IN *HAMDI*

. . . The briefs of petitioners and their *amici* . . . are permeated with a fundamental error—they fail to recognize, let alone address, the constitutional implications of the fact that Hamdi neither was charged with a civilian crime in an American courtroom nor is a civilian noncombatant detained by military or civilian authorities. Rather, Hamdi—although he now claims the protections of United States citizenship by accident of birth—was a soldier for an enemy of this nation captured during wartime on a foreign battlefield while carrying a military assault rifle that he intended to use to kill other U.S. citizens who served as soldiers in our armed forces. . . .

With respect to detention of an enemy belligerent who is a citizen and is captured on a foreign battlefield, the laws of war, constitutional doctrine, and this nation's history are all clear: The military, exercising the President's authority under the Constitution, can detain him at least until the end of hostilities; and a habeas court fulfills its duty under the Due Process Clause to act as a check on Executive arbitrariness by reviewing the evidence on which the military based its detention decision. Judicial inquiry under the Due Process Clause, appropriately delimited by the interests implicated in particular cases, ensures that the government acts in good faith and limits the potential for overbroad action. But trial-type procedures are not appropriate when the indicia of arbitrariness and oppression are nonexistent and the consequences of judicial intervention dire. The Court has previously recognized that due process permits, and Article II compels, substantial deference to military decision making, and it should defer here as well.[*]

III. ORAL ARGUMENT

Oral argument in both *Hamdi* and *Padilla* occurred on April 28, 2004. On behalf of Hamdi, Frank Dunham conceded that, so long as his client had an opportunity to contest his designation as an enemy combatant, an Article 5 hearing might satisfy due process, although Hamdi would still have the right to petition a federal court for a writ of habeas corpus. Hamdi, however, had not received any kind of meaningful review before any sort of neutral decision maker, military or otherwise. Paul Clement, arguing for the government, responded to Dunham's objection by claiming that, even if Hamdi was not represented by counsel, the military officers who screened him were, for all intents and purposes, neutral decision makers. Justice Stevens asked Clement whether there was any law controlling methods of interrogation, an issue not clearly related to the litigation, although a number of press reports had alleged that high level al Qaeda operatives had been subjected to harsh interrogation techniques.[18] Clement responded by referring to both the Convention Against Torture and the Torture Victim Protection Act and insisting that torture was "the last thing" the government would use in the interrogation process. When Justice Ginsburg referred back to the issue of

---

[*] *Amicus* submits that the arguments set forth in this brief generally apply as well in *Rumsfeld* v. *Padilla*. To be sure, in that case respondent José Padilla was not captured on a foreign battlefield. But the Executive's authority to detain enemy belligerents is not limited by geography and the laws of war permit the military to detain enemy combatants—for example, spies and saboteurs—captured behind its own lines. . . . Just as the judiciary lacks institutional competence to second guess battlefield decisions by military commanders, so too should it defer to the expertise of, and the information available to, the expert decision makers in *Padilla*. And the personal involvement of the President in classifying Padilla as an enemy combatant provides a stronger separation-of-powers mandate for deference to that decision.

torture in the *Padilla* argument, Clement said that the courts would simply have to trust the executive during war, not to torture detainees.

Jennifer Martinez, representing Padilla, argued that the AUMF, at most, authorized battlefield detentions. Once such a detainee was returned to the United States, he could not be indefinitely detained without explicit congressional authorization, especially if he was a citizen protected by 4001(a). The executive branch, in her view, could detain citizens for forty-eight hours, but only if there was reasonable suspicion that the detainee was about to commit a violent act. After forty-eight hours of detention, the detainees had to be charged with a crime or released. Only Congress could lengthen the period of time the executive branch could detain a suspected terrorist without criminal charges, but it had not yet done so.

EXCERPTS FROM ORAL ARGUMENT IN *HAMDI*

JUSTICE GINSBURG: . . . In Vietnam and World War II, were there means to entertain the claims of people who said, I wasn't an enemy?

DUNHAM [[Hamdi's Attorney]]: There were regimes then and there are regimes now, but they haven't been used by the military here. There are outstanding military regulations that provide for a hearing for someone captured on the battlefield to determine their status if there is any doubt as to their status.

GINSBURG: Would those military proceedings satisfy your claim? Your point is that Hamdi has not had a chance to be heard on his claim that this was a dreadful mistake, I wasn't an enemy.

DUNHAM: Those proceedings would go a long way towards satisfying the process part of our claim. . . .

JUSTICE SCALIA: What would you expect the military to do? As I understand it, he wasn't even captured by our own forces. He was captured by allied forces and turned over to our forces.

DUNHAM: Well, that's certainly, certainly part of the problem, Your Honor. We have a strong . . .

SCALIA: What if they get a deposition from an American colonel who says this prisoner was turned over to me by allied forces, our Afghan allies in this combat, and I was assured by them that they had captured him in a firefight? Now, is that going to satisfy our habeas corpus review?

DUNHAM: Your Honor, that would be a lot more than what we have now.

SCALIA: Oh, it certainly would, but you wouldn't accept that, would you?

DUNHAM: Well, I wouldn't accept it without Mr. Hamdi . . . [[having]] an opportunity to be heard. Fundamental to—

JUSTICE SOUTER: So your objection is not the hearsay rule, your objection is the right to make some kind of response. That's your basic process claim?

DUNHAM: That's correct, Your Honor. That we have, we have never authorized detention of a citizen in this country without giving him an opportunity to be heard, to say, hey, I am an innocent person. We don't—he hasn't even been able to say that yet. He hasn't been able to look at the facts that have been alleged against him and give any kind of an explanation as to his side of the story, which may well turn out to be true and may well clear up some of the deficiencies in the Mobbs Declaration. . . .

SOUTER: Well, I realize that. . . . And my suggestion is, if I understand your argument, that if . . . your client was found to be entitled to some process, it might be . . . that military process with an opportunity to be heard in response would satisfy your demand.

DUNHAM: Yes. That's correct, Your Honor. . . .

GINSBURG: The person who is locked up, doesn't he have a right to bring before some tribunal himself his own words, rather than have a Government agent say what was told to him that somebody else said.

CLEMENT [[Deputy Solicitor General]]: With respect, Justice Ginsburg, he has an opportunity to explain it in his own words. Now, it may not—

SOUTER: During interrogation?

CLEMENT: During interrogation.

SOUTER: I mean, is that your point?

CLEMENT: During interrogation. During the initial screening. During the screening in Guantanamo.

O'CONNOR: How about to a neutral decision maker of some kind, perhaps in the military? Is that so extreme that it should not be required?

CLEMENT: No, Justice O'Connor. And let me say two things. One is when the initial screening criteria are applied in the field, for all intents and purposes, that is a neutral decision maker. . . .

STEVENS: Yes, but Mr. Clement, you're assuming he has no right to counsel, aren't you? . . .

CLEMENT: Not at the preliminary stages if the Government has made a determination that access to counsel would interfere with the intelligence gathering process. . . .

STEVENS: May I ask just one other question, I think it's just relevant. But do you think there is anything in the law that curtails the method of interrogation that may be employed?

CLEMENT: Well, I think there is, Justice Stevens. I mean—

STEVENS: And what is that?

CLEMENT: Well, just to give one example, I think that the United States is signatory to conventions that prohibit torture and that sort of thing. And the United States is going to honor its treaty obligations. . . . I wouldn't want there to be any misunderstanding about this. It's also the judgment of those involved in this process that the last thing you want to do is torture somebody or try to do something along those lines.

I mean, if there were an artificial—if you did that, you might get information more quickly, but you would really wonder about the reliability of the information you were getting. So the judgment of the people who do this as their responsibility is that the way you would get the best information from individuals is that you interrogate them, you try to develop a relationship of trust. . . .

REHNQUIST: Thank you, Mr. Clement. Mr. Dunham, you have four minutes remaining.

DUNHAM: May it please the Court. Mr. Clement is a worthy advocate and he can stand up here and make the unreasonable sound reasonable. But when you take his argument at core, it is, "Trust us." And who is saying trust us? The executive branch. And why do we have the great writ? We have the great writ because we didn't trust the executive branch when we founded this Government. That's why the Government is saying trust us is no excuse for taking away and driving a truck through the right of habeas corpus and the Fifth Amendment that no man shall be deprived of liberty except upon due process of law.

We have a small problem here. One citizen. We're not talking about thousands. One citizen caught up in a problem in Afghanistan. Is it better to give him rights or is it better to start a new dawn of saying there are circumstances where you can't file a writ of habeas corpus and there are circumstances where you can't get due process. I think not.

I would urge the Court not to go down that road. I would urge the Court to find that citizens can only be detained by law. And here there is no law. If there is any law at all, it is the executive's own secret definition of whatever enemy combatant is. And don't fool yourselves into thinking that that means somebody coming off a battlefield because they've used it in Chicago, they've used it in New York and they've used it in Indiana. . . .

. . .[[T]]these detentions are not lawful. And I would respectfully ask this Court to step up to the plate and say so. . . .

EXCERPTS FROM ORAL ARGUMENT IN *PADILLA*

GINSBURG: . . . So, what is it that would be a check against torture?

CLEMENT: Well, first of all, there are treaty obligations. But the primary check is that just as in every other war, if a U.S. military person commits a war crime by creating some atrocity on a harmless detained enemy combatant or a prisoner of war, that violates our own conception of what's a war crime. And we'll put that U.S. military officer on trial in a court martial. So I think there are plenty of internal reasons—

GINSBURG: Suppose the executive says mild torture, we think will help get this information. . . .

CLEMENT: Well, our executive doesn't. And I think—I mean—

GINSBURG: What's constraining? That's the point. Is it just up to the good will of the executive? Is there any judicial check?

CLEMENT: . . . I think it's very important—I mean, the court in Ludecke against Watkins made clear that the fact that executive discretion in a war situation can be abused is not a good and sufficient reason for judicial micromanagement and overseeing of that authority.

You have to recognize that in situations where there is a war—where the government is on a war footing, that you have to trust the executive to make the kind of quintessential military judgments that are involved in things like that.

MARTINEZ [[Padilla's Attorney]]: If there were a situation where an individual, not like my client, but an individual that were on the verge of engaging in imminent violent conduct, certainly the President would have the power, even under the Fourth Amendment, to seize that individual without a warrant and bring him into custody on the basis that they were about to engage in a violent act.

But that's a far different situation from seizing someone like my client, who is not alleged to be on the verge of imminent lawless activity, was not in the process of hijacking an aircraft, but was simply alleged to be a part of a plot.

STEVENS: Let me interrupt. When you say, it is clear he could do it if the defendant was about to engage in that kind of conduct, by what standard would you decide that he was about to? Probable cause, proof beyond a reasonable doubt, or just suspicion?

MARTINEZ: For the initial seizure, we would say probable cause. . . . But we're not talking about that question of initial seizure here. In this case we're talking about the ongoing detention for two years of someone after there has been—

SCALIA: Well, you wouldn't just say two years. You would certainly say that as soon as the President prevented the act that he feared by taking the person into custody, he immediately had no more authority to detain them, wouldn't you? I mean—

MARTINEZ: Yes, Your—

SCALIA: That's the way the statute you're relying on reads, that he shall not be detained. So two years has nothing to do with it.

MARTINEZ Yes, Your Honor.

SCALIA: The next day, he should, I suppose, you know, hand him over to civil prosecution authorities.

MARTINEZ: Yes, Your Honor. We would say at forty-eight hours under this Court's decisions. If Congress thinks that a longer period of time is appropriate in terrorism cases, it can do as other countries have done and provide for a longer period of time. In the United Kingdom there is a forty-eight hours plus a maximum of seven days without charge for suspected terrorists. . . . But in the absence of that, our normal rule of forty-eight hours . . .would be appropriate. . . .

SCALIA: But we are not just talking about terrorists here. We're talking about terrorists associated with foreign forces.

MARTINEZ: Yes, Your Honor, and let me say that those are exactly the sort of individuals that the passage of 4001 was designed to address. The Emergency Detention Act, which 4001 repealed, specifically talked about the possibility of saboteurs in this country who are under the direction and control of the communist empire. And so there was a specific concern with individuals who might be under that kind of power in 4001. And Congress wanted to make very clear that such individuals could not simply be detained at executive discretion, but could only be detained pursuant to positive law. Positive law that is simply nonexistent in this case. . . .

IV. THE DECISION

On the evening of April 28, just a few hours after Clement had told the Supreme Court that the executive branch would not torture detainees in the war on terrorism, the television program *60 Minutes II* broadcast graphic photos depicting American soldiers of the 372nd Military Police Company, an army reserve unit, abusing Iraqi prisoners at Abu Ghraib, Saddam Hussein's infamous prison. In the days that followed, more of the same images flooded the Internet and the front pages of American newspapers. They showed soldiers taunting naked Iraqi prisoners; hooded prisoners cringing in terror; naked prisoners arranged in a human pyramid; prisoners in sexually humiliating poses; army dogs intimidating prisoners; prisoners with thin wires attached to their extremities, and, finally, a dead body on ice. The parade of depressing photos contributed to the declining popular support for the Iraq war. Bush's job approval rating dropped to 46 percent—the lowest up to that point in time.[19]

American military leaders in Iraq claimed they had not learned about the prisoner abuse until mid-January 2004. A military report prepared by Major General Antonio M. Taguba in February described what had happened at Abu Ghraib as "sadistic, blatant, and criminal abuses." The Senate's Committee on Armed Forces held public hearings on the scandal on May 7, 11, and 19. The military charged the seven MPs who directly participated in the abuse, but there was considerable suspicion that the abuse was far too systematic and pervasive to be the work of a few deviates. By mid-June, portions of leaked classified government memos broadened and deepened the prisoner abuse scandal. One memo dated January 9, 2002, written by Deputy Assistant Attorney General John Yoo (one of the members of the CCD that filed an *amicus* brief in *Hamdi*) and Special Counsel Robert J. Delahunty, both members of the Office of Legal Counsel (OLC) in the Justice Department, provided legal arguments why the Geneva Convention did not apply to members of either al Qaeda or the Taliban. Since the Convention did not apply, it followed that those provisions of the War Crimes Act that punished "grave breaches" of the Convention would also be inapplicable.[20] Based on this OLC analysis, Alberto R. Gonzales, then counsel to the president and later attorney general, sent a memo dated January 25, 2002 to President Bush. The memo described the war against terrorism as "a new kind of war" that "renders obsolete Geneva's strict limitations on questioning of enemy prisoners" and "renders quaint" some of the Convention's provisions. Gonzales also advised Bush that a presidential determination that the Convention did not apply to al Qaeda and the Taliban would substantially reduce "the threat of domestic criminal prosecution under the War Crimes Act. . . ." Guarding against a "misconstruction or misapplication" of the War Crimes Act was important, in Gonzales's view, because "it is difficult to predict the needs and circumstances that could arise in the course of the war on terrorism" and "the motives of prosecutors and independent counsels who may in the future decide to pursue unwarranted charges. . . ."[21]

In another memo dated February 1, 2002, Attorney General John Ashcroft urged Bush to designate Afghanistan "a failed state" and therefore not a party to the Geneva Convention, which would render the Convention completely inapplicable to all Taliban detainees. Such an approach, according to Ashcroft, was preferable to designating all Taliban fighters "unlawful enemy combatants" because it provided "the highest assurance that no court would subsequently entertain charges that American military officers, intelligence officials, or law enforcement officials violated Geneva Convention rules relating to field conduct, detention conduct or interrogation of detainees." Violations of the Geneva Convention were a serious matter, Ashcroft noted, since the War Crimes Act of 1996 made certain violations of the Convention crimes in the United States. In contrast, designating all Taliban fighters as "unlawful enemy combatants" carried "higher risk of liability, criminal prosecution, and judicially-imposed conditions of detainment—including mandated release of a detainee."[22]

The Gonzales and Ashcroft memos left an impression that the Bush administration ruled that the Geneva Convention was inapplicable to al Qaeda and that the Taliban detainees were not entitled to prisoner-of-war status under the Geneva Convention in part to reduce or eliminate the possibility that anyone from the administration could later be prosecuted for war crimes. Two other government documents published while the Court was considering *Hamdi* and *Padilla* focused specifically on standards controlling the interrogations of detainees. [23] In a memo addressed to White House Counsel Gonzales and dated August 1, 2002, Assistant Attorney General Jay S. Bybee construed the federal statute prohibiting torture very narrowly and argued that the anti-torture statute could not be applied in a manner that interfered with the President's Commander-in-Chief authority to interrogate enemy combatants. According to Bybee, Congress could "no more regulate the President's ability to detain and interrogate enemy combatants than it may regulate his ability to direct troop movements on the battlefield." A report authored by a team of administration lawyers dated March 6, 2003 was in general agreement with the conclusions and arguments of the Bybee memo.[24] On June 8, 2004, in testimony before the Senate's Judiciary Committee, Attorney General Ashcroft denied that the Bush administration had ever approved torture, but refused to set any clear limits to the president's war power, claiming that it was not "good government" to do so. Both the Bybee memo and the report came under severe criticism at the Judiciary Committee's hearing and in the media generally. On June 22, at a press briefing White House Counsel Gonzales released complete copies of a number of the partially leaked memos and other relevant documents, insisting throughout the briefing that President Bush had never authorized the use of torture.

The Supreme Court considered *Hamdi* and *Padilla* as the above events unfolded. The Bush administration tried to counteract the political damage caused by the prisoner abuse scandal by highlighting the dangers of terrorism. For example, at a June 1 press conference, Deputy Attorney General James Comey declassified a considerable amount of information in the government's possession supporting Padilla's designation as an enemy combatant. He observed that he could now "for the first time" tell the full "sobering story" about this "highly trained al Qaeda soldier." In March of 2000, Padilla met a recruiter from al Qaeda while on a religious pilgrimage to Saudi Arabia. A few months later he traveled to Afghanistan and attended an al Qaeda training camp in September and October of 2000. Soon thereafter he met Mohammad Atef, al Qaeda's military commander, Abu Zubaydah, a high-ranking al Qaeda leader, and Khalid Sheikh Mohammed (KSM), the mastermind of the 9/11 attacks. KSM urged Padilla to return to the United States and blow up high-rise apartment buildings with natural gas and provided him with $15,000 in cash, travel documents, and a cell phone for this purpose. Padilla still had these items in his possession when he was arrested in Chicago.

The timing of Comey's press briefing raised the question whether the government felt compelled to disclose classified information about Padilla in June of 2004 so that the justices on the Supreme Court would know what a dangerous terrorist he was before they handed down their ruling in his case. The Supreme Court handed down its decisions in both *Padilla* and *Hamdi* on June 28. In the former case, the Court in a 5-4 decision sidestepped the question of whether the Bush administration had the authority to detain an American citizen arrested in Chicago far from any battlefield. Rather than addressing the merits, the Court ruled that Judge Mukasey did not have jurisdiction to hear the case because Padilla was being detained in South Carolina, not New York. The upshot of the decision was that Padilla remained in detention while Donna Newman, his lawyer, refiled his petition for a writ of habeas corpus in the South Carolina district court, delaying a decision in his case for many months. Could it be that Comey's remarks on June 1 had had their desired effect? Did Comey's remarks convince the Court to find some way to delay a substantive ruling in *Padilla*?

Justice Stevens wrote the dissenting opinion in *Padilla*. It argued forcefully that Judge Mukasey and the Second Circuit were proper forums for deciding whether Padilla was being lawfully detained, especially since the government spirited Padilla out of New York to South Carolina without first informing Padilla's attorney. If the government had informed Padilla's attorney, and if a petition for the writ had been filed before Padilla's departure, there was no question that the courts in New York would have had jurisdiction over the case, even if the military would have later moved Padilla. Near the end of his dissent, Stevens conceded that reasonable jurists might differ on whether Padilla was entitled to immediate release, but insisted that there was no question that he was entitled to a hearing on whether his detention was justified. According to Stevens, indefinite incommunicado detention for the purpose of intelligence gathering was unlawful. Even if torture was not involved, any form of detention of this type was the "tool of tyrants." The judiciary had to require an immediate hearing to ensure that no such tool was being used in the Padilla case. Justices Souter, Ginsberg, and Breyer joined Justice Stevens's dissent.

The Supreme Court in *Hamdi* splintered over the question whether the Bush administration could detain citizens captured on foreign battlefields during the war on terrorism. Justice O'Connor wrote a plurality opinion joined by Chief Justice Rehnquist and Justices Kennedy and Breyer, who had dissented in *Padilla*. These four justices concluded that the AUMF, in conjunction with the laws of war, did authorize the detention of enemy combatants captured during the Afghan conflict, but nonetheless insisted that each detainee must be granted an opportunity to contest his designation as an enemy combatant before a neutral decision maker. In contrast, Justice Souter, joined by Justice Ginsburg, denied that the AUMF authorized detention, which meant that, in their view, Hamdi should be released immediately. However, these two justices, despite their conclusion that Hamdi's detention was unlawful, nonetheless joined the plurality in providing Hamdi with a degree of due process. In his dissent, Justice Scalia, joined by Justice Stevens, argued that Congress had not and could not authorize the indefinite detention of citizens as enemy combatants without first suspending the writ of habeas corpus. So long as the writ was not suspended, the government could not indefinitely detain citizens who aided foreign terrorists, but rather could only criminally prosecute them. Lastly, in his dissent, Justice Thomas agreed that the AUMF authorized detention, but rejected the plurality's view that the judiciary could in any way second guess the executive branch's individual designations of who was an enemy combatant.

The following excerpts will provide the context to consider which of these four approaches to the question of the detention of citizen enemy combatants is the most defensible one. Questions worth considering are the following: Can Congress authorize the detention of American citizens who are suspected terrorists? Can it authorize such detention without suspending the writ of habeas corpus? If it can authorize such detention, has it done so through the AUMF? If the AUMF authorizes the detention of citizens, what role does the federal judiciary have in monitoring how the policy is implemented? Is its role simply to say that the executive branch has the authority to detain and leave it to executive officials to decide whom to detain? Or is it the case that the government must produce "some evidence" that the citizen is indeed a terrorist? What kind of due process rights are owed to a citizen who is detained as a terrorist? Does he have a right to an attorney? Must he have an opportunity to rebut the evidence against him? Can a military tribunal make these decisions?

EXCERPTS FROM THE OPINIONS IN *HAMDI*

Justice O'Connor announced the judgment of the Court and delivered an opinion, in which *The Chief Justice, Justice Kennedy*, and *Justice Breyer* join.

[[1. AUMF.]] . . . The threshold question before us is whether the Executive has the authority to detain citizens who qualify as "enemy combatants." There is some debate as to the proper scope of this term, and the Government has never provided any court with the full criteria that it uses in classifying individuals as such. It has made clear, however, that, for purposes of this case, the "enemy combatant" that it is seeking to detain is an individual who, it alleges, was "'part of or supporting forces hostile to the United States or coalition partners'" in Afghanistan and who "'engaged in an armed conflict against the United States'" there. We therefore answer only the narrow question before us: whether the detention of citizens falling within that definition is authorized.

The Government maintains that no explicit congressional authorization is required, because the Executive possesses plenary authority to detain pursuant to Article II of the Constitution. We do not reach the question whether Article II provides such authority, however, because we agree with the Government's alternative position, that Congress has in fact authorized Hamdi's detention, through the AUMF. . . .

Hamdi contends that the AUMF does not authorize indefinite or perpetual detention. Certainly, we agree that indefinite detention for the purpose of interrogation is not authorized. Further, we understand Congress's grant of authority for the use of "necessary and appropriate force" to include the authority to detain for the duration of the relevant conflict, and our understanding is based on longstanding law-of-war principles. If the practical circumstances of a given conflict are entirely unlike those of the conflicts that informed the development of the law of war, that understanding may unravel. But that is not the situation we face as of this date. Active combat operations against Taliban fighters apparently are ongoing in Afghanistan. The United States may detain, for the duration of these hostilities, individuals legitimately determined to be Taliban combatants who "engaged in an armed conflict against the United States." If the record establishes that United States troops are still involved in active combat in Afghanistan, those detentions are part of the exercise of "necessary and appropriate force," and therefore are authorized by the AUMF. . . .

[[2. Due Process.]] Even in cases in which the detention of enemy combatants is legally authorized, there remains the question of what process is constitutionally due to a citizen who disputes his enemy-combatant status. . . .

. . . The Government recognizes the basic procedural protections required by the habeas statute, but asks us to hold that, given both the flexibility of the habeas mechanism and the circumstances presented in this case, the presentation of the Mobbs Declaration to the habeas court completed the required factual development. It suggests two separate reasons for its position that no further process is due.

First, the Government urges the adoption of the Fourth Circuit's holding below—that because it is "undisputed" that Hamdi's seizure took place in a combat zone, the habeas determination can be made purely as a matter of law, with no further hearing or fact-finding necessary. This argument is easily rejected. As the dissenters from the denial of rehearing *en banc* noted, the circumstances surrounding Hamdi's seizure cannot in any way be characterized as "undisputed," as "those circumstances are neither conceded in fact, nor susceptible to concession in law, because Hamdi has not been permitted to speak for himself or even through counsel as to those circumstances." Further, the "facts" that constitute the alleged concession are insufficient to support Hamdi's detention. Under the definition of enemy combatant that we accept today as falling within the scope of Congress' authorization, Hamdi would need to be "part of or supporting forces hostile to the United States or coalition partners" and "engaged in an armed conflict against the United States" to justify his detention in the United States for the duration of the relevant conflict. The habeas petition states only that "[w]hen seized by the United States Government, Mr. Hamdi resided in Afghanistan." An assertion that one *resided* in a country in which combat operations are taking place is not a concession that one was "*captured* in a zone of active combat operations in a foreign theater of war," and certainly is not a concession that one was "part of or supporting forces hostile to the United States or coalition partners" and "engaged in an armed conflict against the United States." Accordingly, we reject any argument that Hamdi has made concessions that eliminate any right to further process.

The Government's second argument requires closer consideration. This is the argument that further factual exploration is unwarranted and inappropriate in light of the extraordinary constitutional interests at stake. Under the Government's most extreme rendition of this argument, "[r]espect for separation of powers and the limited institutional capabilities of courts in matters of military decision-making in connection with an ongoing conflict" ought to eliminate entirely any individual process, restricting the courts to investigating only whether legal authorization exists for the broader detention scheme. Under this review, a court would assume the accuracy of the Government's articulated basis for Hamdi's detention, as set forth in the Mobbs Declaration, and assess only whether that articulated basis was a legitimate one. . . .

Striking the proper constitutional balance here is of great importance to the Nation during this period of ongoing combat. But it is equally vital that our calculus not give short shrift to the values that this country holds dear or to the privilege that is American citizenship. It is during our most challenging and uncertain moments that our Nation's commitment to due process is most severely tested; and it is in those times that we must preserve our commitment at home to the principles for which we fight abroad. . . .

We therefore hold that a citizen-detainee seeking to challenge his classification as an enemy combatant must receive notice of the factual basis for his

classification, and a fair opportunity to rebut the Government's factual assertions before a neutral decision maker. These essential constitutional promises
may not be eroded.

At the same time, the exigencies of the circumstances may demand that,
aside from these core elements, enemy combatant proceedings may be tailored to alleviate their uncommon potential to burden the Executive at a time
of ongoing military conflict. Hearsay, for example, may need to be accepted
as the most reliable available evidence from the Government in such a proceeding. Likewise, the Constitution would not be offended by a presumption
in favor of the Government's evidence, so long as that presumption remained
a rebuttable one and fair opportunity for rebuttal were provided. Thus, once
the Government puts forth credible evidence that the habeas petitioner meets
the enemy-combatant criteria, the onus could shift to the petitioner to rebut
that evidence with more persuasive evidence that he falls outside the criteria.
A burden-shifting scheme of this sort would meet the goal of ensuring that the
errant tourist, embedded journalist, or local aid worker has a chance to prove
military error while giving due regard to the Executive once it has put forth
meaningful support for its conclusion that the detainee is in fact an enemy
combatant. . . .

In so holding, we necessarily reject the Government's assertion that separation of powers principles mandate a heavily circumscribed role for the
courts in such circumstances. Indeed, the position that the courts must forgo
any examination of the individual case and focus exclusively on the legality
of the broader detention scheme cannot be mandated by any reasonable view
of separation of powers, as this approach serves only to *condense* power into
a single branch of government. We have long since made clear that a state of
war is not a blank check for the President when it comes to the rights of the
Nation's citizens. Whatever power the United States Constitution envisions
for the Executive in its exchanges with other nations or with enemy organizations in times of conflict, it most assuredly envisions a role for all three
branches when individual liberties are at stake. . . .

Because we conclude that due process demands some system for a citizen
detainee to refute his classification, the proposed "some evidence" standard is
inadequate. Any process in which the Executive's factual assertions go wholly
unchallenged or are simply presumed correct without any opportunity for the
alleged combatant to demonstrate otherwise falls constitutionally short. . . .

There remains the possibility that the standards we have articulated could be
met by an appropriately authorized and properly constituted military tribunal.
Indeed, it is notable that military regulations already provide for such process
in related instances, dictating that tribunals be made available to determine the
status of enemy detainees who assert prisoner-of-war status under the Geneva

Convention. In the absence of such process, however, a court that receives a petition for a writ of habeas corpus from an alleged enemy combatant must itself ensure that the minimum requirements of due process are achieved. . . .

Hamdi asks us to hold that the Fourth Circuit also erred by denying him immediate access to counsel upon his detention and by disposing of the case without permitting him to meet with an attorney. Since our grant of certiorari in this case, Hamdi has been appointed counsel, with whom he has met for consultation purposes on several occasions, and with whom he is now being granted unmonitored meetings. He unquestionably has the right of access to counsel in connection with the proceedings on remand. No further consideration of this issue is necessary at this stage of the case. . . .

Justice Souter, with whom *Justice Ginsburg* joins, concurring in part, dissenting in part, and concurring in the judgment. . . .

[[1. 4001(a).]] The threshold issue is how broadly or narrowly to read the Non-Detention Act, the tone of which is severe: "No citizen shall be imprisoned or otherwise detained by the United States except pursuant to an Act of Congress." Should the severity of the Act be relieved when the Government's stated factual justification for incommunicado detention is a war on terrorism, so that the Government may be said to act "pursuant" to congressional terms that fall short of explicit authority to imprison individuals? With one possible though important qualification, the answer has to be no. For a number of reasons, the prohibition within § 4001(a) has to be read broadly to accord the statute a long reach and to impose a burden of justification on the Government.

First, the circumstances in which the Act was adopted point the way to this interpretation. The provision superseded a cold war statute, the Emergency Detention Act of 1950, which had authorized the Attorney General, in time of emergency, to detain anyone reasonably thought likely to engage in espionage or sabotage. That statute was repealed in 1971 out of fear that it could authorize a repetition of the World War II internment of citizens of Japanese ancestry; Congress meant to preclude another episode like the one described in *Korematsu v. United States*. . . .

The fact that Congress intended to guard against a repetition of the World War II internments when it repealed the 1950 statute and gave us § 4001(a) provides a powerful reason to think that § 4001(a) was meant to require clear congressional authorization before any citizen can be placed in a cell. . . .

Second, when Congress passed § 4001(a) it was acting in light of an interpretive regime that subjected enactments limiting liberty in wartime to the requirement of a clear statement and it presumably intended § 4001(a) to be read accordingly. This need for clarity was unmistakably expressed in *Ex parte Endo*, decided the same day as *Korematsu* . . . :

In interpreting a wartime measure we must assume that [its] purpose was to allow for the greatest possible accommodation between . . . liberties and the exigencies of war. We must assume, when asked to find implied powers in a grant of legislative or executive authority, that the law makers intended to place no greater restraint on the citizen than was clearly and unmistakably indicated by the language they used.

Congress's understanding of the need for clear authority before citizens are kept detained is itself therefore clear, and § 4001(a) must be read to have teeth in its demand for congressional authorization.

Finally, even if history had spared us the cautionary example of the internments in World War II, even if there had been no *Korematsu*, and *Endo* had set out no principle of statutory interpretation, there would be a compelling reason to read § 4001(a) to demand manifest authority to detain before detention is authorized. The defining character of American constitutional government is its constant tension between security and liberty, serving both by partial helpings of each. In a government of separated powers, deciding finally on what is a reasonable degree of guaranteed liberty whether in peace or war (or some condition in between) is not well entrusted to the Executive Branch of Government, whose particular responsibility is to maintain security. For reasons of inescapable human nature, the branch of the Government asked to counter a serious threat is not the branch on which to rest the Nation's entire reliance in striking the balance between the will to win and the cost in liberty on the way to victory; the responsibility for security will naturally amplify the claim that security legitimately raises. . . . Hence the need for an assessment by Congress before citizens are subject to lockup, and likewise the need for a clearly expressed congressional resolution of the competing claims. . . .

[[2. Laws of War.]] Because the Force Resolution [[the AUMF]] authorizes the use of military force in acts of war by the United States, the argument goes, it is reasonably clear that the military and its Commander in Chief are authorized to deal with enemy belligerents according to the treaties and customs known collectively as the laws of war. Accordingly, the United States may detain captured enemies . . . .

By holding him [[Hamdi]] incommunicado, however, the Government obviously has not been treating him as a prisoner of war, and in fact the Government claims that no Taliban detainee is entitled to prisoner of war status. This treatment appears to be a violation of the Geneva Convention provision that even in cases of doubt, captives are entitled to be treated as prisoners of war "until such time as their status has been determined by a competent tribunal." . . .

Whether, or to what degree, the Government is in fact violating the Geneva Convention and is thus acting outside the customary usages of war are not matters I can resolve at this point. What I can say, though, is that the Government has not made out its claim that in detaining Hamdi in the manner described, it is acting in accord with the laws of war authorized to be applied against citizens by the Force Resolution. I conclude accordingly that the Government has failed to support the position that the Force Resolution authorizes the described detention of Hamdi for purposes of § 4001(a).

It is worth adding a further reason for requiring the Government to bear the burden of clearly justifying its claim to be exercising recognized war powers before declaring § 4001(a) satisfied. Thirty-eight days after adopting the Force Resolution, Congress passed the statute entitled Uniting and Strengthening America by Providing Appropriate Tools Required to Intercept and Obstruct Terrorism Act of 2001 (USA PATRIOT Act); that Act authorized the detention of alien terrorists for no more than seven days in the absence of criminal charges or deportation proceedings. It is very difficult to believe that the same Congress that carefully circumscribed Executive power over alien terrorists on home soil would not have meant to require the Government to justify clearly its detention of an American citizen held on home soil incommunicado. . . .

Because I find Hamdi's detention forbidden by § 4001(a) and unauthorized by the Force Resolution, I would not reach any questions of what process he may be due in litigating disputed issues in a proceeding under the habeas statute or prior to the habeas enquiry itself. . . .

Since this disposition does not command a majority of the Court, however, the need to give practical effect to the conclusions of eight members of the Court rejecting the Government's position calls for me to join with the plurality in ordering remand on terms closest to those I would impose. . . .

It should go without saying that in joining with the plurality to produce a judgment, I do not . . . mean to imply agreement that the Government could claim an evidentiary presumption casting the burden of rebuttal on Hamdi, or that an opportunity to litigate before a military tribunal might obviate or truncate enquiry by a court on habeas. . . .

Justice Scalia, with whom *Justice Stevens* joins, dissenting. . . .

[[1. Habeas Corpus.]] *Justice O'Connor*, writing for a plurality of this Court, asserts that captured enemy combatants (other than those suspected of war crimes) have traditionally been detained until the cessation of hostilities and then released. That is probably an accurate description of wartime practice with respect to enemy *aliens*. The tradition with respect to American citizens, however, has been quite different. Citizens aiding the enemy have been treated as traitors subject to the criminal process. . . .

There are times when military exigency renders resort to the traditional criminal process impracticable. English law accommodated such exigencies by allowing legislative suspension of the writ of habeas corpus for brief periods. . . .

Our Federal Constitution contains a provision explicitly permitting suspension, but limiting the situations in which it may be invoked: "The privilege of the Writ of Habeas Corpus shall not be suspended, unless when in Cases of Rebellion or Invasion the public Safety may require it." Although this provision does not state that suspension must be effected by, or authorized by, a legislative act, it has been so understood, consistent with English practice and the Clause's placement in Article I.

The Suspension Clause was by design a safety valve, the Constitution's only "express provision for exercise of extraordinary authority because of a crisis." . . .

It follows from what I have said that Hamdi is entitled to a habeas decree requiring his release unless (1) criminal proceedings are promptly brought, or (2) Congress has suspended the writ of habeas corpus. . . .

The plurality finds justification for Hamdi's imprisonment in the Authorization for Use of Military Force . . . . This is not remotely a congressional suspension of the writ, and no one claims that it is. Contrary to the plurality's view, I do not think this statute even authorizes detention of a citizen with the clarity necessary to satisfy the interpretive canon that statutes should be construed so as to avoid grave constitutional concerns, or with the clarity necessary to overcome the statutory prescription that "[n]o citizen shall be imprisoned or otherwise detained by the United States except pursuant to an Act of Congress." But even if it did, I would not permit it to overcome Hamdi's entitlement to habeas corpus relief. The Suspension Clause of the Constitution, which carefully circumscribes the conditions under which the writ can be withheld, would be a sham if it could be evaded by congressional prescription of requirements *other than the common-law requirement of committal for criminal prosecution* that render the writ, though available, unavailing. If the Suspension Clause does not guarantee the citizen that he will either be tried or released, unless the conditions for suspending the writ exist and the grave action of suspending the writ has been taken; if it merely guarantees the citizen that he will not be detained unless Congress by ordinary legislation says he can be detained; it guarantees him very little indeed.

. . . Having found a congressional authorization for detention of citizens where none clearly exists; and having discarded the categorical procedural protection of the Suspension Clause; the plurality then proceeds, under the guise of the Due Process Clause, to prescribe what procedural protections *it* thinks appropriate. . . .

. . . The role of habeas corpus is to determine the legality of executive detention, not to supply the omitted process necessary to make it legal. It is not the habeas court's function to make illegal detention legal by supplying a process that the Government could have provided, but chose not to. If Hamdi is being imprisoned in violation of the Constitution (because without due process of law), then his habeas petition should be granted; the Executive may then hand him over to the criminal authorities, whose detention for the purpose of prosecution will be lawful, or else must release him.

There is a certain harmony of approach in the plurality's making up for Congress's failure to invoke the Suspension Clause and its making up for the Executive's failure to apply what it says are needed procedures—an approach that reflects what might be called a Mr. Fix-it Mentality. The plurality seems to view it as its mission to Make Everything Come Out Right, rather than merely to decree the consequences, as far as individual rights are concerned, of the other two branches' actions and omissions. . . . The problem with this approach is not only that it steps out of the courts' modest and limited role in a democratic society; but that by repeatedly doing what it thinks the political branches ought to do it encourages their lassitude and saps the vitality of government by the people. . . .

Justice Thomas, dissenting.

The Executive Branch, acting pursuant to the powers vested in the President by the Constitution and with explicit congressional approval, has determined that Yaser Hamdi is an enemy combatant and should be detained. This detention falls squarely within the Federal Government's war powers, and we lack the expertise and capacity to second-guess that decision. As such, petitioners' habeas challenge should fail, and there is no reason to remand the case. . . .

I agree with the plurality that the Federal Government has power to detain those that the Executive Branch determines to be enemy combatants. But I do not think that the plurality has adequately explained the breadth of the President's authority to detain enemy combatants, an authority that includes making virtually conclusive factual findings. In my view, . . . we lack the capacity and responsibility to second-guess this determination. . . .

. . . "It is 'obvious and unarguable' that no governmental interest is more compelling than the security of the Nation." In *Moyer* [[*v. Peabody* (1909)]], the Court recognized the paramount importance of the Governor's interest in the tranquility of a Colorado town. At issue here is the far more significant interest of the security of the Nation. The Government seeks to further that interest by detaining an enemy soldier not only to prevent him from rejoining the ongoing fight. Rather, as the Government explains, detention can serve to gather critical intelligence regarding the intentions and capabilities of our adversaries, a function that the Government avers has become all the more important in the war on terrorism. . . .

y, the plurality's dismissive treatment of the Government's as-
╵╵╵╵╵ interests arises from its apparent belief that enemy-combatant determinations are not part of "the actual prosecution of a war" or one of the "central
functions of warmaking." This seems wrong: Taking *and holding* enemy combatants is a quintessential aspect of the prosecution of war. Moreover, this
highlights serious difficulties in applying the plurality's balancing approach
here. First, in the war context, we know neither the strength of the Government's interests nor the costs of imposing additional process.

Second, it is at least difficult to explain why the result should be different
for other military operations that the plurality would ostensibly recognize as
"central functions of warmaking." . . . Because a decision to bomb a particular
target might extinguish *life* interests, the plurality's analysis seems to require
notice to potential targets. To take one more example, in November 2002, a
Central Intelligence Agency (CIA) Predator drone fired a Hellfire missile at a
vehicle in Yemen carrying an al Qaeda leader, a citizen of the United States,
and four others. It is not clear whether the CIA knew that an American was in
the vehicle. But the plurality's due process would seem to require notice and
opportunity to respond here as well. I offer these examples not because I think
the plurality would demand additional process in these situations but because
it clearly would not. The result here should be the same. . . .

V. POSTSCRIPT

Hamdi v. Rumsfeld is a landmark decision, if only because the Supreme Court
handed down its ruling while the war against terrorism was ongoing, not after the hostilities were over. Coming when it did, the decision, rightly or
wrongly, rejected the principle of Roman law that during times of war the
laws are silent. However, the decision's splintered character and limited scope
have left many questions unanswered. For example, the decision did not resolve the important question whether Congress has authorized detentions beyond the parameters of the conflict in Afghanistan. It therefore left unanswered whether the Bush administration could detain as an enemy combatant
someone like Padilla, who arguably was not "part of or supporting forces hostile to the United States or coalition partners in Afghanistan and who engaged
in an armed conflict against the United States there." Nor did a majority of the
Court agree as to what level of due process was owed to Afghan battlefield
detainees like Hamdi. The plurality hinted that the burden of proof could be
imposed on the detainee, requiring him to prove his innocence, as it were, and
that due process could be satisfied if a military tribunal made the determinations of who is and who is not an enemy combatant. However, Justices Souter

and Ginsburg, one of whose votes the plurality needed to constitute a majority, not only disagreed with the notion that the AUMF authorized the detention of battlefield detainees, but also rejected the plurality's conclusions regarding the burden of proof and the sufficiency of a military hearing.
Moreover, the three dissenters, not all for the same reason, denied the Court
the authority to impose any due-process requirements. Justice Thomas said it
was an issue for the executive branch; Justices Scalia and Stevens said it was
for Congress, but only if it first suspended the writ of habeas corpus. Accordingly, *Hamdi* reflects the fact that there is little consensus on the Court
regarding the specifics of detaining American citizens as enemy combatants
in the war on terrorism.

Events following the Supreme Court decisions in late June 2004 further
complicated an already confused situation. First, Padilla's lawyers immediately refiled a petition for a writ of habeas corpus in the district court of South
Carolina. Two months later, in September, after a federal grand jury in Florida
indicted Adham Amin Hassoun and Mohamed Hesham Youssef, the two men
who had allegedly recruited Padilla into al Qaeda, the press reported that the
same grand jury had also named Padilla an unindicted co-conspirator. Speculation immediately ensued that the government would either bring criminal
charges against Padilla in the civilian criminal justice system or make a deal
with him so that he would testify against the other two defendants.[25] In the
meantime, after weeks of negotiations between Dunham and Justice Department officials, the government unexpectedly announced that Hamdi would be
permitted to return to Saudi Arabia on condition that he renounce his American citizenship, abandon terrorism, live in Saudi Arabia for five years, stay
out of Afghanistan, Iraq, Israel, Pakistan, and Syria, and not sue the United
States for detaining him for almost three years. Though it was not clear what
government could or would enforce these conditions, the Bush administration
released Hamdi, explaining that he no longer posed a threat to the United
States or possessed any intelligence value in the war on terrorism.[26] It is interesting to speculate whether Hamdi would have been released had the
Supreme Court accepted the government's position in *Hamdi* that courts
could not second-guess the military's enemy combatant designations or that
the military only needed "some evidence" to justify such designations.

Padilla's fate was very different from Hamdi's. Initially, on February 28,
2005, Judge Henry F. Floyd, a South Carolina federal district judge, ruled that
the government had no authority to detain him as an enemy combatant. Quoting from Justice O'Connor's plurality opinion in *Hamdi*, Floyd interpreted the
AUMF narrowly. It only provided authorization for detention of enemy combatants taken prisoner on the battlefields of Afghanistan. Since Padilla was
outside the scope of the AUMF, the Non-Detention Act required his release.[27]

Six months later, however, on September 9, a panel of Fourth Circuit judges unanimously reversed Floyd's decision, holding that the "locus of capture" was not essential to Padilla's designation as an "enemy combatant." In his opinion, Judge Michael Luttig explained that Padilla was properly designated an enemy combatant within the scope of the AUMF because he had met with al Qaeda operatives in Afghanistan, received training in explosives at one of their camps, and served as an armed guard at a Taliban outpost. Because he had done these things, he was "part of or supporting forces hostile to the United States or coalition partners" and he was "engaged in an armed conflict against the United States." He therefore fit the definition of enemy combatant outlined in the Supreme Court's decision in *Hamdi* and it did not matter that civilian authorities had arrested Padilla at a Chicago airport. Luttig could "discern no difference in principle between Hamdi and Padilla,"[28] although Judge Wilkinson, his colleague who had coauthored the Fourth Circuit's decision in *Hamdi*, had written that to "compare this battlefield capture to the domestic arrest in *Padilla v. Bush* is to compare apples and oranges."[29] Luttig concluded that the government could detain Padilla in a military brig in South Carolina for the duration of the conflict without any criminal charges.[30]

Padilla's attorneys appealed to the Supreme Court. However, on November 17, 2005, a few days before the deadline for the submission of the government's brief to the Supreme Court, a federal grand jury indicted Padilla for being a member of a "North American support cell" that provided "material support" to terrorist jihadist groups in Afghanistan and elsewhere. A few days after the indictment, President Bush issued an order transferring Padilla from military to civilian custody. The indictment did not allege the sensationalist acts of terrorism that the Bush administration had previously associated with Padilla's name: exploding a "dirty bomb" and blowing up apartment buildings. Speculation immediately arose that the Bush administration opted for criminal charges to avoid a Supreme Court ruling denying or limiting the president's power to detain citizens arrested far from any battlefield. The Fourth Circuit delayed Padilla's transfer, noting that the charges in the indictment were very different from the claims that had been used to justify his military detention. In response, the government explained that, to avoid constitutional objections, the civilian charges against Padilla had to be limited to those that could be proven without relying on the evidence obtained by military interrogations of Padilla and other detained terrorists.

On December 21, the same panel of Fourth Circuit judges that had upheld the legality of Padilla's military detention in September, unanimously rejected Padilla's transfer to civilian authority. In the court's view, the transfer created the "appearance" that government was "manipulating" the legal system to avoid Supreme Court review of the case. In his opinion, Judge Luttig also warned the Bush administration that its conduct might jeopardize its credibility in other terrorism cases. Padilla's attorneys argued that the Supreme Court should hear the case, even though the government had provided Padilla with the relief he had been requesting all along. The government's position was that the case was moot, but it did not deny that it could reclassify Padilla as an enemy combatant and return him to military detention. In the end, the Supreme Court approved Padilla's transfer on January 4, 2006, but delayed ruling on the status of Padilla's appeal until April 3, 2006, at which time the Court voted 6–3 not to hear the appeal.[32]

The criminal charges against Padilla were that he conspired to murder, maim, and kidnap people, not in the United States, but in a foreign country. While Padilla waited for his trial on these charges, his lawyers in late 2006 claimed that he had been subjected to hooding, stress positions, assaults, threats of imminent execution, and truth serum during his solitary confinement at the military brig in South Carolina. Because of this maltreatment, they argued, he was unable to assist in his defense and was therefore unfit to stand trial. The military denied these allegations, insisting that Padilla had been treated humanely.[33] The judge eventually ruled that the trial could go forward and a jury finally convicted Padilla of three conspiracy charges on August 16, 2007. Defenders of the Bush administration claimed that the conviction justified the three years of military detention that Padilla had served in South Carolina, while critics charged that the verdict proved that Padilla should have been prosecuted immediately. Legal commentators noted that the conviction was based on "thin evidence" and that the conspiracy charges enabled the prosecution to obtain a conviction without proving that a violent crime had occurred or even that the conspirators had agreed on the means by which to carry out a violent act. One law professor claimed that the conviction was "one step away from a thought crime."[34] Despite this concern, Padilla faces a possible life sentence.

NOTES

1. Authorization for Use of Military Force, Pub. L. No. 107-40, 115 Stat. 224 (2001).

2. President Bush also named Ali Saleh Kahlah al-Marri an enemy combatant on June 23, 2003. Eventually al-Marri, Hamdi, and Padilla all ended up in the same naval brig in Charleston, South Carolina. Al-Marri's petition for a writ of habeas corpus will not be considered in detail in this chapter because he is not a citizen of the United States. However, it is worth nothing that, after more than four years of imprisonment for al-Marri, a divided panel of the 4th Circuit Court of Appeals has recently granted his petition for a writ of habeas corpus, thereby overturning the district court's decision and setting the stage for the government to appeal to the Supreme Court. *Ali*

Saleh Kahlah Al-Marri v. Wright, 487 F.3d 160 (4th Cir. June 11, 2007). Also see Susan Schmidt, "Trail of an 'Enemy Combatant': From Desert to Heartland," *Washington Post*, July 20, 2007, A01.

3. *Harris v. Nelson*, 394 U.S. 286, 290–91 (1969).

4. The Mobbs Declaration in *Padilla* included a sealed supplement that Judge Mukasey declined to consider *in camera* until after Padilla had an opportunity to contest his designation as an enemy combatant. *Padilla v. Bush*, 233 F. Supp. 2d 564, 607–10 (S.D.N.Y. 2002).

5. See Judge Doumar's orders in *Hamdi* dated July 31 and August 14, 2002.

6. Brief for Respondents-Appellants at 33–35, *Hamdi v. Rumsfeld*, [[cite to panel decision]].

7. *Hamdi v. Rumsfeld*, 316 F.3d 450 (4th Cir. 2003).

8. Jacoby Declaration, available at www.pegc.us/archive/Padilla_vs_Rumsfeld/Jacoby_declaration_20030109.pdf.

9. Ibid., 50–51, 52–53.

10. *Hamdi v. Rumsfeld*, 337 F.3d 335, 357-68 (4th Cir. 2003).

11. Ibid. At 368–76.

12. *Padilla v. Rumsfeld*, 352 F.3d 695 (2nd Cir. 2003).

13. David W. Moore, "On First Anniversary, Americans Divided Over Impact of Iraq War," March 18, 2004, available at www.gallup.com/content/login.aspx?ci=11029 and Frank Newport, "Update: American Public Opinion and Iraq," Gallup News Service, August 12, 2004, available online at www.gallup.com/content/?ci=12688.

14. 71 U.S. 2 (1866).

15. 343 U.S. 579 (1952).

16. 317 U.S. 1 (1942).

17. *Korematsu v. United States*, 323 U.S. 214 (1944).

18. See, for example, Mark Bowden, "The Dark Art of Interrogation," *Atlantic Monthly* (October 2003): 51–76; Joanne Mariner, "Interrogation, Torture, the Constitution, and the Courts," January 5, 2004, Findlaw's Legal Commentary, available at http://findlaw.com; Don Van Natta Jr., "Questioning Terror Suspects in a Dark and Surreal World," *The New York Times*, March 9, 2004, available at http://nytimes.com; James Risen, David Johnston, and Neil A. Lewis, "Harsh C.I.A. Methods Cited in Top Qaeda Interrogations," *The New York Times*, May 13, 2004, available at http://nytimes.com.

19. See Jeffrey M. Jones, "War Support Unchanged," May 26, 2004, Gallup News Service, available at www.gallup.com/content/login.aspx?ci=11821; David M. Moore, "Bush Job Approval Drops to Record Low, May 11, 2004, Gallup New Service, available at www.gallup.com/content/login.aspx?ci=11668; Lydia Saad, "With Transfer of Sovereignty Looming, Attitude About Iraq Remain Negative," June 14, 2004, Gallup News Service, available at www.gallup.com/content/default.aspx?ci=11977.

20. Memorandum for William J. Haynes II, General Counsel, Department of Defense, from John Yoo, Deputy Assistant Attorney General, and Robert Kelahunty, Special Counsel, Office of Legal Counsel, *Re: Application of Treaties and Laws to al Qaeda and Taliban Detainees* (January 9, 2002).

21. Memorandum for the President, George W. Bush, from Alberto R. Gonzales, Counsel to the President, *Re: Decision Re Application of the Geneva Convention on Prisoners of War to the Conflict with Al Qaeda and the Taliban* (January 25, 2002).

22. Letter from Attorney General John Ashcroft to President George W. Bush, February 1, 2002, in *The Torture Papers*, ed. Karen J. Greenburg and Joshua L. Dratel (New York: Cambridge University Press, 2005), pp. 126–27.

23. It was reported that JAG officers leaked the government documents discussed in the text. Soon after the documents appeared, the Bush administration declassified them, along with a few others, and released them to the public in their entirety.

24. Memorandum for Alberto R. Gonzales, Counsel to the President, from Jay S. Bybee, Assistant Attorney General, *Re: Standards of Conduct for Interrogation under 18 U.S.C. 2340-2340A* (August 1, 2002), pp. 1, 7, 13, 31, and 35; *Working Group Report on Detainee Interrogations in the Global War on Terrorism: Assessment of Legal, Historical, Policy, and Operational Considerations* (March 6, 2003), pp. 7, 8, 17, 33, 35, both documents available in *The Torture Papers*, pp. 172–217 and 241–85.

25. See Vanessa Blum, "Government Implicates Padilla as Terror Conspirator," *Legal Times*, September 17, 2004.

26. "Saudi-American Held for Three Years Back in Saudi Arabia," *The Associated Press*, October 11, 2004; Jerry Markon, "Hamdi Returned to Saudi Arabia," *Washington Post*, October 12, 2004, p. A02.

27. *Padilla v. Hanft*, 2005 U.S. Dist. LEXIS 2921 (D.S.C. 2005).

28. *Padilla v. Hanft*, 2005 U.S. App. LEXIS 19465, 13 (4th Cir. 2005).

29. *Hamdi v. Rumsfeld*, 337 F.3d 335, 344 (4th Cir. 2003).

30. *Padilla v. Hanft*, 2005 U.S. App. LEXIS 19465 (4th Cir. 2005).

31. Deborah Sontag, "A Videotape Offers a Window Into a Terror Suspect's Isolation," *The New York Times*, Dec. 4, 2006, A1, available at http://nytimes.com.

32. See Eric Lichtblau, "In Legal Shift, U.S. Charges Detainee in Terrorism Case," *The New York Times*, November 23, 2005; Mark Sherman, "U.S.: Padilla Can't Challenge His Detention Without Charges Since He's Been Indicted," *Associated Press*, December 12, 2005; Linda Greenhouse, "Justices are Urged to Dismiss Padilla Case," *The New York Times*, December 18, 2005; Neil A. Lewis, "Court Refuses U.S. Bid to Shift Terror Suspect," *The New York Times*, December 22, 2005; *Padilla v. Hanft*, 547 U.S. 1062 (2006).

33. Deborah Sontag, "A Videotape Offers a Window Into a Terror Suspect's Isolation," *The New York Times*, December 4, 2006, A1, available at nytimes.com.

34. Deborah Sontag, "U.S. Judge Finds Padilla Competent to Stand Trial," *The New York Times*, March 1, 2007, A16; Adam Liptak, "Padilla Case Offers a New Model of Terrorism Trial, *The New York Times*, August 18, 2007, both available at nytimes.com.

Chapter 3

Aliens Detained Abroad

Rasul v. Bush (2004)

In the war against the Taliban and al Qaeda in Afghanistan, American-led coalition forces took custody of thousands of alleged enemy combatants, many of whom were initially captured by the Northern Alliance and other local anti-Taliban groups. Beginning in January 2002, the U.S. military forcibly transferred over six hundred of these and other detainees from Afghanistan and forty-three other countries to the Guantanamo Bay Naval Base (GBNB) in Cuba. Two major legal controversies arose concerning the GBNB detainees. First, was it legal for the Bush administration to detain and interrogate these individuals as unlawful enemy combatants or did it violate international law, the United States Constitution, or a federal statute? Second, did the federal courts of the United States have jurisdiction to decide the first question? These two analytically distinct questions were linked together in the litigation that forms the subject matter of this chapter. Though the habeas statute did not explicitly grant federal courts jurisdiction to hear petitions from aliens detained abroad, it did say that federal courts had jurisdiction if someone was detained "under or by color of the authority of the United States or . . . in violation of the Constitution or laws or treaties of the United States." Did this language mean that one cannot decide the issue of jurisdiction without first deciding whether the conduct of the Bush administration violated international, constitutional, or federal law? Critics charged that the Bush administration's detention policies were clear violations of both domestic and international law, including the Geneva Convention Relative to the Treatment of Prisoners of War. In response, defenders of the Bush administration insisted that detention of GBNB detainees was consistent with both domestic and international law, but even if it were not, federal courts had no jurisdiction to hear petitions from aliens detained outside the borders of the United

States. *Rasul v. Bush* provides an excellent forum to consider which of these two views is more defensible.

I. BACKGROUND

According to international law, there are five types of jurisdiction. The most common basis for jurisdiction is the principle of territoriality, according to which the courts of a nation have jurisdiction over any conduct occurring within the nation's borders. No one disputes the legitimacy of the principle of territoriality. Many countries, however, have extended the jurisdiction of their courts beyond the territorial principle by applying domestic law to acts done by citizens abroad (the principle of nationality) and, to a lesser extent, to acts done by aliens that injure citizens abroad (the principle of passive personality). In addition, some states punish acts by citizens or aliens abroad that detrimentally affect the security of the state (the protective principle). All of these types of extraterritorial jurisdiction have some link between the conduct and the state asserting jurisdiction, whether it is the location of the conduct, the citizenship of the offender or victim, or the nature of the offense. The fifth type of jurisdiction, called "universal jurisdiction," has no such linkage; any state can assert jurisdiction over the conduct in question. An example of universal jurisdiction is piracy. For centuries it has been well understood that any country has universal jurisdiction to try a pirate for acts of piracy on the high seas, even if both the pirate and the victim had no relationship to the country in question.

In general, extraterritorial jurisdiction has grown significantly over the last fifty years, including the more unusual form of universal jurisdiction. In addition to piracy, states today assert universal jurisdiction over slave trading, war crimes, acts of genocide, hijackings of aircraft, and "perhaps certain acts of terrorism."[1] Starting in the 1980s, Congress expanded the federal judiciary's extraterritorial jurisdiction over acts of terrorism, but normally confined criminal liability to situations involving the security interests of the United States or to acts involving American nationals, whether as alleged offenders or as victims.[2] For example, in 1986 it became a crime to conspire to kill, attempt to kill, or kill a national of the United States when he or she is outside the country, so long as the attorney general or his representative certified that the offense was intended "to coerce, intimidate, or retaliate against a government or a civilian population."[3] During the 1990s, Congress gave the federal courts jurisdiction over (1) any attempt or conspiracy to use weapons of mass destruction by a U.S. national outside the United States or against a U.S. national abroad;[4] (2) any act of terrorism "transcending national boundaries;"[5] and, lastly, (3) any provision of "material support" to a foreign terrorist organization.[6] Following the 9/11 attacks, Congress enacted the USA PATRIOT Act and legislation to implement the International Convention for the Suppression of Terrorist Bombings.[7] The latter law granted universal jurisdiction to federal courts for anyone charged with bombing a place of public use anywhere in the world or knowingly providing or receiving funds for terrorist purposes.[8]

Against this legislative background, federal judges have not hesitated to assume extraterritorial jurisdiction over acts of terrorism committed abroad. In 1991, the D.C. Circuit ruled that a district court did have jurisdiction to try a hijacker who destroyed a Royal Jordanian airliner on the ground in Beirut, Lebanon.[9] In 1998, the same court said that a Palestinian who hijacked an Egyptian plane on a flight from Athens could be tried in Washington, D.C.[10] In 2000, the alleged bombers of the U.S. embassies in Nairobi, Kenya and Dar es Salaam, Tanzania were tried in New York City.[11] In 2003, the Second Circuit ruled that the district court had jurisdiction, not only over a conspiracy to blow up airliners on their way to destinations in the United States, but also over a related charge involving the placement of a test bomb on a Philippine Airlines flight from Manila to Japan.[12]

It is not clear whether this trend of expanding the extraterritorial jurisdiction of federal courts in an age of terrorism has any bearing on whether federal courts should have jurisdiction to decide the legality of the American government detaining aliens abroad. If torturers, war criminals, and terrorists who commit illegal acts outside the United States can be prosecuted in federal courts, should persons detained by the American armed forces in the war on terrorism have some means of testing the lawfulness of their detention in the same courts? Regarding this question, there is a "longstanding principle of American law" that federal courts are presumed not to have extraterritorial jurisdiction unless Congress's intent to grant it is "clearly manifested" in the statute granting such jurisdiction.[13] Accordingly, there may be nothing inconsistent about broadening the jurisdiction of the federal courts to prosecute terrorists for acts done abroad, but limiting the jurisdiction of the same courts so that they are unable to entertain petitions for writs of habeas corpus from aliens detained abroad. By initiating prosecutions in the former cases, the executive branch has triggered the jurisdiction of the federal courts. It may seem somewhat paradoxical, however, that the executive branch can, so to speak, lock the court room door by simply refusing to prosecute a terrorist who is being detained abroad.

In January 2002, Skina Bibi, a mother of one of the GBNB detainees, Mohammed Iqbal and Terry Hicks, both fathers of detainees, and Maha Habib, a wife of one of the detainees, filed a petition for habeas relief under the name of *Rasul v. Bush* in the federal district court in Washington, D.C. Facts alleged in the petition contradicted the Bush administration's claim that the detainees in question were unlawful enemy combatants. In May, twelve Kuwaiti citizens filed a lawsuit—*Al Odah v. United States*—claiming that their relatives detained at GBNB had been in Afghanistan and Pakistan to provide humanitarian aid to the people of that region. Both *Rasul* and *Al Odah* came before District Judge Colleen Kollar-Kotelly, who dismissed the cases on July 30, 2002 on the ground that federal courts lacked jurisdiction to hear petitions for writs of habeas corpus from aliens detained outside the sovereign territory of the United States.[14] On appeal, a three-judge panel of the D.C. Circuit Court of Appeals affirmed her decision on March 11, 2003.[15] Both lower courts relied heavily on *Johnson v. Eisentrager*, a 1950 Supreme Court decision that had held that federal courts could not provide habeas relief to German nationals tried for war crimes by a military commission in China and imprisoned in Landsberg Prison in Germany. The lawyers for the detainees appealed to the Supreme Court.

A week after the D.C. Circuit handed down its decision in *Rasul* and *Al Odah*, President Bush, in cooperation with a number of allies, initiated the invasion of Iraq. The purpose of the invasion was to destroy the weapons of mass destruction that Saddam Hussein presumably controlled and dismantle his tyrannical regime, which many thought had links to Islamic terrorist groups, perhaps including al Qaeda. American forces encircled Baghdad by April 6. Though President Bush announced that the military phase of Operation Iraqi Freedom was over on May 1, a fierce insurgency raged on during the months that followed. The number of detainees in Iraq sharply increased. By fall 2003, over seven thousand detainees were held at Abu Ghraib, the notorious prison where countless numbers of Saddam's victims had been tortured and killed. The increasing number of detainees abroad heightened the significance of *Rasul* and *Al Odah*. If the Supreme Court were to recognize the possibility of habeas review for the GBNB detainees, it was unclear what implications that decision would have for prisoners held in Afghanistan or Iraq.

While *Rasul* and *Al Odah* were on appeal at the Supreme Court, the Ninth Circuit in *Gherebi v. Bush* decided in a 2–1 decision that *Eisentrager* did not require "sovereignty" as a prerequisite for habeas jurisdiction. "Territorial jurisdiction" was sufficient, according to the majority, which meant that federal courts had jurisdiction over the detainees since no one doubted that the United States exerted territorial jurisdiction over GBNB. In addition, the Ninth Circuit held that, even if *Eisentrager* required sovereignty, the federal courts nonetheless had jurisdiction because the United States was in fact sovereign over GBNB. Though it was true, the panel conceded, that the 1903 lease recognized Cuba's ultimate sovereignty over GBNB, this term had to be understood in a temporal, not a qualitative, sense. In other words, as long as the United States retained control over the GBNB, it exercised all the attributes of sovereignty. All that Cuba retained was a residual sovereignty that would revert back to Cuba if and when the United States decided to surrender actual sovereignty. In dissent, Judge Susan P. Graber rejected both of the above rationales and lamented the fact that the Ninth Circuit had reached out to decide this case after the Supreme Court had already agreed to hear *Rasul* and *Al Odah*.[16]

II. BRIEFS FILED IN *RASUL*

The briefs filed at the Supreme Court in *Rasul* debated the following questions: Was the United States legally sovereign over the GBNB such that *Eisentrager* did not apply? Was *Eisentrager* inapplicable because the detainees of that case are fundamentally different from those of *Rasul* and *Al Odah*? Has so much changed over the past fifty-four years that *Eisentrager* should be overruled or significantly narrowed? Did the detention policy at the GBNB violate federal statutes, the Constitution, or international law and should the answer to this question have any bearing on the issue of the jurisdiction of the federal courts? If the federal courts can entertain petitions for writs of habeas corpus from GBNB detainees, can they also entertain petitions from detainees held in areas of active military hostilities, such as Afghanistan or Iraq? In an age of global terrorism, what role should the federal courts play in monitoring the executive branch's detention policies abroad? Should it be up to Congress to decide these issues or can federal courts act unilaterally?

All of the above questions should be kept in mind as one reads the excerpts from the briefs below. The brief filed by Rasul and his supporting *amici* relied heavily on the statutory language of Congress' grant of habeas jurisdiction to federal courts (28 U.S.C. 2241) and the allegedly unlawful character of the Bush administration's detention policy. The habeas provision in question (see box 3.1) said that the writ should not extend to a "prisoner" unless he was in custody "under or by color of the authority of the United States" or "in violation of the Constitution or laws or treaties of the United States." The GBNB detainees, the brief insisted, satisfied both prongs of the test. They were detained under the authority of the United States and their detention violated the Constitution, federal statutes, and treaties. The statute did not limit the writ to citizens or resident aliens, nor did it explicitly require that the United States have sovereignty over the detention site.

The brief filed by the United States insisted that *Johnson v. Eisentrager* was the controlling precedent governing how the habeas statute should be interpreted. In the government's view, this precedent did not narrow the conditions

---

Box 3.1. 28 U.S.C. 2241: POWER TO GRANT WRITS OF HABEAS CORPUS

(a) Writs of habeas corpus may be granted by the Supreme Court, any justice thereof, the district courts and any circuit judge within their respective jurisdictions. The order of a circuit judge shall be entered in the records of the district court of the district wherein the restraint complained of is had.

(b) The Supreme Court, any justice thereof, and any circuit judge may decline to entertain an application for a writ of habeas corpus and may transfer the application for hearing and determination to the district court having jurisdiction to entertain it.

(c) The writ of habeas corpus shall not extend to a prisoner unless—

(1) He is in custody under or by color of the authority of the United States or is committed for trial before some court thereof; or

(2) He is in custody for an act done or omitted in pursuance of an Act of Congress, or an order, process, judgment or decree of a court or judge of the United States; or

(3) He is in custody in violation of the Constitution or laws or treaties of the United States; or

(4) He, being a citizen of a foreign state and domiciled therein is in custody for an act done or omitted under any alleged right, title, authority, privilege, protection, or exemption claimed under the commission, order or sanction of any foreign state, or under color thereof, the validity and effect of which depend upon the law of nations; or

(5) It is necessary to bring him into court to testify or for trial.

---

under which federal courts should grant writs of habeas corpus, as *Rasul* claimed, but rather substantively limited the jurisdiction of federal courts to aliens detained inside the sovereign territory of the United States. The brief emphasized that Congress has never amended the habeas statute to overturn the Court's result in *Eisentrager*. One 1951 bill was introduced in Congress to effect this result, but it was never voted out of committee. Moreover, later precedents of the Supreme Court, including *Zadvydas v. Davis* (2001) and *United States v. Verdugo-Urquidez* (1990), relied on *Eisentrager* to reject the notion that Fourth and Fifth Amendment rights applied to aliens living abroad.

Justice Robert H. Jackson's majority opinion in *Eisentrager* was therefore a pivotal point in the *Rasul* case (see box 3.2). If the United States was correct in its interpretation of this decision, there was valid precedent for denying the

---

Box 3.2. *Johnson v. Eisentrager* (1950)

MR. JUSTICE JACKSON delivered the opinion of the Court.

The ultimate question in this case is one of jurisdiction of civil courts of the United States vis-à-vis military authorities in dealing with enemy aliens overseas. . . .

We are cited to no instance where a court, in this or any other country where the writ is known, has issued it on behalf of an alien enemy who, at no relevant time and in no stage of his captivity, has been within its territorial jurisdiction. Nothing in the text of the Constitution extends such a right, nor does anything in our statutes. . . .

With the citizen we are now little concerned, except to set his case apart as untouched by this decision and to take measure of the difference between his status and that of all categories of aliens. Citizenship as a head of jurisdiction and a ground of protection was old when Paul invoked it in his appeal to Caesar. The years have not destroyed nor diminished the importance of citizenship nor have they sapped the vitality of a citizen's claims upon his government for protection. . . .

The alien, to whom the United States has been traditionally hospitable, has been accorded a generous and ascending scale of rights as he increases his identity with our society. Mere lawful presence in the country creates an implied assurance of safe conduct and gives him certain rights; they become more extensive and secure when he makes preliminary declaration of intention to become a citizen, and they expand to those of full citizenship upon naturalization. . . .

But in extending constitutional protections beyond the citizenry, the Court has been at pains to point out that it was the alien's presence within its territorial jurisdiction that gave the Judiciary power to act. . . .

It is war that exposes the relative vulnerability of the alien's status. The security and protection enjoyed while the nation of his allegiance remains in amity with the United States are greatly impaired when his nation takes up arms against us. While his lot is far more humane and endurable than the experience of our citizens in some enemy lands, it is still not a happy one. But disabilities this country lays upon the alien who becomes also an enemy are imposed temporarily as an incident of war and not as an incident of alienage. . . .

(Continued)

Box 3.2. *Johnson v. Eisentrager* (1950) (Continued)

The resident enemy alien is constitutionally subject to summary arrest, internment, and deportation whenever a "declared war" exists. Courts will entertain his plea for freedom from Executive custody only to ascertain the existence of a state of war and whether he is an alien enemy and so subject to the Alien Enemy Act. Once these jurisdictional elements have been determined, courts will not inquire into any other issue as to his internment.

The standing of the enemy alien to maintain any action in the courts of the United States has been often challenged and sometimes denied. . . . Our rule of generous access to the resident enemy alien was first laid down by Chancellor Kent in 1813, when, squarely faced with the plea that an alien enemy could not sue upon a debt contracted before the war of 1812, he reviewed the authorities to that time and broadly declared that "A lawful residence implies protection, and a capacity to sue and be sued. A contrary doctrine would be repugnant to sound policy, no less than to justice and humanity." . . .

But the nonresident enemy alien, especially one who has remained in the service of the enemy, does not have even this qualified access to our courts, for he neither has comparable claims upon our institutions nor could his use of them fail to be helpful to the enemy. . . .

The foregoing demonstrated how much further we must go if we are to invest these enemy aliens [[of *Eisentrager*]], resident, captured and imprisoned abroad, with standing to demand access to our courts. We are here confronted with a decision whose basic premise is that these prisoners are entitled, as a constitutional right, to sue in some court of the United States for a writ of habeas corpus. To support that assumption we must hold that a prisoner of our military authorities is constitutionally entitled to the writ, even though he (a) is an enemy alien; (b) has never been or resided in the United States; (c) was captured outside of our territory and there held in military custody as a prisoner of war; (d) was tried and convicted by a Military Commission sitting outside the United States; (e) for offenses against laws of war committed outside the United States; and (f) is at all times imprisoned outside the United States.

We have pointed out that the privilege of litigation has been extended to aliens, whether friendly or enemy, only because permitting their presence in the country implied protection. No such basis can be invoked here, for these prisoners at no relevant time were within any territory over which the United States is sovereign, and the scenes of their offense, their capture, their trial, and their punishment were all beyond the territorial jurisdiction of any court of the United States.

. . . To grant the writ to these prisoners might mean that our army must transport them across the seas for hearing. This would require allocation of shipping space, guarding personnel, billeting, and rations. It might also require transportation for whatever witnesses the prisoners desired to call as well as transportation for those necessary to defend legality of the sentence. The writ, since it is held to be a matter of right, would be equally available to enemies during active hostilities as in the present twilight between war and peace. Such trials would hamper the war effort and bring aid and comfort to the enemy. They would diminish the prestige of our commanders, not only with enemies but with wavering neutrals. It would be difficult to devise more effective fettering of a field commander than to allow the very enemies he is ordered to reduce to submission to call him to account in his own civil courts and divert his efforts and attention from the military offensive abroad to the legal defensive at home. Nor is it unlikely that the result of such enemy litigiousness would be a conflict between judicial and military opinion highly comforting to enemies of the United States. . . .

. . . [[The]] doors of our courts have not been summarily closed upon these prisoners. Three courts have considered their application and have provided their counsel opportunity to advance every argument in their support and to show some reason in the petition why they should not be subject to the usual disabilities of nonresident enemy aliens. This is the same preliminary hearing as to sufficiency of application that was extended in *Quirin, Yamashita,* and *Hirota v. MacArthur.* After hearing all contentions they have seen fit to advance and considering every contention we can base on their application and the holdings below, we arrive at the same conclusion the Court reached in each of those cases, viz., that no right to the writ of habeas corpus appears . . . .

GBNB detainees access to the federal courts. One question was whether Jackson's opinion implied that the federal courts were closed to all aliens detained abroad or only enemy aliens detained abroad because they had been convicted by a military commission. Another was whether Jackson's opinion was only a ruling on jurisdiction or was it also a ruling on the merits, implying that the courts had jurisdiction, even if the petitioners were not entitled to the writ. Read box 3.2 carefully. Which passages of the opinion support the government's position? Which support Rasul's? How should *Johnson v. Eisentrager* be applied to the facts of *Rasul* and *Al Odah*?

Although ambiguous, Justice Jackson's opinion in *Eisentrager* expressed three important principles of American law. First, aliens inside the United States, whether inside legally or illegally, not only have the right to petition a court for a writ of habeas corpus if detained, but also have additional procedural and substantive rights under federal immigration law and the Due Process Clauses of the Fifth and Fourteenth Amendments. Second, a resident enemy alien in a declared war was subject to the Alien Enemy Act. The executive branch could detain him or her and any review by courts would be limited to whether there was a declared state of war and whether the detainee was an enemy alien. Third, a writ of habeas corpus was not available to a nonresident enemy alien convicted of war crimes during a declared war by a U.S. military commission outside the United States and imprisoned abroad.

Rasul's brief highlighted the broad language of the habeas statute and insisted that *Eisentrager* should be interpreted as a decision denying that the German war criminals had a right to the writ, not as a decision denying that federal courts had the jurisdiction to decide the issue. Moreover, unlike the detainees of *Eisentrager*, the GBNB detainees are neither convicted war criminals nor enemies in a declared war. The government has detained them without any legal process whatsoever in violation of international law and the Suspension Clause of Constitution, which prohibits suspending the writ of habeas corpus "unless when in Cases of Rebellion or Invasion the public safety may require it." Accordingly, the courts not only have jurisdiction to entertain petitions for writs of habeas corpus from GBNB detainees, but the detainees have a right to the writ itself. The fact that the detention is taking place outside the formal boundaries of the United States makes no difference. Not only is GBNB "practically . . . a part of the Government of the United States," but the degree of jurisdiction exercised by the United States is far greater than the allied military occupation over Germany that was considered in *Eisentrager*. The United States has exclusive territorial jurisdiction over GBNB, which is all that is required to establish the federal judiciary's jurisdiction.

In response, the brief for the United States argued that the GBNB detainees were clearly "detained abroad" because the lease agreement with Cuba explicitly stated that Cuba retained "ultimate sovereignty" over Guantanamo Bay. *Ex parte Quirin* (1942) and *In re Yamashita* (1948) were consistent with the Bush administration's position that federal courts lacked jurisdiction in *Rasul* because the enemy aliens in those two earlier cases were detained within the United States or the Philippines, at that time a territory of the United States. Sovereignty, according to the U.S. brief, had to be the correct criterion for determining jurisdiction. If de facto control of a detention site were the criterion, it would grant access to federal courts to any alien detained by the American military anywhere in the world, including those detained on battlefields during actual hostilities. Such a broad understanding of federal jurisdiction would entangle courts in "political questions," the government's brief insisted, and violate the principle of separation of powers by permitting judicial interference with the president's duties as commander in chief.

The U.S. brief also addressed the argument that the Bush administration was violating international law by detaining suspected members of the Taliban and al Qaeda at the GBNB. It argued that these claims were both wrong and irrelevant. President Bush had the authority under international law to deny the GBNB detainees POW status and the issue of jurisdiction did not depend on the merits because the Geneva Convention and the other relevant international treaties were not "self-executing." According to American law, a self-executing treaty granted individuals a private right of action to sue for violations of the treaty. If a treaty was not self-executing, a right of action would exist only if Congress enacted appropriate implementation legislation. Since the Geneva Convention was not self-executing, and since Congress had not enacted a private cause of action, American courts had no jurisdiction, even if one wrongly assumed that the Bush administration was violating an international treaty. According to the U.S. brief, the GBNB detainees only had political remedies, such as diplomatic negotiations, congressional inquiries, or the scrutiny of an interested public. Courts had no right to interfere.

Short excerpts from a number of additional briefs are included below. First, the main brief filed in *Al Odah* argued forcefully that the system of detention at GBNB clearly violated international law and that American courts should follow the example of the Israel High Court of Justice and review all forms of executive detention or, at a minimum, insist that the military itself provide individualized hearings. An *amicus* brief submitted by a group of law professors defended the Bush administration's authority to hold unlawful enemy combatants indefinitely. Another, by retired military officers, argued that the Bush administration should abide by the Geneva Conventions to protect American troops from arbitrary treatment in future conflicts abroad. Three of the *amici curiae* briefs that supported the petitioners came from abroad, including a brief filed by 175 members of both houses of the Parliament of the United Kingdom of Great Britain and Northern Ireland, the first such brief ever submitted to the Supreme Court of the United States. Fatima El-Samnah filed a brief on behalf of her fifteen-year-old grandson, the only Canadian citizen detained at the GBNB and presumably the youngest. Lastly, Abdullah Al-Joaid submitted a brief on behalf of his brother, one of the approximately 127 nationals of Saudi Arabia detained at GBNB, the largest contingent of detainees from a single country. These three foreign *amici* briefs highlighted issues of international law and legal precedents of other countries, thereby underlining the international character of the litigation involving the GBNB detainees.

In evaluating whether GBNB is within the legal sovereignty of the United States, a central issue of the case, it is certainly relevant that the United States exercises criminal jurisdiction over both citizens and aliens on the base.[17] For example, the U.S. military recently brought espionage charges against an army chaplain, an intelligence officer, and two translators at the GBNB.[18] Moreover, in the past military courts have issued writs of habeas corpus against officers in charge of detaining American soldiers at GBNB?[19] In a case dealing with Haitian refugees interdicted on the high seas and detained at GBNB during the early 1990s, the Second Circuit Court of Appeals held that the Bill of Rights protected the aliens. However, the Supreme Court later vacated this case as moot and the Eleventh Circuit came to the opposite conclusion in 1995, holding that the Constitution was inapplicable to the Haitian refugees because they were outside the country.[20] Lastly, in 1993 a New York district judge ruled that the government violated the Fourteenth Amendment by not providing adequate medical facilities to HIV-positive refugees held at a detention camp at the GBNB.[21]

EXCERPTS FROM RASUL'S BRIEF

[[1. Habeas Corpus statute.]] . . . [[T]]he Executive argues that the federal courts are powerless to review these prisoners' indefinite detentions because they are foreign nationals brought by the military to a prison beyond the "ultimate sovereignty" of the United States. The Government is mistaken. First, nothing in the habeas statute supports such a limitation, nor has Congress manifested an intention to strip the federal courts of their jurisdiction under these circumstances. The Court has routinely taken jurisdiction of habeas petitions filed by persons in custody under the authority of the United States in places beyond its "ultimate sovereignty," even during times of armed conflict. And the Court has never suggested that the Executive can incarcerate people indefinitely, beyond the reach of judicial recourse, simply by confining them in a facility that the United States Government controls through some arrangement other than "ultimate sovereignty."

Second, the Executive's argument—if accepted—would raise "serious constitutional problem[s]." It would permit "an indefinite, perhaps permanent, deprivation of human liberty without any [judicial] protection," and would suspend the writ for an entire class of detainees on no firmer basis than Executive fiat. The Executive would have the Court "close our doors to a class of habeas petitioners seeking review without any clear indication that such was Congress's intent." This country has rejected imprisonment without legal process, even during times of war, and the Court should not interpret the habeas statute in a manner that permits the creation of an offshore prison for foreign nationals that operates entirely outside the law. . . .

Title 28 U.S.C. § 2241 (c)(1) and (c)(3) confer jurisdiction on the district court to hear applications for habeas corpus filed by any person imprisoned "under or by color of the authority of the United States," or "in violation of the Constitution or laws or treaties of the United States." Nothing in the text purports to exclude habeas jurisdiction on the basis of nationality or territory. On the contrary, "[t]his legislation is of the most comprehensive character. It brings within the habeas corpus jurisdiction of every court and of every judge every possible case of privation of liberty contrary to the National Constitution, treaties, or laws. It is impossible to widen this jurisdiction." . . .

The Court should also avoid an interpretation of the habeas statute that suspends the writ for an entire class of claimants based solely on Executive proclamation. In [[*INS v.*]] *St. Cyr*, the Government argued that certain provisions of the Anti-Terrorism and Effective Death Penalty Act of 1996 should be construed as denying the alien petitioners the right to habeas review of their deportation proceedings. The Court rejected this position, noting that such a construction would raise grave constitutional doubts under the Suspension Clause. [[The Constitution states that the writ of habeas corpus can only be suspended "when in Cases of Rebellion or Invasion the public safety may require it." See Article I, Section 9.]] . . .

The constitutional questions are even more "difficult and significant" here. Because the prisoners in this case "are nonenemy aliens"—they are citizens of allied nations—the writ would have been available to them even at the Founding. In addition, the detentions here are the very sort that the Government conceded in *St. Cyr* must, under the Suspension Clause, be subject to testing by habeas corpus because they are supported by no statutory authorization. There is no evidence that Congress meant to suspend the writ during the current hostilities, let alone the plain and unambiguous statement required by the Court.

These grave constitutional questions would confront the Court if the habeas statute were read as the Executive suggests—to close the courthouse doors to an entire class of habeas petitioners "without any clear indication that such was Congress' intent." It should not be read that way. . . .

[[2. International Law.]] . . . Over 190 countries, including the United States, are parties to the Geneva Conventions. Under the Conventions, the rights due to an individual vary with the person's legal status. The Official Commentary to the Fourth Geneva Convention makes clear that "every person in enemy hands must have some status under international law. . . . [N]obody in enemy hands can be outside the law." To implement this command, Article 5 of the Third Geneva Convention, governing prisoners of war, requires that any doubt regarding the status of a person captured by the detaining power must be resolved by a "competent tribunal," and that all detainees enjoy prisoner of war status unless and until an Article 5 tribunal determines otherwise. . . .

The Executive's proposed reading of the habeas statute would thus put the United States in flagrant disregard of globally recognized norms. Just as the Court should avoid an interpretation of the statute that runs afoul of the Constitution, it should avoid an interpretation in conflict with international law. . . .

[[3. *Johnson v. Eisentrager.*]] *Johnson* is best understood not as a limitation on the *power* of the federal judiciary, but as a restraint on the *exercise* of habeas based on the factors present in that case. The Court limited the exercise of habeas to a determination that the prisoners were enemy aliens imprisoned in occupied territory who had received a lawful trial before a properly constituted military commission. Because these threshold questions were not in dispute, the Court refused to countenance any further interference with the operation of a lawful and independent system of military justice.

The present case stands on entirely different footing. Congress has not authorized trials by military commission, and, even if it had, the prisoners here have been detained for two years with no legal process. They are not enemy aliens, but citizens of our closest allies who allege they have committed no wrong against the United States, and whose allegations at this stage must be accepted as true. Because there have been no proceedings, they do not seek post conviction relief from an overseas trial by a lawfully constituted tribunal. Instead, they challenge the fact that they have been cast into a legal limbo, held by the Executive without charges, without recourse to any legal process, and with no opportunity to establish their innocence. . . .

. . . [[T]]he Court in *Johnson* restrained the exercise of habeas to avoid interfering with the military commissions. Thus, the Court refused to provide the prisoners with the right to appear before the District Court, "[a] basic consideration in habeas corpus practice" as it existed at that time. The Court, however, did not consider itself powerless to inquire into the lawfulness of the prisoners' detention. On the contrary, the Court stated that "the doors of our courts have not been summarily closed upon these prisoners."

First, the Court reviewed at great length the legal disabilities imposed upon enemy aliens, and took pains to emphasize that these disabilities are "imposed temporarily as an incident of war and not as an incident of alienage." . . .

Second, the Court reviewed the prisoners' challenge to the "jurisdiction" of the military commissions, and ultimately concluded that it failed. . . .

And third, the Court in *Johnson* adjudicated the merits of the prisoners' claims under both the Constitution and the 1929 Geneva Convention. The Court rejected the prisoners' contention that the Fifth Amendment conferred "a right of personal security or an immunity from military trial and punishment upon an enemy alien engaged in the hostile service of a government at war with the United States," as well as their other arguments under the Constitution and the Convention.

This extensive and multifaceted review of the prisoners' claims cannot be squared with the Government's contention that the Court did not have jurisdiction. "Without jurisdiction the court cannot proceed at all in any cause. Jurisdiction is power to declare the law, and when it ceases to exist, the only function remaining to the court is that of announcing the fact and dismissing the cause." . . .

[[4. U.S. Sovereignty over the GBNB.]] Here, unlike in *Johnson*, the petitioners are held at Guantanamo. The Executive concedes that if the petitioners were being held in the United States, the federal courts would be open to them. It offers no persuasive reason why an area subject to the complete, exclusive, and indefinite jurisdiction and control of the United States, where this country alone has wielded power for more than a century, should be treated the same as occupied enemy territory, temporarily controlled as an incident of wartime operations. . . .

To suggest that . . . Guantanamo is no more amenable to federal habeas jurisdiction than occupied enemy territory defies reality. The Government has long considered Guantanamo to be "practically . . . a part of the Government of the United States." Solicitor General Olson once described the base as part of our "territorial jurisdiction" and "under exclusive United States jurisdiction." The same treaty article that reserves an undefined quantum of "ultimate sovereignty" for Cuba grants the United States "complete jurisdiction and control" over the base. . . .

Consistent with the Treaty language, the United States has long exercised prescriptive and adjudicative jurisdiction over Guantanamo. In *Vermilya-Brown v. Connell*, the Court made clear that Guantanamo is presumptively covered by federal statutes regulating conduct in "territories and possessions" and that the rule against "extraterritorial application" of federal law has no provenance in a case arising from Guantanamo. . . .

Equally important, Cuba's laws are wholly ineffectual in Guantanamo. United States governance, now entering its second century, is potentially permanent and in no way dependent on the wishes or consent of the Cuban Government. . . .

The extent of our jurisdiction and control in Guantanamo, and its amenability to judicial process, stands in stark contrast to the situation in *Johnson*. The

Executive could not convene a military commission to try the *Johnson* petitioners unless it first secured permission from the Chinese Government. The same is true of Landsberg prison, where the *Johnson* petitioners were detained. The United States shared jurisdiction and control over detentions in occupied Germany with the United Kingdom and France. . . .

> Respectfully submitted,
> JOSEPH MARGULIES,
> Counsel of Record

EXCERPTS FROM U.S. BRIEF

[[1. *Eisentrager*.]] . . . In an opinion written by Justice Jackson, the Court held that U.S. courts lacked jurisdiction to consider the habeas petition in *Eisentrager* because the prisoners were aliens who were seized abroad and detained outside the sovereign territory of the United States.

In the first sentence of the Court's decision, the Court framed the basic question before it as "one of jurisdiction of civil courts." In the following pages, the Court repeatedly underscored the fundamental jurisdictional nature of its ruling. The Court referred in broad terms to the Judiciary's "power to act" vis-à-vis military authorities with respect to aliens held abroad, the standing of such individuals "to maintain any action in the courts of the United States," the "standing [of such individuals] to demand access to our courts," and the "capacity and standing [of such individuals] to invoke the process of federal courts." Similarly, the Court discussed "the privilege of litigation" in U.S. courts and the use of "litigation [as a] weapon" by aliens held by military authorities. . . .

. . . The Court emphasized that aliens are accorded rights under the Constitution and federal law only as a consequence of their *presence* within the territory of the United States. Accordingly, the Court explained that the "privilege of litigation" was unavailable to the aliens in *Eisentrager* because they "at no relevant time were within any territory over which the United States is sovereign, and the scenes of their offense, their capture, their trial and their punishment were all beyond the territorial jurisdiction of any court of the United States." The Court also emphasized that, as aliens held abroad, the prisoners in *Eisentrager* had no Fifth Amendment rights to invoke.

At the same time, the Court stressed the separation-of-powers problems inherent in any exercise of jurisdiction in this uniquely military context. The Court explained that judicial review of claims filed on behalf of aliens captured by the U.S. military and detained in connection with an armed conflict would directly interfere with the President's authority as Commander in

Chief, which "has been deemed, throughout our history, as essential to wartime security." Likewise, the Court observed that "[i]t would be difficult to devise more effective fettering of a field commander than to allow the very enemies he is ordered to reduce to submission to call him to account in his own civil courts and divert his efforts and attention from the military offensive abroad to the legal defensive at home." . . .

In at least three key respects, the force of the Court's decision in *Eisentrager* has only grown with time.

1. As explained above, the Court in *Eisentrager* held that "nothing . . . in our statutes" conferred jurisdiction over the habeas petition at issue. Congress is presumed to be aware of this Court's decisions. It has legislated in the area of federal habeas jurisdiction on several occasions since 1950. Yet Congress has never amended the habeas statutes to provide the jurisdiction that this Court held was absent in *Eisentrager*. . . .

There was, however, one failed legislative attempt to create such jurisdiction in the immediate aftermath of *Eisentrager*. In February 1951, a bill was introduced in Congress "[p]roviding for the increased jurisdiction of Federal courts in regard to the power to issue writs of habeas corpus in cases where officers of the United States are detaining persons in foreign countries, regardless of their status as citizens." The bill provided "[t]hat the district court of the United States is given jurisdiction to issue writs of habeas corpus inquiring into the legality of any detention by any officer, agent, or employee of the United States, *irrespective of whether the detention is in the United States or in any other part of the world, and irrespective of whether the person seeking the writ is a citizen or an alien.*" (emphasis added). The bill was never voted out of committee, much less enacted into law.

Principles of separation of powers and stare decisis strongly counsel against revisiting *Eisentrager* and revising the habeas statutes in a manner that Congress itself considered and rejected. . . .

2. During the past fifty years, the Court also has repeatedly reaffirmed the principle that the Fifth Amendment does not apply to aliens abroad. Three terms ago in *Zadvydas* v. *Davis*, the Court stated that "it is well established that certain constitutional protections available to persons inside the United States are unavailable to aliens outside of our geographic borders." In support of that proposition, the Court cited *Eisentrager* and *United States* v. *Verdugo-Urquidez* (1990), with the parenthetical explanation that the "Fifth Amendment's protections do not extend to aliens outside the territorial boundaries" of the United States. . . .

3. The actions of the U.S. armed forces and courts since *Eisentrager* also have reinforced the basic principles reflected in that decision. In *Eisentrager*, the Court emphasized that there was no historical practice of U.S. courts

exercising jurisdiction over the claims of aliens held by the military outside the territory of the United States. Since *Eisentrager*, this Nation has engaged the armed forces in numerous armed conflicts, including in Korea, Vietnam, Iraq, and Bosnia. The military has captured and detained thousands of aliens abroad in connection with those conflicts. Yet, until the Ninth Circuit's divided panel decision in *Gherebi* v. *Bush* (2003), no court had ever recognized jurisdiction over a claim filed on behalf of such a detainee.

[[2. Sovereignty over GBNB.]] Both the court of appeals and the district court below carefully examined *Eisentrager* and correctly concluded that it applies with full force to the Guantanamo detainees. First, the Guantanamo detainees, like the detainees in *Eisentrager*, are aliens with no connection to the United States. . . .

Second, the Guantanamo detainees, like the detainees in *Eisentrager*, are being held by the U.S. military outside the sovereign territory of the United States. . . . That conclusion is compelled by the terms of the Lease Agreements pursuant to which the United States occupies Guantanamo, and the Executive Branch's definitive construction of those agreements. . . .

The 1903 Lease Agreement was executed in both English and Spanish, and both authoritative texts confirm Cuba's ongoing sovereignty over Guantanamo Bay. . . .

In *Gherebi* v. *Bush*, a divided panel of the Ninth Circuit held "that, *at least for habeas purposes*, Guantanamo is a part of the sovereign territory of the United States." This Court has never distinguished between sovereignty *for habeas purposes* and sovereignty *for all other purposes*. Moreover, the judicial recognition of even limited sovereignty in contravention of the Executive's position is problematic. As Judge Graber observed in [[his dissent in]] *Gherebi*, "[t]he majority today declares that the United States has sovereignty over territory of a foreign state, over the objections of the executive branch," and despite the fact that "both parties to the Guantanamo Lease and its associated treaties—Cuba and the United States (through the executive branch)—maintain that Guantanamo is part of *Cuba*." In light of those practical problems and the unambiguous terms of the Lease Agreements, there is no basis for adopting the Ninth Circuit's novel conception of sovereignty. . . .

Although they have conceded that Guantanamo is outside the sovereign territory of the United States, petitioners nonetheless argue that *Eisentrager* is inapplicable on the ground that Guantanamo is "under U.S. jurisdiction and control." . . .

To begin with, petitioners' argument cannot be squared with *Eisentrager*'s own terms. As discussed above, *Eisentrager* makes clear that its jurisdictional holding is based on sovereignty, and not on malleable concepts like de facto control. In particular, in explaining why "the privilege of litigation" did not extend to the aliens in *Eisentrager*, the Court stated that the "prisoners at no relevant time were within any *territory over which the United States is sovereign.*" . . .

[[If]] . . . U.S. jurisdiction or control over foreign territory, and not sovereignty, were the benchmark, then the prisoners in *Eisentrager* themselves would have been entitled to judicial review of their habeas claims. The Landsberg prison in Germany was unmistakably under the control of the United States when Eisentrager was held there. Indeed, it is hard to imagine that the United States would ever detain military prisoners in a facility over which it *lacked* control. The Court in *Eisentrager* noted that the prisoners at issue in *Eisentrager* were under the custody of the "American Army officer" who was the "Commandant of Landsberg Prison" and it referred to the hundreds of cases—like *Eisentrager*—involving "aliens confined by *American* military authorities abroad." . . . The United States controls Guantanamo subject to the terms and conditions of its Lease Agreements with Cuba, but—as this Court made clear in *Eisentrager*—in the absence of *sovereignty*, the exercise of such control does not entitle the aliens held at Guantanamo to the privilege of litigating in U.S. courts. . . .

[[3. Enemy Alien Status: A Political Question.]] The "enemy" status of aliens captured and detained during war is a quintessential political question on which the courts respect the actions of the political branches. The U.S. military has determined that the Guantanamo detainees are enemy combatants. The President, in his capacity as Commander in Chief, has conclusively determined that the Guantanamo detainees—both al Qaeda and Taliban—are not entitled to prisoner-of-war status under the Geneva Conventions. Any effort to look beyond such executive determinations concerning aliens held abroad would conflict with the rationale of *Eisentrager*.

Petitioners attempt to distinguish *Eisentrager* on the ground that the detainees in that case had been convicted by a military commission. As the district court observed, "[w]hile it is true that the petitioners in *Eisentrager* had already been convicted by a military commission, the *Eisentrager* Court did not base its decision on that distinction. Rather, *Eisentrager* broadly applies to prevent aliens detained outside the sovereign territory of the United States from invoking a petition for a writ of habeas corpus."

Moreover, petitioners cannot make a virtue of the relative prematurity of their claims. Under petitioners' reading of *Eisentrager*, aliens captured and held abroad would have access to U.S. courts in the earliest stages of their detention, but not after hostilities had ended and the detainees had been convicted of military charges years later. Nothing in *Eisentrager* supports, much less compels, that counterintuitive result. To the contrary, even the dissenters in *Eisentrager* recognized the profound separation of powers difficulties occasioned by an exercise of judicial jurisdiction "while hostilities are in progress." Thus, far from curing the jurisdictional defect that this Court recognized in *Eisentrager*, the fact that petitioners in this case are being held while active fighting is still ongoing in Afghanistan and elsewhere and before they have been tried or convicted by a military commission, only demonstrates that this litigation implicates political questions that the Constitution leaves to the President as Commander in Chief.

Petitioners' argument also creates a practical anomaly. The vast majority of aliens who are captured overseas by the military in connection with an armed conflict are detained during the course of hostilities without being charged with any war crime and without being tried or punished by a military commission. Such preventative detention is by definition not penal. The relatively small percentage of aliens who are actually tried and convicted for war crimes often receive severe punishments, including death. Yet, under petitioners' construction of *Eisentrager*, habeas jurisdiction would *not* be available for those aliens who face the most drastic punishments—including death—as a result of their capture, and such jurisdiction *would* be available for the vastly greater number of aliens who are simply detained during the conflict without charge in order to prevent them from returning to the battlefield to aid the enemy.

[[4. International Law.]] Petitioners argue that jurisdiction must be available because the Guantanamo detentions allegedly violate the United States's international obligations. That is incorrect. The Guantanamo detentions are fully consistent with applicable principles of international law. But more important for present purposes, the availability of habeas jurisdiction does not turn on a threshold inquiry into the merits of a detainee's claims under international or domestic law.

The federal habeas statute has allowed treaty-based international law claims since at least 1867, and the prisoners in *Eisentrager* themselves raised claims under the Geneva Convention. Nonetheless, *Eisentrager* held that the U.S. courts lacked jurisdiction over such claims and further emphasized that the Geneva Convention did not create any privately enforceable rights. Indeed, it would have made little sense for the *Eisentrager* Court to conclude that the same courts that are closed to constitutional claims nonetheless remain open to claims based on international law. . . .

. . . The Geneva Convention does not create privately enforceable rights, and Congress has never sought to create such rights through implementing legislation. Rather, as this Court recognized in *Eisentrager* with respect to the 1929 Geneva Convention, the "obvious scheme" of the Geneva Convention is that the "responsibility for observance and enforcement" of its provisions is "upon political and military authorities." . . .

[[5. Separation of Powers.]] Exercising jurisdiction over habeas actions filed on behalf of the Guantanamo detainees would directly interfere with the Executive's conduct of the military campaign against al Qaeda and its supporters. The detention of captured combatants in order to prevent them from rejoining the enemy during hostilities is a classic and time-honored military practice, and one that falls squarely within the President's authority as Commander in Chief. Moreover, collecting and evaluating intelligence from captured combatants about the enemy or its plans of attack is a common sense and critical element of virtually any successful military campaign.

The intelligence-gathering operations at Guantanamo are an integral component of the military's efforts to "repel and defeat the enemy" in the ongoing military campaign being waged not only in Afghanistan but around the globe. Any judicial review of the military's operations at Guantanamo would directly intrude on those important intelligence-gathering operations. Moreover, any judicial demand that the Guantanamo detainees be granted access to counsel to maintain a habeas action would in all likelihood put an end to those operations—a result that not only would be very damaging to the military's ability to win the war, but no doubt be "highly comforting to enemies of the United States."

More generally, exercising jurisdiction over actions filed on behalf of the Guantanamo detainees would thrust the federal courts into the extraordinary role of reviewing the military's conduct of hostilities overseas, second-guessing the military's determination as to which captured aliens pose a threat to the United States or have strategic intelligence value, and, in practical effect, superintending the Executive's conduct of an armed conflict—even while American troops are on the ground in Afghanistan and engaged in daily combat operations. . . .

. . . Petitioners seem to recognize that a ruling that the Constitution "follows the flag" for *all* aliens abroad would impermissibly hamper the Executive's conduct of foreign affairs. But there is no manageable and defensible basis, other than sovereignty (i.e., the line drawn by this Court in *Eisentrager* and subsequent cases), for limiting the reach of the arguments that petitioners advance. Certainly, a "de facto control and jurisdiction" test would serve no limiting function at all, because the U.S. military exercises control over the detainees at Bagram Air Force Base [[in Afghanistan]] as well—and would not detain prisoners in a facility that it did not control.

Moreover, drawing an arbitrary legal distinction between aliens held at a facility, such as the Bagram Air Force Base in Afghanistan, which is controlled by the U.S. military and located outside the sovereign territory of the United States, and aliens held at a facility, such as the Guantanamo Naval

Base in Cuba, which is controlled by the U.S. military and located outside the sovereign territory of the United States, would create a perverse incentive to detain large numbers of captured combatants in close proximity to the hostilities where both American soldiers *and* the detainees themselves are more likely to be in harm's way. Indeed, the Geneva Convention itself calls for the movement of prisoners of war "as soon as possible after their capture, to camps situated in an area far enough from the combat zone for them to be out of danger." . . .

The Executive's military operations at Guantanamo and, more generally, its efforts to eradicate the al Qaeda terrorist network and prevent additional terrorist attacks are the subject of intense public scrutiny as well. By constitutional design, the political branches are directly accountable to the people for foreign policy decisions made on their watch. In that regard, the political branches occupy an entirely different position in our constitutional system than this Court. As the number of amicus briefs filed in this case underscore, the Guantanamo detentions are subject of intense public interest in this country and, indeed, the international community. The political branches ultimately are accountable for the conduct of the ongoing military campaign against al Qaeda and protecting the Nation from additional attacks. The military operations at Guantanamo are a critical component of the Executive's efforts to accomplish those objectives. . . .

Respectfully submitted.
THEODORE B. OLSON,
Solicitor General

EXCERPTS FROM AL ODAH'S BRIEF

[[1. International Law.]] For almost 100 years, the United States has been the international leader in efforts to promote adoption of the rule of law around the world. It has championed the rule of law in fighting wars against totalitarian regimes and in seeking to contain and roll back the adoption of totalitarian ideologies. It has publicly rebuked and condemned regimes that fail to adhere to the rule of law. It has fought for the global recognition of the rule of law through advocacy of the adoption of the Geneva Conventions, the Universal Declaration of Human Rights, the International Covenant on Civil and Political Rights (ICCPR), and the American Declaration of the Rights and Duties of Man. These international agreements and covenants seek to make universal the principle, first adopted in the Magna Carta, that no person may be deprived of liberty without access to an impartial tribunal administered in accordance with law. As these authorities demonstrate, the proposition that a nation may round up aliens and imprison them outside the rule of law and without court review is anathema to the law of civilized nations and to the principles the United States has promoted around the world. . . .

. . . [[I]]t would place the United States outside the established norms of international law should this Court accede to the executive's contention that detaining petitioners outside the territorial sovereignty of the United States insulates the detention from judicial review and deprives the petitioners of all legal recourse. It would also send a dangerous signal to those around the world committed, as the United States has been, to upholding the rule of law, and an even more dangerous signal to those countries whose commitment to the rule of law has been tenuous at best. . . .

The experience of other nations facing ongoing threats of terrorism demonstrates that executive action aimed at protecting the nation's safety can be subject to judicial examination consistently with national security. Perhaps more than any other nation, the State of Israel has faced terrorism, both within and outside its territorial sovereignty, but it has never closed its courts to challenges to the legality of national security measures alleged to infringe fundamental rights. Although the Israel High Court of Justice has ruled that "the court will not take any stance on the manner of conducting the combat," the court has ruled on various petitions challenging administrative detention of suspected terrorists.

Last fall, the [[Israel High]] court struck down an order issued in the midst of a terrorist crisis that allowed suspected terrorists to be detained for up to thirty days without access to an impartial judicial official. . . . The court recognized that "there is room to postpone the beginning of the investigation, and naturally also the judicial intervention until after detainees are taken out of the battlefield to a place where the initial investigation and judicial intervention can be carried out properly." Once that happened, however, access to a judicial official cannot be delayed. The court held that allowing detention for thirty days without access to judicial authority "unlawfully infringes upon the judge's authority, thus infringing upon the detainee's liberty, which the international and Israeli legal frameworks are intended to protect."

The war on terrorism, like all other governmental actions, can be conducted only within the bounds of law. The President of the Israel high court emphasized that judges must not shrink from applying the law in the face of terrorism: "[T]he struggle against terrorism is not conducted outside the law, but within the law, using tools that the law makes available to a democratic state. Terrorism does not justify the neglect of accepted legal norms. This is how we distinguish ourselves from the terrorists themselves." Our country, no less than Israel, is committed to the rule of law. Terrorism must not be allowed to destroy that commitment.

[[2. Individualized Hearings.]] Petitioners ask only that the courts ensure that an adequate process be put in place so that their detentions are not arbitrary. They do not contend that an Article III court must itself conduct that process and review the basis for each individual detention. Rather, they contend that some legal process must apply and that the courts must have the authority to ensure that one does. Because petitioners seek a judicial forum to ensure that the government establishes a fair process, rather than to review the validity of particular detentions, acceptance of jurisdiction will not open the floodgates of litigation.

In fact, the government's existing regulations, incorporating the requirements of the Geneva Conventions, establish such a process; they require that an impartial panel review the claim of any detainee who asserts an entitlement to treatment as a prisoner of war or as to whom there is any doubt as to his or her status. That process has been applied in each of our recent conflicts, from Vietnam to the current conflict in Iraq. Indeed, in the prior Gulf War, the government held 1,196 individual hearings to assess the status of captured persons. In 886 of those hearings, the individuals detained were found not to be combatants at all, but displaced civilians or refugees. Only 310 were found to be enemy combatants, and all of those were determined to be "privileged" or legal combatants.

At Guantanamo, the government has conducted no individual hearings. It has simply disregarded its regulations. Yet, because the Guantanamo detainees were all taken into custody dressed as civilians, and because many were turned over by bounty hunters, the danger of mistake is at least as great as in the prior Gulf War—as is the need for a process to distinguish and prevent the prolonged and unjustified detention of the innocent. Detaining people without such a process can be justified only for so long as it takes to put a process in place. The executive may conduct that process, as its regulations require, but the judiciary must stand watch. Barring it from doing so authorizes the executive to engage in just the sort of unrestrained and arbitrary conduct that the framers of our Constitution were intent upon preventing. . . .

> Respectfully submitted,
> THOMAS B WILNER,
> Counsel of Record

EXCERPTS FROM THE LAW PROFESSORS' *AMICUS CURIAE* BRIEF SUPPORTING THE UNITED STATES

As Commander-in-Chief, President Bush has determined that the al Qaeda and Taliban fighters detained at Guantanamo Bay are "unprivileged" or "unlawful" combatants. Because of this determination, the detainees are not entitled to the full rights and privileges of prisoners of war (POWs) under the Geneva Conventions. The President properly based this conclusion on the traditional prerequisites of lawful belligerency, as recognized by the Geneva Conventions. Al Qaeda is "an international terrorist group and cannot be considered a state party to the Geneva Convention," and both al Qaeda and the Taliban have failed to satisfy the [[Geneva Convention's]] traditional four-part [[POW]] test of having a responsible commander, wearing a uniform or distinctive insignia, carrying arms openly, and conducting military operations "in accordance with the laws and customs of war." . . .

The President's conclusion that the members of al Qaeda, and the Taliban, are unlawful combatants is clearly correct. Neither group satisfied the four critical criteria. Indeed, al Qaeda is nothing but a private organization. The law of armed conflict does not authorize violence by private individuals, and private groups are not entitled to the privileges of belligerency—regardless of whether the motivation is ideological, religious, or political. The Taliban's status also presents anomalous facts. . . . As one widely respected military law expert has noted, the Taliban was at most "a faction engaged in a civil war in a failed state."

Moreover, even if the Taliban had been a legitimate government, it did not prosecute war in a legitimate way. Taliban combatants targeted civilians, killed journalists, and used civilians and mosques as shields. They acted with perfidy by pretending to surrender—for example, in the Taliban/al Qaeda rebellion at the Mazar-i-Sherif fortress. . . .

. . . Unlawful combatants are denied the full rights of lawful belligerents so as to create an incentive system for appropriate behavior in wartime. Unlawful combatants cannot exploit legal asymmetry, demanding the privileges that they fail to accord to their adversary. The matter was put plainly by Professor Richard Baxter of Harvard: "International law deliberately neglects to protect unprivileged belligerents because of the danger their acts present to their opponents." . . .

Further, alien enemy combatants have not been entitled to challenge their detention in court. During World War II, some 400,000 German and Italian prisoners of war were captured and transported to the continental United States for internment, and were repatriated only at the end of the war. Initially, their internment was "indefinite," since neither they nor their captors knew when the war would end. Nevertheless, so far as the case reports reveal, the federal courts did not entertain any habeas petitions challenging this civil internment, which is simply a normal prerogative of war. The only reported exception is *In re Territo*, which concerned an Italian-American enemy combatant who unsuccessfully asserted that his citizenship should prevent his detention. This dearth of litigation is consistent with the history of the common law. In English common law, alien enemy combatants and alien prisoners of war were plainly excluded from access to the writ of habeas corpus, no matter where they were detained. . . .

The American commitment to the decent treatment of all persons in its custody remains a centerpiece of our foreign policy, including in the war against terrorism. The struggle against terrorism will be won in large part by our devotion to the ideals of this country's founding. But we must also win on the battlefield. Even lawful foreign enemy combatants are not entitled to use the courts of their adversary in order to fight the war. It would be an extraordinary extension of the judicial role for the courts to create a roving supervisory jurisdiction over the conduct of American foreign policy and military operations around the globe. The President's determination to abide by the principles of Geneva gives no occasion for this Court to revolutionize the reach of statutory habeas corpus. . . .

Respectfully submitted,
DAVID B. RIVKIN,
Counsel of Record

EXCERPTS FROM THE RETIRED MILITARY OFFICERS' BRIEF SUPPORTING THE GBNB DETAINEES

. . . In past conflicts the United States has insisted that American soldiers held by the enemy be accorded the basic protections of the Geneva Conventions.

The United States has also demanded application of the principles codified in the Geneva Conventions to captured U.S. service personnel, even when they were taken prisoner under circumstances when the Conventions, technically, did not apply. For example, following the capture of U.S. Warrant Officer Michael Durant by forces under the control of Somali warlord Mohamed Farah Aideed in 1993, the United States demanded assurances that Durant's treatment would be consistent with the broad protections afforded under the Conventions, even though, "[u]nder a strict interpretation of the Third Geneva Convention's applicability, Durant's captors would not be bound to follow the convention because they were not a 'state.'"

Invoking international human rights standards, the United States also has condemned foreign governments that have held detainees incommunicado, depriving them of the ability to seek judicial review of their confinements. . . .

Yet even as American officials condemn other nations for detaining people indefinitely without access to a court or tribunal, authoritarian regimes elsewhere are pointing to U.S. treatment of the Guantanamo prisoners as justification for such actions. Eritrea's ambassador to the United States defended his own government's roundup of journalists by claiming that their detention without charge was consistent with the United States's detention of material witnesses and aliens suspected by the United States of terrorist activities.

If American detention of the Guantanamo prisoners—indefinite confinement without any type of review by a court or tribunal—is regarded as precedent for similar actions by countries with which we are at *peace*, it is obvious that it may be similarly regarded by *enemies* who capture American soldiers in an existing or future conflict. As a result, the lives of captured American military forces may well be endangered by the United States's failure to grant foreign prisoners in its custody the same rights that the United States insists be accorded to American prisoners held by foreigners. . . .

Respectfully submitted.
JAMES C. SCHROEDER,
Counsel of Record

EXCERPTS FROM THE *AMICUS CURIAE* BRIEF OF 175 MEMBERS OF PARLIAMENT

. . . Courts have a duty to vindicate the rule of law when it is circumvented or abused by legislative or executive fiat. History harshly judges attempts to detain individuals beyond the reach of the rule of law even in times of crisis. Japanese-American internment during the Second World War has become the paradigm for the pitfalls of judicial deference to arbitrary executive detention. The U.K. has its regrettable equivalent to the military order used to imprison Fred Korematsu. Under the auspices of Section 18B of the Wartime Defense Regulation, approximately 27,000 persons were detained between 1939 and 1945 in the U.K. without charge, trial, or set term. This abuse of executive power allowed arrest and detention on the Home Secretary's "reasonable belief" that an individual posed a threat to the nation—judicial deference was presumed. The most conspicuous case thereunder, *Liversidge v. Anderson*, also provides the most vigorous and insightful dissent. Expressing his deep concern to safeguard the role of the judiciary in the scheme of the government, Lord Atkin stated, "in this country, amid the clash of arms, the laws are not silent. They may be changed, but they speak the same language in war as in peace." Lord Atkin's comments, largely disfavored by his fellow Law Lords, are now universally viewed as an accurate reflection of the rule of law even in times of war.

The U.K.'s recent experience with terrorism is equally instructive. In answering charges that it violated the human rights of Irish citizens held in the U.K. because of suspected involvement in terrorism, the U.K. government claimed that it was compelled to take severe measures. However, the powers of detention exercised over suspected Irish terrorists were eventually criticized by the European Court of Human Rights as disproportionate violations of human rights.

Such examples stand out "as a caution that in times of distress the shield of military necessity and national security must not be used to protect government institutions from close scrutiny and accountability." Moreover, these examples from both the U.S. and U.K. are no more shocking than the situation in Guantanamo, where detainees have been precluded from even being informed of the grounds for their detention or having their rights brought before any court of law. . . .

> Respectfully submitted,
> EDWIN S. MATTHEWS JR.,
> Counsel of Record

AMICUS BRIEF OF FATIMA EL-SAMNAH

Between the United States and Canada lies the longest undefended border in the world. Each nation shares an interest in ensuring the fair treatment of its citizens by its neighbor's government, and each has a proud constitutional tradition of recognizing basic human rights. In assessing the issues in this case, this Court ought to consider and adopt the jurisprudence recently developed by the Supreme Court of Canada in relation to the treatment of U.S. citizens by Canadian government officials outside Canada's sovereign territory. . . .

Having declined to follow [[*R. v.*]] T*erry*, the Court in [[*R. v.*]] *Cook* enunciated a new approach to the extraterritorial application of the Canadian *Charter*. The domestic courts of Canada may now apply the *Charter* beyond Canada's sovereign territory where a two part test is satisfied: (1) the conduct in question was that of Canadian government officials, and (2) the application of the *Charter* will not interfere with the sovereign authority of the foreign state and thereby generate an objectionable extraterritorial effect. . . .

The *amicus curiae* respectfully submits that this Court ought to adopt an approach to the extraterritorial application of the Constitution similar to that established by the Supreme Court of Canada in *R. v. Cook*. This approach has been developed in the context of today's global economy where people and goods travel across borders at rates previously unimagined. It is carefully crafted to strike an appropriate balance between the basic human rights of the individual and the need to avoid interference with the sovereign legal authority of foreign governments.

. . . [[In]] the present case, there can be no serious suggestion that the application of the law of the United States to the government officials who are currently detaining the Petitioners and *amicus curiae* would generate an objectional extraterritorial effect. The government of Cuba, while technically retaining "ultimate sovereignty" under the terms of the lease of Guantanamo Bay, does not purport to exercise legal authority over the persons detained therein. In the absence of such an objectionable extraterritorial effect, it is appropriate for this Court . . . [[to apply the Constitution extraterritorially.]]

. . . Other constitutional democracies, sharing traditional common law notions of sovereignty, have so held. . . .

Respectfully submitted
JOHN A. E. POTTOW,
Counsel of Record

AMICUS BRIEF OF ABDULLA AL-JOAID

. . . The Saudi families' specific objectives have included, first and foremost, the release of any innocent persons detained in Guantanamo. With regard to those who might have committed offenses, the families have requested, to the extent possible, their repatriation for interrogation, trial, and punishment by Saudi authorities and courts. The Saudi families have not suggested that any of the detainees who have committed punishable offenses escape justice. The legal systems in Saudi Arabia and the United States share a common view of such acts, and punishment could be even more severe in Saudi Arabia under Islamic law than in the United States. . . .

One reason that the families of the Saudi detainees have advocated that the detainees be repatriated for interrogation, criminal proceedings, and punishment in accordance with Islamic law is because a judgment by a Saudi court would be more readily accepted by the Saudi people, including the families of the detainees. A verdict by a Shari'a court would prevent concerns or misunderstanding by the families and citizens of the Kingdom that justice is not being fairly administered, perceptions which can often occur between cultures even if such is not the case. However, it is very difficult to expect any country to accept a legal judgment of another if the government of the other country is free to do with foreign nationals "as it will, when it pleases, without any compliance with any rule of law of any kind, without permitting him to consult counsel, and without acknowledging any judicial forum in which its actions may be challenged." . . .

> Respectfully submitted,
> MARY PATRICIA MICHEL,
> Counsel of Record

III. ORAL ARGUMENT

Oral argument in *Rasul* took place on April 20, 2004, approximately six weeks after the al Qaeda–inspired bombing attacks on commuter trains in Madrid, Spain. John J. Gibbons, a former federal judge who was representing the GBNB detainees, began by addressing the argument that the Geneva Convention did not grant a private cause of action because the treaty was not self-executing. In his response, Gibbons claimed that it was the habeas statute, not the Geneva Convention, that granted Rasul a cause of action, though it was the Convention that provided courts with a "rule of decision." In other words, the Bush administration's policy of detention at the GBNB was illegal because it violated the Geneva Convention, but Rasul could sue as a detainee because of the jurisdiction provisions of the habeas statute. Some of the justices suggested that Gibbons was confusing jurisdiction (a court's right to hear a case) with the merits (a particular detainee's right to the writ). Justice Souter wondered why, if jurisdiction rested on the habeas statute, Gibbons emphasized that the GBNB detainees were not "admitted enemy aliens" and were not given any kind of hearing before a military tribunal. If Gibbons argument was correct, the federal courts would have jurisdiction even if Rasul was an enemy alien who had been tried by a military court.

Justice Kennedy focused on what he saw as a troublesome implication of Gibbon's argument: if the habeas statute was read the way that Gibbons was urging, then a lawful combatant detained in a declared war would have a right to petition a federal court for a writ of habeas corpus a few weeks after he was captured. Gibbons replied that the writ had never been granted to battlefield detainees, but he never really explained why courts would not nonetheless have jurisdiction in such cases. His position appeared to be that federal courts had jurisdiction to receive petitions from all persons detained abroad by the United States, but that some of these petitions could be summarily dismissed on the merits, especially those coming from battlefield detainees. Justice Scalia highlighted the fact that the treaty with Cuba, which (like the Geneva Convention) was the "supreme law of the land," recognized the continuance of the "ultimate sovereignty" of Cuba.

In comparison to Gibbons, Solicitor General Theodore B. Olson's argument relied heavily on *Johnson v. Eisentrager*. He claimed this case drew a sharp distinction between the rights of citizens under the habeas statute and the rights of aliens who had no contact with the United States. Justice Souter probed how Olson could rely on the statements in *Johnson* regarding the rights of citizens, since such statements implied that the Court had jurisdiction in the case, which is just what Olson was denying in *Rasul*. Olson countered by resting jurisdiction in the case of a detained citizen on the Constitution, rather than the habeas statute. Justice Breyer conceded that Olson's position had the "virtue of clarity," but that it also left the executive branch "unchecked." Olson replied that Congress could check the executive branch through legislation, oversight, and appropriations. Justice Souter demanded to know why legal sovereignty, rather than actual control, was the key to determining the reach of the habeas statute. Olson responded that the line of legal sovereignty, like the line of citizenship, had the virtue of "relative certainty." It would be improper, he implied, for courts to draw a jurisdictional line based on whether the United States was in control of the area of detention. Such a line was a matter of degree and would grant courts jurisdiction over all military detainees, including the two million who were in custody at the end of World War II and the thousands currently detained in Afghanistan and Iraq.

Justice Stevens injected an issue into the oral argument that had not been debated in the written briefs.[22] Through his questions and comments, Stevens implied that the Court denied jurisdiction in *Eisentrager* only because *Ahrens v. Clark* (1948) was at that time the controlling precedent. *Ahrens*, a 6–3 decision, dealt with the case of 120 German detainees held on Ellis Island, who had petitioned the D.C. District Court for a writ of habeas corpus. In a majority opinion written by Justice William O. Douglas, the Court held that the habeas statute allowed federal judges to issue writs of habeas corpus only "within their respective jurisdictions" (see the language of the habeas statute in box 3.1 above). Accordingly, Douglas concluded, the D.C. District Court lacked statutory jurisdiction to issue the writ because the detainees were held in New York. Justice Wiley B. Rutledge issued a strong dissent in *Ahrens*, arguing that "a great contraction of the writ's classic scope and exposition has taken place, and much of its historic efficacy may have been destroyed."[23]

Since *Ahrens* was the controlling precedent governing the scope of the federal judiciary's jurisdiction under the habeas statute, the petitioners in *Eisentrager* could only claim that federal courts had jurisdiction over their petitions if that jurisdiction was rooted in the Constitution, not the habeas statute. The Court then arguably held that there was no constitutional basis for jurisdiction in *Eisentrager* and therefore refused to issue the writ. However, twenty-three years after *Eisentrager*, the Supreme Court in *Braden v. 30th Judicial Circuit*

Court of Kentucky (1973) considered the case of a prisoner held in Alabama at the request of Kentucky. The prisoner filed a petition for the writ in Kentucky, challenging a criminal indictment. The Court held that the federal court in Kentucky had statutory jurisdiction to entertain the petition because the persons who were ultimately responsible for the indictment were "within the respective jurisdictions" of federal judges in Kentucky, not in Alabama.[24] At the oral argument in *Rasul*, Stevens was suggesting that *Braden* overturned *Ahrens*, which meant that *Eisentrager* was not a valid precedent for denying statutory jurisdiction in *Rasul*, so long as the persons responsible for the GBNB detainees were within the territorial jurisdiction of the D.C. District Court, the court in which Rasul and the other detainees had filed their petitions. Of course, President Bush resided at the White House, squarely within the territorial jurisdiction of the D.C. District Court.

As the transcript below makes clear, Gibbons did not know what to do with Steven's suggestion that *Braden* overturned *Ahrens*. He hesitated, stammering "Well—in any event" before Stevens interrupted him by saying, "Let me help you." Very few people in the courtroom that day, if any, knew what Stevens was doing with his offer to help Gibbons or why he was doing it, but within a few days the *Washington Post* published an article revealing that Stevens had been Rutledge's law clerk at the time *Ahrens* was decided and that Rutledge's papers at the Library of Congress contained a memo from Stevens urging Rutledge to support a "fair hearing" for the Germans detained on Ellis Island. The *Post* article claimed that the following language inside quotation marks came directly from a draft of Rutledge's dissent written by Stevens.

> There "may be instances arising in the future where persons are wrongfully detained in places unknown to those who would apply for habeas corpus in their behalf. . . ." "Without knowing the district of confinement, a petitioner would be unable to sustain the burden of establishing jurisdiction in any court in the land. Such a situation might arise from military detention . . . as a result of mass evacuation of groups from a given area in time of emergency . . . or possibly, though it is to be hoped not often, even from willful misconduct by arbitrary executive officials overreaching their constitutional or statutory authority. These dangers may seem unreal in the United States," the Rutledge-Stevens opinion continued. But the experience of less fortunate countries should serve as a warning against the unwarranted curtailment of the jurisdiction of our courts to protect the liberty of the individual by means of the writ of habeas corpus.[25]

The twenty-seven-year-old law clerk who had helped write Rutledge's dissent in *Ahrens* was now an eighty-four-year-old Supreme Court justice deciding whether federal courts had jurisdiction to review whether arbitrary executive officials in the Bush administration were overreaching their constitutional or statutory authority. By injecting the *Ahrens/Braden* issue into the question of whether the federal judiciary had jurisdiction to entertain petitions for writs of habeas corpus from the GBNB detainees, Stevens fundamentally reoriented the litigation, making it possible for the Court to resolve the case in favor of the GBNB detainees without explicitly overturning *Eisentrager*.

EXCERPTS FROM THE ORAL ARGUMENT

CHIEF JUSTICE REHNQUIST: But now in *Johnson v. Eisentrager*, we said that the Geneva Convention did not confer a private right of action.

JOHN GIBBONS [[counsel for Rasul]]: Your Honor, the question of the private right of action really is not presented in this case. We are not asking to imply a private right of action from the Geneva Convention or any other treaty. What we are saying is that the cause of action is created by the Habeas Corpus Statute. . . . The treaty provides a rule of decision, not a cause of action.

JUSTICE O'CONNOR: Well, I guess, at least the question presented is just whether the Federal court has jurisdiction under the Habeas Statute, Section 2241, is that right?

GIBBONS: That's correct.

O'CONNOR: And you don't raise the issue of any potential jurisdiction on the basis of the Constitution alone. We are here debating the jurisdiction under the Habeas Statute, is that right?

GIBBONS: That's correct, Justice O'Connor. . . .

KENNEDY: Well, but other than producing the person before the court so that the system is satisfied that we know where the person is, surely you have to go beyond that and assert some sort of right. And you—you say that—

GIBBONS: Of course.

KENNEDY:—the Geneva Convention is really not the basis for the cause of action, which I agree, so where do we go after that? So he is here in front of the court. Now what?

GIBBONS: Your Honor, the Geneva Convention is the supreme law of the land. That's what the Constitution says about habeas.

O'CONNOR: But it may not be self-executing. That's the problem, I guess. The indications are it's not.

GIBBONS: Your Honor, Your Honor—

KENNEDY: Forgetting the Geneva Convention, what happens when the person comes before the court? You prevail and there is a writ of habeas corpus, it comes here, and the judge says, now what am I supposed to do.

GIBBONS: What the judge is supposed to do is determine first whether or not the government's response that the detention is legal is in fact an adequate response. Now, the government in this case probably will respond, we don't have to give the hearings required by the Geneva Convention. But if you're going to treat a binding United States treaty as the supreme law of the land, that is not an adequate answer.

Now, this question of, is the treaty self-executing or not self-executing, I suggest is a straw man. Since 1813, if a treaty provides a rule of decision and something else provides a cause of action, the treaty nevertheless provides the rule of decision. . . .

GIBBONS: It's our position that *Eisentrager* was a decision on the merits as a matter of fact. The Court says that they—Petitioners were extended the same preliminary hearing as the sufficiency application that was extended in *Quirin, Yamashita and Hirota versus McArthur*, all of which were decisions on the merits.

REHNQUIST: But in several different places, Mr. Gibbons, in *Eisentrager*, the Court says that we are talking about the Habeas Statute, and we are saying these Petitioners are not entitled to habeas.

GIBBONS: Well, they are not as a matter—let me be clear about that. The result on the merits in *Eisentrager* is perfectly correct. What the Court did in *Eisentrager* was apply the scope of review on habeas corpus, which was standard at that time. If the military tribunal had lawful jurisdiction, that ended the habeas inquiry.

JUSTICE STEVENS: Well, there is another problem. At that time, that case was decided when *Ahrens against Clark* was the statement of the law, so there is no statutory basis for jurisdiction there, and the issue is whether the Constitution by itself provided jurisdiction. And of course, all that's changed now.

GIBBONS: Well, Your Honor, in *Eisentrager*, both the Court of Appeals and the Supreme Court made it clear that they disapproved, they were not adopting the ruling of the District Court based on *Ahrens v. Clark*. . . .

STEVENS: Well, you raised the question of whether the territorial jurisdiction provision covered it. There was no territorial jurisdiction if they were outside the district under the ruling in *Ahrens against Clark*, which means they had to rely on the Constitution to support jurisdiction, which in turn means that once they have overruled *Ahrens against Clark*, which they did, there is now a statutory basis for jurisdiction that did not then exist.

GIBBONS: Your Honor, respectfully, I don't think you can fairly read Justice Jackson's opinion as adopting the *Ahrens v. Clark* position.

STEVENS: No. But *Ahrens v. Clark* was the law at the time of that decision, and it was subsequently overruled. So that—that case was decided when the legal climate was different than it has been since *Ahrens against Clark* was overruled.

GIBBONS: Well—in any event—

STEVENS: Let me help you. . . .

KENNEDY: What do you do if you have a lawful combatant in a declared war, and the combatant, an enemy of the United States is captured and detained, habeas?

GIBBONS: Habeas, you mean on the battlefield? Absolutely not.

KENNEDY: We'll take it from the battlefield, and a week later, ten miles away, then six months later, a thousand miles away.

GIBBONS: In the zone of active military operations or in an occupied area under martial law, habeas corpus jurisdiction has never extended.

KENNEDY: Suppose it's Guantanamo.

GIBBONS: Well, the—

KENNEDY: A declared war and a lawful combatant. . . .

GIBBONS: Your Honor, what I'm suggesting is that whether you call it jurisdiction or whether you call it the merits, in the battlefield situation, it's going to go out under Rule 12, in any event.

REHNQUIST: But that's, that's quite different. I mean, all we are theoretically talking about here is jurisdiction. And the idea that, you know, you have Justice Kennedy's example, a lawful combatant, a declared war, detained at Guantanamo maybe two months after he is captured, and an action's brought here in the District of Columbia for habeas corpus and what does a—what does a judge say when he considers that sort of petition?

GIBBONS: When he sees that petition, he should dismiss it summarily, whether he dismisses it under 12(b)(1) or 12(b)(6), it won't take him any more time. Habeas corpus, as the historians' brief, and others among the *amici* point out, has never run to the battlefield, as a matter of habeas corpus common law. And it is, after all, a common law writ. It has never run to any place except where the sovereign issuing the writ has some undisputed control. . . .

STEVENS: Mr. Olson, supposing the war had ended, could you continue to detain these people on Guantanamo? Would there then be jurisdiction?

SOLICITOR GENERAL THEODORE B. OLSON [[On behalf of the Bush administration]]: We believe that there would not be jurisdiction, just—

STEVENS: So the existence of the war is really irrelevant to the legal issue?

OLSON: It is not irrelevant, because it is in this context that that question is raised. . . . [[In]] the case of *Johnson v. Eisentrager*, which we have discussed here, even the dissent in that case said that it would be fantastic to assume that habeas corpus jurisdiction would exist in the time of war. So that that case is not—

STEVENS: No, but your position does not depend on the existence of a war?

OLSON: It doesn't depend upon that, Justice Stevens, but it's even more forceful. And more compelling. Because all of the Justices in the *Eisentrager* case would have held that there was no jurisdiction under these circumstances.

O'CONNOR: What if one of the Plaintiffs were an American citizen here, being held in Guantanamo. . . .

OLSON: We would acknowledge that there would be jurisdiction—

BREYER: Why?

OLSON:—under the Habeas Corpus Statute for the reasons that are explained in *Eisentrager* itself, that citizenship is a foundation for a relationship between the nation and the individual and a foundation for—

STEVENS: Is that sufficient to give us jurisdiction over Guantanamo, which is another sovereign?

OLSON: With respect to the individual. We would, we would still argue—

STEVENS: What if the American citizen was in the middle of the battlefield in Iraq?

OLSON: We would still argue that the jurisdiction under the Habeas Statute would not extend under these circumstances to a wartime situation, Justice Stevens, but that the—what the *Eisentrager* Court said, that there is enhanced power of the Court under the habeas corpus jurisdiction with respect to questions involving citizenship.

But what was unquestionable with respect to that case is that an alien who had never had any relationship to the United States and who was being held as a result of a combat situation or a war situation in a foreign jurisdiction, there was no jurisdiction under the Habeas Statute. . . .

O'CONNOR: But the *Eisentrager* Court never once mentioned the statute, the Habeas Statute in its opinion. What it seemed to do was to reach the merits and say at the end of the day, these people have no rights. They have had a trial under the military tribunal and they have no rights that could be granted at the end of the day, and no mention of the Habeas Statute.

OLSON: The Court specifically . . . did not mention the statute, Justice O'Connor, but the statute is mentioned throughout the briefs. . . . The statute that exists today is the same statute that the *Eisentrager* Court was considering. . . .

KENNEDY: That gets me back to your statement that if this had been a citizen held in Guantanamo, that habeas would be available. But the statute doesn't talk about citizens. It says prisoners held under the authority of the United States. Now, if the citizen can say that he is a prisoner held under the authority of the United States in Guantanamo, why couldn't a noncitizen under the statute say the same thing?

OLSON: I think, Justice Kennedy, . . . we are not . . . we are not saying that there necessarily would be jurisdiction there, but we are saying that the Court . . . will find more protection for citizens as a result of the relationship going back . . .

KENNEDY: . . . I had thought you said at the outset that if this had been a citizen of the United States held in Guantanamo, there would be habeas corpus.

OLSON: We are not—we are saying that we would not be contesting it, Justice Kennedy, and the Court will be dealing with other issues involving citizens.

STEVENS: You don't have to contest the jurisdictional objection. If there is no jurisdiction, there is no jurisdiction, whether you contest it or not. . . .

SCALIA: Certainly the argument is available that in that situation, the Constitution requires jurisdiction. The Constitution requires that an American citizen who has the protection of the Constitution have some manner of vindicating his rights under the Constitution. That would be the argument. . . .

OLSON: I agree with that, Justice Scalia, and this Court has said again and again that . . .

SOUTER: Is that your answer to Justice Kennedy, that there would be jurisdiction because due process would require it for citizens, but there would not be statutory jurisdiction in the case of the citizen at Guantanamo?

OLSON: I think it would be an interpretation. . . .

BREYER: . . . So what I'm thinking now, assuming that it's very hard to interpret *Eisentrager*, is that if we go with you, it has a virtue of clarity. There is a clear rule. Not a citizen, outside the United States, you don't get your foot in the door. But against you is that same fact. It seems rather contrary to an idea of a Constitution with three branches that the executive would be free to do whatever they want, whatever they want without a check. That's problem one. Problem two is that we have several hundred years of British history where the cases interpreting habeas corpus said to the contrary anyway. And then we have the possibility of really helping you with what you're really worried about, which is undue court interference by shaping the substantive right to deal with all those problems of the military that led you to begin your talk by reminding us of those problems.

So if it's that choice, why not say, sure, you get your foot in the door, prisoners in Guantanamo, and we'll use the substantive rights to work out something that's protective but practical.

OLSON: Well, Justice Breyer, there are several answers to that. You started with the proposition that there was no check and that the executive is asserting no check. This is the interpretation of the scope of a Habeas Statute. Congress had—has had fifty-four years with full awareness of the decision to change it.

Indeed, as we point out in our brief, eight months after the *Eisentrager* decision, a bill was introduced that would have changed that statute, H.R. 2812, which would specifically have changed the statute to deal with the *Eisentrager* situation, so there is a check.

GINSBURG: . . . As you well know, the fact that a bill was introduced and not passed carries very little weight on what law that exists means.

OLSON: Well, I understand that, but the bill was—came eight months after *Eisentrager*.

SCALIA: You're not using it to say what the law was. You're using it to show that there was available, and is available, a perfectly good check upon the executive branch. If the people think that this is unfair, if Congress thinks it's unfair, with a stroke of the pen, they can change the Habeas Statute.

OLSON: That's precisely correct. . . .

GINSBURG: Why doesn't complete jurisdiction [[work]]? No one else has jurisdiction. [[Why isn't]] complete jurisdiction a satisfactory line. . . .

OLSON: Because . . . the question of sovereignty is a political decision. It would be remarkable for the judiciary to start deciding where the United States is sovereign and where the United States has control—

GINSBURG: The word is physical control, power.

OLSON: We have that, Justice Ginsburg, in every place where we would put military detainees, in a field of combat where there are prisons in Afghanistan where we have complete control with respect to the circumstances.

SOUTER: But those—Afghanistan is not a place where American law is, and for a century, has customarily been applied to all aspects of life. We even protect the Cuban iguana. We bring—in bringing people from Afghanistan or wherever they were brought to Guantanamo, we are doing in functional terms exactly what we would do if we brought them to the District of Columbia, in a functional sense, leaving aside the metaphysics of ultimate sovereignty. If the metaphysics of ultimate sovereignty do not preclude us from doing what we have been doing for the last 100 years, why is it a bar to the exercise of judicial jurisdiction under the Habeas Statute? . . .

OLSON: With respect to a certain area, a military base in Germany, a military base in Afghanistan, the United States must have and does exercise relatively complete control. Every argument that's being made here today could be made by the two million persons that were in custody at the end of World War II, and judges would have to decide the circumstances of their detention, whether there had been adequate military process, what control existed over the territory in which they were being kept. What this is—

SOUTER: Are you saying that there is no statutory regime that applies to Guantanamo which is different from the statutory or legal regime that applied to occupied territories after World War II or indeed that applies to territory under the control of the American military in Afghanistan or Iraq?

OLSON: There is a great deal of difference in connection with every area over which the United States has some degree of control. . . .

IV. THE DECISION

As discussed in the preceding chapter, events during April, May, and June of 2004 transformed the political background of the Supreme Court's deliberations in *Hamdi v. Rumsfeld*, *Padilla v. Bush*, and *Rasul v. Bush*. On April 28, only eight days after the oral argument in *Rasul* and on the same day the Court heard argument in *Hamdi* and *Padilla*, the graphic photos depicting American soldiers abusing Iraqi prisoners at Abu Ghraib Prison appeared on television and the Internet. By mid-June, a number of classified government memos that had been leaked to the press left an impression that the Bush administration had perhaps ruled that the Geneva Convention was inapplicable to al Qaeda and that the Taliban detainees were not entitled to prisoner-of-war status in part to reduce or eliminate the possibility that anyone from the administration could later be prosecuted for war crimes. This impression in turn raised the possibility that the administration's rulings on the applicability of the Geneva Convention might have indirectly encouraged harsh interrogation tactics in Afghanistan, which might have migrated to the Abu Ghraib prison despite the fact that the Geneva Conventions were fully applicable to the Iraq War.

One of the classified documents leaked to the press—a March 6, 2003 report authored by a working group of Bush administration lawyers—had an indirect bearing on the question of jurisdiction presented in *Rasul*. The report claimed that the U.S. Torture Statute (18 U.S.C. 2340 and 2340A) that Congress had enacted to implement the 1994 Convention Against Torture was only applicable to torture that occurred "outside the United States." The report then went on to conclude that any torture that occurred at the GBNB would not be covered by the Torture statute since the military base was within the "special maritime and territorial jurisdiction" of the United States. Accordingly, in early 2003 government lawyers were arguing that federal courts would have no jurisdiction under the Torture statute over U.S. officials or military personnel who allegedly mistreated GBNB detainees. Since the mistreatment occurred inside the United States, federal courts had no jurisdiction. A year later in *Rasul* other government lawyers argued that federal courts would have no jurisdiction to hear petitions from GBNB detainees, even if they were allegedly being tortured by U.S. officials, because the base was outside the sovereignty of the United States.[26] It seemed that the GBNB was inside or outside the United States, depending upon what outcome served the interests of the administration.

Whether any justice read the March 6, 2003 report is unknown, but it, along with the other leaked classified memos, received a great deal of attention in the public media and in more specialized legal circles, whether in print or on the Internet. At a minimum, the justices had to have been aware of the Abu Ghraib photos that established beyond doubt that American soldiers had abused Iraqi prisoners, which of course underscored the danger of turning the GBNB into what Rasul's lawyers called a legal "black hole"—a prison from which there was no appeal to any court.

On June 28, 2004, the Supreme Court handed down its decision in *Rasul v. Bush*. Six of the nine justices ruled in favor of the petitioners, holding that federal courts did have jurisdiction to hear petitions for writs of habeas corpus from the GBNB detainees. In his majority opinion, Justice Stevens, joined by Justices Souter, Breyer, Ginsburg, and O'Connor, discussed whether federal courts had a constitutional or statutory foundation for jurisdiction, or both. In regard to the former alternative, Stevens pointed out that the *Rasul* detainees were very different from the petitioners in *Eisentrager*: they were not nationals of countries at war with the United States; they denied that they had engaged in any aggression against the United States; they had had no access to any sort of tribunal; and they were imprisoned in territory over which the United States exercised exclusive jurisdiction and control. Because of these differences, Stevens hinted that federal courts might have a constitutionally rooted form of jurisdiction over the GBNB detainees. However, despite this hint, in the end he rested jurisdiction in *Rasul* squarely on a statutory foundation. In his view, consistent with what he had suggested at oral argument, Section 2241 granted the federal courts jurisdiction because *Braden v. 30th Judicial Circuit Court of Kentucky* had overturned *Ahrens v. Clark*. His basic conclusion was that Section 2241 required "nothing more" than that the district court have jurisdiction over the custodian of the petitioner. Accordingly, without specifying in any way what kind of proceedings were appropriate at the district court level to determine the lawfulness of detaining suspected enemy combatants in the war on terrorism, Stevens concluded that the district court had jurisdiction to hear petitions for writs of habeas corpus from GBNB detainees.

Justice Kennedy concurred in the result, but not in Justice Stevens's reasoning. In contrast to the emphasis that Stevens placed on the habeas statute, Kennedy stressed the validity and meaning of *Eisentrager*. In his view, this key precedent recognized two spheres of political authority over military affairs: one in which the judiciary could not interfere and one in which it could. The facts of *Eisentrager* were within the former sphere; the facts of *Rasul*, the latter. The key differences between the two cases that justified this conclusion, according to Kennedy, were, first, the GBNB was "in every practical respect a United States territory" that was "far removed from any hostilities," and, second, the GBNB detainees were subject to indefinite detention without the benefit of any sort of legal proceeding. Federal courts had jurisdiction over the GBNB detainees because of these special circumstances, not because the ultimate custodian of the detainees, President Bush, was within the territorial jurisdiction of a federal court. The problem with the majority's reasoning, according to Kennedy, was that it gave every detainee held abroad by the American military a statutory right to petition a federal judge for a writ of habeas corpus. Such a result violated *Eisentrager*'s framework by allowing judges to interfere with military matters over which the political authorities should have exclusive control.

Joined by Chief Justice Rehnquist and Justice Thomas, Justice Scalia wrote a bitter dissent that called the majority's opinion "an irresponsible overturning of settled law in a matter of extreme importance to our forces currently in the field." According to Scalia, the statutory language of Section 2241 clearly required that a detainee must be within the jurisdiction of a federal district court before a different district court could assert jurisdiction over the detainee's custodian. The only Supreme Court case that considered whether a federal court could have jurisdiction over a detainee held outside the territorial jurisdiction of all federal courts was *Eisentrager*, which denied jurisdiction if the detainee was a noncitizen. *Braden* did not overrule either *Eisentrager* or *Ahrens*; rather it made an exception to the *Ahrens* rule in cases in which a prisoner was indicted in one federal court's jurisdiction but held within the jurisdiction of another. By abandoning *Eisentrager*, the majority, according to Scalia, had "boldly" extended the scope of the habeas statute "to the four corners of the earth," thereby permitting any alien "captured in a foreign theater of active combat" to petition a federal court for his or her release.

Congress had the power to change the law in this fashion, but Scalia thought it was "unthinkable" that the Court would depart from the rule of *stare decisis* during a time of war.

One of the most important aspects of the Supreme Court's decision in *Rasul* was that five justices signed an opinion that granted federal courts jurisdiction to hear petitions for writs of habeas corpus from anyone detained by American armed forces, no matter where that person was detained around the world. The majority could have, as Justice Kennedy had urged, limited its ruling to situations comparable to the one at GBNB, where the United States, though not legally sovereign, had exercised exclusive territorial jurisdiction for many years. It chose instead to take a more radical course by concluding that jurisdiction under the habeas corpus statute only required that the custodian of the detainee be within the jurisdiction of a federal district court. What consequences this ruling will have for the war on terrorism is impossible to say at this time, if only because the Court said nothing whatsoever concerning the standards of measuring the lawfulness of detentions of this type. However, the Court's decision in *Rasul*, unless Congress revises the habeas statute, more or less insures that it will eventually issue substantive rulings establishing what constitutes lawful detention of aliens in the war on terrorism. Whether or not the Court's future rulings will make it easy or difficult for the executive branch to justify the detention of suspected alien terrorists abroad, the Court in *Rasul* substantially increased the likelihood that it would have an impact on the resolution of this question. And, it made this ruling, not after the war was over, as it did in *Ex parte Milligan*, but during the war itself. For this reason alone, *Rasul* is a landmark case regarding the Court's role during times of war.

EXCERPTS FROM THE OPINIONS

Justice Stevens delivered the opinion of the Court. . . .

Respondents' primary submission is that the answer to the jurisdictional question is controlled by our decision in *Eisentrager*. In that case, we held that a Federal District Court lacked authority to issue a writ of habeas corpus to twenty-one German citizens who had been captured by U.S. forces in China, tried, and convicted of war crimes by an American military commission headquartered in Nanking, and incarcerated in the Landsberg Prison in occupied Germany. The Court of Appeals in *Eisentrager* had found jurisdiction, reasoning that "any person who is deprived of his liberty by officials of the United States, acting under purported authority of that Government, and who can show that his confinement is in violation of a prohibition of the Constitution, has a right to the writ." In reversing that determination, this Court summarized the six critical facts in the case:

> We are here confronted with a decision whose basic premise is that these prisoners are entitled, as a constitutional right, to sue in some court of the United States for a writ of *habeas corpus.* To support that assumption we must hold that a prisoner of our military authorities is constitutionally entitled to the writ, even though he (a) is an enemy alien; (b) has never been or resided in the United States; (c) was captured outside of our territory and there held in military custody as a prisoner of war; (d) was tried and convicted by a Military Commission sitting outside the United States; (e) for offenses against laws of war committed outside the United States; (f) and is at all times imprisoned outside the United States."

On this set of facts, the Court concluded, "no right to the writ of *habeas corpus* appears." Petitioners in these cases differ from the *Eisentrager* detainees in important respects: They are not nationals of countries at war with the United States, and they deny that they have engaged in or plotted acts of aggression against the United States; they have never been afforded access to any tribunal, much less charged with and convicted of wrongdoing; and for more than two years they have been imprisoned in territory over which the United States exercises exclusive jurisdiction and control.

Not only are petitioners differently situated from the *Eisentrager* detainees, but the Court in *Eisentrager* made quite clear that all six of the facts critical to its disposition were relevant only to the question of the prisoners' *constitutional* entitlement to habeas corpus. The Court had far less to say on the question of the petitioners' *statutory* entitlement to habeas review. Its only statement on the subject was a passing reference to the absence of statutory authorization. . . .

Reference to the historical context in which *Eisentrager* was decided explains why the opinion devoted so little attention to question of statutory jurisdiction. In 1948, just two months after the *Eisentrager* petitioners filed their petition for habeas corpus in the U.S. District Court for the District of Columbia, this Court issued its decision in *Ahrens v. Clark,* a case concerning the application of the habeas statute to the petitions of 120 Germans who were then being detained at Ellis Island, New York, for deportation to Germany. The *Ahrens* detainees had also filed their petitions in the U.S. District Court for the District of Columbia, naming the Attorney General as the respondent. Reading the phrase "within their respective jurisdictions" as used in the habeas statute to require the petitioners' presence within the district court's territorial jurisdiction, the Court held that the District of Columbia court lacked jurisdiction to entertain the detainees' claims. . . .

Because subsequent decisions of this Court have filled the statutory gap that had occasioned *Eisentrager's* resort to "fundamentals," persons detained outside the territorial jurisdiction of any federal district court no longer need rely on the Constitution as the source of their right to federal habeas review. In *Braden v. 30th Judicial Circuit Court of Ky.* (1973), this Court held, contrary to Ahrens, that the prisoner's presence within the territorial jurisdiction of the district court is not "an invariable prerequisite" to the exercise of district court jurisdiction under the federal habeas statute. Rather, because "the writ of habeas corpus does not act upon the prisoner who seeks relief, but upon the person who holds him in what is alleged to be unlawful custody," a district court acts "within [its] respective jurisdiction" within the meaning of § 2241 as long as "the custodian can be reached by service of process." *Braden* reasoned that its departure from the rule of *Ahrens* was warranted in light of developments that "had a profound impact on the continuing vitality of that decision." These developments included, notably, decisions of this Court in cases involving habeas petitioners "confined overseas (and thus outside the territory of any district court)," in which the Court "held, if only implicitly, that the petitioners' absence from the district does not present a jurisdictional obstacle to the consideration of the claim." *Braden* thus established that *Ahrens* can no longer be viewed as establishing "an inflexible jurisdictional rule," and is strictly relevant only to the question of the appropriate forum, not to whether the claim can be heard at all.

Because *Braden* overruled the statutory predicate to *Eisentrager's* holding, *Eisentrager* plainly does not preclude the exercise of § 2241 jurisdiction over petitioners' claims.

Putting *Eisentrager* and *Ahrens* to one side, respondents contend that we can discern a limit on § 2241 through application of the "longstanding principle of American law" that congressional legislation is presumed not to have extraterritorial application unless such intent is clearly manifested. Whatever traction the presumption against extraterritoriality might have in other contexts, it certainly has no application to the operation of the habeas statute with respect to persons detained within "the territorial jurisdiction" of the United States. By the express terms of its agreements with Cuba, the United States exercises "complete jurisdiction and control" over the Guantanamo Bay Naval Base, and may continue to exercise such control permanently if it so chooses. Respondents themselves concede that the habeas statute would create federal court jurisdiction over the claims of an American citizen held at the base. Considering that the statute draws no distinction between Americans and aliens held in federal custody, there is little reason to think that Congress intended the geographical coverage of the statute to vary depending on the detainee's citizenship. Aliens held at the base, no less than American citizens, are entitled to invoke the federal courts' authority under § 2241. . . .

In the end, the answer to the question presented is clear. Petitioners contend that they are being held in federal custody in violation of the laws of the United States.* No party questions the District Court's jurisdiction over petitioners' custodians. Section 2241, by its terms, requires nothing more. We therefore hold that § 2241 confers on the District Court jurisdiction to hear petitioners' habeas corpus challenges to the legality of their detention at the Guantanamo Bay Naval Base. . . .

Whether and what further proceedings may become necessary after respondents make their response to the merits of petitioners' claims are matters that we need not address now. What is presently at stake is only whether the federal courts have jurisdiction to determine the legality of the Executive's potentially indefinite detention of individuals who claim to be wholly innocent of wrongdoing. Answering that question in the affirmative, we reverse the judgment of the Court of Appeals and remand for the District Court to consider in the first instance the merits of petitioners' claims.

Justice Kennedy, concurring in the judgment.

The Court is correct, in my view, to conclude that federal courts have jurisdiction to consider challenges to the legality of the detention of foreign nationals held at the Guantanamo Bay Naval Base in Cuba. While I reach the same conclusion, my analysis follows a different course. . . . In my view, the correct course is to follow the framework of *Eisentrager.*

Eisentrager considered the scope of the right to petition for a writ of habeas corpus against the backdrop of the constitutional command of the separation of powers. The issue before the Court was whether the Judiciary could exercise jurisdiction over the claims of German prisoners held in the Landsberg prison in Germany following the cessation of hostilities in Europe. The Court concluded the petition could not be entertained. The petition was not within the proper realm of the judicial power. It concerned matters within the exclusive province of the Executive, or the Executive and Congress, to determine. . . .

The decision in *Eisentrager* indicates that there is a realm of political authority over military affairs where the judicial power may not enter. The existence of this realm acknowledges the power of the President as Commander in Chief, and the joint role of the President and the Congress, in the conduct of military affairs. A faithful application of *Eisentrager,* then, requires an ini-

---

* [[Footnote by Justice Stevens]] Petitioners' allegations—that, although they have engaged neither in combat nor in acts of terrorism against the United States, they have been held in Executive detention for more than two years in territory subject to the long-term, exclusive jurisdiction and control of the United States, without access to counsel and without being charged with any wrongdoing—unquestionably describe "custody in violation of the Constitution or laws or treaties of the United States." 28 U.S.C. 2241(c)(3).

tial inquiry into the general circumstances of the detention to determine whether the Court has the authority to entertain the petition and to grant relief after considering all of the facts presented. A necessary corollary of *Eisentrager* is that there are circumstances in which the courts maintain the power and the responsibility to protect persons from unlawful detention even where military affairs are implicated.

The facts here are distinguishable from those in *Eisentrager* in two critical ways, leading to the conclusion that a federal court may entertain the petitions. First, Guantanamo Bay is in every practical respect a United States territory, and it is one far removed from any hostilities. The opinion of the Court well explains the history of its possession by the United States. In a formal sense, the United States leases the Bay; the 1903 lease agreement states that Cuba retains "ultimate sovereignty" over it. At the same time, this lease is no ordinary lease. Its term is indefinite and at the discretion of the United States. What matters is the unchallenged and indefinite control that the United States has long exercised over Guantanamo Bay. From a practical perspective, the indefinite lease of Guantanamo Bay has produced a place that belongs to the United States, extending the "implied protection" of the United States to it.

The second critical set of facts is that the detainees at Guantanamo Bay are being held indefinitely, and without benefit of any legal proceeding to determine their status. In *Eisentrager*, the prisoners were tried and convicted by a military commission of violating the laws of war and were sentenced to prison terms. Having already been subject to procedures establishing their status, they could not justify "a limited opening of our courts" to show that they were "of friendly personal disposition" and not enemy aliens. Indefinite detention without trial or other proceeding presents altogether different considerations. It allows friends and foes alike to remain in detention. It suggests a weaker case of military necessity and much greater alignment with the traditional function of habeas corpus. Perhaps, where detainees are taken from a zone of hostilities, detention without proceedings or trial would be justified by military necessity for a matter of weeks; but as the period of detention stretches from months to years, the case for continued detention to meet military exigencies becomes weaker.

. . . [[The above]] approach would avoid creating automatic statutory authority to adjudicate the claims of persons located outside the United States, and remains true to the reasoning of *Eisentrager*. For these reasons, I concur in the judgment of the Court.

Justice Scalia, with whom the *Chief Justice* and *Justice Thomas* join, dissenting.

The Court today holds that the habeas statute extends to aliens detained by the United States military overseas, outside the sovereign borders of the

United States and beyond the territorial jurisdictions of all its courts. This is not only a novel holding; it contradicts a half-century-old precedent on which the military undoubtedly relied, *Johnson v. Eisentrager*. The Court's contention that *Eisentrager* was somehow negated by *Braden v. 30th Judicial Circuit Court of Ky.* (1973)—a decision that dealt with a different issue and did not so much as mention *Eisentrager*—is implausible in the extreme. This is an irresponsible overturning of settled law in a matter of extreme importance to our forces currently in the field. I would leave it to Congress to change § 2241, and dissent from the Court's unprecedented holding.

. . . [[T]]his case turns on the words of § 2241, a text the Court today largely ignores. Even a cursory reading of the habeas statute shows that it presupposes a federal district court with territorial jurisdiction over the detainee. Section 2241(a) states:

> Writs of habeas corpus may be granted by the Supreme Court, any justice thereof, the district courts and any circuit judge *within their respective jurisdictions*. (Emphasis added).

It further requires that "[t]he order of a circuit judge shall be entered in the records of *the* district court of *the district wherein the restraint complained of is had.*" And § 2242 provides that a petition "addressed to the Supreme Court, a justice thereof or a circuit judge . . . shall state the reasons for not making application to *the* district court of *the district in which the applicant is held.*" (Emphases added). No matter to whom the writ is directed, custodian or detainee, the statute could not be clearer that a necessary requirement for issuing the writ is that *some* federal district court have territorial jurisdiction over the detainee. Here, as the Court allows, the Guantanamo Bay detainees are not located within the territorial jurisdiction of any federal district court. One would think that is the end of this case.

The Court asserts, however, that the decisions of this Court have placed a gloss on the phrase "within their respective jurisdictions" in § 2241 which allows jurisdiction in this case. That is not so. In fact, the only case in point holds just the opposite (and just what the statute plainly says). That case is *Eisentrager*. . . .

Eisentrager's directly-on-point statutory holding makes it exceedingly difficult for the Court to reach the result it desires today. To do so neatly and cleanly, it must either argue that our decision in *Braden* overruled *Eisentrager*, or admit that *it* is overruling *Eisentrager*. The former course would not pass the laugh test, inasmuch as *Braden* dealt with a detainee held within the territorial jurisdiction of a district court, and never *mentioned Eisentrager*. And the latter course would require the Court to explain why our almost categorical rule of *stare decisis* in statutory cases should be set aside in order to complicate the present war, *and*, having set it aside, to explain why the habeas statute does not mean what it plainly says. . . .

But in fact *Braden* did not overrule *Ahrens*; it distinguished *Ahrens*. *Braden* dealt with a habeas petitioner incarcerated in Alabama. The petitioner filed an application for a writ of habeas corpus in Kentucky, challenging an indictment that had been filed against him in that Commonwealth and naming as respondent the Kentucky court in which the proceedings were pending. This Court held that Braden was in custody because a detainer had been issued against him by Kentucky, and was being executed by Alabama, serving as an agent for Kentucky. We found that jurisdiction existed in Kentucky for Braden's petition challenging the Kentucky detainer, notwithstanding his physical confinement in Alabama. *Braden* was careful to *distinguish* that situation from the general rule established in *Ahrens*. . . .

The reality is this: Today's opinion, and today's opinion alone, overrules *Eisentrager*; today's opinion, and today's opinion alone, extends the habeas statute, for the first time, to aliens held beyond the sovereign territory of the United States and beyond the territorial jurisdiction of its courts. No reasons are given for this result; no acknowledgment of its consequences made. . . .

In abandoning the venerable statutory line drawn in *Eisentrager*, the Court boldly extends the scope of the habeas statute to the four corners of the earth . . . [[by asserting]] that *Braden* stands for the proposition that "a district court acts 'within [its] respective jurisdiction' within the meaning of § 2241 as long as 'the custodian can be reached by service of process.'" . . .

Departure from our rule of *stare decisis* in statutory cases is always extraordinary; it ought to be unthinkable when the departure has a potentially harmful effect upon the Nation's conduct of a war. The Commander in Chief and his subordinates had every reason to expect that the internment of combatants at Guantanamo Bay would not have the consequence of bringing the cumbersome machinery of our domestic courts into military affairs. Congress is in session. If it wished to change federal judges' habeas jurisdiction from what this Court had previously held that to be, it could have done so. And it could have done so by intelligent revision of the statute, instead of by today's clumsy, counter textual reinterpretation that confers upon wartime prisoners greater habeas rights than domestic detainees. The latter must challenge their present physical confinement in the district of their confinement, see *Rumsfeld v. Padilla*, whereas under today's strange holding Guantanamo Bay detainees can petition in any of the ninety-four federal judicial districts. The fact that extraterritorially located detainees lack the district of detention that the statute requires has been converted from a factor that precludes their ability to bring a petition at all into a factor that frees them to petition wherever they wish—and, as a result, to forum shop. For this Court to create such a monstrous scheme in time of war, and in frustration of our military commanders' reliance upon clearly stated prior law, is judicial adventurism of the worst sort. I dissent.

V. POSTSCRIPT

Within a few days of the Supreme Court's decision in *Rasul*, lawyers affiliated with the Center for Constitutional Rights (CCR), a public-interest law firm in New York City that had played a pivotal role in the earlier litigation, demanded that the Pentagon grant them access to their clients, arguing that each detainee had a right to an attorney since federal courts had jurisdiction over their petitions for writs of habeas corpus. On July 2, the Bush administration agreed to such access, but limited it to the GBNB detainees who were litigants in *Rasul* and *Al Odah*. The CCR ratcheted up the pressure by filing new habeas corpus petitions for new clients and by recruiting other law firms to file additional petitions. Partly in response to these developments, but also in response to the due process rights that the Supreme Court had recognized in *Hamdi*, the Defense Department on July 7 announced a new review process for the GBNB detainees. Each detainee would be provided, not with a lawyer, but with a "personal representative," who would be a military officer above the rank of major; each detainee would be able to contest his status as an "unlawful enemy combatant" before a Combatant Status Review Tribunal (CSRT) consisting of three military officers; and each would be informed of his right to contest his status in federal court by way of a petition for a writ of habeas corpus.[27]

CCR lawyers denounced the CSRT review process as inadequate if only because it did not provide all GBNB detainees with immediate access to attorneys. In addition, CCR lawyers objected to the monitoring and review procedures imposed by the government on the attorneys for the *Rasul* and *Al Odah* petitioners. The procedures included audio and video taping of attorney-client meetings and a "classification review" of any notes that were taken during such meetings and any mail between the attorneys and their detainee clients. The government claimed that such procedures were necessary for national security and were permissible because access to legal counsel at GBNB was discretionary. Since the detainees had no legal right to counsel, the government argued it could impose conditions as it saw fit.

In *Al Odah v. United States*, District Judge Kollar-Kotelly on October 20, 2004 ruled against the government, holding that the detainees had a statutory right to counsel since they could not fairly litigate their habeas claims in federal court without representation. Since the detainees had a statutory right to counsel, Kollar-Kotelly rejected the "real-time monitoring" of attorney-detainee meetings and both types of classification review. Acknowledging the government's legitimate national security concerns, Kollar-Kotelly established a framework that allowed only one attorney to have unmonitored meetings with each detainee. All attorneys were forbidden to disclose to anyone any information obtained from a detainee, unless it was cleared beforehand by the government. As an additional requirement, the judge ordered all attorneys who had access to GBNB detainees to report to the government any information from a detainee that threatened national security or involved immediate violence. Lastly, all the attorneys seeking access to GBNB detainees had to have the requisite security clearances and be properly trained in handling classified information, a requirement that produced considerable delay.[28]

The purpose of the CSRT review process was to provide a minimal level of due process to the GBNB detainees so that the government could defend the lawfulness of their detention in the expanding number of habeas cases. However, by not referring to the CSRTs as Article 5 hearings, the Bush administration refused to reconsider its decision not to grant POW status to any of the GBNB detainees. Detainees found not to be unlawful enemy combatants were therefore innocent civilians who were entitled to be released. By March 2005, approximately one hundred detainees had filed habeas petitions in federal court, while CSRT reviews by July had found that thirty-eight of the detainees had been improperly designated as enemy combatants. However, some of these detainees remained at the GBNB since they could not be returned to their home countries because of well-founded fears of persecution.[29]

During late 2004, GBNB military authorities also established Administrative Review Boards (ARB) that were to function as a complement to the CSRTs. The purpose of the ARBs was to decide each year whether a detainee still had valuable intelligence or was a threat to the United States. A key feature of the ARBs was that they could order a detainee's release without any admission that the U.S. military had made a mistake. By March 2005, ARBs reviewed sixty-four detainees, but thirty-nine of these detainees refused to attend the hearings. By July, three detainees were released through ARB review.[30] The Bush administration also transferred a number of GBNB detainees to their home countries for prosecution or release. In fact, both Shafiq Rasul and Isif Iqbal were transferred to Great Britain in March 2004 and Mamdouh Habib was transferred to Australia in January 2005. Their home countries eventually released all three of them. However, despite the safe character of these three releases, it is worth noting that at least ten GBNB detainees who were released after their transfer to their home countries have rejoined terrorist groups.[31]

In September 2004, eight of the nine judges on Washington, D.C.'s federal district court who were assigned habeas cases from GBNB transferred them to Senior Judge Joyce Hens Green, a Jimmy Carter appointee, so that she could rule on all common issues, including the government's motion to dismiss all the cases pretrial. However, Judge Richard Leon, a George W. Bush appointee, kept the two cases that had initially been assigned to him, thereby exhibiting an interesting form of judicial independence. There was no way for the other judges on the district court to force him to follow Green's rulings on the government's motion to dismiss or other pretrial issues.[32] The price of this form of judicial independence is that two judges on the same court could hand down completely opposite rulings in related or identical cases. This is just what happened in January 2005. Judge Leon granted the government's motion, holding that, though he had jurisdiction to hear the petition on the basis of *Rasul*, the GBNB detainees had no right to a writ of habeas corpus. According to Leon, the president had the authority to detain enemy combatants under the Authorization for the Use of Military Force, even if they were captured far from the battlefields of Afghanistan. In addition, Leon ruled that nonresident aliens detained outside the sovereign territory of the United States had no constitutional, statutory, or treaty-based rights that were enforceable in a federal court. "In the final analysis," Leon concluded, "the Court's role in reviewing the military's decision to capture and detain a nonresident alien is, and must be, highly circumscribed" since the "judiciary should not insinuate itself into foreign affairs and national security issues."[33]

In contrast to Judge Leon's decision, Judge Green denied the government's motion to dismiss the other pending habeas petitions, holding that, because GBNB was "the equivalent of a U.S. territory," the detainees did have enforceable due process rights under the Fifth Amendment and that the CSRT review process was constitutionally inadequate. First, the CSRTs often relied on classified evidence to find that detainees were enemy combatants, but refused to give the detainees access to this evidence or a fair opportunity to rebut it. Second, the CSRTs could base their designations on statements that were possibly coerced from detainees. Third, the government's definition of enemy combatant was vague and overly broad, permitting the possibility that GBNB detainees were being held, perhaps for life, on the basis of their contacts and associations, not on the basis of any terrorist acts. For these reasons, Judge Green concluded that the GBNB detainees had presented potentially viable arguments supporting the illegality of their detentions. She therefore declined to grant the government's motion to dismiss.[34]

The fact that two judges on the same federal district court disagreed so fundamentally on whether the GBNB detainees were entitled to a writ of habeas corpus underscored the complexity of the underlying issues and the unprecedented character of the litigation. The habeas cases were immediately appealed to the D.C. Circuit, which heard oral argument on September 8, 2005. In late December, however, Congress enacted the Detainee Treatment Act of 2005 (DTA): a major piece of legislation in the ongoing war on terrorism. It established uniform standards of interrogation for all persons held in U.S. custody and prohibited "cruel, inhuman, or degrading treatment." Second, the DTA purportedly eliminated the jurisdiction of federal courts over all habeas petitions from the detainees held at GBNB and left the detainees without any access to the federal judiciary except for two exceptions. One court, the D.C. Circuit Court of Appeals, was granted exclusive jurisdiction to review the validity of both the enemy combatant designations made by the CSRTs and the final decisions of military commissions that convicted detainees of violating the laws of war.[35] Following the enactment of the DTA, these were the only two avenues of access to the federal judiciary that were left open to the GBNB detainees, but it was unclear whether the law applied to pending habeas cases or only to future ones.

The Bush administration moved for the dismissal of all pending habeas cases from the detainees, including those before the D.C. Circuit. Since these cases were neither reviews of designations by CSRTs or convictions by military commissions, the government claimed that D.C. Circuit did not have jurisdiction. The court should dismiss them all without any decision on the merits. This jurisdictional question regarding pending cases was complicated by the fact that the Supreme Court had already agreed in November 2005 to hear *Hamdan v. Rumsfeld*, the litigation that will be considered in chapter 5. *Hamdan* was a habeas case from a detainee who objected pretrial to the legality of the military commission that was going to try him for violations of the laws of war. In February 2006, the government filed a motion with the Supreme Court arguing that the case should be dismissed because the DTA had eliminated the federal judiciary's jurisdiction over all habeas petitions from GBNB detainees, including those pending at the nation's highest court. The Supreme Court could review the legality of Hamdan's military commission, the government argued, but only posttrial, after the D.C. Circuit had reviewed the case on direct appeal. The Supreme Court decided to consider the issue of jurisdiction along with the substantive issues of the case. The D.C. Circuit therefore had little incentive to decide how the DTA applied to pending habeas cases since the Supreme Court was about to decide a very similar question in *Hamdan*. Accordingly, the impact of the DTA on the jurisdiction of D.C. Circuit will be considered in the postscript of chapter 5, after the issues of *Hamdan* and the Supreme Court's resolution of them have been fully explored.

NOTES

1. For further elaboration of these five principles of jurisdiction, see *Restatement (Third) of Foreign Relations Law*, Sections 401-404 (1987). See also The Princeton Project on Universal Jurisdiction, available online at www.law.uc.edu/morgan/newsdir/univjuris.html.

2. See The Omnibus Diplomatic Security and Antiterrorism Act of 1986, Pub. L. No. 99-399; the Antiterrorism and Effective Death Penalty Act of 1996, Pub. L. No. 104-132; and the Military Extraterritorial Jurisdiction Act of 2000, Pub. L. No. 106-523.

3. 18 U.S.C. 2332.

4. 18 U.S.C. 2332a.

5. 18 U.S.C. 2332b (e).

6. 18 U.S.C. 2339B (d).

7. See Pub. L. No. 107-56 and Pub. L. No. 107-197.

8. See 18 U.S.C. 2332f (b) (2) (C) and 2339C (b) (2) (B), enacted into law June 25, 2002, Pub. L. No. 107-197, available at thomas.loc.gov/.

9. *United States v. Yunis*, 924 F. 2d 1086 (D.C. Cir. 1991).

10. *United States v. Rezaq*, 134 F. 3d 1121 (D.C. Cir. 1998).

11. See *United States v. Usama bin Laden*, 92 F. Supp. 2d 189 (2d. Cir. 2000).

12. *United States v. Yousef*, 327 F.3d 56 (2d Cir. 2003).

13. See *EEOC v. Arabian American Oil Company*, 499 U.S. 244, 248 (1991).

14. *Rasul v. Bush*, 215 F. Supp. 2d 55, 63, 65 (D.D.C. 2002).

15. See generally *Al Odah v. United States*, 321 F.3d 1134 (D.C. Cir. 2003).

16. *Gherebi v. Bush*, 352 F. 3d 1278 (9th Cir. 2003).

17. See *United States v. Lee* 906 F.2d117 (4th Cir. 1990) and *United States v. Rogers*, 388 F. Supp. 298, 301 (E.D. VA. 1975).

18. These espionage cases eventually fell apart. See Kim Curtiss, "Plea Deal Approved in Guantanamo Spy Case," *Associated Press*, September 22, 2004, available online at Findlaw: Legal News and Commentary; "Judge Rules Spy Charges May Proceed," *Washington Post*, September 21, 2004, p. A07; Neil A. Lewis and Thom Shanker, "Missteps Seen in Muslim Chaplain's Spy Case," *The New York Times*, January, 4, 2004.

19. See Burtt v. Schick, 23 M.J. 140 (1986).

20. See *Haitian Centers Council v. McNary*, 969 F. 2d1326, 1343 (2nd Cir. 1992), vacated as moot sub nom. *Sale v. Haitian Centers Council, Inc.*, 509 U.S. 918 (1993); *Cuban-American Bar Ass'n v. Christopher*, 43 F. 3d 1412 (11th Cir. 1995).

21. See *Haitian Centers Council, Inc. v. Sale*, 823 F. Supp. 1028 (E.D.N.Y 1993).

22. In *Rasul*, the government's brief did not cite either *Ahrens* or *Braden* and the petitioner's brief only mentioned these two cases in footnotes. See Petitioner's Brief on the Merits, f.n. 8 and 41.

23. *Ahrens v. Clark*, 335 U.S. 188, 195 (1948).

24. *Braden v. 30th Judicial Circuit Court of Kentucky*, 410 U.S. 484 (1973).

25. See Charles Lane, "Stevens Brings a Historical Perspective to Detainee' Case," *Washington Post*, May 3, 2004, p. A19, available at http://washingtonpost.com.

26. See *Working Group Report on Detainee Interrogations in the Global War on Terrorism: Assessment of Legal, Historical, Policy, and Operational Considerations* (March 6, 2003), pp. 7, 8, 17, 33, 35. Also see Memorandum for Alberto R. Gonzales, Counsel to the President, from Jay S. Bybee, Assistant Attorney General, *Re: Standards of Conduct for Interrogation under 18 U.S.C. 2340-2340A* (August 1, 2002), pp 1, 7, 13, 31, and 35;

27. Josh White, "Lawyers Seek Access to 53 at Guantanamo," *Washington Post*, July 2, 2004, available online at http://washingtonpost.com; Neil A. Lewis, "U.S. Allows Lawyers to Meet Detainees," *The New York Times*, July 3, 2004, available online at http://nytimes.com; Christopher Marquis, "Pentagon Will Permit Captives at Cuba Base to Appeal Status," *The New York Times*, July 8, 2004, available online at http://nytimes.com; Kathleen T. Rhem, "Detainee Status Review Tribunals to Begin Within Weeks," *American Forces Press Service*, July 9, 2004, available online at American Forces Information Service: News Articles.

28. 346 F. Supp. 2d 1 (D.D.C. 2004).

29. Neil A. Lewis, "Guantanamo Detainees Make Their Case," *The New York Times*, March 24, 2005, available at http://nytimes.com; Josh White, "3 Guantanamo Detainees Freed," *Washington Post*, July 21, 2005, A02, available at http://washingtonpost.com; Josh White, "5 Chinese Detainees Given More Freedom at Guantanamo," *Washington Post*, August 26, 2005, A22, available at http://washingtonpost.com.

30. Ibid.

31. Paisley Dodds, "Guantanamo Takes on Look of Permanence," *Associated Press*, January 10, 2005; Carol D. Leonnig and Glenn Frankel, "U.S. to Send 5 Detainees Home from Guantanamo," *Washington Post*, January 12, 2005; John Mintz, "Released Detainees Rejoining the Fight," *Washington Post*, October 22, 2004, available at http://washingonpost.com.

32. See Vaness Blum, "Guantanamo Detainee Cases Torn Between Two Judges," *Legal Times*, November 30, 2004.

33. *Khalid v. Bush*, 2005 U.S. Dist. LEXIS 749, 46-47, 48 (D.D.C. 2005).

34. *In re* Guantanamo Detainee Cases, 344 F. Supp. 2d 174 (D.D.C. 2005).

35. See Department of Defense Appropriations Act of 2006, Pub. L. No. 109-148, § 1005 (signed by President Bush on December 30, 2005), also known as the Detainee Treatment Act of 2005.

Chapter 4

Civilian Trials of High-Profile Terrorists

U.S. v. Moussaoui

The case of Zacarias Moussaoui, who was at one time thought to be the "twentieth hijacker," raises the question whether terrorist suspects can be fairly prosecuted in civilian courts, especially if their goal is to put the American legal system on trial. The most troubling constitutional problem regarding the Moussaoui case was that the government refused to give the defendant access to a number of al Qaeda operatives detained abroad, despite the fact that they could testify favourably on his behalf. Moussaoui argued repeatedly that this refusal of access to potential defense witnesses was a violation of his Sixth Amendment right "to have compulsory process for obtaining witnesses in his favour." In 2003 District Judge Leonie Brinkema declined to give Moussaoui *personal* access to the detainees, but she did order the government to permit videotaped depositions of them. The government, however, refused to comply with this order, whereupon the judge eliminated the death penalty from the case and prohibited the government from linking Moussaoui to the events of 9/11. The government appealed to the Fourth Circuit Court of Appeals, which in September 2004 upheld Brinkema's conclusion that the government was violating Moussaoui's Sixth Amendment rights, but reversed her ruling on sanctions. The government could link Moussaoui to the events of 9/11 and seek the death penalty in his case without giving him the opportunity to depose the detainees, whether in person or by videotape. According to the Fourth Circuit, the proper sanction for the government's conduct was to permit Moussaoui to use written "substitutions" compiled from classified "intelligence reports" of the interrogations of the detainees in lieu of videotaped depositions. The Supreme Court declined to hear the case, perhaps because at the time of the appeal Moussaoui had not yet been convicted or sentenced.

In April 2005, Moussaoui unexpectedly pleaded guilty to all the charges the government had filed against him, including those that made him eligible for the death penalty. Although his motives for pleading guilty were far from clear, Moussaoui still had the right to present the above substitutions during the sentencing phase of his trial. However, following his plea, Moussaoui kept his distance from the process of compiling the substitutions, leaving the entire matter to his court-appointed attorneys, with whom he had little or no contact. During his March 2006 sentencing hearing, Moussaoui unexpectedly testified under oath that he knew in August 2001 that al Qaeda operatives were planning to fly airplanes into the World Trade Center and that his role on 9/11 was to fly a plane into the White House. One conceivable explanation of Moussaoui's bizarre behavior was that he was seeking a death sentence so that he could increase the likelihood that the Supreme Court would eventually hear his case. On this assumption, Moussaoui wanted to die for his cause, but he wanted to die fighting an "unjust" American legal system. The case therefore raised a fundamental question: Can the American legal system provide due process to a terrorist who is trying to tarnish the United States in the court of world opinion by doing his utmost to become, or to appear to become, its victim?

I. BACKGROUND

At the time of the 9/11 attacks, the government had already detained Moussaoui based on immigration violations. A federal grand jury sitting in Virginia nonetheless indicted him on December 11, 2001 with six counts of conspiracy: conspiracy to commit terrorist acts transcending national boundaries; to engage in aircraft piracy; to destroy aircraft; to use weapons of mass destruction; to murder United States employees; and to destroy property. A conviction on any of the first four charges carried the possibility of a death sentence. By the end of January 2002, Moussaoui was completely at odds with his court-appointed defense team (which included Frank Dunham, Edward B. MacMahon, and Gerald Zherkin) over strategy and tactics. At a hearing before Judge Brinkema on April 22, 2002, Moussaoui, against the advice of counsel, denigrated the United States, its judicial system, his defense lawyers, and Judge Brinkema and insisted that he wanted to proceed *pro se*, that is, as his own lawyer. His fifty-minute speech left the impression that Moussaoui wanted to be in complete charge of his case so that he could put the American criminal justice system on trial (see box 4.1).

On June 13, Judge Brinkema ruled that Moussaoui was competent to represent himself. Dunham, MacMahon, and Zerkin would function only as standby counsel: they were to assist Moussaoui with his case if he let them and they had to be prepared to take over the defense if Brinkema ever ruled that Moussaoui was

Box 4.1. ZACARIAS MOUSSAOUI'S APRIL 22, 2002 REMARKS IN OPEN COURT

. . . I will not entertain the illusion that a U.S. District Judge Leonie Brinkema is an honest broker. Reality tells me that this judge is here as a field general, entrusted with the mission to get this matter over quickly. Every general has a commander in chief, and I know how much the U.S. commander in chief wants me to be over quickly. . . .

My experience tells me that the U.S. will not hesitate to have a trial without me. After all, they only need me for the gas chamber. But Allah is my witness. Nobody will ever represent me, *inshallah*, because suicide is forbidden in Islam. . . .

I pray to Allah, the protector, for the destruction of Russia and the return of the Islamic Emirates of Chechnia. I pray to Allah, the powerful, for the return of the Islamic Emirates of Afghanistan and the destruction of the United States of America. . . .

So, America, America, I'm ready to fight in your Don King fight, even both hands tied behind the back in court. And be sure, *inshallah*, that all your ingenuity will not prevent me to be in court in October. *Inshallah*, you will get the point. . . .

So at first MacMahon have a very relaxed attitude. He say, "This is our defense, Mr. Moussaoui. We are here to help you, OK and we will do as you wish. You want to do this according to Islam principle," so on and so forth, OK. Nice talk. The same for Mr. Dunham.

But on January 30, the last day of the month, I believe, after like something of great importance, we have an argument, a divergence of opinion about a tactical point, OK, and Frank send them, MacMahon and Zerkin, to visit me, OK, to clarify a situation.

When they came, they didn't discuss the point they were supposed to discuss. They wanted to assert their right as a lawyer to define the strategy and the tactic on the defense of my life. . . . They say, "From now on, finished. We are going to do as we wish." I say, "This is my life, and you have not any understanding of the situation. You have no information. You have nothing from the FBI. You have nothing, and you want to be in charge." He says, "We are the lawyer, and we are, by statute or whatever, we are in charge."

So I say, "So are you sure?" So I asked three time, because this is the manner of the Muslim, to assert something, we used to—we ask three

(Continued)

unable to continue as his own lawyer. Since these attorneys had the necessary security clearances, they would have access to classified information, but they could not discuss any classified information with Moussaoui without the permission of the government or the court. Moussaoui's decision to proceed *pro se* therefore placed him in a dilemma: he was his own lawyer, but he would have little access to much of the evidence that the government intended to use against him. Moussaoui continued as his own lawyer until November 2003, at which point Brinkema turned his defense over to standby counsel. The legal tactics Moussaoui pursued while he was his own lawyer were highly questionable. At a hearing on July 18, 2002, Moussaoui unexpectedly declared that he was ready to plead guilty to the charges against him, that he was a member of al Qaeda, and that he had pledged allegiance (*bayat*) to Osama bin Laden. Judge Brinkema refused to accept the guilty plea because Moussouai would not accept responsibility for the essence of the conspiracy charges filed against him, but the incriminating statements were nonetheless very damaging to Moussaoui's case.

The capture by Pakistani authorities of Abu Zubaydah, al Qaeda's chief of operations, in March 2002, and Ramzi Binalshibh, an organizer of the 9/11 attacks, in September complicated the Moussaoui case immeasurably. Once it became common knowledge that the two detainees had been transferred to U.S. custody for interrogation, Moussaoui, relying on his Sixth Amendment right "to have compulsory process for obtaining witnesses in his favour," filed motions with Judge Brinkema to produce both detainees as defense witnesses at his trial.[1] Citing national security concerns, the government immediately objected to Moussaoui's request. For months the issues were debated in a number of legal filings with the district court. Finally, on January 13, 2003, the government filed a seventy-one-page brief under seal and Moussaoui's standby counsel responded with a fifty-one-page reply on January 23.[2] If Moussaoui ever saw the government's brief, it presumably was a version akin to the heavily redacted brief that appeared on the district court's website on June 2, 2003, of which fifty of the seventy-one pages were completely blank. Standby counsel's brief, which appeared on the district court's website on August 6, 2003, was not as heavily redacted as the government's, but at best Moussaoui could only infer the government's arguments from what standby counsel wrote in their brief. Moreover, even standby counsel were not permitted to see a number of "declarations" that the government had filed *ex parte* in support of its January 13 brief. Judge Brinkema only ordered the government to turn over "summaries" of any statements in the "declarations" that were exculpable.[3] Oral argument was held on the question of defense access to the al Qaeda detainees on January 30. Since classified information was discussed at the session, Moussaoui was barred from attending, though his standby counsel were present.[4]

On January 31, Judge Brinkema denied the defense any trial or personal pretrial access to the detainees, but she did order the government to arrange videotaped depositions. Both Moussaoui and his lawyers would be allowed to ask the detainees questions via a closed-circuit television hook-up. Transmission would be time-delayed so that Brinkema would have an opportunity to rule on the permissibility of the questions.[5] The deposition was to be completed before April 30, 2003 and the resulting videotape would be available for use by the defense at the scheduled June trial in lieu of live testimony. The government immediately appealed Judge Brinkema's ruling to the Fourth Circuit, but the appellate court remanded the case back to Judge Brinkema and instructed her to use the procedures of the Classified Information Procedures Act (CIPA) as a model to evaluate whether the government could propose substitutions for the videotaped depositions of the detainees. CIPA was a statutory framework that Congress had established to protect a defendant's right to a fair trial and the confidentiality of classified information. Rather than disclosing a classified document at trial, the statute permitted the government to propose a "substitution" that was either a "statement admitting relevant facts" or a "summary of the classified information." A judge decided if the substitution was adequate based on whether it provided "the defendant with substantially the same ability to make his defense." In effect, the Fourth Circuit was asking Judge Brinkema to consider whether the government could come up with a comparable substitute for a videotaped deposition, rather than a classified document.

The government submitted its proposed substitutions, which were classified as "Top Secret/Codeword," to Brinkema under seal on April 24. The prosecution team had prepared the proposed substitutions from intelligence summaries of intelligence reports. Officers from the intelligence agencies had composed the intelligence reports for the purpose of distributing actionable foreign intelligence concerning the war on terrorism within the intelligence community. The reports summarized what the detainees had told their interrogators, but no special effort had been made to ensure that these reports contained any information that was exculpable regarding Moussaoui. Such information would have been included only if it was thought to be actionable foreign intelligence. The intelligence summaries were those portions of the intelligence reports that had a bearing on Moussaoui's culpability. Lawyers in the Justice Department had prepared these classified documents and gave copies of them to Moussaoui's standby counsel, but not to Moussaoui himself.

On May 15, Brinkema ruled that the government's proposed substitutions were "unreliable," "incomplete," and "inaccurate." They were unreliable because the detainees' statements to interrogators were neither taken under oath nor subject to cross-examination. In addition, the court had no way to evaluate the accuracy of the underlying intelligence reports, which were the basis for both the intelligence summaries and the substitutions. The proposed substitutions were incomplete because they omitted some exculpatory information contained in the classified intelligence summaries and the summaries themselves included statements suggesting that more exculpatory testimony could be obtained from the detainees if Moussaoui and his standby counsel could ask them additional questions at a deposition. And, lastly, the substitutions were inaccurate because they were an organized distillation of information, rather than a verbatim compilation of the detainees' statements. Brinkema concluded that the government's "Proposed Substitution would not 'provide the defendant with substantially the same ability to make his defense' as would the videotaped deposition ordered on January 31, 2003."[6]

The government immediately appealed Judge Brinkema's ruling to the Fourth Circuit, which held a public and a secret session of oral argument on June 3. Aspects of the case that were in some way dependent on classified information were reserved for the secret session, although a redacted transcript of this session was later made public. The transcript revealed interesting exchanges between the judges and assistant attorney general Michael Chertoff, who later became secretary of the Department of Homeland Security, and Edward B. MacMahon, one of Moussaoui's standby counsel. In reaction to the claim that it would be a field day for the government if it could control what evidence was important for the defense, Chertoff argued that Moussaoui was seeking access to the detainees, not to obtain exculpatory evidence, but to continue his war against the United States by interfering with the interrogations of the detainees and forcing the United States to disclose classified information. In response, MacMahon insisted that the government's proposed substitution could in no way be an adequate substitute for live testimony, since only Moussaoui knew what he wanted to ask the detainees, and that, if the substitution was permitted, the prosecution would have become "the architect" of Moussaoui's defense, an unacceptable result in the American adversarial system of justice (see box 4.2).

**Box 4.2. EXCERPTS FROM TRANSCRIPT
OF CIPA PROCEEDINGS, JUNE 3, 2003**

JUDGE GREGORY: Well, don't we have to credit to a great extent the defendant? . . . [[The]] sword of Damocles is over . . . [[his]] head, isn't it, if . . . [[a detainee]] says something that's opposite and hurtful? So what interest would the . . . [[defense]] have to speculate if they really didn't believe that they have some feeling and a good reason to believe it's going to be good? If it's bad, it's good for you.

MR. CHERTOFF: You know, Your Honor, . . . one might make that argument in a world in which we're dealing with ordinary criminals. The reality is it may very well be the case that a defendant who has openly acknowledged in a court he was, is, and remains a committed member of a terrorist organization might very well be prepared to hurt himself by triggering a deposition if he thought he could help one of his colleagues overseas or destroy a military operation, because after all, someone who has indicated that their dream was to fly an airplane into a building and kill himself would probably not have a lot of difficulty hurting his criminal case in a U.S. court in order to have the opportunity to sabotage our _____.

And that is why these cases [[are]] unlike any other case, because everybody in the American court system . . . operate in the normal rules of what the criminal justice system requires. To people who are [[at]] war with this country, the system is merely another weapon or potentially another weapon for achieving their ends, and they may even be prepared to hurt themselves or destroy themselves if they can use the system to destroy something that we're doing. . . .

JUDGE WILKINS: In . . . the district court's view, . . . substitutions would never work.

MR. MAC MAHON: Well, . . . government counsel was asked, "Do you have any authority that says that you can substitute the testimony for an entire witness with a CIPA substitute?" And that question was actually never answered by the government in the record to my recollection.

(Continued)

Box 4.2. EXCERPTS FROM TRANSCRIPT
OF CIPA PROCEEDINGS, JUNE 3, 2003 (Continued)

And the answer is there is no such—there's no case where anybody's ever tried to do this. In the [[*United States v.*]] *Fernandez* case, . . . this Court found that it was improper, it was detrimental to the defense to force him to accept a script written by the government.

And when . . . I go back and read *Brady* [[*v. Maryland*]] . . . , somewhere near the end of Brady, it says that allowing the government to suppress favorable testimony in a trial puts the prosecutor, even if it's for good reasons, in the position of becoming the architect of the defense, and that's something that this Court, I would hope, would keep in mind in this case.

Now, what the government wants to do here is disqualify this witness. They [[are]] . . . saying that we're at war, and Mr. Moussaoui is a committed terrorist, an admitted member of al Qaeda, and therefore, we shouldn't give him this witness.

And that makes them the architect of his defense, and we think that that's just entirely inappropriate and that the judge was correct to, to reject that effort. . . .

Following the oral argument, the Fourth Circuit delayed considering Moussaoui's case until Judge Brinkema sanctioned the government for its refusal to go forward with the videotaped depositions of the detainees. Judge Brinkema handed down her decision on sanctions on October 2, 2003. She held that due process and the right to a fair trial included the right to compel "the trial testimony of witnesses . . . who may be able to provide favourable testimony" on the defendant's behalf. However, somewhat unexpectedly, Brinkema did not dismiss the charges against Moussaoui. On the ground that the "interests of justice would not be well served" by a dismissal, she instead permitted the case to go forward, but eliminated the death penalty as a possible sentence for Moussaoui and precluded the government from making any argument or offering any evidence that Moussaoui "had any involvement in, or knowledge of, the September 11 attacks." The government could continue to prosecute Moussaoui for his membership in a general al Qaeda conspiracy to attack the United States, including evidence that Moussaoui had been trained to fly planes into American buildings, but it could not refer to 9/11 and it could only seek a life sentence.

II. BRIEFS FILED IN MOUSSAOUI

The government immediately appealed Judge Brinkema's ruling on sanctions to the Fourth Circuit and both sides soon thereafter submitted briefs that articulated their respective positions on whether Moussaoui could be tried in accordance with the Constitution if he was denied the opportunity to either call the three detainees as witnesses at his trial or, at a minimum, conduct videotaped depositions. In its brief, the government first claimed that Judge Brinkema's ruling unjustifiably placed it on the horns of a dilemma: if the ruling was not reversed, the government had to choose between gathering intelligence to prevent future terrorist attacks or prosecuting terrorists for past terrorist attacks. In response, the government argued that Moussaoui had no Sixth Amendment right to depose the three detainees. Relying heavily on *Johnson v. Eisentrager* (1953), the Supreme Court's decision discussed in chapter 3 that denied habeas relief to Germans convicted of war crimes abroad and imprisoned in Germany after World War II, the government argued that alien enemy combatants detained overseas were beyond the jurisdiction of the federal judiciary. Just as a federal judge could not in a criminal case subpoena an alien living abroad, even if the alien could testify on the behalf of a defendant, so also a federal judge had no jurisdiction over an alien enemy combatant detained abroad by the United States. Moreover, the order to conduct videotaped depositions of the three detainees violated basic separation-of-powers principles because it constituted judicial interference with the executive branch's war-making powers, just as a judicial order requiring the prosecution to immunize a certain witness so that he or she could testify on the behalf of the defendant would constitute judicial interference with the executive branch's prosecutorial responsibilities. Lastly, the government insisted that national security concerns outweighed Moussaoui's need for the evidence, partly because the detainees would, if they testified truthfully, incriminate rather than exculpate Moussaoui, and partly because of the likelihood that the detainees would invoke their Fifth Amendment right against self incrimination and refuse to testify. In any case, according to the government, the national security interests in the Moussaoui case were weightier than the interests that often justified withholding the identity of a confidential informant from a defendant.

Although the government refused to permit videotaped depositions of the three detainees, it conceded in its brief to the Fourth Circuit that it had an obligation under the Due Process Clause to turn over to Moussaoui any exculpatory evidence in its possession, including any written summaries of exculpatory statements made by the detainees to their interrogators. The Supreme Court had established this obligation in *Brady v. Maryland* (1963).[7] In its brief, the government acknowledged its obligation to turn over such exculpatory information to Moussaoui, but insisted that its compliance would be in accordance with the relevant provisions of CIPA. Although Judge Brinkema had found the government's substitutions in the Moussaoui case to be unreliable, incomplete, and inaccurate, she had not applied the proper standards because CIPA only required that the substitutions give a defendant "substantially the same ability" to present his defense, not "precisely" the same ability. Moreover, she had failed to appreciate that the "intelligence reports" of the detainees' interrogations were in fact reliable because they were distributed inside the intelligence community for the very purpose of preventing future terrorist attacks.

Lastly, the government argued that Judge Brinkema had abused her discretion by barring the government from introducing any evidence of Moussoui's involvement in the 9/11 attacks and by setting aside the death penalty. According to the government, Moussaoui was death eligible under the Federal Death Penalty Act because he was a major participant in the 9/11 attacks and because he did two acts that directly resulted in the 9/11 deaths (he joined the general al Qaeda conspiracy to kill Americans and he did not inform authorities of the upcoming attacks after he was arrested on immigration violations). Moreover, the government argued that the procedures and standards of CIPA offered a satisfactory solution to the defense's Eighth Amendment objection to the government's pursuit of the death penalty in Moussaoui's case. Although the Supreme Court had ruled in *Lockett v. Ohio* (1978) that a state could not restrict what a defendant convicted of a capital crime could present as mitigating evidence during the sentencing phase of the trial,[8] the evidence did not have to be in the form of direct or videotaped testimony. The government's proposed substitutions under CIPA would enable Moussaoui to get the relevant information to the sentencing jury, thereby avoiding an Eighth Amendment violation. In short, the government's compelling interest in national security justified limiting the form, but not the substance, of any mitigating evidence that Moussaoui decided to present at his sentencing hearing.

Moussaoui's lawyers sharply disputed the above arguments in the brief they filed with the Fourth Circuit in late November 2003. First, they insisted that Moussaoui's right of access to the detainees was grounded on the Fifth, Sixth, and Eighth Amendments. They rejected the relevance of *Johnson v. Eisentrager* and argued that Judge Brinkema was not intruding into the executive's war power, but rather was simply defending the autonomy of the judicial branch of government by insuring that Moussaoui received a fair trial. Moussaoui's brief denigrated the notion that there was any "national security exception" to the basic principle that criminal trials had to be fair, noting that the executive branch also had a constitutional obligation to provide defendants with a fair trial and that, under CIPA, the judge's focus was on whether the classified information was material and exculpatory, not on how seriously national security would be affected if the classified information was disclosed at trial. The latter issue was left to the attorney general, who could always decide that it was more important to protect the confidentiality of the classified information than it was to proceed with a trial that required its disclosure. In fact, if judges were to balance national security concerns against a defendant's need for exculpatory evidence, they would be doing exactly what government decried elsewhere: intruding into the functions of the executive branch.

In regard to the government's proposed substitutions, Moussaoui's lawyers endorsed Judge Brinkema's characterization of them as unreliable, incomplete, and inaccurate and highlighted the fact that they would not provide the jury with any basis to assess the credibility of the detainees. Moreover, some of the substitutions contained information adverse to Moussaoui. Their use at trial by the prosecution would violate Moussaoui's Sixth Amendment right to confront witnesses against him because he would have no opportunity to cross-examine a substitution. In contrast to the inadequacy of the government's proposed substitutions, Moussaoui's lawyers argued that Judge Brinkema's sanctions were perfectly appropriate, far removed from any sort of abuse of discretion. The elimination of the death penalty was justified since the government was refusing to produce witnesses whose testimony could make Moussaoui ineligible for the death penalty. The testimony of the three detainees was relevant to both whether Moussaoui was a major participant in the 9/11 attacks and whether any of his acts directly resulted in the 9/11 deaths. Also, excluding evidence of Moussaoui's participation in the 9/11 attacks was justified because the government was denying him access to witnesses who could testify regarding his non-involvement.

EXCERPTS FROM THE GOVERNMENT'S BRIEF

[[*Editor's note*: Single bracketed material in the excerpts from the briefs, transcripts of oral argument, and the opinion itself are from the original. Anything in double brackets has been added. Standard ellipses indicate material deleted from quotations in the original or, if the ellipses appear outside quotations, material that the editor has deleted from the excerpts. Underlined blank text shows the amount of text that the government has redacted from the published versions of the briefs, transcripts, or opinions on grounds of national security. Since it is not impossible to discern the meaning of certain of these redacted passages, the reader is urged to consider what specific words have been redacted. It would seem that certain words or phrases, such as "statement," "interrogation," "interrogation process," "intelligence reports," "intelligence summaries," and "intelligence officials," were routinely redacted from the briefs, transcripts of oral arguments, and the judicial opinion itself. Footnotes in the excerpts are from the original source. All citations, subsection titles, and parenthetical passages from the briefs and the opinion have been deleted.]]

[[1. Sixth Amendment Right to Compulsory Process.]] . . . Under the district court's decision, any defendant charged with criminal responsibility for terrorist operation related to al Qaeda will be able to make a plausible claim to have access to these combatants. The district court's analysis puts the Government to the choice of either gathering intelligence to maximize the prospect for avoiding future terrorist attacks *or* prosecuting terrorists. However, nothing in the Constitution puts the Government on the horns of this dilemma. . . .

The district court's unprecedented plan for deposing enemy combatants overseas ignores fundamental limits on its authority and provides defendant a breathtaking right to interfere with the conduct of warfare—a right that the Compulsory Process Clause simply does not grant. The Compulsory Process Clause does not provide an absolute guarantee of the ability to secure witnesses. Rather, it is well settled that "the right to compulsory process is not absolute."

In particular, the Clause guarantees a defendant only the right to the process a court can provide consistent with its jurisdiction. As a result, it is settled, for example, that compulsory process provides no right to secure alien witnesses from overseas, who are beyond the court's reach. The Sixth Amendment ensures that the court's process is available to the defendant; it does not guarantee the presence of every witness. . . .

The district court erred by failing to recognize that the witnesses at issue here are beyond the reach of its process. . . . As alien enemy combatants seized and detained overseas, _____ are beyond the power of the Court to compel their testimony. As explained below, no United States court has the authority to exercise jurisdiction over such alien enemy combatants, even by means of a writ of habeas corpus. And defendant's compulsory process rights provide no ground for extending the court's authority to interfere in an area—the conduct of war—where it otherwise would be powerless to act.

In *Johnson v. Eisentrager* (1950), a case involving German prisoners held overseas in the aftermath of World War II, the Supreme Court definitively established that there is no basis for exercising federal judicial power in habeas corpus over alien enemy combatants held overseas. There, the German prisoners sought to challenge their detention by means of habeas corpus. In con-

cluding that the courts had no authority to entertain their claims, the Supreme
Court explained that the exercise of such power by the court would exceed
their proper role, interfere with military operations, and thereby "hamper the
war effort and bring aid and comfort to the enemy." . . .

The separation-of-powers principles that dictated the result in *Eisentrager*
apply equally in this case. . . .

The district court's unprecedented plan . . . enables the defense to interfere
with the determination that military _____ officers have made concerning the best means for pursuing their critical mission of obtaining intelligence from the combatants. The plan, and the court's dismissal of the Executive Branch's concerns with it, highlight the dangers of permitting courts
managing domestic litigation to assert piecemeal control over military
_____ operations.

First, and foremost, the depositions will critically undermine efforts

_____

_____

_____

_____ would irretrievably
cripple painstaking efforts for securing the flow of information. The district
court disregarded the Government's submissions on this point in favour of its
own assessment of the impact the depositions would have. In the court's view

_____

_____

_____

_____. This assessment took precedence over the declaration
of a senior Government _____ official detailing how interference
_____ would jeopardize national security. The
courts, however, are in no position to second-guess such Executive Branch
judgments.

Indeed, the district court went so far as to suggest that removing these enemy combatants from their current carefully structured environment and putting them in front of a video camera to answer questions from defendant and
American criminal defense lawyers would actually enhance efforts to obtain
intelligence. . . . But here again, the judgment of military _____ ex-
perts who have experience in securing valuable intelligence from enemy combatants should not be disregarded by judges more familiar with ordinary criminal defendants. . . .

Second, the court rejected the Government's concern that ordering access
to the combatants would "divert the military's attention from its offensive efforts abroad" with the dismissive observation that _____

_____

_____. Again, assessments of the responsibilities of _____ officers in the field and their relative importance to the war effort are paradigmatically matters that are not for federal district courts to second-guess. Equally important, the asserted dichotomy between "offensive efforts abroad" (which the court equated with "decisions on the battlefield") and the detention of prisoners is a false one. The detention of enemy combatants is part and parcel of the ongoing struggle with al Qaeda. Here, in a war where the enemy refuses to engage our regular forces in the field and instead attacks only by stealth, the intelligence front is the critical battleground, and the officers who are intimately involved in the detention and interrogation of key al Qaeda leaders are precisely those who make the vital "daily decisions on the battlefield." The district court's flawed assumptions thus simply reinforce a point this Court recently emphasized: "[t]he federal courts have many strengths, but the conduct of combat operations has been left to others."

Third, as explained in _____ Declarations, the depositions will undermine _____

_____

_____

_____

_____

_____. As the Court in *Eisentrager* warned, having judges countermand military decisions "would diminish the prestige of our commanders," particularly in the eyes of "wavering neutrals," who might come to see assurances of our officers as ineffective and unreliable.

Finally, the district court failed to anticipate a host of other issues that will inevitably arise in connection with the depositions and could further undermine efforts to gather intelligence. For example, are _____ entitled to counsel and would they invoke the privilege against self-incrimination in this criminal proceeding? Defense counsel will, after all, ask them questions under oath that will squarely implicate them in capital crimes, and it seems unlikely that—at least in an ordinary case—the district court would permit a witness under oath to answer such questions without counsel and advice of rights. Providing these enemy combatants a lawyer, of course, will likely end forever the possibility of securing further intelligence from them. _____. The Government takes no position on any of these questions; but they demonstrate how disruptive the unprecedented plan for deposing enemy combatants will be and the dangers of disregarding the views of those charged with gathering intelligence.

It makes no sense, furthermore, to think that the apprehension of an enemy combatant by our forces overseas should somehow bring that prisoner within the authority of a federal court hearing a criminal case or expand the rights of a criminal defendant to obtain witnesses. Before his capture, such an overseas alien was a fugitive member of an enemy force wholly beyond the court's power and unavailable to any defendant as a witness. The action of our _____ officers abroad—unconnected with domestic law enforcement—in capturing such a person provides no logical basis for concluding that federal district courts hearing criminal cases should suddenly be able to exert authority over such a prisoner through the processes of the criminal law at the behest of a criminal defendant in disregard of the war-related imperatives that led to the capture. . . .

Finally, the district court's approach would permit al Qaeda terrorists on trial in the United States to hold the conduct of the war hostage to claims that refusal to produce various detainees violated their constitutional rights. Indeed, as more and more high-level leaders of al Qaeda are detained by our forces, claims identical to the one in this case, if permitted, would undoubtedly become terrorist defendants' favorite trump card, for they would guarantee either the hobbling of a prosecution or the hobbling of interrogation efforts directed at al Qaeda leaders overseas. In short, the district court's approach would allow terrorists on trial to manufacture precisely the "conflict between judicial and military opinion highly comforting to the enemies of the United States" that the Supreme Court decisively foreclosed by restricting federal court authority in habeas corpus in *Eisentrager*. As in *Eisentrager*, the proper rule here is that federal courts lack authority to issue a writ controlling the disposition of alien enemy combatants overseas. . . .

. . . [[T]]he rule that a defendant has no right to obtain alien witnesses from overseas reflects both the limits on the courts' jurisdiction and fundamental separation-of-powers principles. It is often not impossible for the Executive to take steps to secure an alien's presence at a trial—perhaps through requests under a mutual legal assistance treaty. Nevertheless, courts have refused to read the Compulsory Process Clause to confer on a criminal defendant a right to have a court order the Executive to undertake diplomatic efforts to obtain a witness from abroad. As the D.C. Circuit has explained in rejecting a request to direct the State Department to enter negotiations with France to free an American from prison there, "the commencement of diplomatic negotiations with a foreign power is completely in the discretion of the President and the head of the Department of State, who is a political agent. The Executive is not subject to judicial control or direction in such matters."

Similar separation-of-powers principles limit the scope of compulsory process when defendants seek to force the Government to grant a witness immunity. Courts routinely reject the claim that a defendant's compulsory process rights can give the court the power to order the prosecution to grant immunity. . . .

[[2. Due Process.]] It is important to recognize that if the Court rules that the Compulsory Process Clause does not give defendant the right to elicit trial testimony from alien enemy combatants held overseas, that ruling will not conclusively resolve the question whether any information from these combatants can ever be presented in some form to the jury. In compliance with its obligations under *Brady v. Maryland*, the Government has been providing, as necessary, classified summaries _____ to the defense. If, at trial, the defense believes it has material exculpatory evidence, including evidence derived from the classified summaries _____, it can seek to have that evidence admitted. In evaluating defendant's request, the district court will apply the rules of evidence in light of the guarantees of a fundamentally fair trial under the Due Process Clause and with an understanding that evidentiary rules cannot be applied "mechanistically" to exclude reliable exculpatory evidence. Moreover, . . . if there is a penalty phase in this trial, the Eighth Amendment may provide defendant even more flexibility with regard to the introduction of mitigating evidence.

To be sure, the evidence may not be available in precisely the form—direct testimony—the defendant would prefer. But, . . . while the Due Process Clause ensures fundamental fairness, it does not require the government to ensure that all evidence the defendant wants is placed before the jury.

[[3. Balancing of Interests.]] Even if the enemy combatants were within the reach of the district court's process; that would not provide defendant an absolute right to secure their presence at trial. Rather, compulsory process rights may give way to "countervailing public interests." It is settled that where the Government has a legitimate interest in foreclosing access to a potential witness—even the routine interest in protecting the identity of a police informant or ensuring the timely identification of defense witnesses—a court must "balance[e] the public interest in protecting the flow of information against the individual's right to prepare his defense." . . .

Here, the district court failed to give any serious consideration to the required balancing. . . .

Had the district court properly balanced the competing interests, it would have been obvious that the balance overwhelmingly tips in favour of the vital national security interests that demand foreclosing any access _____ _____. The Nation is currently engaged in an armed conflict with an enemy force that has already killed more than 3,000 individuals in attacks carried out within the continental United States and hundreds more in attacks on U.S. embassies, warships, and other interests abroad. The interest at stake in this case involves paramount concerns of protecting national security by preserving the Government's ability to gather intelligence vital to saving American lives and winning this ongoing war. As the Supreme Court has admonished, it is "'obvious and unarguable' that no government interest is more compelling than the security of the Nation." . . .

. . . It requires no stretch to recognize that, once al Qaeda operatives realize that they can use the legal system to disrupt _____ by claiming a right to secure their testimony, they will eagerly exploit the opportunity to put the Government to the choice between effective intelligence gathering and effective prosecution.* Moreover, once al Qaeda combatants realize that any false exculpatory statements could result in the dismissal of prosecutions against their comrades, the abuses would only multiply.

The national security interests at stake in this case overwhelmingly tip the balance in favor of denying the defense requests for the trial testimony of the combatants. In fact, courts have routinely found that government interests far less compelling than those present here permit foreclosing access to witnesses or other information. For example, courts have concluded that threats to the Government's ability to root out conventional criminal activity merit denying the defendant the disclosure of the identity of an informant. If the threat to one witness's safety or protecting ordinary ongoing criminal investigations can be sufficiently compelling to deny a defendant access to witnesses, it follows *a fortiori* that the grave national security risks posed here are sufficiently compelling to reject the defense motions, especially where defendant has not demonstrated a countervailing compelling need for testimony from these combatants. . . .

[[4. Adequacy of Substitutions.]] . . . [[According to CIPA, the]] district court must allow a substitution if it will provide the defendant with "substantially the same ability" to present his defense as would disclosure of the specific classified information. However, "substantially" does not mean precisely. Therefore a substitution is sufficient if it "provide[s] the gist of the defense in virtual entirety although not necessarily the minutia." . . .

The Government's proposed substitutions fully satisfy the standard under CIPA because they provide defendant with substantially the same ability to make his defense as if the combatants provided the allegedly material statements during depositions. Simply put, the substitutions incorporate the specific statements the district court identified as being material. As such, they allow the defense to make use of the classified information identified as material by the district court, even if not presented in the form of deposition testimony. . . .

[[6. Sanctions.]] . . . The basic logic behind the district court's approach seems to have been that if defendant was not himself a part of the specific

---

* These are only some of the primary dangers raised by the defense motions. _____ Declarations explain in more detail both the concerns outlined in text and other risks to national security that are too sensitive to be set forth here.

September 11 attacks (the proposition that the district court concluded the enemy combatants' testimony would support), he cannot be eligible for the death penalty based on the deaths that resulted on September 11. But that fundamentally misunderstands the applicable law and the two specific bases on which the Government has sought the death penalty in this case. The Government has argued that defendant is eligible for the death penalty because: (i) he lied at the time of his arrest to conceal the forthcoming attacks and, (ii) while possessing an admitted specific intent to kill Americans, he played a significant role in an overall conspiracy that resulted in the deaths of 3,000 innocent victims. Whether defendant was to participate in the first (September 11) or second wave of attacks by flying a plane into an American building is irrelevant to either basis for seeking the death penalty. Thus, for example, the purported testimony, which, at best, suggests that defendant was part of a second wave of members of al Qaeda flying planes into American buildings, has no impact upon defendant's death eligibility.

Moreover, as to evidence of mitigating factors, even taking _____ statements in the light most favorable to defendant, the relaxed evidentiary standard for the penalty phase . . . might permit the defense to introduce relevant information gathered from the combatants to show that defendant played a "minor role" in the September 11 plot. . . . However, the same relaxed evidentiary standard which allows for the broader introduction of information at the penalty phase also provides for a relaxed evidentiary standard as to the *form* of the information. The use of substitutions, summarily rejected by the district court, properly could be used by the defense in their efforts to establish the mitigating factor of "minor role." Thus, the district court abused its discretion when it dismissed the death penalty notice and thereby deprived the community of an opportunity to consider a proper sentence in this case.

The district court's sanction deprives the community of its voice in sentencing defendant, an admitted member of al Qaeda, who participated in the most heinous crime ever committed on American soil. . . .

Dismissal of the death notice and all evidence related to September 11 also sends a troubling message to the family members of the victims. Not only will they no longer be able to testify concerning the impact of the crime during the capital sentencing hearing . . . , but the district court's ruling also casts substantial doubt on whether they will be allowed to allocute during defendant's noncapital sentencing hearing, given the apparent wholesale exclusion of the September 11 attack from this case. While the rights of this admitted terrorist undoubtedly deserve protection, the criminal justice system ought to work for the victims as well. . . .

Defendant's own judicial admissions demonstrate . . . [[that he]] was an active participant in a coordinated plan of attack upon the United States that included flying planes into American buildings, regardless of whether the attack was to come in one or two waves. Instead of his lying at the time of his arrest, defendant should have truthfully answered, at the very minimum, that: (1) I am a member of al Qaeda and I have pledged *bayat* (allegiance) to Usama bin Laden; (2) I was sent to the United States to take flight training to fly a plane into a building in the U.S.;* (3) Bin Laden personally approved my participation in the attack; (4) I am part of an attack that includes others who will fly planes into American buildings; and (5) my contacts are KSM and Ahad Sabet (a/k/a Bin al-Shibh). . . .

Respectfully submitted,
PAUL J. MCNULTY,
United States Attorney

EXCERPTS FROM MOUSSAOUI'S BRIEF

No matter how well the Government dresses up its arguments, the truth is that it seeks absolute power to withhold material, exculpatory witnesses in a death penalty case without suffering sanctions. This absolute power extends to all matters of inquiry related to the witnesses. We cannot know their current location, or the circumstances or conditions under which they are being held _____. We surely cannot talk to them, communicate with them, or use their testimony live in court. In the name of national security, the Government would have us pretend that these critical witnesses simply do not exist and try this capital case anyway. In place of the constitutional protections that have been erected to give a defendant a fair trial, we are told to just trust summaries authored by the Government of what it says these witnesses would say. Courts have done this in the past to their peril. . . .

The Government says that the district court's analysis threatens the Government's ability to prosecute any terrorists for the crimes of September 11 in other cases. It argues that "any defendant charged with criminal responsibility for terrorist operations related to al-Qaeda will be able to make a plausible claim [for] access to [enemy] combatants" and that the logical extension of the district court's analysis to *other cases* put the Government to "the choice of either gathering intelligence to maximize the prospects for avoiding future terrorist attacks or prosecuting terrorists." The Government is simply "crying wolf." . . .

---

* Other evidence regarding defendant's statements prove that the White House was his intended target.

[[1. Moussaoui's Constitutional Rights.]] The district court's ruling that Moussaoui has a right of access to the testimony of _____ favourable witnesses _____ is rooted in the Sixth Amendment, the Due Process Clause, and the Eighth Amendment. . . .

The power to issue a writ *ad testificandum* [[an order compelling a witness to appear at a judicial proceeding]] comes from the Sixth Amendment's Compulsory Process Clause. As the Supreme Court has indicated, whether a prisoner/witness can be procured by this means turns on whether the custodian of the prisoner, not the prisoner himself, is within the reach of the court's process, for it is upon the custodian that the writ is directed and served, not the prisoner. . . .

. . . Accordingly, the issue of whether the testimony of the witnesses can be procured by writ *ad testificandum*, as the district court held, turns on whether a U.S. custodian of the prisoner witnesses held abroad, not the witnesses themselves, are reachable by the process of the district court. _____ _____. Here, of course, the ultimate custodian of the witnesses is within the reach of the district court's process.

Citing *United States v. Zabaneh* (1988), the Government argues that "compulsory process provides no right to secure alien witnesses from overseas, who are beyond the court's reach." This, of course, states the obvious and is not the issue here. The issue is whether alien witnesses abroad *in the _____ control of the Government* are "beyond the court's reach." That the witnesses here are in the Government's _____ control, and could be produced for testimony if the Government wanted to produce them, is conceded. Compulsory process can be used to obtain such evidence when all that is required is for the Government to act. . . .

It is the right of a defendant to a fair trial in a case initiated by the Government that the district court is protecting when it acts to issue a writ *ad testificandum*, not rights asserted by enemy alien combatant witnesses. In doing so, the district court does not question the judgment of the Executive to detain the enemy combatant witnesses; it seeks their testimony so that it can perform its own Article III function. The Government's position rests on the flawed premise that a district court order issued to ensure a fair trial in proceedings before it violates separation-of-powers principles if it somehow interferes with the Executive's national security prerogatives. However, to deny Moussaoui access to these witnesses on national security grounds, without a sufficiently compensating sanction, would be a separation-of-powers concern of a different kind. The intrusion would be by the Executive upon the Article III court's quintessential duty to insure a fair trial, not an intrusion by the court on the Executive war-making power.

The Government's flawed separation-of-powers premise is grounded upon its unwarranted extension of the rationale used in *Johnson v. Eisentrager* (1950). Whatever role separation-of-powers concerns may have played in denying Great Writ relief to the alien enemy petitioners abroad in *Eisentrager* where Article II powers were used as a "shield," they certainly do not come into play to deny a writ *ad testificandum* to Moussaoui where the Government itself has invoked the jurisdiction of the court as a "sword."

The signal distinction between this capital case and *Eisentrager*, is that the latter is a civil habeas corpus case where petitioners initiated the litigation seeking to invoke the jurisdiction of the Article III courts to second-guess military decisions relating to their detention. . . .

Further, none of the specific holdings in *Eisentrager* apply here. That Court held that the petitioners had no "standing to . . . sue . . . for a writ of *habeas corpus*." Conversely, the petitioner here is a defendant in a capital case and certainly has standing to seek a writ of habeas corpus *ad testificandum* in exercise of his rights under the Constitution.

Second, in *Eisentrager*, the Court held that the petitioners, as enemy aliens detained abroad, had no Fifth Amendment protection. Contrary to those petitioners, Moussaoui, a criminal defendant, has Fifth Amendment protection.

Finally, *Eisentrager* concludes that the petition in that case did not state a claim for relief. Here, Moussaoui's petition, by making a substantial showing of his need for the testimony of these witnesses, has made a facially valid claim. . . .

It is likewise of no moment to say that "many individual rights guaranteed by the Constitution will not be construed to reach so far as to interfere with the Executive's conduct of war." Even the President, when exercising his constitutionally bestowed powers to wage war, maintain national security, and conduct foreign affairs, is constrained by other provisions of the Constitution.

Thus, the Executive, even in the midst of war, does not have the power to avoid, by withholding relevant and material evidence, its own constitutional obligations to see that justice is served in a criminal case. . . .*

---

* The Government's analogy to defense witness immunity cases as an example of where separation-of-powers principles limit the scope of compulsory process is misplaced. A defendant does not have a right to defense witness immunity, so he has no basis to demand it. This contrasts sharply with the instant situation where Moussoui has a constitutional and statutory right to use the processes of the court to obtain the testimony of witnesses. In the immunity context, it is not the Government that is depriving the defendant of the evidence, but the witness who is asserting his privilege against self-incrimination. In such a situation, the defendant is powerless to demand production of the evidence as his right to exculpatory evidence cannot displace a constitutional claim of Fifth Amendment right by the witness. The Government, which is constitutionally obligated to assist in obtaining the presence of that witness, is not obligated to provide that witness protection from his own criminal acts by providing immunity.

The Government, thus, is wrong when it implies that it cannot be forced to choose between competing Executive Branch responsibilities, namely, between executing Moussaoui and gathering additional intelligence. . . . When the Government, because of some competing interest, chooses to withhold exculpatory evidence that the district court has ordered produced, the Supreme Court has specifically stated that the Government cannot avoid choosing between safeguarding its secrets and its prosecution. . . .

. . . [[The]] district court's ruling hardly amounts, as the Government describes it, to "micro-managing the conduct of the war [on terrorism]," or as an unwarranted intrusion on the Executive's ability to conduct war. Indeed, the district court strove to minimize the impact of its rulings on national security. First, the court denied any access to _____ witnesses sought by the defense. Second, pretrial access to _____ witnesses as well as trial access was denied. Finally, all the district court ordered the Government to do was to make the witnesses available for depositions, and even then under most restrictive circumstances. _____
_____. The district court could hardly have been more deferential to the Government's national security concerns without compromising its own duty and obligation to assure the Defendant a fair trial. . . .

Finally, it is worth remembering that an important component of a defendant's due process rights is *Brady*'s obligation requiring the production of favorable evidence. *Brady* "is not a discovery rule, but a rule of fairness and minimum prosecutorial obligation." Under *Brady*, the Government is obligated to produce to the defense all exculpatory evidence in its possession. The witnesses here are exculpatory, so they must be produced. There is no exception to this rule _____.

Even assuming that the district court was required to proceed without the witnesses in the event the Government's Sixth Amendment/separation-of-powers arguments were to prevail, the Eighth Amendment would nevertheless bar imposition of the death penalty. Simply put, even assuming that the Government may be entitled to withhold the witnesses because the Sixth Amendment Compulsory Process Clause does not reach overseas, the Eighth cannot tolerate a death sentence where the Government has control over, but will not produce, witnesses who could exculpate the Defendant on the issue of death. . . .

What is clear is that the Eighth Amendment—the Constitution's embodiment of "the dignity of man"—cannot, on the one hand, prohibit the execution of one who has, at most, played a minor role in a capital offense, and on the other hand, countenance a proceeding in which the Government seeks the death penalty even as it declines to provide trial access to the very witnesses whose testimony could render the Defendant ineligible for the death penalty *under that same constitutional provision.* . . .

[[2. Balancing of Interests.]] The district court found that to deny the limited access to the witnesses it has ordered would deny the Defendant a fair trial. Notwithstanding, the Government argues that its national security interests are particularly vital in this case. It says the district court should have weighed the Government's particular national security interests here differently than it did and that the court should have denied access to the witnesses because the national security concerns are so overwhelming.

[[The Government's position]] . . . is breathtaking in that it suggests that a criminal defendant's due process rights can be eclipsed if the court finds that the Government's national security interests in a given case are particularly compelling. It is unprecedented in that neither the courts nor Congress have ever suggested that the Government can protect its national security interests by denying a fair trial, no matter how compelling those interests might be.

Requiring courts to evaluate the seriousness of particular national security implications in order to weigh them against a defendant's need for exculpatory evidence invites the courts into the very separation-of-powers thicket the Government so decries. How is the court to distinguish an "ordinary" national security claim from an extraordinary one? How is an appellate court to determine whether a district court gave too little or too much weight to the Government's national security concerns? Total deference to the Executive in this regard is not the answer because it would inexorably lead to executive veto power over defense witnesses in the name of national security. This is a proposition explicitly rejected by the Founders and which is ripe for prosecutorial abuse.

The district court here, faced with a Government claim that national security would be adversely affected by granting defense access to the witnesses at issue, followed traditional methods for untangling national security concerns from fair trial rights and protected both by analogizing to CIPA procedures. Under CIPA, this Court has said "courts must not be remiss in protecting a defendant's right to a full and meaningful presentation of his claim of innocence." Nothing in CIPA requires the district court to consider the potential damage from a particular disclosure of classified information when determining whether to authorize disclosure. Thus, it matters not under CIPA whether the classified information at issue consists of the most sensitive technical details of our most advanced nuclear missile or information which appear to border on the innocuous, as classified information often does.

Whether a Defendant is entitled to use the evidence or not turns on whether it can be shown that it is material and exculpatory, not on how seriously national security would be impaired by its disclosure. CIPA protects all classified information against unauthorized disclosure for reasons of national security. If it is classified, it is protected by CIPA which treats all classified information, insofar as the courts are concerned, as fungible and leaves it to the Attorney General to decide whether damage from a particular disclosure ordered by the court can be tolerated. In following those procedures as closely as it could, even though its initial access orders were discovery orders, not CIPA disclosure orders, the district court's order protects the Defendant's right to a fair trial while preserving the Government's ability to proceed with its prosecution.

[[3. Government's Substitutions.]] . . . The district court rejected the . . . Substitutions _____ because . . . [[they are]] unreliable, incomplete, and inaccurate/misleading. . . .

. . . [[T]]he district court's ruling on the adequacy of [[the Substitutions]] . . . is correct, well supported, and by any measure, not an abuse of discretion. Likewise, the district court's rejection of the proposed Substitutions for the deposition testimony _____ is not an abuse of discretion. These Substitutes suffer from the same core deficiencies. . . .

In addition, live testimony _____

_____

_____would make any jury verdict and sentence much more reliable because it would provide some basis for assessing demeanor. It is for this reason, no doubt, that the district court insisted that the Substitutions "accommodate some form of defense interaction or input." It is also why the law prefers live testimony over hearsay.

The Government's proposed Substitutions _____ would eliminate demeanor evidence altogether. The proposed faceless, colorless, inanimate Substitutions provide no basis for the jury to evaluate _____ credibility. All the Substitutions offer are hearsay recitations of what the Government says its summaries _____ and they do so without any concession as to the truth of information favorable to Moussaoui appearing therein. This leaves the Government free to ask the jury to infer and/or find facts contrary to the Substitutions—and indeed, free to introduce evidence in contradiction to the Substitutions. At least with a live witness, Moussaoui can reap the benefit of whatever credibility the jury assigns to the witness' testimony in order to mitigate the force of any contrary evidence the Government might adduce. . . .

Finally, _____ Substitutions, _____ include adverse information that the Government would endeavor to elicit _____ not just information that the defense would seek to elicit. The Substitutions thus contain information from statements _____ that the defense would not even seek to use. Accordingly, the Government's approach results in substitutes that are far too broad, violating Moussaoui's Confrontation Clause rights.

The Government argues that Moussaoui's Confrontation Clause rights are not implicated because the defense, not the Government, is the proponent of the witnesses' testimony. However, Moussaoui has a constitutional right under the Confrontation Clause to confront adverse evidence in the Substitutions even though _____ defense witnesses. As the district court held, the confrontation right "include[s] the opportunity to examine a witness on redirect who inculpates the accused on cross-examination."

On this point the district court is entirely correct. The fact _____ _____ "defense" witnesses is not the critical determinant for Confrontation Clause purposes. As this Court has noted, "[t]he critical matter is not the formal status of a witness but the actual content of his testimony." What is critical is whether the testimony to be confronted is adverse to the Defendant, that is, whether the testimony is incriminatory. Thus, the mere fact _____ are called by the defense does not invalidate operation of the Confrontation Clause, particularly given that the Government is "the proponent of the Substitution[s].". . .

[[4. The Sanctions.]] As a sanction for the Government's refusal to obey the district court's orders directing access to the witnesses, the district court declined to dismiss the indictment, which was the remedy the defense requested and the Government did not oppose. Instead, the court struck the death penalty and precluded the Government from presenting "any evidence or argument that the defendant was involved in, or had knowledge of, the planning or execution of the attacks of September 11, 2001.". . .

The Government asserts that the district court abused its discretion in striking the death penalty because the Eighth Amendment does not expand the scope of the Compulsory Process Clause. But, that is not the issue. Rather, the issue is whether, once the Government refuses to make available witnesses whose testimony could make the Defendant ineligible for the death penalty, or could otherwise significantly influence the jury's ultimate penalty decision, does the trial court abuse its discretion when it strikes the death penalty from the case as a sanction. The answer to that question clearly is "no" . . . .

The Government . . . asserts that the district court's decision was premised on the erroneous belief that the Defendant's death eligibility may not be predicated on the deaths inflicted on September 11 if "[he] was not himself part of [those] attacks." Yet, the Government has not cited a single case in which a defendant, convicted *solely* of conspiracy, has been found death eligible in relation to a homicide committed by other members of the conspiracy in an event in which the Defendant did not actually participate. The district court, likewise, could find no such authority.

The implications of the Government's argument are dangerous and far-reaching. If accepted, the Government's position would make every member of al-Qaeda who "played a significant role in [the] *overall conspiracy*," death eligible in relation to every killing committed by another member of the conspiracy, irrespective of his knowledge or participation in the homicide at issue. So, too, it would render every "significant" member of the Mafia or a drug conspiracy death eligible for every murder committed by every other member of the organization. Indeed, the Government concedes as much when it argues that Moussaoui's death eligibility may be predicated solely on his participation in the overall conspiracy. Nothing in the Supreme Court's jurisprudence suggests that the Eighth Amendment would countenance such a broad rule of vicarious death eligibility, as the district court properly held. To the contrary, it would be inconsistent with the basic principles of personal culpability that underlie the Supreme Court's capital jurisprudence.

The ramification of the Government's theory of death eligibility are made starkly apparent by its argument that the Defendant's death eligibility also may be predicated on his alleged lies to Government agents while in custody, even though it appears to concede that those lies alone could not satisfy the constitutional requirement of major participation. Thus, while these lies provide an "act" upon which the Government relies to establish statutory liability, that is, an act which directly resulted in the deaths of the victims, it relies not on the act, but on his conduct within the broader al-Qaeda conspiracy to establish major participation. It cites no case that supports such a disjointed theory of death eligibility.

Moreover, even assuming such a theory is legally supportable, the Government's factual argument is not. The Government's argument that testimony that the Defendant lacked detailed information about the September 11 plot "would be *utterly irrelevant*" to its position that his lies "prevented discovery of the September 11 attacks" is inexplicable. Since the Government must prove not only that the Defendant lied, but that the victims died as a "direct result" of those lies, testimony tending to undermine the causal link between Moussaoui's alleged deceptions and the success of the September 11 attacks is plainly relevant and material to the question of death eligibility. . . .

Finally, it appears to be the Government's position that Moussaoui's right to fairly defend himself may be sacrificed on the alter of public "retribution." Distilled to its essence, the Government's argument is that, however unfair the process may be for the Defendant as a result of the Government's decision to deny him access to the witnesses, dismissal of the death notice was inappropriate because it will deprive the victims of their entitlement to the ultimate punishment. While the Government may make such consideration part of its calculus in determining whether to risk its ability to seek the death penalty, it surely can not elevate the victims' retributive interests to a factor to be balanced by the district court against Moussaoui's right to a fair trial. If as the Government says, "the punishment should fit the crime," so too the process should fit the punishment. That is precisely why the Supreme Court adopted the principle of "heightened reliability" in capital cases. Surely, the Court should reject the Government's invitation to tread upon this slippery slope. . . .

Similarly, the district court did not err in imposing evidentiary sanctions . . . [[by precluding evidence of Moussaouoi's involvement in the 9/11 attacks.]]

. . . This action was entirely appropriate. The court found that it is unfair to allow the Government to rely on the events of September 11 to prove its case while simultaneously preventing Moussaoui from relying on witnesses who could disprove his involvement in or knowledge of those events. The district court did not "ignore[ ] fundamental axioms of conspiracy law, rather, it correctly applied them to protect Moussaoui's fair trial rights. . . .

Respectfully submitted this 14th day of November, 2003,

FRANK W. DUNHAM,
Federal Public Defender

III. ORAL ARGUMENT

The Fourth Circuit heard oral argument in the Moussaoui case on December 3, 2003, two weeks after truck bombs went off in Istanbul, Turkey, killing fifty-seven and wounding seven hundred people. As in June, the argument was split into two parts: a secret classified session in the morning and an open public one in the afternoon. The excerpts below are from the afternoon session. What transpired in the morning session is unknown, but traces of what issues were debated occasionally appear in passages from the public session. One such oblique reference to the morning session concerned the government's argument that the capture of the three detainees should not be a windfall for Moussaoui. Judge Wilkins suggested that this argument was not all that persuasive since the government conceded that the detainees would be subject to a court's jurisdiction if they were detained inside the United States, a result that would also be a windfall for Moussaoui. Deputy Solicitor General Paul Clement argued that the difference was that in the latter case the courts were not expanding their powers, but Judge Wilkins referred to a hypothetical example that had been discussed in the morning session: an American prison in Mexico whose warden was a citizen. If a federal judge could order the warden to appear and testify on behalf of a criminal defendant on trial in the United States, why could the judge not order the warden to produce an alien in his custody for the same purpose? Clement claimed a judge could order the warden to appear, but could not order the warden to produce the alien. Judge

Gregory was unconvinced because, in his view, the "purpose of our courts is to seek truth." The fact that the capture of the three detainees was a windfall for Moussaoui was irrelevant. For Gregory, the crux of the matter was the independent nature of the judiciary and its constitutional obligation to provide criminal defendants with fair trials.

In a second exchange with Judge Gregory, Clement tried to clarify the government's rationale for seeking the death penalty for Moussaoui by introducing an analogy of a general conspiracy to rob two banks. If there was a general conspiracy to rob two banks and leave no witnesses alive, and if co-conspirator A only had a role in killing witnesses at the second robbery, and if this conspirator was arrested before the first bank robbery but refused to tell the police anything about the conspiracy, then he would have been a conspirator who had engaged in conduct that directly resulted in all the deaths at the first bank robbery, even if the second bank robbery never took place. Referring to this analogy, Clement argued that, even if co-conspirators B, C, and D would testify that co-conspirator A only had a role in the second bank robbery, they would nonetheless be providing inculpatory evidence of his guilt for conspiracy to commit bank robbery. The implication of Clement's analogy was that Moussaoui only had a right to the testimony of the detainees at the sentencing phase of his trial, at which time, according to the Federal Death Penalty Statute, the defense's objections to the use of substitutions had little weight.

The exchanges between the Fourth Circuit judges and Edward B. MacMahon, one of Moussaoui's standby counsel, also raised interesting issues. First, Judge Williams wanted to know why the defense were demanding live interaction with the detainee witnesses when Moussaoui himself, in open court and in various court filings, had stated that he knew about the September 11 attacks, that he was a member of al Qaeda, and that Osama bin Laden had personally sent Moussaoui to the United States to take flight training for the purpose of flying a plane into a building. MacMahon tried to explain away the significance of Moussaoui's statements by claiming that at least some of them were his foolish attempts to chide the government. But since Moussaoui had made all these incriminating statements, Judge Williams asked, why should the Fourth Circuit not wait until after the trial to review the constitutionality of the government's use of substitutions. After the trial, the appellate court would have a full record to review and it would know the exact character of the substitutions. Trying once again to defuse the significance of Moussaoui's incriminating statements, MacMahon suggested that Moussaoui was a "wannabe," someone who wished he had participated in the 9/11 attacks but who could not be fairly tried for what happened on 9/11 on that basis, at least not without the videotaped testimony of the detainees. What Judge Brinkema was saying, MacMahon claimed, was that the government could not use Moussaoui's incriminating statements to prove that he had lied when he had the opportunity to stop the 9/11 attacks and also to prevent the videotaped testimony of the three detainees. The incriminating statements could not be both the basis for Mousssaoui's death eligibility and the basis for denying him access to exculpatory evidence. Such a result, according to MacMahon, was unfair and a violation of due process.

Judge Wilkins wanted to know why properly drafted substitutions would not be strategically valuable for the defense, since live witnesses were often unpredictable or not very credible, especially under cross-examination. MacMahon did not deny Wilkins's point, but argued that the problem was that the government was "imposing" this alternative on Moussaoui, thus becoming "the architect of the defense," the same charge MacMahon had levelled at the session of oral argument in June 2003. Even if reliance on substitutions was not a great burden in itself, it was intolerable because it was the government that was imposing it. In addition, MacMahon argued, a jury could not assess the demeanor of the detainee witnesses through written substitutions and the government would deflate the credibility of the substitutions at trial by claiming that "these are just terrorists lying for each other."

Judge Wilkins hinted that perhaps the substitutions would be adequate if the defense, rather than the prosecution, crafted them from the intelligence summaries. MacMahon expressed his reservations about crafting substitutions for a witness that he had never met, but Judge Wilkins opined that MacMahon could craft such substitutions if there was a deceased witness who had left some writing behind that was relevant and material to a criminal case. MacMahon objected that the two cases were different because the writings of a deceased witness "was the entirety of what I had to work with," while, if given an opportunity to depose them, he could ask the detainee witnesses questions beyond the information contained in the intelligence summaries. Moreover, since the interrogations of the three detainees were ongoing, the detainees could yet disclose information that was exculpatory for Moussaoi, but it would not be included in the summaries or the substitutions. The advantage of a live witness, MacMahon urged, was that "you could put on all the questions and all the answers at one time." Lastly, MacMahon defended the sanctions that Judge Brinkema had imposed on the government. Far from being an abuse of discretion, the sanctions showed how well the judge knew the facts of the case.

EXCERPTS FROM THE TRANSCRIPT
OF THE ORAL ARGUMENT

JUDGE WILKINS: Let me ask you this: Do you remember our federal penitentiary in Mexico this morning?

MR. CLEMENT: I do remember it.

JUDGE WILKINS: Let's assume that the warden is an American citizen and the defendant in this country wants that warden's testimony and it is material to the defense. We agree, I think, that the court would have the power to issue a subpoena compelling that attendance of that warden.

MR. CLEMENT: I think that's right. . . .

JUDGE WILKINS: Now, why does the fact that the court wants to issue a testimonial writ directed at the warden to produce a non-U.S. citizen inmate in his custody, why does that change? The court can issue the subpoena to the warden because it has jurisdiction over the warden. It surely should have jurisdiction over that same warden to issue the testimonial writ.

MR. CLEMENT: With respect, Your Honor, I disagree, and I think it would be quite clear that as we discussed this morning, if there is an individual in that hypothetical Mexican prison who let's say he's an excludable alien that was stopped at the border and then we're incarcerating there in Mexico, the writ—compulsory process would not reach that individual even though, as you say, the writ can certainly reach the warden, and if the person who was sought is the warden, the warden can come.

But I do think that this area of the law reflects the importance of citizenship and sort of territorial reach, and I think that this—that this area of the law, consistent with the great writ, recognizes that it's sort of a two-variable analysis. With respect to a United States citizen, when that's at issue, the writ applies and reaches abroad no matter what, but with respect to an alien, the writ does not extend extraterritorially, but it does apply with full force territorially. . . .

JUDGE GREGORY: Well, counsel, how could that be? The purpose of our courts is to seek truth. Is the search for truth any less because the person is an alien? . . .

MR. CLEMENT: If the witness is an alien, the interest in the search for truth is not any less—

JUDGE GREGORY: All right.

MR. CLEMENT: —but the rules that apply are no different whether the defendant is an alien or a citizen, but nothing guarantees a perfect trial or a perfect truth-seeking process, and so the law allows a criminal trial to go forward when there is even a material witness who is an alien abroad.

JUDGE GREGORY: Well, the problem is, the question is, control. You have control over the alien witness, and you are standing, for good reason in this case, between that search for truth because of national security. Nobody's blaming you for that, but then the court has to fashion an appropriate remedy to counterbalance that good reason that you have, and that's what the court is trying to do and did here.

I suppose it's beyond just the Sixth Amendment; it's the Fifth Amendment. If you look in her order, she says that I'm trying to determine now how can we have a fair trial with death being a possible punishment given that we cannot search completely for truth. . . . And that's where we are in the case.

But for you to go back and forth whether it's a windfall, what does a windfall have to do with it? It's not a windfall. That's the search for truth.

If the person popped out of Mars and popped here, that's a windfall, but if they have something that's relevant to the case, then you come here and you testify, and you have control over them, but you can't give them to us, and we understand. We're not going to quibble over that.

MR. CLEMENT: Right, Your Honor. And—

JUDGE GREGORY: But we . . . have as an independent judiciary, not answering to the executive or the legislature, we—as an independent judiciary, we have to ensure fair trials. . . .

MR CLEMENT: . . . [[I]]f I could just use an analogy that I found helpful in sort of simplifying it, if you think about an overall conspiracy, the design of which is to rob banks, and the innovation of this conspiracy is that there will be no witnesses, because it's planned from the get-go that all the witnesses will be killed, and it's a plan that encompasses two banks, and they're going to first kill all the witnesses at the first bank, drive to the second bank, kill all the witnesses at the second bank.

If you have co-conspirators who are testifying that this defendant was definitely part of the second bank, his job was to stand there armed, ready to kill people at the second bank, and you had a situation where maybe they got pulled over for speeding between the first and second bank so they never fulfilled the second part of the conspiracy, co-conspirator after co-conspirator that testified that this defendant, yes, second bank, that's a second bank individual, that is inculpatory as to guilt, not exculpatory. It may be exculpatory as to death—

JUDGE WILLIAMS: Well, it's inculpatory and it's exculpatory as to the death on the first conspiracy.

MR. CLEMENT: It is exculpatory as to the death penalty to the extent that the argument is that there's an overall conspiracy that produced the first deaths, and I think that we would argue that it's death eligible, but we would say that the fact that this individual—I think we would concede that with respect to this individual, the fact that he was involved in the second bank, that has—that goes to a mitigating factor, a minor role, and we would say that that information should go before the jury.

JUDGE GREGORY: So therefore, then you concede then that something can be inculpatory but still favorable. . . .

MR. CLEMENT: I agree that testimony can be inculpatory as to guilt and exculpatory as to the death phase of the case.

JUDGE GREGORY: So then for you to say that this evidence is mostly inculpatory does not resolve the issue of whether or not there is a right to it.

MR. CLEMENT: I dis—well, no, I don't disagree in the sense that we do not take issue with the possibility that this material in one form or another can go before the jury in the penalty phase of this case and that it is in that sense exculpatory evidence that go in front of the jury. But I think the important point and the reason I'm resisting pushing together the guilt phase and the penalty phase is that I think that in the penalty phase, all of the sort of evidentiary objections that might be raised to substitutions, to using the summaries as a basis for substitutions, are not well taken. Because as I was answering a question before, I used the word "information" in describing what would go before the jury, and I use that term advisedly, because the Federal Death Penalty Act, when it talks about the penalty phase, uses the term "information," not "evidence." And so the substitutions based on the summary can go before the jury, and I think that the Federal Death Penalty Act reflects less of this concern about information going in testimonial form versus another form, because the rules of sentencing have generally allowed more flexibility as to how information goes before the jury. . . .

JUDGE WILLIAM: . . . Mr. Mousaoui said . . . when he was attempting to enter his guilty plea, "I will be able to prove that I have certain knowledge about September 11 and I know exactly who done it. I know which group, who participated, when it was decided. I have many information."

And then on page 20 of the recent *pro se* filing that was entitled "In the World Top Combat for Global Supremacy," he writes, "20th hijacker, 9/11 American dream. Truthfully answered that I am Zacarias Moussaoui, a member of al Qaeda, and I, Zacarias Moussaoui, have pledged *bayat* to Usama Bin Laden, and I, Zacarias Moussaoui, was sent to the U.S. to take flight training to fly a plane into a building in the U.S. Bin Laden personally approved my participation in the attack."

Now, why do we need to give him access to detainees to contradict what he's saying himself?

MR. MacMAHON: Well, on the first one, what he said in his plea colloquy, . . . [[we]] don't know when it was that he learned this information. He's had access to all the discovery in this case. He's had time . . . to talk to me and Mr. Dunham and Mr. Yamamoto about the fruits of our investigation. He's—he saw television the day of 9/11. He's had access to newspaper articles that we send him. . . . But the second issue, the writing that you've read is troublesome. What you have to do with that is lay it down next to the government's brief, and what I take that is Mr. Moussaoui foolishly, in my regard, trying to chide the government, because that's a verbatim transcript of what the government says in their brief that was delivered to him on a redacted basis, and it says that if Mr. Moussaoui had been honest, he would have answered the following questions, and all Moussaoui does there, sitting in his cell, is take that pleading and fill in "I, Z.M."

I don't take that to be a confession as much as him just chiding the government or being foolish. And the more important—

JUDGE WILLIAMS: So you've got to disparage what he writes and rely upon what the summaries, I guess, are.

MR. MacMAHON: We've you know, we've had to disparage a lot of what Mr. Moussaoui's written, Your Honor, but the point of what—what I'm saying is that I don't believe that the two items . . . contradict what these witnesses are saying. . . .

MR. MacMAHON: . . . You know, Moussaoui, he's a—some have speculated that he's a wannabe that would love to have been involved in this thing, and he would have done it in a second, and the district court found that he can't be executed on something that he would have liked to have done or, as he sits in his cell in Alexandria, wishes that he could have done and writes to you. . . .

JUDGE WILLIAMS: He can't be executed on the fact that he knew about this, deliberately lied, didn't tell them what could have prevented all of this?

MR. MacMAHON: If the government can prove that, Your Honor, and the judge finds that Moussaoui under those circumstances is eligible for the death penalty, we would assume that that could happen, but what the judge is saying here is that it's fundamentally unfair for the government to rely on these supposed lies of what Mr. Moussaoui said in order to make him both death eligible and to defeat the use of the mitigators [[the testimony of the detainees]]. . . .

JUDGE WILKINS: Let me ask you this: Why aren't the substitutions, if they were properly drafted, an appropriate instruction given, and the defense can pick and choose from among them what it would like the jury to see or not or hear or not, why wouldn't the substitutions be an appropriate remedy for the violation of Moussaoui's Sixth Amendment right that you claim occurred?

MR. MacMAHON: Well, the government's already tried that, Your Honor.

JUDGE WILKINS: I know, but I'm asking you why doesn't the defense want that? I mean, having one of these witnesses testify, you know, I don't know whether I'd rather have the witness testify or being able to stand before the jury or talk _____

_____.

I mean, that's pretty compelling, I think, just from a trial strategy standpoint.

MR. MacMAHON: It is, Your Honor, but the problem is that the government is putting us in that position. In *Brady*, you read that the problem with the government suppressing favorable evidence is that they become the architect of the defense, and that's what they want. . . .

JUDGE WILLIAMS: You couldn't have done it for a deceased witness based on writing that you had?

MR. MacMAHON: Sure.

JUDGE WILLIAMS: Sure you could. You've probably done it.

MR. MacMAHON: I could, Your Honor, with a deceased witness, because I would know that that was the entirety of what I had to work with.

Mr. Clement just told you that this, this _____ process is ongoing. You know, when is it going to end? Is it going to end after this trial is over? Are we going to get another stipulation after—

JUDGE WILLIAMS: Well, I assume you'd come back on a newly discovered evidence motion.

MR. MacMAHON: It seems there's the constitutional protection for when you put on a live witness, you could resolve—you could put on all the questions and all the answers at one time.

The government has said we can't do that. We know that. We're not going to get to take these depositions. And so the government—the judge in what I think is a novel order entered sanctions against the government. She, she said that if you're going to take away that right from him, you have to pay a price, and that happens to litigants, both criminal and civil, in this court every day.

JUDGE WILKINS: If we're there then, the question to us is—is that the right price to pay. Do you agree?

MR. MacMAHON: Yes. . . .

IV. THE DECISION

The Fourth Circuit handed down its initial decision in the Moussaoui case on April 22, 2004, approximately six weeks after the bombing attacks of commuter trains in Madrid, Spain. It was a divided decision, with each of the three judges writing an opinion. Chief Judge Wilkins and Judge Gregory rejected the government's claims that Judge Brinkema had exceeded her authority by granting access to the detainees and that her rulings had violated the principle of separation of powers. In their view, despite the fact that the detainees were detained abroad, the Sixth Amendment gave Moussaoui the right to have judicial compulsory process for obtaining their testimony because the detainees' chief custodian, Secretary of Defense Donald Rumsfeld, was within the jurisdiction of the federal court. Moreover, ordering such access did not violate separation of powers since a defendant's right to a trial that "comports with the Fifth and Sixth Amendment" always prevailed over any governmental privilege. If the testimony of the detainees was "material" and "favorable" to Moussaoui, the court had no choice but to issue the order providing access. If the government chose not to comply, then the court had to sanction the government's conduct. The normal sanction was dismissal of the indictment.

Although dismissal of the indictment was the normal sanction for a government's refusal to produce a defense witness in its custody, Wilkins and Gregory thought that "a more measured approach" was required in the Moussaoui case, noting that CIPA required dismissal only if the government failed to produce an "adequate substitute" for classified information and only if a lesser sanction would not serve the "interests of justice." Both judges thought there was a lesser sanction that would serve the interests of justice, but they parted ways on what that sanction should be. Although Judge Wilkins believed that the specific substitutions that the government had proposed in the Moussaoui case were inadequate, he argued that proper substitutions could be compiled through an "interactive process among the parties and the district court" if the actual language of the summaries was used "to the greatest extent possible." Wilkins recommended that defense counsel should first identify those portions of the intelligence summaries that Moussaoui might want to admit into evidence at trial. Then the government should be given an opportunity to argue that additional portions of the summaries should be included for the sake of completeness, but that the government should not be permitted to bolster its case by including independent inculpatory statements. Based on the defense's submissions and the government's objections, the district judge, according to Wilkins, could then create "an appropriate set of substitutions." Wilkins added that at Moussaoui's trial the judge should instruct the jury that the substitutions were ultimately compiled from intelligence reports of the interrogations of the detainees, that the detainees' statements were obtained under conditions that tended to support their reliability, and that no one involved in the litigation had been privy to the interrogation process or had any input into it.

Even though Judge Gregory refused to go along with Judge Wilkins's approach to sanctions, Wilkins kept his majority on the Fourth Circuit panel because Judge Williams, the third judge, agreed with his approach as to the proper remedy for the government's refusal to give Moussaoui access to the detainees. In regard to the substantive merits of the case, Williams had a view of the Moussaoui case that was very different from Wilkins's. She argued that Moussaoui had no Sixth Amendment right to the detainees' testimony because any court order compelling access to the detainees violated separation of powers. In her view, the court's lack of power to issue the order implied that Moussaoui had no Sixth Amendment right of access. The court lacked the power to issue the order because it would "prevent the Executive from accomplishing its war-making, military, and foreign relations duties." It was therefore an error to infer that Moussaoui had a right to compel the production of witnesses who were in the government's custody. The "need to promote objectives within the constitutional authority of the Judiciary" did not justify the "grave risks to national security" posed by giving Moussaoui access to the detainees. The right of a criminal defendant "to offer witnesses in his favor and to compel their attendance" was "fundamental to our adversarial system," Williams agreed, but it was not absolute. For example, absent prosecutorial misconduct, a court cannot order the government to immunize a defense witness who invoked the Fifth Amendment right against self-incrimination. Absent such misconduct, the principle of separation of power insulated the government from any judicial control of its immunity decisions.

Despite Judge William's denial of Moussaoui's Sixth Amendment right of access to the detainees, she did uphold his Fifth Amendment Due Process right to any exculpable information contained in the intelligence reports of the interrogations of the three detainees. In other words, Moussaoui had a constitutional right to the exculpatory information, but he did not have a corresponding right to compel the production of the detainees as witnesses. However, the intelligence summaries were not "admissible *in toto*," Williams insisted. Only statements that were based on the personal knowledge of the detainees and that were relevant to Moussaoui's culpability could be admitted into evidence. Williams agreed with both Wilkins and Gregory that the specific substitutions that the government had proposed in the Moussaoui case were inadequate. However, she shared Wilkins's view that the district court could remedy the inadequacies of the existing substitutions by following the interactive process outlined above.

Judge Gregory disagreed. He claimed that the interactive process put the district court in a "thoroughly untenable position." Judge Brinkema had already ruled that the intelligence reports from which the substitutions were derived were "inherently unreliable" because the detainees' statements were not taken under oath, were taken in circumstances "not designed to guarantee reliability," and were "not responsive to questions posed by the defense." Accordingly, the Fourth Circuit was directing Judge Brinkema to do what she had already stated could not be done. Moreover, under CIPA, the government was responsible for preparing the substitutions, not the court, whose role was limited to deciding whether a substitution was adequate. According to Gregory, the interactive process ordered by the Fourth Circuit turned the CIPA procedure upside down and transformed the judge's role into that of an advocate. Lastly, the majority's reliance on substitutions, in Gregory's view, was misplaced because they could never be the "functional equivalent of live (or deposition) testimony." For that reason, Judge Brinkema's sanction of striking the death penalty from the case should be upheld. The government could not constitutionally seek the ultimate sanction if it denied Moussaoui access to witnesses who might be able to save his life.

The Fourth Circuit's April 22 decision was noteworthy in a number of respects. First, all three judges concluded that the government's specific substitutions in the Moussaoui case were inadequate. This finding was a significant blow to the government and, presumably, a subtle warning. On the other hand, all three judges refused to give much consideration to the option of dismissing the indictment against Moussaoui, despite the fact that dismissal was the normal sanction for such cases. Even the two judges (Wilkins and Gregory) who concluded that the government was violating Moussaoui's Sixth Amendment rights, refused to take this step, claiming that a "more measured approach was required." The measured approach that the Court came up with was the CIPA-option of substitutions, but this option had never before been used in the context of live witnesses. Accordingly, it was unclear how these two judges reconciled their bold recognition of Moussaoui's Sixth Amendment rights with the relatively tepid sanctions that they imposed on the government for its refusal to respect the right. Constitutional rights lose some or much of their value if the government can violate them at little cost.

Judge Williams avoided these problems by denying that Moussaoui had any Sixth Amendment right to produce the detainee witnesses. Her approach, however, raised a different problem. In her view, Moussaoui did not have a Sixth Amendment right to produce the witnesses because recognizing the court's power to produce them would interfere with the executive's "warmaking, military, and foreign relations duties," but he did have a Fifth Amendment Due Process right to an adequate substitution for those portions of the intelligence reports that contained exculpable information. To compile these adequate substitutions, Williams endorsed reducing the government's control over classified information by expanding the role of the judge in compiling the substitutions. But controlling classified information would seem to be one of the executive branch's war-making, military, and foreign relations duties. If judges could not interfere with this duty in the context of an alleged Sixth Amendment violation, as Williams had argued, then it was not clear why judges should have a more intrusive role in the context of an alleged Fifth Amendment violation.

One of the more interesting aspects of the April 22 decision was that the Fourth Circuit replaced it with an amended opinion on September 13, 2004, just four days after the Australian embassy was bombed in Jakarta, Indonesia, killing eight people. One reason for the amended opinion was rather straightforward: the Supreme Court's decision in *Rasul v. Bush* (discussed in chapter 3), in which the Court held that the federal courts did have statutory jurisdiction to entertain habeas corpus petitions from detainees held at the Guantanamo Bay Naval Base. If the federal courts had statutory jurisdiction to hear such petitions, then the principle of separation of powers could not bar federal courts from exercising jurisdiction over detainees held abroad who happened to be potential witnesses in criminal cases. In her new concurring opinion on September 13, Judge Williams grudgingly admitted that Moussaoui had a Sixth Amendment right to compulsory process of the three witnesses. The Fourth Circuit was now unanimous on this major point.

Although amended opinions are not that unusual in the American legal system, some of the factors that induced the Fourth Circuit to amend its initial Moussaoui opinion were highly irregular. In a heavily redacted section of the September 13 decision, the Fourth Circuit gave a partial explanation of what had happened. On May 12, the government filed a letter with the Fourth Circuit that purported to "clarify certain factual matters." In this letter, the government told the court that its assertion in the April 22 opinion that neither side had any input into the interrogations of the three detainees was not true. Members of the prosecution team had submitted questions to the interrogators of the detainees, although it was up to the sole discretion of the interrogator to ask the questions or not.

This admission by the government was of fundamental importance. Even if the prosecutors did not have ultimate control over whether their questions were asked of the detainees, they had a degree of indirect access to the detainees that Moussaoui had been denied. Moreover, the indirect access gave the government an opportunity to increase the likelihood that the intelligence reports would contain inculpatory statements regarding Moussaoui participation in al Qaeda and the 9/11 attacks. The latter possibility compromised to some extent the validity of the Court's April 22 holding that properly compiled substitutions were adequate sanctions for the government's refusal to provide Moussaoui with access to the detainees. The adequacy of this remedy was possibly compromised if the government had exercised a unilateral opportunity "to fish" for inculpatory statements against Moussaoui. The substitutions were tainted because the government had tainted the underlying intelligence reports.

At the same time that the Fourth Circuit found out that Moussaoui's prosecution team had indirect access to the interrogators of the detainees, they also discovered that the government had permitted the 9/11 Commission to submit written questions to unidentified al Qaeda detainees. Press reports of this arrangement appeared on May 12, the same day the government had sent the letter to the Fourth Circuit to "clarify certain factual matters."[9] It was not clear whether the government disclosed the existence of this arrangement with the 9/11 Commission in its May 12 letter or whether the Fourth Circuit learned of it from the press, but the fact that the letter and the press reports arrived at the Court on the same day was a noteworthy coincidence. It suggested that the press reports may have compelled the government to concede not only that it had permitted the 9/11 Commission to submit written questions to the detainees, but also that members of the prosecution team had been granted a comparable level of access. After all, once the Fourth Circuit had found out about the 9/11 Commission's access to the detainees, it would have been natural for the judges to ask the government whether comparable access had been granted to anyone else. At that point, the government's lawyers would have had to tell the truth or lie to the judges, thereby risking disbarment.

The troubling question was the following: Why had the government denied Moussaoui, who was on trial for his life, all access to the detainees, while it had allowed limited access to both the prosecution and a governmental commission? In response to the situation, the Fourth Circuit ordered the government to answer the following questions: "Why was the information in the May 12 Letter not provided to this court or the district court prior to May 12?" "In light of the information contained in the Letter and any other pertinent developments, would it now be appropriate to submit written questions to any of the enemy combatant witnesses?" "What restrictions would apply to such a process and how should it be conducted?" "If access is granted by written questions, is the Compulsory Process Clause satisfied?" "If access is granted by written questions, what effect, if any, would *Crawford v. Washington* have on such a process?" "If circumstances have changed such that submissions of written questions are now possible, when did the circumstances change and why was neither this court nor the district court so informed at that time?"[10]

The reference to *Crawford v. Washington* was understandable because it was a decision on the Sixth Amendment right to confront witnesses that the Supreme Court had handed down on March 8, 2004. The case concerned the admission of a tape-recorded statement that the defendant's wife had made to the police. State law barred the wife from testifying against her husband without his consent at the trial, but the prosecution used the tape to convict the defendant of assault. The Supreme Court held that the admission of the tape violated the Sixth Amendment because the testimony was completely *ex parte.*

The defendant never had an opportunity to cross-examine his wife during her police interrogation. Even if the statement was reliable, it could not be admitted. "Dispensing with confrontation because testimony is obviously reliable," Justice Scalia wrote in his majority opinion, "is akin to dispensing with jury trial because a defendant is obviously guilty."[11]

Because *Crawford* dealt with a defendant's right to confront the prosecution's witnesses, not the right of the defendant to rely on compulsory judicial process to produce his own witnesses, it was arguably not exactly on point regarding the Sixth Amendment at issue in the Moussaoui case. However, the cases were analogous enough to see why the Fourth Circuit wanted to know how the government would respond to the recent Supreme Court decision. In the words of Justice Scalia, "statements of witnesses absent from trial have been admitted only where the declarant is unavailable, and only where the defendant has had a prior opportunity to cross-examine."[12] Since the government was responsible for both the "unavailability" of the detainees and Moussaoui's lack of opportunity to cross-examine them, it was arguable that his Sixth Amendment claim was within the scope of *Crawford*. Even if the government's substitutions in the Moussaoui case were reliable, *Crawford* suggested that dispensing with Moussouai's right to depose the detainees was perhaps tantamount to dispensing with a jury trial because he was obviously guilty.

On May 19 the government filed its answers to the above questions, a classified joint appendix, and a classified *ex parte* appendix, about which the defense raised a concern on May 24. The court conducted a sealed oral argument on June 3, 2004, at which time the panel asked the government to provide additional information in the form of another *ex parte* document. In its amended September 13 opinion, the panel summarized the additional facts that were contained in the government's submissions, but the section was heavily redacted because much of the information was classified. Little can be learned from it except that Special Agent Aaron Zebley was a member of the FBI "Penttbom team" that was investigating the 9/11 terrorist attacks, that he was the FBI's expert on the al Qaeda cell operating in Hamburg, Germany, that he had "special expertise and knowledge" regarding Witness A (presumably Ramzi Binalshibh), and that he became a case agent for Moussaoui's prosecution team in November 2001, one month prior to his indictment. Presumably, Zebley, as a member of both the Penttbom team and the Moussaoui prosecution team, functioned as a link between the prosecutors of Moussaoui and the interrogators of the detainees. Although the two subsections of the amended opinion that summarized Zebley's role were completely redacted, the titles for the two subsections were "2. Oral Communications" and "3. Written Communications." It was possible that these subsections summarized the oral and written communications that Zebley had earlier had with the interrogators.

The Fourth Circuit's discovery that both the 9/11 Commission and the prosecution had had more access to the detainees than Moussaoui had been granted took place in the context of the Abu Ghraib prisoner abuse scandal. The Abu Ghraib photos first appeared on April 28, just two weeks before the government's May 12 letter. In the weeks that followed, the story cascaded throughout the media. The Senate's Committee on Armed Forces held public hearings on the subject in May, the same month Islamic extremists massacred twenty-two people in Al-Khobar, a city in eastern Saudi Arabia and the location of the 1996 Khobar Tower bombings. In June classified government memos regarding the inapplicability of the Geneva Convention to the war in Afghanistan were leaked to the press. On June 22 the government released redacted copies of many of these memos, including Jay Bybee's August 1 memo and the Working Group Report on Detainee Interrogations in the Global War on Terrorism dated March 6, 2003. Both the memo and the report narrowly defined torture and authorized the use of coercive interrogation techniques. The official Department of Defense reports on the prisoner abuse scandal began to appear in August.

The Fourth Circuit was therefore assessing the significance of the revelations that the prosecution and the 9/11 Commission had had a form of access to the detainees that had been denied Moussaoui at the same time that the detainee abuse scandal was unfolding. Of course, if coercive interrogation techniques had been used on Moussaoui's exculpatory witnesses, it could be argued that the intelligence reports could no longer be used as the basis for the substitutions. However, despite this possible argument, Judges Wilkins and Williams did not abandon their position that properly compiled substitutions could be an adequate sanction for the government's violation of Moussaoui's Sixth Amendment rights. In language that had not been in the initial April 22 opinion, the two judges argued that the substitutions were nonetheless a viable sanction because the interrogators of the detainees "have a profound interest in obtaining accurate information from the witnesses and in reporting that information accurately to those who can use it to prevent acts of terrorism and to capture other al Qaeda operatives." In a footnote, they added that "we are even more persuaded that the _____ process is carefully designed to elicit truthful and accurate information from the witnesses,"[13] language suggesting that the two judges were more persuaded of the reliability of the intelligence reports after they had examined the *ex parte* documents that the government had submitted to the court in May and June than they had been before. It seemed that the two judges preferred the option of substitutions, rather than the elimination of the death penalty, even though there was the distinct possibility that substitutions were compiled from coerced statements.

Regarding the fact that the prosecution had submitted questions to the interrogators of the detainees, Judges Wilkins and Williams concluded in the amended opinion of September 13 that the input had "worked no unfairness on Moussaoui."[14] The opinion, however, did not shed any light on why the prosecution had not informed the court of its indirect access to the three detainees earlier than it did. Nor did it explain if or when the circumstances had changed so that such indirect access was acceptable. However, without finding any fault with the government's conduct, the court did order the district court "to provide Moussaoui with an opportunity to _____ _____ for ___ discretionary use _____ of the witnesses,"[15] language hinting that Moussaoui would be given the option of submitting written questions to the interrogators of the three detainees. A footnote explained that the defense had expressed concern at a hearing that such a procedure would "result in the disclosure of trial strategy to the Government," but the government had assured the court that measures could be taken to avoid such an eventuality, presumably by adopting procedures that prevented lawyers on the Moussaoui prosecution team from seeing the written questions submitted by Moussaoui's defense team.[16] In his concurrence to the September 13 opinion, Judge Gregory objected to the above type of substitutions, claiming that their use would mean that justice had taken "a long stride backward."

Although the Fourth Circuit gave Moussaoui the opportunity to submit written questions to the interrogators of the detainees, the interrogators would have the sole discretion to decide whether to ask them or not. A cynic might argue that the interrogators would have had more incentive to ask the questions submitted by the prosecution/investigation team than those submitted by Moussaoui and his defense team. Moreover, if questions submitted by the defense were asked, the court's amended opinion did not make it clear whether the answers would be sent directly to Moussoui's defense team or if they would be filtered in the normal way through the intelligence reports and summaries. If the defense received the answers by the latter method, then presumably the answers would be included in the report only if they contained actionable intelligence. The opportunity to submit written questions to the detainees therefore did not insure that the substitutions would be more favorable for Moussaoui than they otherwise would have been.

EXCERPTS FROM THE FOURTH CIRCUIT'S OPINIONS

[[*Editor's note*: The shaded parts of the excerpts from Judge Wilkins's majority opinion indicate passages of the September 13 opinion that were not in the earlier April 22 opinion. These passages were either redacted from the earlier April 22 opinion or (more likely) added by the Fourth Circuit to the September 13 opinion. It is worthwhile noting what changes were made. Excerpts from both Judge William's April 22 opinion and her September 13 opinion are included separately without any shading. Excerpts from Judge Gregory's opinion follow the above rules regarding Judge Wilkins's opinion. Material that has been redacted from the opinion is indicated by four stars (* * * *) or, when it is possible to do so, by underlined blank text. A limited number of footnotes from the September 13 opinion are also included.]]

WILKINS, Chief Judge (September 13 amended opinion):
. . . We are presented with questions of grave significance—questions that test the commitment of this nation to an independent judiciary, to the constitutional guarantee of a fair trial even to one accused of the most heinous of crimes, and to the protection of our citizens against additional terrorist attacks. These questions do not admit of easy answers. . . .

[[1. Sixth Amendment.]] The Sixth Amendment guarantees that "in all criminal prosecutions, the accused shall enjoy the right . . . to have compulsory process for obtaining witnesses in his favor." The compulsory process right is circumscribed, however, by the ability of the district court to obtain the presence of a witness through service of process. The Government maintains that because the enemy combatant witnesses are foreign nationals outside the boundaries of the United States, they are beyond the process power of the district court and, hence, unavailable to Moussaoui.

The Government's argument rests primarily on the well established and undisputed principle that the process power of the district court does not extend to foreign nationals abroad. Were this the governing rule, Moussaoui clearly would have no claim under the Sixth Amendment. This is not the controlling principle, however.

The Government's argument overlooks the critical fact that the enemy combatant witnesses are _____ of the United States Government. Therefore, we are concerned not with the ability of the district court to issue a subpoena to the witnesses, but rather with its power to issue a writ of habeas corpus *ad testificandum* (testimonial writ) to the witnesses' custodian.

In determining whether a district court possesses the power to serve a writ of habeas corpus, the critical principle is that the writ is served not upon the prisoner, but upon the custodian. As the Supreme Court has noted, "The important fact to be observed in regard to the mode of procedure upon this writ is, that it is directed to, and served upon, not the person confined, but his jailer. It does not reach the former except through the latter." Therefore, the relevant question is not whether the district court can serve the *witnesses*, but rather whether the court can serve the *custodian*. . . .

[[2. Separation of Powers.]] The Government next argues that even if the district court would otherwise have the power to order the production of the witnesses, the January 30 and August 29 orders are improper because they infringe on the Executive's war-making authority, in violation of separation of powers principles.

We begin by examining the Government's reliance on cases concerning governmental refusal to grant immunity to potential defense witnesses. The Government argues that these cases stand for the proposition that the district court may be precluded from issuing certain orders that implicate the separation of powers. We reject this characterization of these cases. . . .

The circuit courts, including the Fourth Circuit, have uniformly held that district courts do not have any authority to grant immunity, even when a grant of immunity would allow a defendant to present material, favorable testimony. These holdings have been based on the facts that no power to grant immunity is found in the Constitution and that Congress reserved the statutory immunity power to the Attorney General. Because a district court has no power to grant immunity to compel the testimony of a potential witness who has invoked the privilege against self-incrimination, a defendant has no Sixth Amendment right to such testimony.

The circuits are divided with respect to the question of whether a district court can ever compel the government, on pain of dismissal, to grant immunity to a potential defense witness. The Fourth Circuit, consistent with the majority [[of the circuits,]] . . . has held that a district court may compel the government to grant immunity upon a showing of prosecutorial misconduct and materiality. . . .

. . . A showing of misconduct is necessary because . . . a defendant has no Sixth Amendment right to the testimony of a potential witness who has invoked the Fifth Amendment right against self-incrimination; therefore, the defendant has no Sixth Amendment right that could outweigh the Government's interest in using its immunity power sparingly. Governmental abuse of the immunity power, however, vitiates this interest because when the Government's misconduct threatens to impair the defendant's right to a fair trial, it is proper for the district court to protect that right by compelling the Government to immunize the witness.

For these reasons, the analogy between this case and the immunity cases is inapt. The witnesses at issue here, unlike potential witnesses who have invoked their Fifth Amendment rights, are within the process power of the district court, and Moussaoui therefore has a Sixth Amendment right to their testimony. . . .

This is not a case involving arrogation of the powers or duties of another branch. The district court orders requiring production of enemy combatant witnesses involved the resolution of questions properly—indeed, exclusively—reserved to the judiciary. Therefore, if there is a separation of powers problem at all, it arises only from the burden the actions of the district court place on the Executive's performance of its duties.

[[3. Balancing.]] The Supreme Court has explained on several occasions that determining whether a judicial act places impermissible burdens on another branch of government requires balancing the competing interests. . . .

The Constitution charges the Congress and the Executive with the making and conduct of war. It is not an exaggeration to state that the effective performance of these duties is essential to our continued existence as a sovereign nation. . . .

The Government alleges—and we accept as true—that _____ the enemy combatant witnesses is critical to the ongoing effort to combat terrorism by al Qaeda. The witnesses are _____ al Qaeda operatives who have extensive knowledge concerning not just the September 11 attacks, but also other past attacks, future operations, and the structure, personnel, and tactics of al Qaeda. Their value as intelligence sources can hardly be overstated. And, we must defer to the Government's assertion that interruption _____ of these witnesses will have devastating effects on the ability to gather information from them. _____ _____, it is not unreasonable to suppose that interruption _____ could result in the loss of information that might prevent future terrorist attacks.

The Government also asserts that production of the witnesses would burden the Executive's ability to conduct foreign relations. The Government claims that if the Executive's assurances of confidentiality can be abrogated by the judiciary, the vital ability to obtain the cooperation of other governments will be devastated.

The Government also reminds us of the bolstering effect production of the witnesses might have on our enemies. . . .*

In summary, the burdens that would arise from production of the enemy combatant witnesses are substantial.

The importance of the Sixth Amendment right to compulsory process is not [[, however,]] subject to question—it is integral to our adversarial criminal justice system. . . . To state the matter more succinctly, "[f]ew rights are more fundamental than that of an accused to present witnesses in his own defense." . . .

. . . In all cases of this type—cases falling into "what might loosely be called the area of constitutionally guaranteed access to evidence"—the

---

* [[*Editor's note*: In the Fourth Circuit's April 22 opinion, this paragraph ended with the following sentence: "For example, al Qaeda operatives are trained to disrupt the legal process in whatever manner possible; indications that such techniques may be successful will only cause a redoubling of their efforts." The sentence was redacted from the September 13 opinion.]]

Supreme Court has held that the defendant's right to a trial that comports with the Fifth and Sixth Amendments prevails over the governmental privilege. Ultimately, as these cases make clear, the appropriate procedure is for the district court to order production of the evidence or witness and leave to the Government the choice of whether to comply with that order. If the government refuses to produce the information at issue—as it may properly do—the result is ordinarily dismissal [[of the charges]]. . . .

[[4. Sanctions.]] As noted previously, the Government has stated that it will not produce the enemy combatant witnesses for depositions (or, we presume, for any other purpose related to this litigation). We are thus left in the following situation: the district court has the power to order production of the enemy combatant witnesses and has properly determined that they could offer material testimony on Moussaoui's behalf, but the Government has refused to produce the witnesses. Under such circumstances, dismissal of the indictment is the usual course. Like the district court, however, we believe that a more measured approach is required. Additionally, we emphasize that no punitive sanction is warranted here because the Government has rightfully exercised its prerogative to protect national security interests by refusing to produce the witnesses.[*]

Although, as explained above, this is not a CIPA case, that act nevertheless provides useful guidance in determining the nature of the remedies that may be available. Under CIPA, dismissal of an indictment is authorized only if the government has failed to produce an adequate substitute for the classified information, and the interests of justice would not be served by imposition of a lesser sanction. CIPA thus enjoins district courts to seek a solution that neither disadvantages the defendant nor penalizes the government (and the public) for protecting classified information that may be vital to national security.

A similar approach is appropriate here. Under such an approach, the first question is whether there is any appropriate substitution for the witnesses' testimony. . . .

The conclusion of the district court that the proposed substitutions are inherently inadequate is tantamount to a declaration that there could be no adequate substitution for the witnesses' deposition testimony. We reject this conclusion. The answer to the concerns of the district court regarding the accuracy of the _____ reports is that those who are _____ the witnesses have a profound interest in obtaining information accurately to those who can use it to prevent acts of terrorism and to capture other al Qaeda

---

[*] We emphasize that by all appearances, the Government's refusal to produce the witnesses is done in the utmost good faith. The Government is charged not only with the task of bringing wrongdoers to justice, but also with the grave responsibility of protecting the lives of the citizenry. The choice the government has made is not without consequences, but those consequences are not punitive in nature.

operatives. These considerations provide sufficient indicia of reliability to alleviate the concerns of the district court.

Next, the district court noted that the substitutions do not indicate that they are summaries of statements made over the course of several months. We agree with the district court that in order to adequately protect Moussaoui's right to a fair trial, the jury must be made aware of certain information concerning the substitutions. The particular content of any instruction to the jury regarding the substitutions lies within the discretion of the district court. However, at the very least the jury should be informed that the substitutions are derived from reports _____ of the witnesses. The instructions must account for the fact that members of the prosecution team have provided information and suggested _____ _____. The jury should also be instructed that the statements were obtained under circumstances that support a conclusion that the statements are reliable.**

. . .

The Government's submissions in response to the Petition make clear that members of the prosecution team, _____ _____ _____ have had some input _____ the enemy combatant witnesses. Our review of the circumstances of this access indicates that the input by the prosecution team into the _____ process has worked no unfairness on Moussaoui. Nevertheless, in order to provide Moussaoui with the fullest possible range of information from the witnesses, we direct the district court to provide Moussaoui with an opportunity to _____ for _____ discretionary use _____ of the witnesses.***

For the reasons set forth above, we conclude that the district court erred in ruling that any substitution for the witnesses' testimony is inherently inadequate

---

** Nothing in the Government's submissions in connection with the Petition contradicts our conclusion that those _____ the witnesses have a profound interest in obtaining truthful information. To the contrary, we are even more persuaded that the _____ process is carefully designed to elicit truthful and accurate information from the witnesses.

We emphasize that we have never held, nor do we now hold, that the witnesses' statements are *in fact* truthful, and the jury should not be so instructed. Instead, the jury should be informed that the circumstances were designed to elicit truthful statements from the witnesses. We offer no opinion regarding whether this instruction may include information regarding _____.

*** During the hearing regarding the Petition, defense counsel expressed concern over whether _____ would result in the disclosure of trial strategy to the Government. The Government, in its June 16 filing, informs us that measures can be taken to avoid such disclosures. We leave the particulars of any such process to the discretion of the district court. At an absolute minimum, however, whatever process is adopted must ensure that the prosecution team is not privy to _____ propounded by the defense, just as the defense was unaware of _____ propounded by the prosecution team.

to the extent it is derived from the _____ reports. To the contrary, we hold that the _____ summaries (which, as the district court determined, accurately recapitulate the _____ reports) provide an adequate basis for the creation of written statements that may be submitted to the jury in lieu of the witnesses' deposition testimony.

The compiling of substitutions is a task best suited to the district court, given its greater familiarity with the facts of the case and its authority to manage the presentation of evidence. Nevertheless, we think it is appropriate to provide some guidance to the court and the parties.

First, the circumstances of this case—most notably, the fact that the substitutions may very well support Moussaoui's defense—dictate that the crafting of substitutions be an interactive process among the parties and the district court.+ Second, we think that accuracy and fairness are best achieved by crafting substitutions that use the exact language of the _____ summaries to the greatest extent possible. We believe that the best means of achieving both of these objectives is for defense counsel to identify particular portions of the _____ _____ summaries that Moussaoui may want to admit into evidence at trial. The Government may then offer any objections and argue that additional portions must be included in the interest of completeness, as discussed below. If the substitutions are to be admitted at all (we leave open the possibility that Moussaoui may decide not to use the substitutions in his defense), they may be admitted only by Moussaoui. Based on defense counsel's submissions and the Government's objections, the district court could then compile an appropriate

---

+ We disagree with Judge Gregory's view that, by assigning the district court a role in the crafting of substitutions, we have "place[d] the district court in the position of being an advocate in the proceedings," and that "we are setting ourselves out as super-arbiters of the admission of evidence in this case." In fact, what we are asking the district court to do is little removed from the quite ordinary judicial task of assessing the admissibility of evidence. And, any subsequent review by this court on these matters will involve nothing more than review of evidentiary rulings—a routine function of an appellate court.

We also reject the notion that we are improperly "asking the [district] court to do something that it has stated cannot be done." The district court ruled that the _____ reports were unreliable; we have reached a contrary conclusion. There is no reason to suppose that the district court is incapable of proceeding on the premise that the _____ reports are reliable. We are also confident that it lies well within the competence of the district court to forestall any attempt, by either party, to "offer a distorted version of the witnesses' statements" [[Editor's note: This paragraph appeared in the April 22 opinion, but was redacted from the amended September 13 opinion]].

Finally, we are not "transferring to the court the authority that CIPA vests in the Government," by mandating that the district court be involved in crafting substitutions. CIPA authorizes the Government to move for an order approving substitutions for classified information, but it does not mandate that the Government draft proposed substitutions. While we imagine that substitutions will be drafted by the Government in the vast majority of cases, nothing in CIPA expressly or implicitly precludes the involvement of defense counsel or the district court.

set of substitutions.++ We leave to the discretion of the district court the question of whether to rule on the admissibility of a particular substitution (e.g., whether a substitution is relevant) at trial or during pre-trial proceedings. . . .

Moussaoui asserts that allowing the Government to argue that additional portions of the summaries must be included in the substitutions will result in substitutions "larded with inculpatory information under the guise of 'completeness,'" in violation of the Confrontation Clause. And, indeed, the Government has indicated its view that the rule of completeness would allow it to designate an inculpatory portion of a witness' statement to counter an exculpatory statement by the same witness designated by Moussaoui.+++

The common law "rule of' completeness" is partially codified in Federal Rule of Evidence 106, which provides, "When a writing or recorded statement or part thereof is introduced by a party, an adverse party may require the introduction at that time of any other part or any other writing or recorded statement which ought in fairness to be considered contemporaneously with it." The purpose of Rule 106 is "to prevent a party from misleading the jury by allowing into the record relevant portions of [a writing or recorded statement] which clarify or explain the part already received." The rule is protective, merely. It goes only so far as is necessary to shield a party from adverse inferences, and only allows an explanation or rebuttal of the evidence received." . . .

In short, we wish to make clear that the rule of completeness is not to be used by the Government as a means of seeking the admission of inculpatory statements that neither explain nor clarify the statements designated by Moussaoui. On the other hand, the defense's ability to propose substitutions based on the language of the _____ summaries is not a license to mislead the jury.

On rehearing, both parties acknowledged our holding that CIPA does not apply here but indicated their belief that once the district court has approved substitutions for the witnesses' testimony, CIPA comes into play, with the result that the Government may object to the disclosure of the classified information in the substitutions and request that the district court adopt an alternative form of evidence. We disagree.

It must be remembered that the substitution process we here order is a *replacement* for the testimony of the enemy combatant witnesses. Because the Government will not allow Moussaoui to have contact with the witnesses, we

---

++ We leave it to the district court to determine whether national security mandates non-substantive changes, such as designating alternate names for people or places, in order to accommodate national security concerns articulated by the Government when the substitutions are being compiled.

+++ The Government acknowledges that, under the circumstances here, the rule of completeness would not allow it to use a statement by one witness to "complete" a statement by another.

must provide a remedy adequate to protect Moussaoui's constitutional rights. Here, that remedy is substitutions. Once Moussaoui has selected the portions of the _____ summaries he wishes to submit to the jury and the Government has been given an opportunity to be heard, the district court will compile the substitutions, using such additional language as may be necessary to aid the understanding of the jury. Once this process is complete, the matter is at an end—there are to be no additional or supplementary proceedings under CIPA regarding the substitutions. . . .

WILLIAMS, Circuit Judge, concurring in part and dissenting in part (April 22 opinion):

[[1. Sixth Amendment right.]] . . . I believe that separation of powers principles place the enemy combatant witnesses beyond the reach of the district court. Accordingly, Moussaoui does not have a Sixth Amendment right to their compulsion. . . .

. . . In my view, the district court's orders prevent the Executive from accomplishing its war-making, military, and foreign relations duties. . . .

The Executive war-making authority is one of "extraordinary breadth." This authority includes the power to capture and detain individuals involved in hostilities against the United States. Indeed, the capture, detention, and interrogation of enemy aliens, like the designation of a detainee as an enemy combatant, "bears the closest imaginable connection to the President's constitutional responsibilities during the actual conduct of hostilities." . . .

Additionally, as was the case in *Eisentrager*, the district court's orders are likely to bolster our enemies and undermine the Executive's war-making efforts. Although some of the concerns with the Great Writ that the *Eisentrager* Court identified are not present with a testimonial writ, many of the concerns are equally present in this context, including: the custodian would have to transport the witness to the location of the deposition; the writ would be equally available during active hostilities as during the times between war and peace (and the writ would be equally available immediately after capture as well as months after capture); moreover, granting a testimonial writ could bring aid and comfort to our enemies; it would diminish the prestige of our commanders with enemies and wavering neutrals; the logistics and security concerns of coordinating production of the detainee to testify will divert the attention of at least some military or intelligence personnel, perhaps even the field commander; and finally, it is highly likely that the result of a court being able to force the custodian * * * * of an alien enemy combatant detained abroad would be a conflict between judicial and military opinion highly comforting to enemies of the United States. In this regard, I note that the Government has articulated more than a generalized interest in unfettered pursuit of the war effort. Rather, the Government has offered a case-specific analysis of the harm that will be done by interruption * * * *. . . .

I therefore conclude that requiring the Government to produce for depositions alien enemy combatants detained abroad * * * *, the goals of which is to protect the security of American lives from future terrorist attacks, would prevent the Executive from exercising its war and foreign relations powers. I also conclude that the grave risks to national security that would arise from granting access to the witnesses cannot be justified by the need to promote objectives within the constitutional authority of the Judiciary.

I agree that the right of a defendant to offer testimony of witnesses in his favor and to compel their attendance "if necessary" is fundamental to our adversarial system. We have recognized, however, that "the right to compulsory process is not absolute."

The "immunity cases" provide a helpful, albeit imperfect, analogy here. . . .

I disagree with my colleagues' conclusion that these immunity cases stand for the proposition that "legitimate separation of powers concerns [cannot] effectively insulate the Government from being compelled to produce evidence or witnesses." I interpret the immunity cases as standing for the proposition that the Executive, acting through the prosecution, forfeits its right to rely on the separation of powers as a bar to compelled judicial immunity when it exceeds the bounds of its authority by overreaching or some other type of prosecutorial misconduct. In these circumstances, compelled judicial immunity is akin to a punishment of the Executive for failing to perform properly the duties assigned to it by the Constitution. This conclusion is bolstered by the cases . . . that hold unequivocally that a showing that the evidence sought is material, favorable, and unavailable from any other source is insufficient to require a grant of immunity. Thus, absent bad faith by the government, legitimate separation of powers concerns *can* restrict the court's authority to compel the government to make the testimony of certain witnesses available. I note that Moussaoui has conceded that there has been no prosecutorial misconduct, overreaching, or other abuse in this case.

. . . I conclude that separation of powers principles prohibited the district court from issuing its January 30 and August 29 orders granting access to the witnesses. Where the court lacks the authority to compel production or testimony of a witness, the defendant is not entitled to any remedy for that lack of authority.

Even though Moussaoui does not have a right of access to the witnesses, I agree with Moussaoui that in the circumstances of this case the Government may not proceed (and, in fact, has not proceeded) as if it does not have information from these detainees. In compliance with its obligation under *Brady v. Maryland*, the Government has been providing summaries * * * * to the defense. . . .

In analyzing whether to admit the information in the * * * * summaries, we are faced with a request to admit information whether the declarants of the information are completely unavailable because of legitimate separation of powers reasons. . . . Thus, to the extent that the information gives Moussaoui an opportunity to defend against the Government's accusations, the materiality and favorability of the information remains relevant. . . .

Given this conclusion and the fact that legitimate separation of powers reasons prohibit the defendant from having any access to the detainees, I believe that the Fifth Amendment's guarantee of a fundamentally fair trial gives Moussaoui the right to introduce at least some of this information at trial. This is not to say that the summaries are admissible *in toto*. I agree with my colleagues that "Moussaoui should not be allowed to rely on obviously inadmissible statements (e.g., statements resting on a witness' belief rather than his personal knowledge)." Similarly, the district court retains the power to exclude irrelevant information and to require inclusion of additional portions of the summaries, over and above what Moussaoui seeks to introduce, in the interest of completeness. However, the Government may not, consistent with due process, rely on legitimate separation of powers principles to prohibit any access to the detainees, and at the same time, argue that the statements in the summaries that are based on personal knowledge are inadmissible because they were made out-of-court and not under oath.

Given that Moussaoui has a right to introduce the *information*, which is itself classified, I come to the issue of substitutions. I concur [[in the parts]] . . . of Chief Judge Wilkins's opinion, which direct the district court to aid the parties in crafting acceptable substitutes based on the * * * * and to give appropriate instructions to the jury regarding the source of the information.

WILLIAMS, Circuit Judge, concurring (September 13 opinion):

[[T]]he Supreme Court has recently resolved the question of whether the district court has the authority to grant access to aliens detained abroad. . . .

Thus, Moussaoui has a Sixth Amendment right to compulsory process of these witnesses because (1) under *Rasul*, the district court has the power to grant a testimonial writ directed to _____ of these witnesses, and (2) Moussaoui has made a sufficient showing that the witnesses would provide material and favorable testimony based on the charges in the indictment. The Government, however, has refused to provide access to the witnesses. Although I am troubled by the lack of interactivity in the process that generated the substitutions,* that lack of interactivity is compelled by the substantial national security concerns surrounding these witnesses. I feel that in light of those concerns, the fact that the substitutions will not materially disadvantage the defendant—because he will be permitted to introduce every favorable statement from the witnesses while the Government will be precluded from introducing any inculpatory statements—adequately protects his Sixth Amendment rights. Accordingly, I concur in Part V of Chief Judge Wilkins's opinion.

GREGORY, Circuit Judge, concurring in part and dissenting in part (September 13 opinion): . . .

After we issued our opinion, the Government filed a letter dated May 12, 2004, purporting to "clarify certain factual matters." In that letter, the Government stated that this court's opinion erroneously relied on a presumption that the Government's attorneys had not been privy to, nor had any input into, the _____ witnesses at issue. The Government had argued, in both the district court and this court, that Moussaoui could not question the witnesses because any interference in the _____ process would be devastating to national security. _____
_____.
_____.

The Government now concedes in the May 12 letter that members of the prosecution team have in fact _____
_____
_____

pertaining to the prosecution of Moussaoui. _____
_____
_____
_____. While the
May 12 letter does not necessarily contradict the Government's previous pleadings and statements during oral argument, it is easy to see why the court concluded, based on the Government's prior representations, _____
_____
_____

_____ information with actionable foreign intelligence value,
_____ that information is passed to the prosecutors, who in turn will pass the information to Moussaoui's defense team in accordance with their obligation under *Brady v. Maryland*. Until now,

---

* I note that this lack of interactivity could be ameliorated in part by utilizing a process similar to that used by the 9/11 Commission.

no parallel access to the _____ process has been available to Moussaoui.

The Government's May 12 letter, and its positions taken during the hearing before the panel on June 3, 2004, only serve to reinforce my conclusion that the district court was correct in holding that the death penalty should not be within the range of sentencing options available when, as here, the Defendant's ability to mount a defense is severely impaired. As the Government has made clear, the summaries of witness statements provided to the defense are not a complete account of the witnesses' responses _____ the only _____ responses passed to the prosecution, and subsequently provided to the defense, are those responses deemed _____ to have actionable foreign intelligence value. Thus, as the majority acknowledges, it is certainly possible that the witnesses, _____ _____ may have provided information that, although exculpatory as to Moussaoui, was not passed on to the prosecution, and in turn to the defense team, because _____ _____ the information had no actionable foreign intelligence value.[*] As the majority further recognizes, if _____ have exculpatory evidence that they have not passed on to the prosecution, Moussaoui's due process rights may be implicated. The majority downplays this possibility, calling it unlikely, and states that it need not be further explored because "there is no evidence before us that the Government possesses exculpatory material that has not been disclosed to the defense." This conclusion is, at best, misguided. Because of the highly classified nature of the evidence at issue in this case, there is no way this court or Moussaoui could know whether an arm of the Government possesses exculpatory evidence that does not have foreign intelligence value; indeed, even the prosecution would not have access to any such evidence, _____ distribute only those witness summaries that have foreign intelligence value. How there could ever be any evidence before us from which we could conduct a *Brady* analysis under these circumstances is a mystery.

Further, the reliability (or lack thereof) of the witnesses' statements poses real stumbling blocks to the admission of those statements. The Government admits that the summaries are simply accurate reflections of the witnesses' re-

---

[*] Although the prosecutorial function is to achieve justice, and as such prosecutors must seek out both inculpatory and exculpatory evidence, the Government makes clear that _____. _____ have no duty _____ _____ exculpatory evidence unless that evidence would have actionable foreign intelligence value. Accordingly, even though _____ "have a profound interest in obtaining truthful information," they do not have an interest in ensuring that justice is achieved in this case.

sponses _____. However, we do not have all of the witnesses' statements; instead, we are privy only to those portions of their statements that are deemed to have actionable foreign intelligence value. We do not have _____; we do not have _____ _____; we do not know _____ _____. Although the Government assures us that the statements have some indicia of reliability _____ _____ _____ _____ _____ _____. Without this context, however, we have only the bare statement, which the jury may consider to be true _____. This is a slim reed indeed upon which to base a jury verdict, especially where a man's life hangs in the balance.

I cannot disagree with the majority's statement that "because the Government will not allow Moussaoui to have contact with the witnesses, this court must provide a remedy adequate to protect Moussaoui's constitutional rights." However, the majority's effort to craft such a remedy rings hollow. The majority boldly states that "input by the prosecution team into the _____ process has worked no unfairness on Moussaoui," but directs that, "to provide Moussaoui with the fullest possible range of information from the witnesses," the district court must permit Moussaoui to _____ _____ _____ _____.* To say this is a "remedy" must be of cold comfort to Moussaoui. Although he may propose _____ _____ _____ _____ _____ _____. The entire process is cloaked in secrecy, making it difficult, if not impossible,

---

* The prosecution has had one distinct advantage not afforded to Moussaoui: it has been able to _____ over the course of many months, _____ _____ which may have aided the shaping of its trial strategy. This fact alone belies the majority's assertion that no unfairness has befallen Moussaoui.

for the courts to ensure the provision of Moussaoui's rights. Although the prosecution is laboring under the same constraints _____.
Moussaoui has constitutional rights, not extended to the prosecution, that are implicated by this procedure. Because the majority decrees that this so-called "remedy" will fulfill this court's obligation to protect Moussaoui's constitutional rights, today justice has taken a long stride backward.

To leave open the possibility of a sentence of death given these constraints on Moussaoui's ability to defend himself would, in my view, subvert the well-established rule that a defendant cannot be sentenced to death if the jury is precluded from considering mitigating evidence pertaining to the defendant's role in the offense. A sentence of death requires "a greater degree of reliability" than any lesser sentence.

Here, the reliability of a death sentence would be significantly impaired by the limitations on the evidence available for Moussaoui's use in proving mitigating factors (if he is found guilty). Although it has been repeated often enough to have the ring of cliché, death is different. It is the ultimate penalty, and once carried out, it is irrevocable. A sentence of death cannot be imposed unless the defendant has been accorded the opportunity to defend himself fully; it cannot be imposed without the utmost certainty, the fundamental belief in the fairness of the result. Because Moussaoui will not have access to the witnesses who could answer the question of his involvement, he should not face the ultimate penalty of death. Accordingly, I would uphold the district court's sanction to the extent that it struck the Government's death notice. On this basis, I dissent.

V. POSTSCRIPT

After the Supreme Court declined to hear his pretrial appeal, Moussaoui, for reasons known only to himself, pleaded guilty to the charges against him in April 2005. Perhaps his decision was the result of his unstable mental condition, or of his desire for immediate martyrdom, or perhaps of his fear that the government would transfer him to military custody and place him on trial in front of a military commission. In any case, whatever Moussaoui's motive for pleading guilty, the plea itself did not change the Fourth Circuit's September 13 decision regarding the use of substitutions in his case. During his sentencing hearing on March 27, 2006, excerpts from the intelligence reports of the interrogations of three al Qaeda detainees were read to the jury that was to decide whether Moussaoui should be executed or spend the rest of his life in prison. The substitutions indicated that Khalid Sheikh Mohammad would have testified that Moussaoui was to be part of a second wave of attacks on the White House and the Sears Tower in Chicago, that Mustafa al-Hawsawi would have testified that he had not helped Moussaoui arrange his travel to the United States as he had done with the other 9/11 hijackers and that Nurjaman Riduan Isamuddin (a.k.a. "Hambali") would have testified that Moussaoui was "very troubled, not right in the head" and that he "managed to annoy everyone he came into contact with."[17] Despite the potential exculpatory impact of these substitutions, their significance paled before the inculpatory significance of what Moussaoui said on the stand the very same day the substitutions were read to the jury. Although Moussaoui had denied in earlier proceedings that he had anything to do with the 9/11 attacks, he now testified that he knew prior to 9/11 that al Qaeda operatives were planning to fly planes into the World Trade Center and that his role in the attack was to fly a plane into the White House. Asked if he had lied to an FBI agent in August 2001 so that he "could allow the operation to go forward," Moussaoui defiantly answered, "That is correct."[18]

Moussaoui's testimony at his sentencing hearing suggested that he was actively seeking a death sentence, possibly because such an outcome would increase the likelihood that the Supreme Court would eventually hear his case on appeal. His goal was ultimately martyrdom, but he also wanted to put the American criminal justice system on trial in the court of world public opinion by taking his Sixth Amendment objection to his sentencing hearing to the Supreme Court. It was a near certainty that international public opinion would not accept the legitimacy of a death sentence for Moussaoui if he was not permitted any personal access to witnesses who could provide exculpable testimony on his behalf. Moussaoui's strategy backfired, however, when the jury, after deliberating for forty-one hours over seven days, returned a sentence of life imprisonment on May 4, 2006. It was later reported that one holdout juror stood between Moussaoui and the unanimous verdict that was required for a death sentence.[19] If true, one American citizen stymied both Moussaoui's plan to put the American criminal justice system on trial and the Bush administration's efforts to bring closure to the tragedy of the 9/11 attacks by executing a known member of al Qaeda: a remarkable end to a remarkable case.

On May 9, Moussoui filed a motion to withdraw his guilty plea, arguing that he deserved a new trial because he had not been involved with the 9/11 attacks in any way, which of course contradicted what he had said at his sentencing hearing. Judge Brinkema summarily rejected the motion and Moussaoui was transferred to the Supermax federal prison in southern Colorado, where he will spend the rest of his days in solitary confinement. Moussaoui's future obscurity, however, does not detract from the significance of the decision that carries his name. The September 13 decision in the Moussaoui case will be the controlling precedent for any future prosecution of an al Qaeda terrorist in a civilian federal court, at least one that is within the jurisdiction of the Fourth Circuit. If that is so, then it will still be possible for the government to deny such a terrorist access to detainees who could provide exculpatory evidence on his behalf, so long as the defense can read to the jury substitutions from summaries of the intelligence reports of the interrogations of the detainees. Whether such a practice is consistent with the Sixth Amendment and due process of law remains a live and significant controversy in the context of the war on terrorism.

NOTES

1. District Court, Docket Nos. 491 and 557.

2. District Court, Docket Nos. 594, 616, and 711.

3. District Court, Docket Nos. 717 and 722.

4. District Court, Docket No. 725.

5. District Court, Docket No. 732. Also see Toni Locy, "Court Papers Reveal Specifics of Moussaoui Ruling," *USA Today*, April 24, 2003, 2A. In January 2003, Judge Brinkema's ordered a videotaped deposition of Binalshibh. On August 29, 2003, Brinkema granted defense motions seeking comparable access to two additional detainees: Khalid Sheik Mohammad, al Qaeda's former chief of operations and mastermind behind the 9/11 attacks, and Mustafa Ahmed Hawsawi, the paymaster of the attacks. Throughout the chapter, Binalshibh, Mohammad, and Hawsawi will be referred to as the detainees.

6. District Court, Docket No. 925.

7. 373 U.S. 83 (1963).

8. 438 U.S. 586 (1978). Also see *Gardner v. Florida*, 430 U.S. 349, 361 (1977).

9. The Fourth Circuit's amended opinion identifies the following press reports that highlighted the 9/11 Commission's access to al Qaeda detainees: Philip Shenon, "Accord Near for 9/11 Panel to Question Qaeda Leaders," *The New York Times*, May 12, 2004, at A20 and "Vice Chairman Expects Responses to Written Questions Soon," *Associated Press*, May 13, 2004.

10. Id. at 460–61.

11. 541 U.S. 36, 62 (2004).

12. Id. at 59.

13. Id. at 478, footnote 31.

14. Id. at 479.

15. Id. The length of the redacted material is estimated from the slip opinion available at http://findlaw.com

16. Id., footnote 34.

17. Markon and Dwyer, "Moussaoui Offered to Implicate Himself," A01; "Moussaoui Says He Was to Fly 5th Plane," *Washington Post*, March 28, 2006, A01; Neil A. Lewis, "Moussaoui Now Ties Himself to 9/11 Plot," *The New York Times*, March 28, 2006.

18. Neil A. Lewis, "Moussaoui Now Ties Himself to 9/11 Plot," *The New York Times*, March 28, 2006.

19. Timothy Dwyer, "One Juror Between Terrorist and Death," *Washington Post*, May 12, 2006, A01.

Chapter 5

Trial by Military Commissions

Hamdan v. Rumsfeld

Courts-martial are military courts with jurisdiction over members of the American armed forces charged with violating the Uniform Code of Military Justice (UCMJ). They are well established and defined proceedings that embody high standards of fairness and due process.[1] In contrast, military commissions throughout American history have been temporary and flexible tribunals that have replaced civilian courts in times of martial law or military occupation or in trials of combatants who allegedly violated the laws of war. The level of due process achieved by these types of military commissions has varied in American history, depending on the circumstances of their use and the purpose for which they were established, but they tended not to achieve the level of fairness embodied in modern courts-martial or civilian trials. Of course, despite this shortcoming, trying terrorists by military commissions, rather than by civilian courts, would arguably be an effective way to bring terrorists to justice without running the risk of eroding American constitutional rights, such as the defendant's Sixth Amendment right to compel the attendance of witnesses, the subject of the preceding chapter.

On November 13, 2001, two months after the 9/11 attacks, President George W. Bush issued a military order authorizing the use of military commissions to try noncitizens "for violations of the laws of war and other applicable laws," the third type of commission noted above. The order stated that it was "not practicable" for these commissions to adhere to "the principles of law and rules of evidence generally recognized in the trial of criminal cases in the United States district courts." Accordingly, the order empowered the presiding officer of a commission to admit evidence that had "probative value to a reasonable person," regardless if the evidence would have been excluded from a civilian trial because it was, for example, hearsay or coerced from the defendant.[2] The order also directed the secretary of defense to issue more specific rules governing the protection of classified information and the removal of the defendant from the trial. This provision raised the possibility that a commission could convict a defendant on the basis of classified information that the defendant had not seen. Later regulations issued by Secretary of Defense Donald Rumsfeld confirmed this possibility, although the final version of these regulations permitted the exclusion of the defendant only if it would not deny "a full and fair trial."[3]

One of the first Guantanamo Bay Naval Base (GBNB) detainees charged under President Bush's system of military commissions was Salim Ahmed Hamdan, allegedly Osama bin Laden's former driver and bodyguard. Coalition forces captured Hamdan in Afghanistan in late 2001 and turned him over to American personnel soon thereafter. The military transferred him to GBNB in June 2002. President Bush found Hamdan eligible for trial by military commission in July 2003, at which point he was placed in solitary confinement. A year later the appointing authority for military commissions charged Hamdan with conspiring to attack and murder civilians, destroy civilian property, and engage in acts of terrorism. In a petition for a writ of habeas corpus, Hamdan objected to his upcoming trial by military commission, claiming that it would violate the UCMJ and the Geneva Conventions. Hamdan's petition triggered two years of litigation on the legality of Bush's policy of using military commissions to convict and punish terrorists in the war on terrorism, resulting in a Supreme Court decision in late June 2006. An exploration of the arguments on both sides of this debate provide a valuable opportunity, with the Moussaoui case in the background, to consider the question of how high-level terrorists should be prosecuted.

I. BACKGROUND

In American history the use of military commissions has been atypical, but there has been little or no doubt about their legitimacy or their legality in special circumstances. In 1780, General George Washington ordered a board of fourteen military officers to try Major John André, a British officer, for spying. André was convicted and hanged. In 1818 General Andrew Jackson constituted a court of eleven officers to try two British subjects for spying and inciting the Creek Indians to make war against the United States. One was hanged and the other shot. During the Mexican War, General Winfield Scott declared martial law and created a system of military tribunals that tried soldiers and civilians of both sides of the conflict. A distinction arose between courts-martial and military commissions during the Civil War. Courts-martial were for the purpose of trying American soldiers for offenses against the Articles of War that Congress had enacted, while military commissions tried offenses against "the law of war," a vague body of customary international rules that prohibited, for example, spying, assassinations, or sabotage.[4] There were over four thousand trials by military commissions during the Civil War. Most of them were convened in "the strife-torn border states of Missouri, Kentucky, and Maryland" to deal with "guerilla activities, horse stealing, and bridge-burning."[5] However, the composition and procedure of a military commission during the Civil War generally resembled that of a court-martial.

In 1865, a nine-member commission convicted Confederate Captain Henry Wirz, the former superintendent of the notorious Andersonville prison in Georgia, of conspiracy "to injure the health and destroy the lives of soldiers in the military service of the United States . . . to the end that the armies of the United States might be weakened and impaired, in violation of the laws and customs of war."[6] In the same year, President Andrew Johnson established a nine-member commission to try eight individuals for conspiring to kill Abraham Lincoln, Johnson himself, Secretary of State William H. Seward, and General Ulysses S. Grant, despite the fact that the civilian courts in Washington, D.C. were open and functioning. All the defendants were convicted and four were hanged, including Mary E. Surratt. On the day of her execution, her lawyers challenged the jurisdiction of the military commission, but her petition was denied after government lawyers informed the judge that Johnson had suspended the writ of habeas corpus.

The Supreme Court addressed the legality of military commissions for the first time in 1865. In the preceding year, a military commission had convicted Lambdin P. Milligan, a resident of Indiana, of conspiring against the United States, providing aid and comfort to the rebels, inciting insurrection, disloyal practices, and violating the laws of war. The sentence was death. Milligan filed a petition for a writ of habeas corpus and the Supreme Court ruled that military courts could not constitutionally try civilians in states where civilian courts were open and functioning. The Court emphasized the fact that Milligan had never been a member of the armed forces of either the North or the South and had never resided in any of the rebellious states. Accordingly, although military commissions could not try civilians in nonrebellious states if courts were open, the Court indirectly implied that military trials of civilians in rebellious states might not be illegal and that military commissions might be able to try enemy soldiers who violated the laws of war.[7]

Two years after the Supreme Court handed down *Milligan*, Samuel A. Mudd, the physician who had set John Wilkes Booth's broken leg during his flight from Washington, D.C., challenged the jurisdiction of the military commission that had convicted him and sentenced him to life imprisonment at hard labor. He relied heavily on the *Milligan* rule that military trials were unconstitutional if civilian courts were open. In response, Judge Thomas

Boynton denied that the precedent was "a case in point," noting that the assassination, unlike Milligan's actions, took place "in a fortified city, which had been invaded during the war" and that the assassins had acted, not from any private motive, but from "a desire to impair the effectiveness of military operations." Johnson eventually pardoned Mudd, but his conviction by a military commission was never overturned, despite years of litigation.[8]

In 1920 Congress granted courts-martial the jurisdiction to try violations of the laws of war, but Article 15 also recognized the concurrent jurisdiction of military commissions.

> ART. 15 JURISDICTION NOT EXCLUSIVE.—The provisions of these articles conferring jurisdiction upon courts-martial shall not be construed as depriving military commissions, provost courts, or other military tribunals of concurrent jurisdiction in respect of offenders or offenses that by statute or by the law of war may be triable by such military commissions, provost courts, or other military tribunals.

Relying in part on Article 15, President Franklin D. Roosevelt in 1942 appointed a seven-member commission to try eight German saboteurs who had secretly entered the country for the purpose of destroying war-related factories and other strategic targets. During the trial, military counsel for the saboteurs petitioned the Supreme Court for a writ of habeas corpus. The Court heard argument over July 29 and 30 and issued its decision upholding the jurisdiction of the military commission the following day. The commission thereupon convicted all eight men and sentenced six of them to death.[9] The Supreme Court did not issue an opinion in *Ex Parte Quirin* until October 29, 1942, well after the burial of the six executed saboteurs. The Court's primary concern was the jurisdiction of the military commission. Regarding that question, the Court had no doubt that the first charge of violating the "law of war" was proper since the defendants had passed surreptitiously into the country without uniforms to commit acts of sabotage. In such an instance, trial by military commission was lawful despite the fact that the civilian courts were open and functioning. The *Milligan* rule did not apply to enemy belligerents who violated the law of war (see box 5.1).[10]

Box 5.1. EXCERPTS FROM *EX PARTE QUIRIN*

. . . By the Articles of War, and especially Article 15, Congress has explicitly provided, so far as it may constitutionally do so, that military tribunals shall have jurisdiction to try offenders or offenses against the law of war in appropriate cases.

. . . We are concerned only with the question whether it is within the constitutional power of the national government to place petitioners upon trial before a military commission for the offenses with which they are charged. . . .

By universal agreement and practice the law of war draws a distinction between . . . lawful and unlawful combatants. Lawful combatants are subject to capture and detention as prisoners of war by opposing military forces. Unlawful combatants are likewise subject to capture and detention, but in addition they are subject to trial and punishment by military tribunals for acts which render their belligerency unlawful. . . .

Specification 1 states that petitioners "being enemies of the United States and acting for . . . the German Reich, a belligerent enemy nation, secretly and covertly passed, in civilian dress, contrary to the law of war, through the military and naval lines and defenses of the United States . . . and went behind such lines, contrary to the law of war, in civilian dress . . . for the purpose of committing . . . hostile acts, and, in particular, to destroy certain war industries, war utilities and war materials within the United States." . . . .

Petitioners . . . stress the pronouncement of this Court in the *Milligan* case that the law of war "can never be applied to citizens in states which have upheld the authority of the government, and where the courts are open and their process unobstructed." . . . We construe the Court's statement as to the inapplicability of the law of war to *Milligan*'s case as having particular reference to the facts before it. From them the Court concluded that Milligan, not being a part of or associated with the armed forces of the enemy, was a non-belligerent, not subject to the law of war. . . .

. . . We have no occasion now to define with meticulous care the ultimate boundaries of the jurisdiction of military tribunals to try persons according to the law of war. It is enough that petitioners here, upon the conceded facts, were plainly within those boundaries, and were held in good faith for trial by military commission, charged with being enemies who, with the purpose of destroying war materials and utilities, entered or after entry remained in our territory without uniform—an offense against the law of war. We hold only that those particular acts constitute an offense against the law of war which the Constitution authorizes to be tried by military commission. . . .

In September 1945 the American military convened a law-of-war commission in the Philippines to try Tomoyuki Yamashita for not stopping his
troops from committing war crimes against civilians and prisoners of war.
There was no evidence that Yamashita had participated in any of the atrocities or even that he knew about them. The charge was rather that he should
have stopped the atrocities because he should have known about them. A
five-member commission convicted Yamashita, at least in part, on the basis
of hearsay evidence that would never have been admitted in an American
civilian trial. In a 6–2 decision, the Supreme Court held that Yamashita's
failure to control his troops was a violation of the law of war that could be
tried by a military commission and that the procedures of the trial, including the admission of hearsay evidence, was lawful because none of the protections for defendants embedded in the Articles of War applied to unlawful enemy combatants. The dissents charged both that the commission
violated the Due Process Clause and the Articles of War and that the allegation against Yamashita had never been considered a violation of the law of
war prior to his prosecution. Despite these objections, Yamashita was hanged
on February 23, 1946.[11]

Following World War II, the law of war was revised and updated by the
four Geneva Conventions of 1949, which the United States ratified in 1955.
The Third Convention dealt with the treatment of prisoners of war (GPW) and
the Fourth with the treatment of civilians, both of which were potentially relevant to the legality of future military commissions. However, all four Conventions also included a Common Article 3 (CA3) that applied to cases of
armed conflict "not of an international character occurring in the territory of
one of the High Contracting Parties." CA 3 established a minimal set of protections for those who were "taking no active part in hostilities," presumably
including captured war criminals. "Cruel treatment," "torture," "outrages on
personal dignity," and "humiliating and degrading treatment" were all prohibited. In addition, the Article prohibited the imposition of any punishments
without the previous judgment of a "regularly constituted court affording all
the judicial guarantees which are recognized as indispensable by civilized
peoples." Following the U.S. ratification of the Conventions, it was not entirely clear whether only political and military authorities were responsible
for enforcement of CA3 or whether federal judges could also enforce it in judicial proceedings. (See box 5.2.)

In 1950 Congress enacted the Uniform Code of Military Justice (UCMJ).
The UCMJ revised, unified, and consolidated the Articles of War, the Articles
for the Navy, and the Disciplinary Laws of the Coast Guard. The revised
UCMJ reenacted Article 15 (quoted above) as Article 21, thereby maintain-
ing the principle that military commissions had concurrent jurisdiction with

---

Box 5.2. COMMON ARTICLE 3

In the case of armed conflict not of an international character occurring in the territory of one of the High Contracting Parties, each Party to the conflict shall be bound to apply, as a minimum, the following provisions:

(1) Persons taking no active part in the hostilities, including members of armed forces who have laid down their arms and those placed hors de combat by sickness, wounds, detention, or any other cause, shall in all circumstances be treated humanely, without any adverse distinction founded on race, color, religion or faith, sex, birth or wealth, or any other similar criteria. To this end the following acts are and shall remain prohibited at any time and in any place whatsoever with respect to the above-mentioned persons:

(a) violence to life and person, in particular murder of all kinds, mutilation, cruel treatment and torture;

(b) taking of hostages;

(c) outrages upon personal dignity, in particular, humiliating and degrading treatment;

(d) the passing of sentences and the carrying out of executions without previous judgment pronounced by a regularly constituted court affording all the judicial guarantees which are recognized as indispensable by civilized peoples. . . .

---

courts-martial.[12] Second, a new Article 36 slightly revised the old Article 38 that had granted the president the authority to adapt the procedures and the rules of evidence of both courts-martial and military commissions from those used in civilian trials. The president was under an obligation to use the civilian rules, but only so far as he considered them "practicable."

(a) Pretrial, trial, and post-trial procedures, including modes of proof, for cases arising under this chapter triable in courts-martial, military commissions and other military tribunals, and procedures for courts of inquiry, may be prescribed by the President by regulations which shall, so far as he considers practicable, apply the principles of law and the rules of evidence generally recognized in the trial of criminal cases in the United States district courts, but which may not be contrary to or inconsistent with this chapter.

(b) All rules and regulations made under this article shall be uniform insofar as practicable.[13]

Although Article 36 granted the president latitude to depart from "impracticable" procedures of civilian courts, paragraph (b) of Article 36 was ambiguous. Did it mean that the procedures of military commissions had to be "uniform" with all the rules that the UCMJ mandated for courts-martial or with only the nine provisions of the UCMJ that referred specifically to military commissions? The first interpretation required substantial uniformity between the two types of tribunals; the second did not. Also, Article 36 was unclear about who assessed the requirement in (b) that all rules and regulations of courts-martial and military commissions be uniform "insofar as practicable." Both issues became important points of contention in *Hamdan v. Rumsfeld*.

II. BRIEFS FILED IN *HAMDAM*

The conspiracy charge against Hamdan was composed of thirteen numbered paragraphs, nine of which identified Usama bin Laden and described the goals and activities of al Qaeda, while only two addressed Hamdan's conduct. The first of these two paragraphs alleged that Hamdan "knowingly joined an enterprise of persons who shared a common criminal purpose" and "conspired and agreed" with others to commit offenses "triable by military commission." The second of the two described the "overt acts" that Hamdan had allegedly committed in furtherance of the conspiracy (see box 5.3). It was not

---

Box 5.3. HAMDAN'S CONSPIRACY CHARGE*

12. Salim Ahmed Hamdan (a/k/a Salim Ahmad Hamdan, a/k/a Salem Ahmed Salem Hamdan, a/k/a Saqr al Jadawy, a/k/a Saqr al Jaddawi, Khalid bin Abdallah, a/k/a Khalid wl'd Abdallah, hereinafter "Hamdan"), in Afghanistan, Pakistan, Yemen, and other countries, from on or about February 1996 to on or about November 24, 2001, willfully and knowingly joined an enterprise of persons who shared a common criminal purpose and conspired and agreed with Usama bin Laden, Saif al Adel, Dr. Ayman al Zawahari (a/k/a "the Doctor"), Muhammad Atef (a/k/a Abu Hafs al Masri), and other members and associates of the al Qaida organization, known and unknown, to commit the following offenses triable by military commission: attacking civilians; attacking civilian objects; murder by an unprivileged belligerent; destruction of property by an unprivileged belligerent; and terrorism.

13. In furtherance of this enterprise and conspiracy, Hamdan and other members of associates of al Qaida committed the following overt acts:

a. In 1996, Hamdan met with Usama bin Laden in Qandahar, Afghanistan and ultimately became a bodyguard and personal driver for Usama bin Laden. Hamdan served in this capacity until his capture in November of 2001. Based on his contact with Usama bin Laden and members or associates of al Qaida during this period, Hamdan believed that Usama bin Laden and his associates were involved in the attacks on the U.S. embassies in Kenya and Tanzania in August 1998, the attack on the USS *Cole* in October 2000, and the attacks on the United States on September 11, 2001.

b. From 1996 through 2001, Hamdan:

1) delivered weapons, ammunition or other supplies to al Qaida members and associates;

2) picked up weapons at Taliban warehouses for al Qaida use and delivered them directly to Saif al Adel, the head of al Qaida's security committee, in Qandahar, Afghanistan; and

3) served as a driver for Usama bin Laden and other high ranking al Qaida members and associates. At the time of the al Qaida-sponsored attacks on the U.S. embassies in Tanzania and Kenya in August of 1998, and the attacks on the United States on September 11, 2001, Hamdan served as a driver in a convoy of three to nine vehicles in which Usama bin Laden and others were transported to various areas in Afghanistan. Such convoys were utilized to ensure the safety of Usama bin Laden and the others. Bodyguards in these convoys were armed with Kalishnikov rifles, rocket propelled grenades, hand-held radios, and handguns.

c. On diverse occasions between 1996 and November of 2001, Hamdan drove or accompanied Usama bin Laden to various al Qaida-sponsored training camps, press conferences, or lectures. During these trips, Usama bin Laden would give speeches in which he would encourage others to conduct "martyr missions" (meaning an attack wherein one would kill himself as well as the targets of the attack) against the Americans, to engage in war against the Americans, and to drive the "infidels" out of the Arabian Peninsula.

d. Between 1996 and November of 2001, Hamdan, on diverse occasions received training on rifles, handguns and machine guns at the al Qaida-sponsored al Farouq campus in Afghanistan.

---

* The complete charge against Hamdan is available at www.defenselink.mil /news/Jul2004/d20040714hcc.pdf

clear from the charge whether the government was alleging that any of these alleged overt acts, by itself or in combination with any of the others, constituted a violation of the law of war.

During the summer of 2004, newspaper reports speculated that harsh interrogation techniques had "migrated" to Iraq from both Afghanistan and the GBNB and that this migration was partly responsible for the abuse at Abu Ghraib prison.[14] The graphic reality of the Abu Ghraib photos lent credibility to the claim that coercive interrogations might have been used at GBNB and indirectly highlighted the possibility that a military commission could convict Hamdan based on "probative" evidence that had been obtained through coercive interrogations of Hamdan himself or some other detainee. In October 2004, the presiding officer of Hamdan's commission excluded him from the *voir dire* process, depriving him of the opportunity to personally challenge the members of the panel that was scheduled to try him in December. Secretary of Defense's Military Commission Order No. 1 permitted the exclusion of the defendant (but not his assigned military counsel) to protect "classified or classifiable" information; other information "protected by law or rule from unauthorized disclosure;" "the physical safety of participants of the Commission proceedings, including witnesses"; "intelligence and law enforcement sources, methods, and activities"; and, finally, "other national security interests."[15] Hamdan's exclusion from the *voir dire* process once again raised the possibility that he could be convicted on the basis of evidence that he had no opportunity to rebut.

Hamdan's appointed military defense lawyer, Navy Lieutenant Commander Charles Swift, adapted Hamdan's pending petition for a writ of habeas corpus into a general challenge of the lawfulness of the military commission that was about to try him. Neal Katyal, a civilian and a law professor at Georgetown Law School, joined the defense team. Hamdan's habeas petition came before James Robertson, a federal district judge in the District of Columbia, in early September of 2004. On November 8, Robertson held that Article 21 of the UCMJ limited the jurisdictions of military commissions to "offenders or offenses that by statute or by the *law of war* may be tried by military commissions" (emphasis added). Since the Third Geneva Convention (GPW) was a part of the "law of war," Hamdan had to be tried by a court-martial so long as his prisoner-of-war status was in doubt.[16] Robertson also held that Hamdan's military commission was illegal because it violated his rights under the UCMJ to be present at his trial and to see all the evidence admitted against him. Citing Article 36 (see above), Robertson argued that the procedures of any military commission could be "different" from those of the UCMJ, but they could not be "contrary to or inconsistent with" the UCMJ. Although Robertson had indicated that certain provisions of the Geneva Conventions were self-executing, he did not base his ruling regarding the illegality of the commission's procedures on Common Article 3, which he described as having no "fixed" meaning.[17]

The government immediately appealed Judge Robertson's decision to the D.C. Circuit Court of Appeals. The judges on the panel were Stephen Williams, Arthur Randolph, and John Roberts, whom President Bush would soon nominate to Chief Justice of the United States. These three judges gave President Bush a huge victory when it handed down their decision on July 15, 2005, one week after bombs exploded in three of London's underground trains and one double-decker bus, killing fifty-six people and injuring over seven hundred. Regarding every substantive issue of the case, the panel sided with the government. First, in its view, Congress had, by the Authorization for Use of Military Force and two relevant provisions of the UCMJ (10 U.S.C. 821 and 836), granted President Bush the authority to create military commissions. Second, the Geneva Conventions of 1949 were not judicially enforceable. Third, even if the Conventions were enforceable, Hamdan had no rights under them because he did not qualify as a prisoner of war and, more broadly, because the Conventions did not apply to a nonstate actor like al Qaeda, especially one that was not abiding by the Conventions. Fourth, CA3 provided no protections to Hamdan because the conflict with al Qaeda was of an international character. Fifth, even if CA3 applied, objections based to the procedures of a commission could only be considered after Hamdan had exhausted all his military appeals following his conviction. Sixth, the procedures of a military commission did not have to conform to all the provisions of the UCMJ, but only to those that explicitly referred to military commissions. Seventh, army regulations implementing the Geneva Conventions did not give Hamdan a right to an Article 5 hearing because President Bush had the authority to determine that he was not a POW and also because a military commission was a "competent tribunal" to make such a determination.[18]

Four days after the D.C. Circuit handed down its *Hamdan* decision, President Bush nominated Judge Roberts to fill the seat on the Supreme Court left vacant by the retirement of Sandra Day O'Connor. Then, six weeks later, when Chief Justice Rehnquist died on September 5, 2005, Bush nominated Roberts to occupy the Court's center seat. The Senate confirmed Roberts on September 29, even though it had become known that Roberts had a number of White House interviews for a possible Supreme Court appointment while *Hamdan* was under active consideration by the D.C. Circuit. Although no one suggested that Roberts voted in *Hamdan* to increase his chances of receiving a Supreme Court nomination, legal commentators claimed that "to avoid even the appearance of impropriety whenever possible" Roberts should have withdrawn from the case or informed Swift and Katyal of the interviews.[19] On November 7, the Supreme Court agreed to hear *Hamdan* and Chief Justice Roberts shortly thereafter recused himself from any further participation in the case. Two days after the Court took the case, bombs exploded at three hotels in Amman, Jordan, leaving 60 dead and 120 wounded.

On December 16, 2005, as Congress was considering the renewal of the controversial USA PATRIOT Act, *The New York Times* reported that President Bush had signed an order soon after the 9/11 attacks that authorized the National Security Agency (NSA; a secret agency based at Fort Meade, Maryland, nicknamed "No Such Agency") to intercept the international phone calls and e-mails of persons residing inside the United States, including American citizens. The program was operating without a FISA warrant, despite the fact that FISA criminally prohibited any foreign intelligence surveillance not in compliance with its provisions. Only a few members of Congress knew about the NSA's program and they had been pledged to secrecy. The White House had asked *The New York Times* not to publish the story because it would endanger ongoing investigations and warn possible terrorists that they were under surveillance. The newspaper delayed the story for a year, but decided to publish it while Hamdan's attorneys and the government were preparing to submit their briefs to the Supreme Court and while Congress was debating whether to extend controversial provisions of the USA PATRIOT Act, including the one that granted the Federal Bureau of Investigation relatively easy access to Internet, library, and medical records.[20]

The briefs in *Hamdan* focused on the following issues: (1) Did the president have constitutional authority to establish military commissions or could they only be created by Congress? (2) Has Congress authorized commissions by the AUMF and relevant provisions of the UCMJ? (3) Was Hamdan a type of offender and was conspiracy a type of offense that could be tried by a military commission? (4) Has Congress enacted laws that have implemented any of Hamdan's rights under the Geneva Conventions? (5) Were the Geneva Conventions, including CA3, self-executing and therefore judicially enforceable without any implementation legislation? (6) Were the Conventions applicable to the conflict against al Qaeda? (7) Must a military commission respect the defendant's right to be present and the right to confront the evidence against him? The government and Hamdan's attorneys squared off on each of these issues, joined by over thirty *amici curiae*, most of whom filed briefs on behalf of Hamdan. The stakes of the litigation were high because how the Supreme Court answered the above questions could have implications for the war on terrorism beyond the lawfulness of military commissions. For example, if the Court held that the Geneva Conventions were self-executing, then Common Article 3 would be judicially enforceable against all aspects of the ongoing war on terrorism, including the Bush administration's detention and interrogation policies.

EXCERPTS FROM HAMDAN'S BRIEF

[[1. Limits on Commissions.]] This Court has repeatedly recognized that "the Framers harbored a deep distrust of executive military power and military tribunals." The traditions of this country favor civilian courts and courts-martial, not commissions, for the prosecution of war crimes. . . .

The jurisdiction of commissions has always been strictly confined. They have been permitted only as courts of necessity, convened temporarily by commanders in zones of active military operations and used to try war crimes or enforce justice in occupied territory when no other courts were open or had jurisdiction. . . .

Petitioner's commission does not fall within any of these traditional uses of commissions. Among other things, it was convened at Guantanamo Bay, which is neither a zone of combat nor occupied territory. Even *Quirin*, which marked the absolute outer bounds of the commissions used in World War II, recognized that war crimes tribunals have been exceptionally limited by constitutional tradition, specific legislation, and the laws of war. Here, however, the President has given the commission a jurisdiction that far exceeds any ever previously exercised. . . .

The court of appeals held that Congress had authorized the commission in the AUMF and two long-standing UCMJ provisions. None of these provisions authorize a commission; nor do they authorize the President to employ tribunals unfettered by tradition or the law of war. To whatever extent Congress *may* lawfully create commissions, none of the three statutes invoked by the President may be read to do so. . . .

The court of appeals erred in holding that these [[two]] provisions [[of the UCMJ (Articles 821 and 836)]] authorized this commission. At most, the provisions acknowledge that the President may, on occasion, be authorized to establish commissions, but *restrict* how the President may implement that authority. . . .

The object of the AUMF was to authorize military action. It said nothing about criminal punishment. In *Quirin*, even the Declaration of War was not enough to authorize a commission; the Court relied instead on other statutes. If commissions qualify as a "use [of] force," then those words permit any action the President believes related to terrorism, however tangential. Indeed, the President has, in this case and elsewhere, claimed precisely such unlimited powers under his broad reading of the AUMF.

A plurality of this Court recently rejected the idea that "a state of war" can be "a blank check for the President." It reached that conclusion in the far less onerous context of detention. It is wholly consistent with wartime precedent to interpret the AUMF as authority for one thing (detention) but not another (trial and punishment). "Congress in drafting laws may decide that the Nation may be 'at war' for one purpose and at peace' for another"; the "attitude of a free society toward the jurisdiction of military tribunals—our reluctance to give them authority to try people for nonmilitary offenses—has a long history.

Even if "force" were stretched to mean something it does not, the AUMF only authorizes "necessary and appropriate" force. The government has not shown that resurrecting a tribunal eschewed in Korea and Vietnam (and which four years after the September 11 attacks has not even completed one trial) is somehow necessary or appropriate, let alone both. . . .

Finally, assuming that "force" includes military tribunals, the AUMF only permits action necessary "to prevent" terrorism. In light of Respondent's separate claim of power to detain Hamdan indefinitely as an enemy combatant, the burden can only be met if his trial serves general deterrence. Terrorists fear being killed by our Armed Forces and intelligence community. If they cannot deter a terrorist, it is far-fetched to think that a prosecution of Hamdan at Guantanamo five years after his supposed crime would do so. . . .

Even if this Court were to conclude that the President possesses some inherent authority to convene military commissions, or that Congress has implicitly authorized their use, that authority must be strictly confined to safeguard liberty and our constitutional division of authority between the executive, legislative, and judicial branches. This Court has thus long construed authorizations for commissions to allow the President at most to employ them in accordance with their traditional use. . . .

The commissions created by the President fail to provide essential protections long afforded under the law of war and mandated in the UCMJ and Geneva Conventions. . . .

a. . . . 10 U.S.C. 836(a) codifies the longstanding requirement of consistency between commissions and courts-martial; it precludes the President from employing procedures in commissions that are "contrary to or inconsistent with" the UCMJ. It states that if Hamdan is merely "triable" in a court-martial, the UCMJ cannot be set aside. A commission that circumvents the procedural requirements of the UCMJ "exceeds the President's authority." . . .

b. The commission's procedures are avowedly "contrary to or inconsistent with" the procedural protections afforded by the UCMJ and by historical practice. For example, the proceedings can "exclude the Accused." As the district court concluded, this rule, which has already been used to bar Hamdan's presence, is fatally inconsistent with 10 U.S.C. 839(b). . . .

Similarly, this Court has held that "a criminal trial is not just unless one can confront his accusers." Although the right to confront witnesses is reflected in the Sixth Amendment, it has a genesis in natural law and has been recognized as essential in military courts and international law. Our Government, in fact, took the position during World War II that conducting a commission without the participation of the accused was a punishable violation of the laws of war.

In the face of this precedent, the Government has offered no authority that permits a commission to be convened without rights of presence and confrontation. Nor have they offered anything to suggest that Congress has authorized a commission whose own procedures violate the laws of war. . . .

Finally, this commission takes place outside of occupied territory or a zone of war, deviations from practice that Congress would not have anticipated and that this Court has not approved. Geographic limitations on jurisdiction ensure that commissions are used out of necessity, not to avoid procedural protections. . . . The government argued that "present threats to peace" and "world tension" justified expanding the "battlefront" concept. Yet the "exigencies which have required military rule on the battlefront are not present in areas where no conflict exists." . . .

Although Congress has authorized the President to promulgate *procedures* for trials within the jurisdiction of commissions, it withheld the power to define the offenses subject to such trial. Rather, 10 U.S.C. 821 ordains that, at most, the jurisdiction of commissions would be defined by the law of war. This jurisdictional limitation is the defining feature of military tribunals and the most important protection against the threat to liberty and our constitutional separation of powers posed by the existence of military trials.

Quirin recognized that a court must examine if "it is within the constitutional power of the National Government to place petitioners upon trial before a military commission for the offenses with which they are charged." The Court "*must therefore first inquire* whether any of the acts charged is an offense against the law of war cognizable before a military tribunal." The sole charge in this case, conspiracy, is not such an offense.

The charge [[against Hamdan]] fails to state a violation of the law of war for two reasons: (1) "conspiracy" is not an offense recognized by the laws of war; and (2) while acts of stateless terrorism are justifiably subject to severe punishment under civilian criminal law, they do not constitute war crimes falling within the jurisdiction of a military commission.

Neither the 1907 Hague Convention Respecting the Laws and Customs of War on Land, nor the Geneva Conventions of 1929 or 1949, make any mention of conspiracy as an offense against the law of war. The failure of the 1949 Geneva Conventions to identify conspiracy is particularly significant, since those treaties require signatories to punish so-called "grave breaches" of the

Conventions by criminal prosecutions. To fulfill this obligation, Congress passed the War Crimes Act of 1996 and the Expanded War Crimes Act of 1997. The Acts define a war crime as any "grave breach" of the Geneva Conventions, or violation of select provisions of the 1907 Hague Convention or the Landmine Protocol.

Thus, Congress no longer relies on the "common law of war" to define war crimes (as it did in World War II); it now has "crystalliz[ed]" and occupied the field with legislation identifying such crimes. Reflecting the universal disregard of conspiracy in international law, conspiracy is not on that large congressional list of offenses.

Likewise, the statutes and treaties establishing the major tribunals punishing war crimes in Rwanda and Yugoslavia, as well as the International Criminal Court, do not regard conspiracy as a war crime. The absence of conspiracy as a stand-alone crime is deliberate—conspiracy is seen as an abusive tool of prosecutors and rejected throughout the world. Customary international law evidences the same refusal. . . .

In short, there is no stand-alone war crime of conspiracy that permits Petitioner's trial. Accordingly, the commission lacks jurisdiction because Hamdan has not been charged with an offense that a commission may try. . . .

[[2. Third Geneva Convention (GPW).]] Article 5 of the GPW requires a hearing to determine POW status "[s]hould any doubt arise." Until a "competent tribunal" decides otherwise, those captured "shall enjoy" its "protections." Hamdan was apprehended in a theater of military operations and asserts a right to GPW protection. It is undisputed that no such Article 5 hearing has occurred. Thus, as the district court correctly concluded, Hamdan is entitled to presumptive POW status. One right POWs hold is the Article 102 right to be tried by "the same courts, according to the same procedure as in the case of members of the armed forces of the Detaining Power." As such, even if Hamdan's commission is otherwise consistent with federal law, the Geneva Conventions bar his trial. . . .

The court of appeals did not reject Hamdan's GPW claim on the merits, but rather because the "Convention does not confer upon Hamdan a right to enforce its provisions in court." That conclusion is in error.

As an initial matter, the court of appeals was wrong in concluding that the rights to which petitioner lays claim are embodied solely in the GPW. To the contrary, the United States has implemented its obligations under the GPW by statute and regulation, both of which are subject to enforcement through a mandamus or habeas corpus petition.

Second, the GPW is part of the law of war and limits the jurisdiction of commissions, a limitation this Court has repeatedly enforced. Thus, for example, in *Quirin*, this Court carefully considered the petitioners' status to discern whether they were, in fact, unlawful belligerents triable by commission. . . .

Hamdan's rights are separately enforceable under the Supremacy Clause because the GPW is self-executing. A treaty is self-executing when "no domestic legislation is required to give the Convention the force of law in the United States." Treaties that "by their terms confer rights upon individual citizens," are generally self-executing, unless a contrary intention is manifest.

"To ascertain whether [a provision] confers a right on individuals, we first look to the treaty's text as we would with a statute's." The GPW's text plainly confers individual rights; it does not merely regulate relations among states. Nothing in the relevant GPW provisions (particularly Arts. 3, 5, and 102) calls for legislation. Congress knew "that very little in the way of new legislative enactments will be required to give effect to the provisions." . . .

In this country, the mechanism for "ensur[ing] respect" for treaty rights includes the independent judiciary. . . .

The court of appeals concluded that Hamdan was chargeable under the law of war but not protected by it. The propositions are backward. The laws of war do not apply in the allegedly separate "war on terror" in which Hamdan's commission has been convened, but they do protect those *captured* in the conflict in *Afghanistan*, including Hamdan. GPW Article 2 provides, in pertinent part:

> [T]he present Convention shall apply to all cases of declared war or of any other armed conflict which may arise between two or more of the High Contracting Parties. . . . The Convention shall also apply to all cases of partial or total occupation of the territory of a High Contracting Party.

Afghanistan and the United States are High Parties. Yet Respondents claim that Hamdan is not protected because the "war against terror" is a separate conflict. This position ignores the undisputed facts of Hamdan's capture, is inconsistent with Article 2, and departs from American practice. . . .

Accordingly, under GPW Article 102, those committing offenses in the Afghan conflict may be tried by courts-martial for war crimes, not by commissions. . . .

In short, Respondents' contention that no individual assessment of Hamdan's status is required, and that he can be denied POW status by presidential fiat, is irreconcilable with text of Article 5, defeats its purpose, and departs from past American practice. This undermines "respect for the present Convention" and compromises our ability to insist on GPW observance when American personnel fall into enemy hands. The Court should reject that position, and consistent with longstanding tradition, adopt the treaty interpretation that faithfully enforces the protections the United States has promised to others and expects for its own forces.

[[3. Common Article 3.]] The commission is also invalid because it violates GPW Article 3, which prohibits "the passing of sentences and the carrying out of executions without previous judgment pronounced by a regularly constituted court affording all the judicial guarantees which are recognized as indispensable by civilized peoples" in "the case of armed conflict not of an international character occurring in the territory of one of the High Contracting Parties." . . .

Even if Hamdan does not qualify as a POW under GPW Article 4, he is nonetheless protected by these provisions. The commission clearly does not comply with them because it is not a "regularly constituted court." As the ICRC's definitive recent work explains, a "court is regularly constituted if it has been established and organized in accordance with the laws and procedures already in force in a country." The "court must be able to perform its functions independently of any other branch of the government, especially the executive."

Instead, the commission is an ad hoc tribunal fatally compromised by command influence, lack of independence and impartiality, and lack of competence to adjudicate the complex issues of domestic and international law. The rules for trial change arbitrarily—and even changed after the Petition for Certiorari was filed. It is not regularly constituted; its defects cannot be cured without a complete structural overhaul and fixed rules.

Commission procedures also fail to provide adequate "judicial guarantees" in many ways, including admitting evidence extracted under duress and denying the fundamental rights of confrontation and presence. These flaws are not theoretical; they have already had practical consequence, as Hamdan's exclusion from *voir dire* reveals.

The divided [[Court of Appeals]] panel nonetheless held that Article 3 does not apply because the conflict against al Qaeda is "international," and Article 3 only applies to internal conflicts. Even were that true, Article 3 extends to all conflicts as a matter of customary international law. And as Judge Williams recognized: "the logical reading of 'international character' is one that matches the basic derivation of the word 'international,' i.e., *between* nations."

> Respectfully submitted,
> NEAL KATYAL,
> Counsel of Record

EXCERPTS FROM THE GOVERNMENT'S BRIEF

Petitioner's central submission is that the President lacked the authority to establish military commissions to try and punish captured enemy combatants in the ongoing armed conflict against al Qaeda. That contention is refuted by

Congress's actions, this Court's precedents, and the war powers vested in the President by the Constitution. . . .

[[1. Congressional Authorization.]] In *Hamdi v. Rumsfeld*, a plurality of this Court concluded that the AUMF authorized the President to exercise his traditional war powers, and it relied on *Quirin* for the proposition that "the capture, detention, *and trial* of unlawful combatants, by 'universal agreement and practice,' are 'important incident[s] of war.'" Likewise, in *Yamashita*, the Court explained that an "important incident to the conduct of war is the adoption of measures by the military commander, not only to repel and defeat the enemy, but to seize and subject to disciplinary measures those enemies who, in their attempt to thwart or impede our military effort, have violated the law of war." Because "[t]he trial and punishment of enemy combatants" is a fundamental incident of war, it follows that, in authorizing the President "to use all necessary and appropriate force" against al Qaeda, the AUMF authorized the use of military commissions against enemy combatants, such as petitioner.

Congress has not only authorized the President to exercise his traditional war powers in the specific context of the armed conflict with al Qaeda; it has also specifically recognized his ongoing authority to invoke military commissions when he deems them necessary. Article 21 of the UCMJ, 10 U.S.C. 821, states that "[t]he provisions [of the UCMJ] conferring jurisdiction upon courts-martial do not deprive military commissions . . . of concurrent jurisdiction with respect to offenders or offenses that by the law of war may be tried by military commissions." That language originated in, and is identical in all material respects to, Article 15 of the Articles of War, which were enacted during World War I. . . .

[[This]] . . . Court has construed Article 15 as having "*authorized* trial of offenses against the laws of war before such commissions." Although the language of this authorization in Article 15 seems indirect, that simply recognizes that Congress was adding its imprimatur to a practice with a long history which did not depend on express statutory authorization. When Congress enacted Article 21 of the UCMJ, it merely recodified Article 15 of the Articles of War. Consequently, this Court's interpretation of Article 15 controls the interpretation of Article 21.

Article 36 of the UCMJ, 10 U.S.C. 836, provides even further statutory recognition of the President's authority to use military commissions. It authorizes the President to establish procedures "for cases arising under this chapter triable in . . . military commissions." . . .

Petitioner's attempts to undermine the obvious import of those congressional enactments are unavailing. The fact that Congress has not issued a formal declaration of war against al Qaeda is irrelevant. The President's prerogative to invoke the law of war in a time of armed conflict, including with respect to the trial and punishment of war criminals, in no way turns on the existence of such a declaration. The Court in *Hamdi* rejected a similar contention and found that the AUMF was sufficient to confirm Congress's support for the President's exercise of his war powers. . . .

Petitioner also errs in arguing that the use of military commissions is not "necessary" to prevent terrorism and therefore unauthorized by the AUMF. This Court has recognized that courts are not competent to second-guess judgments of the political branches regarding the extent of force necessary to prosecute a war. In any event, this Court has also recognized the general principle, in *Quirin*, *Yamashita*, and other cases, that trying unlawful combatants for violating the law of war is a fundamental part of the conduct of the war itself. The punishment of persons who have violated the law of war is an appropriate and time-honored means of deterring or incapacitating them from doing so in the future.

[[2. President's Constitutional Authority.]] Congress's multiple authorizations of the President's use of military commissions in the ongoing conflict with al Qaeda obviate the need to consider the President's inherent authority to act in the absence of such authorization. Nevertheless, the President undoubtedly possesses that authority, as history, Congress's enactments, and this Court's precedents make clear.

As this Court has noted, "[t]he first of the enumerated powers of the President is that he shall be Commander-in-Chief of the Army and Navy of the United States." The President's war power under Article II, Section 2, of the Constitution includes the inherent authority to create military commissions even in the absence of any statutory authorization, because that authority is a necessary and longstanding component of his war powers. The war power thus includes "the power . . . to punish those enemies who violated the law of war," because that power is "part of the prosecution of the war" and "a furtherance of the hostilities directed to a dilution of enemy power and involving retribution for wrongs done." . . .

The well-established executive practice of using military commissions confirms this conclusion. Throughout our Nation's history, Presidents have exercised their inherent commander-in-chief authority to establish military commissions without any specific authorization from Congress. For example, during the Mexican-American War in the 1840s, tribunals called "council[s] of war" were convened to try offenses under the law of war; other tribunals, called "military commission[s]," were created to administer justice in occupied areas. Likewise, during the Civil War, military commissions were convened to try offenses against the law of war, despite the lack of statutory authorization.

As this Court has repeatedly explained, "'traditional ways of conducting government . . . give meaning' to the Constitution." . . .

[[3. Law of War and Geneva Conventions.]] Petitioner contends that the law of war does not apply to the current conflict with al Qaeda, a foreign terrorist organization that engages in systematic violations of the law of war to accomplish its ideological and political goals. That contention is seriously mistaken.

The Constitution vests in the President the authority to determine whether a state of armed conflict exists against an enemy to which the law of war applies.

The President's determination that "members of al Qaida . . . have carried out attacks . . . on a scale that has created a state of armed conflict" is thus conclusive in establishing the applicability of the law of war to the conflict. Moreover, Congress itself determined that the law of war was applicable to al Qaeda when it authorized the President to use all "necessary and appropriate force" against the "nations, organizations, or persons he determines" were responsible for the September 11 attacks or those who "aided" them. There is no basis for this Court to invalidate the judgments made by both political branches that the law of war applies to al Qaeda. . . .

Petitioner suggests that, if the Geneva Convention does not apply to al Qaeda, the law of war does not apply either. That suggestion is baseless. There is no field preemption under the Geneva Convention. The Convention seeks to *regulate* the conduct of warfare to which it applies with respect to nation-states that have entered the Convention and agreed to abide by its terms, but it does not purport to apply to every armed conflict that might arise or to crowd out the common law of war. Instead, . . . the Convention applies only to conflicts identified in Articles 2 and 3. If an armed conflict, therefore, does not fall within the Convention, the Convention simply does not regulate it. Nothing in the Convention prohibits a belligerent party from applying the law of war to a conflict to which the Convention does not apply. . . .

[[4. Legality of Hamdan's Commission.]] Petitioner contends that his commission is invalid because it is located outside a zone of combat or occupied territory. That contention is unsound. The commission in *Quirin* was held in Washington, D.C., while the commission in *Yamashita* was held in the Philippines, which was a U.S. territory at the time. . . . [[There]] is no requirement that commissions established for the . . . purpose of prosecuting violations of the law of war must be confined to a war zone. . . .

Petitioner [[also]] contends that conspiracy, the offense with which he has been charged, is not a cognizable offense under the law of war. That is not so. Individuals have been tried before military commissions for conspiracy to commit war crimes throughout this Nation's history. The *Quirin* saboteurs were charged with conspiracy, as was another Nazi saboteur whose convictions were subsequently upheld. That long-standing practice suffices to defeat petitioner's claim. . . .

[[5. Judicial Enforceability of the Geneva Convention.]] Petitioner argues that subjecting him to a military commission would violate the Geneva Convention. For several reasons, that argument is mistaken.

As the court of appeals held, the Geneva Convention is not individually enforceable. The long-established presumption is that treaties and other international agreements do not create judicially enforceable rights. As the Court has observed: "A treaty is primarily a compact between independent nations. It depends for the enforcement of its provisions on the interest and the honor of the governments which are parties to it." When a violation of a treaty nonetheless occurs, it "becomes the subject of international negotiations and reclamations," not of judicial redress.

To be sure, treaties can, and on occasion do, create judicially enforceable private rights. But since such treaties are the exception, rather than the rule, there is a presumption that a treaty will be enforced through political and diplomatic channels, rather than through the courts. That background principle applies even when a treaty benefits private individuals.

In *Eisentrager*, this Court held that captured Nazi combatants challenging the jurisdiction of a military tribunal could not invoke the 1929 version of the Geneva Convention because the Convention was not judicially enforceable. Like the current version of the Convention, the 1929 version contained various provisions that protected individual rights. The Court explained, however, that the Convention's protections, like those of most treaties, "are vindicated under it only through protests and intervention of protecting powers." Although petitioner seeks to characterize this analysis as dictum, it was an alternative holding that formed the basis for the Court's rejection of the respondents' claims that the military commission violated their rights under the Convention. . . .

[[A]] . . . contrary construction of the Geneva Convention would severely encumber the President's authority as Commander in Chief. Indeed, petitioner's argument suggests that the hundreds of thousands of POWs held by the United States in this country during World War II were entitled to enforce the 1929 version of the Convention through private legal actions in our courts. The Executive Branch's construction of the Convention avoids such absurd consequences and is entitled to "great weight." . . .

Petitioner contends that, even if the Geneva Convention does not *itself* create judicially enforceable rights, it has been made enforceable by a variety of provisions of domestic law. That argument lacks merit. . . .

. . . Army regulations concerning the implementation of the Geneva Conventions . . . do not extend any substantive rights; instead, they merely establish internal policies. And, of course, it would be quite remarkable to construe an Army regulation to create rights for enemy combatants that can be enforced in *civilian* courts. . . .

[[6. GPW is not Applicable to al Qaeda.]] Even if the Geneva Convention were judicially enforceable, it is inapplicable to the ongoing conflict with al Qaeda and thus does not assist petitioner. The President has determined that the Geneva Convention does not "apply to our conflict with al Qaeda in Afghanistan or elsewhere throughout the world because, among other reasons, al Qaeda is not a High Contracting Party to [the Convention]." . . .

The decision whether the Geneva Convention applies to a terrorist network like al Qaeda is akin to the decision whether a foreign government has sufficient control over an area to merit recognition or whether a foreign state has ratified a treaty. In each case, the decision is solely for the Executive.

Even if some judicial review of the President's determination were appropriate, moreover, the standard of review would surely be extraordinarily deferential to the President. And, under any standard, the President's determination is manifestly correct. . .

Petitioner observes that he was captured in Afghanistan and that Afghanistan, unlike al Qaeda, is a party to the Geneva Convention. But the Convention does not apply based on where a particular conflict occurs, or a particular combatant is captured. Instead, Article 2 specifies that the Convention "shall apply to all cases of declared war or of any other armed conflict which may arise *between two or more of the High Contracting Parties.*" Because the United States and Afghanistan are both "High Contracting Parties," the President determined that the Convention could potentially apply to Afghanistan's Taliban regime. It does not follow, however, that the Convention would cover al Qaeda combatants who happen to be located in Afghanistan, because the conflict between the United States and al Qaeda is discrete and different from the conflict between the United States and the Taliban (and because al Qaeda is not a "High Contracting Party" or "Power" for purposes of Article 2). For the reasons discussed above, the question whether there is one conflict or two is precisely the kind of foreign-policy judgment that is committed to the President's discretion.

[[7. Commission's Consistency with GPW.]] Even if this Court were to conclude (notwithstanding the President's determination) that the Convention is applicable to al Qaeda, petitioner's trial by military commission would not violate the substantive terms of the Convention. Petitioner relies on Article 102 of the Convention, which provides that "[a] prisoner of war can be validly sentenced only if the sentence has been pronounced by the same courts according to the same procedure as in the case of members of the armed forces of the Detaining Power."

Article 102, however, applies only to a "prisoner of war." And petitioner does not qualify as a POW for purposes of Article 102 because he does not meet the requirements set out in Article 4 for POW status. The relevant subsection, Article 4(A)(2), provides that members of militias or volunteer corps are eligible for POW status only if the *group* in question displays "a fixed distinctive sign," "carr[ies] arms openly," and "conduct[s] [its] operations in accordance with the laws and customs of war." "[T]he widely accepted view" is that, "if the group does not meet the first three criteria . . . [an] individual member cannot qualify for privileged status as a POW." Al Qaeda does not remotely satisfy those criteria.

Petitioner contends that his assertion of POW status is itself sufficient to establish "doubt" as to whether he is a POW, and that he must be treated as a POW until a tribunal constituted under Article 5 of the Convention eliminates that doubt. . . . In this case, however, the CSRT process, which clearly discharges any obligation under Article 5, has removed any conceivable doubt by confirming prior military determinations and finding that petitioner is an enemy combatant who is a member or affiliate of al Qaeda.

[[8. Commission's Consistency with U.S. Law.]] . . . As an alien enemy combatant detained outside the United States, petitioner does not enjoy the protection of our Constitution.

Petitioner argues that the UCMJ requires that any military commission proceeding must conform to the rules for courts-martial. . . .

Petitioner's theory rests on a fundamental misunderstanding of the UCMJ. The UCMJ is directed almost exclusively to establishing the rules for courts-martial. The UCMJ does not purport to establish comprehensive procedures for military commissions, which are preserved by the UCMJ as "our common-law war courts" with a distinct tradition that dates from the earliest days of the Republic. . . . In fact, only nine of the statute's 158 articles even mention military commissions and specify particular safeguards that must be provided in military commissions as well as in the more comprehensively regulated courts-martial. If military commissions must replicate all of the procedures employed in courts-martial, it is not at all clear why Congress bothered to preserve them. . . .

[[10) Common Article 3.]] Finally, Petitioner argues that the procedures governing his military commission do not comport with the requirements of Article 3 of the Geneva Convention. As a preliminary matter, that contention fails because the Geneva Convention is not judicially enforceable. In any event, Article 3, by its plain terms does not apply to the ongoing conflict with al Qaeda. Article 3 applies only "[I]n the case of armed conflict *not of an international character* occurring in the territory of *one* of the High Contracting Parties." As the President determined, because the conflict between the United States and al Qaeda has taken place and is ongoing in several countries, the conflict is "of an international character," and Article 3 is thus inapplicable. Once again, the President's determination is dispositive or, at a minimum, entitled to great weight. . . .

In any event, petitioner's military commission complies with Article 3. In relevant part, Article 3 prohibits "[t]he passing of sentences and the carrying out of execution without previous judgment pronounced by a regularly constituted court affording all the judicial guarantees which are recognized as indispensable by civilized peoples." Petitioner's military commission, governed by . . . extensive procedural protections . . . and subject to judicial review under the DTA readily meets this standard. And the longstanding statutory recognition of the military commission as a legitimate body to try violations of the law of war and the repeated use of commissions throughout this Nation's history further refute petitioner's contention that the commission is not a regularly constituted court, as well as refuting his broader contention that use of a military commission is not authorized. . . .

> Respectfully submitted,
> PAUL D. CLEMENT,
> Solicitor General

EXCERPTS FROM HAMDAN'S REPLY BRIEF

The longstanding restrictions on commissions are not . . . disposable niceties. Rather, they are time-tested barriers to the dangerous seepage of martial law into our civilian order. To fail to enforce these limits would be to allow a dangerous and unprecedented expansion of Executive authority whose legal premise must be that the fight against terrorism justifies a reallocation of constitutional power. There would be no principled way to prevent that precedent from becoming the edifice upon which any number of actions could be grounded, even against U.S. citizens, from surveillance to indefinite detention, on the mere allegation that they are affiliates in that "war." If fighting terrorism requires such a basic shift in our legal order, it is for Congress, not the Executive, to say so; and Congress must say so in the most explicit of terms. . . .

The inescapable fact is that the conflict with al Qaeda is not equivalent to the only war [[World War II]] in which this Court approved commissions. Congress has not declared war; the laws of war have not been extended to these nonstate, nonterritorial actors; the conflict is in its fifth year; and Congress stands ready to act. So far, Congress has only authorized "force," conditioning even that grant by requiring it to be "necessary and appropriate" to promote specific (not general) deterrence. . . .

. . . Common Article 3's minimal guarantees are binding as customary international law in all conflicts. . . . [[T]]he President has never been able to break with customary international law when customary law is the basis for the President's action in the first place. Since the President claims the power to enforce laws of war through commissions, it cannot be that the President can then disregard those laws when they forbid the tribunal. To hold otherwise writes the "blank check" that *Hamdi* rejected. . . .

> Respectfully submitted,
> NEAL KATYAL,
> Counsel of Record

III. ORAL ARGUMENT

In late 2005 congressional concerns about President Bush's secret NSA domestic surveillance program derailed the administration's efforts to renew the USA PATRIOT Act prior to the December recess. Bush had to content himself with a one-month extension of the law that had significantly expanded the FBI's domestic surveillance powers (see chapter 1). However, Congress in late December did enact the Detainee Treatment Act (DTA), which President Bush signed on December 30. Largely the work of Senators John Warner (R-VA), John McCain (R-AZ), and Lindsey Graham (R-SC), the law established two important principles regarding future interrogations during the war on terrorism: first, anyone detained by the American military could only be interrogated in accordance with the terms of a new United States Army Field Manual on Intelligence Interrogation; second, anyone detained by the U.S. government, including those detained at secret CIA overseas facilities, shall not be subject to "cruel, inhuman, or degrading treatment or punishment," which the statute equated with the "shock-the-conscience" standard of the Fifth, Eighth, and Fourteenth Amendments.[21] The upshot was that, even if an interrogation technique did not constitute torture, it would be a violation of domestic law if it shocked the conscience. The law made such techniques illegal, though it did not impose criminal liability, whether or not the Geneva Conventions or the War Crimes Act was applicable to the war on terrorism. Although President Bush signed the DTA into law, he issued a "signing statement" that said he would interpret the legislation in a manner consistent with his power as president "to supervise the unitary executive branch" and as commander in chief to protect "the American people from further terrorist attacks."[22] The three Republican sponsors of the legislation immediately disputed Bush's apparent contention that he could sidestep the law if he thought it was necessary.[23]

One of the provisions of the DTA had enormous significance for the *Hamdan* litigation because it arguably took away from the Supreme Court its jurisdiction to hear the case. Based on this provision, the government filed a motion to dismiss the case on January 13, 2006. The Court asked both sides to brief the issue. The relevant provision was Section 1005(e), which amended the habeas corpus statute (28 U.S.C. 2241) by adding the following section:

> (e) Except as provided in section 1005 of the Detainee Treatment Act of 2005, no court, justice, or judge shall have jurisdiction to hear or consider—
>> (1) an application for a writ of habeas corpus filed by or on behalf of an alien detained by the Department of Defense at Guantanamo Bay, Cuba; or
>> (2) any other action against the United States or its agents relating to any aspect of the detention by the Department of Defense of an alien at Guantanamo Bay, Cuba, who—
>> (A) is currently in military custody; or
>> (B) has been determined by the United States Court of Appeals for the District of Columbia Circuit in accordance with the procedures set forth in Section 1005(e) of the Detainee Treatment Act of 2005 to have been properly detained as an enemy combatant.

The DTA stated that the above "jurisdiction-stripping" provision "shall take effect on the date of the enactment of this Act." Accordingly, the law was unclear as to whether the law was to be applied retroactively to the hundreds of habeas cases that were already pending in federal courts, including *Hamdan*, or only prospectively to future petitions filed by GBNB detainees. If the law did not take effect until December 30, then it was arguable, Hamdan's attorneys insisted, that it had no effect on existing habeas cases. The government, of course, took the opposite position. It claimed that, once the DTA went into effect, jurisdiction over every pending habeas case evaporated.

At about the time that the briefs on the jurisdiction-stripping provisions of the DTA were submitted to the Supreme Court, confirmation hearings were held for Samuel Alito, President Bush's nominee for the seat on the Supreme Court vacated by Sandra Day O'Connor after Harriet Miers withdrew her name from consideration in October 2005. The nomination was important because O'Connor had been a pivotal swing justice on the Supreme Court on many controversial constitutional issues, including questions involving presidential power. A group of Democratic senators mounted a feeble attempt to filibuster Alito's appointment, but the Senate confirmed Alito by a rough 58–42 party-line vote on January 31, with one Republican crossing over to vote against Alito and four Democrats voting in favor. Since he was confirmed prior to oral argument in *Hamdan*, Alito would participate fully in the decision.

In early February, newspaper reports circulated that military authorities at GBNB had begun to force-feed detainees to break hunger strikes. Lawyers for the detainees complained, but the government responded that a degree of coercion was necessary to prevent suicides.[24] Another study reported that Pentagon documents filed in court cases suggested that most of the detainees at GBNB had not engaged in any hostilities against the United States and that very few were associated directly with al Qaeda.[25] The ACLU also released fifty-four e-mails from 2002–2003 that the organization had acquired through its FOIA-based lawsuit against FBI and the Department of Defense. The e-mails were from FBI agents working at GBNB who had complained to their superiors in Washington that the military was using an assortment of abusive interrogation techniques at GBNB, including pornography, strobe lights, impersonations of FBI agents, loud music, extended interrogations, and cold temperatures.[26]

Lastly, a twenty-two-page memo that Alberto J. Mora, General Counsel of the Navy, had written on June 18, 2004 was leaked to the press. The memo summarized the formation of interrogation policy from December 2002 until June of 2003. Mora indicated in the memo that unlawful coercive interrogation techniques at GBNB "did not represent simply rogue activity . . . , but had been reportedly authorized at a 'high level' in Washington" and that some of the interrogation techniques that Secretary of Defense Donald Rumsfeld had approved "could produce effects reaching to the level of torture" and "certainly would constitute 'cruel, inhuman, or degrading treatment,' another class of unlawful treatment." Mora speculated that defendants in military commissions would call Rumsfeld as a witness because he had signed a memo authorizing "forced standing" as an interrogation technique and had, in addition, written in his own handwriting at the bottom of the memo the following notation: "However, I stand for 8-10 hours a day. Why is standing limited to 4 hours?" There was cause to be concerned, in Mora's opinion, that the notation could be seen as implicit encouragement to go beyond the approved techniques. Whether or not the notation could reasonably be read in this light, Mora's memo, once it became public, provided additional support to the conclusion that serious detainee abuse had more than likely occurred at GBNB.[27]

The above newspaper reports and Mora's leaked memo shaped the context of the session of oral argument that was held in *Hamdan* on March 28, 2006, a few weeks after an American diplomat was killed in Karachi, Pakistan. The session covered both the jurisdictional questions that the passage of the DTA had raised and the substantive ones that had been earlier debated in the main briefs filed by the parties. The following excerpts from the oral argument will generally focus on the substantive arguments for and against the legality of the military commissions. Neal Katyal emphasized that Hamdan was not challenging any ruling, but rather the "lawfulness of the tribunal itself" and insisted that conspiracy was not recognized by contemporary international law as a violation of the laws of war. Lastly, Katyal also argued that the procedures of the military commission, in particular the rule that allowed the exclusion of the defendant from his trial, was in violation of the UCMJ and CA3. In his portion of the oral argument, Katyal repeatedly borrowed the phrase "blank check" from Justice O'Connor's *Hamdi* opinion to underscore the depth of his objections to Bush's system of military commissions. Paul Clement responded that President Bush could deny that the Geneva Conventions applied to Hamdan at the same time that he prosecuted him for violating the laws of war. Hamdan had no right to challenge pretrial the lawfulness of his military commission because the commission was more than just "a group of people." Lastly, the charge of conspiracy was legitimate, according to Clement, because comparable charges had been tried as war crimes during the Civil War. In rebuttal, Katyal argued that if the Bush administration was insisting that the law of war had to adapt to the new type of war reflected in the war on terrorism, then it also had to recognize that the law of war has evolved since the Civil War and that conspiracy, according to contemporary international standards, was no longer a legitimate offense.

EXCERPTS FROM THE ORAL ARGUMENT

MR. KATYAL: . . . The whole point of this is to say we're challenging the lawfulness of the tribunal itself. This isn't a challenge to some decision that a court makes. This is a challenge to the court itself. . . . In *Quirin*, this Court rushed in to hear a military-commission challenge before the commission was over, and the reason why it did so was, it said that the public interest required adjudication of these issues. And the public interest is no less severe in that case than it is here. That is, this is a military commission that is literally unbounded by the laws, Constitution, and treaties of the United States. And if you adopt the Government's position here, it effectively replicates the blank check that this Court rejected in *Hamdi*. . . .

So, if I could turn to the merits . . . , the first thing I'd like to discuss . . . is . . . whether this military commission states a charge that violates the laws of war. And we believe it doesn't, for two essential reasons.

First, the only charge in this case is one of conspiracy. And conspiracy has been rejected as a violation of the laws of war . . . in every tribunal to consider the issue since World War II. It has been rejected in Nuremberg, it's been rejected in the Tokyo tribunals, it's been rejected in the international tribunals for Rwanda and Yugoslavia, and, most importantly, it's been rejected by the Congress of the United States, in 1997. . . . [[The]] problem . . . is compounded by the fact that the tribunal itself is charging a violation of the laws of war, when the military commission has never operated to try violations of

terrorism in stateless, territoryless conflicts. . . . [[The]] commission is operating in totally uncharted waters . . . , something as to which the full laws of
war have never applied. . . .

JUSTICE ALITO: Isn't this contrary to the way legal proceedings and appeals are normally handled? You have a—essentially, a pretrial appeal concerning the validity of the charge that may not even be the final charge.

MR. KATYAL: No . . . because [[this]] is a challenge to the lawfulness of
the underlying tribunal and the charge that's against them. . . . The world rejects conspiracy, because if it's adopted it allows so many individuals to get
swept up within its net. . . . And so, for example, under the Government's theory, a little old lady in Switzerland who donates money to al Qaeda, and that
turns out to be a front for terrorists acts and so on, might be swept up within
this broad definition of conspiracy. And that's why international law has so
rejected the concept of conspiracy. . . .

MR. KATYAL: . . . If I could turn to a second argument for why we believe
this military commission is impermissible, and that is that it defies the Uniform Code of Military Justice. The Uniform Code of Military Justice, in Article 36, sets minimal ground rules for military justice, writ large. And it says
that the President can't act in ways that are contrary to, or inconsistent with,
this chapter. . . .

JUSTICE SCALIA: What is the use of them if they have to follow all of
the procedures required by the UCMJ? I mean, I thought that the whole object was to have a different procedure.

MR. KATYAL: Justice Scalia, that's what the Government would like you
to believe. I don't think that's true. The historical relationship has been that
military commissions and courts-martial follow the same procedures. . . .

Now, to be clear, our position is not that military commissions must follow
all the rules for courts-martial. Not at all. They must require—must follow the
minimal baseline rules set in the Uniform Code of Military Justice by Congress.
They can depart from the panoply of rules, the 867 pages of rules in the Manual for Courts-Martial, so long as they don't depart from the UCMJ itself. . . .

JUSTICE KENNEDY: What fundamental, other than personal presence,
are you concerned with in this case? . . . Is there a requirement of prompt convening of the proceedings?

MR. KATYAL: Absolutely. There's an Article 10 right for speedy charges.
There is also an Article 67 right for independent Court of Appeals for the
Armed Forces review, which is something that is not guaranteed by this com-
mission. . . .

JUSTICE BREYER: But if you have . . . approximately the same procedures, what's the point of having a military commission? I think that was implicit in Justice Scalia's question. So, if you go back—Revolution, Seminoles, Medoc, Mexican War, World War II—why have them?

MR. KATYAL: Well, we had them before . . . because we couldn't find military court-martial jurisdiction. They were situations of absolute necessity. The reason was that the Articles of War, for one reason or another, didn't cover particular individuals. And, therefore, we needed to craft a separate procedure. But, whenever we did so, Justice Breyer, we always said that court-martial rules apply. . . . And, essentially, the worry is one of forum shopping, that you give the President the ability to pick a forum and define the rules. And that . . . is what I believe this Court rejected in *Hamdi* . . . when it rejected the blank check. . . .

MR. KATYAL: If I could turn to . . . the Geneva Conventions, I'd like to start with Common Article 3 and its minimal baseline requirements that a regularly constituted court be set up, and one that . . . affords the rights indispensable to civilized peoples. . . . [[That]] article does apply to Mr. Hamdan, and protects him. It's the most minimal rudimentary requirements that the United States Senate adhered to when it ratified the convention in 1955. And those requirements—

JUSTICE SCALIA: It depends on what you mean by "regularly constituted." In your brief, I gather you—what you meant is that a court that was pre-existing. It doesn't necessarily mean that. It just—it could mean one that was set up for the occasion, but was set up for the occasion by proper procedures. Wouldn't that be a "regularly constituted court"?

MR. KATYAL: Well, I think the way that it has been interpreted, "regularly constituted court," is not an ad hoc court with ad hoc rules. So, that is to say, Justice Scalia, if they resuscitated—

JUSTICE SCALIA: Well, I mean, not ad hoc in that sense, "I'm creating one court for this defendant, another court for the other defendant," but setting up for the occasion, and for trying numerous defendants, a new court. I don't think that, just because it's a new court, you can say that it's not a "regularly constituted court."

MR. KATYAL: So long as it is, (a) independent of the executive, which is what it's been interpreted to be, and, (b) affords the rights known to civilized peoples. And here, we think this military commission strays from both of those—from both of those. It's not independent of the executive—

JUSTICE GINSBURG: . . . What are the other rights recognized by all civilized people that these tribunals do not guarantee?

MR. KATYAL: . . . We're not talking about, you know, *Miranda* rights or something like that. We're talking about just a set of core ideas that every country on the world—every country in the world is supposed to dispense when they create war-crimes trials. And, even that minimal standard, the Government says they don't want to apply here.

And why we think this is enforceable is that Mr. Hamdan is being prosecuted in the name of the laws of war. And he has the right to invoke the Geneva Conventions defensively as a—as a way to constrain the tribunal. . . . If I could reserve the balance of my time.

JUSTICE STEVENS: Yes, you certainly may.

GENERAL CLEMENT: Justice Stevens, and may it please the Court:

The executive branch has long exercised the authority to try enemy combatants by military commissions. That authority was part and parcel of George Washington's authority as Commander in Chief of the Revolutionary Forces, as dramatically illustrated by the case of Major André. And that authority was incorporated into the Constitution.

Congress has repeatedly recognized and sanctioned that authority. Indeed, each time Congress has extended the jurisdiction of the court-martials, Congress was at pains to emphasize that that extension did not come in derogation of the jurisdiction of military commissions. . . .

JUSTICE STEVENS: . . . What sources of law have the commissions generally enforced over the years, beginning with George Washington and so forth? . . .

GENERAL CLEMENT: Well, what I would say, Justice Stevens, is, they basically enforce the laws of war. . . .

JUSTICE STEVENS: And what we have here is enforcement of the laws of war.

GENERAL CLEMENT: That is right. And, of course, in this context, you have a controlling executive act in the form of the regulations themselves that make it clear that the executive views things like conspiracy to violate the laws of war to be actionable under the laws of war. Now . . .

JUSTICE STEVENS: So, the basic position you're asserting is that . . . this commission intends to try a violation of the laws of war. And do the laws of war then have any application to the procedures that they have to follow?

GENERAL CLEMENT: Yes . . . , [[but]] I don't think that the law of war . . . extensively regulates procedure. . . . If . . . this Court follows the precedents in *Madsen*, it will recognize that only those nine provisions of the UCMJ that expressly reference military commissions will apply, and the rest is left to a much more common-law, war-court approach, where there's much greater flexibility.

JUSTICE SOUTER: What do you . . . make of the argument that Mr. Katyal just alluded to, that if you take . . . the position that the commissions are operating under the laws of war, you've got to accept that one law of war here is the Geneva Convention . . . with the . . . the rights that that carries? . . .

GENERAL CLEMENT: Well, I don't think, consistent with the position of the executive, that the Geneva Convention applies in this particular conflict.

JUSTICE SOUTER: But that, I guess, is the problem that I'm having. For purposes of determining the domestic authority to set up a commission, you say, the President is operating under the laws of war recognized by Congress, but for purposes of a claim to status, and, hence, the procedural rights that go with that status, you're saying the laws of war don't apply. And I don't see how you can have it both ways.

GENERAL CLEMENT: We're not trying to have it both ways, Justice Souter. The fact that the Geneva Conventions are part of the law of war doesn't mean that the Petitioner is entitled to any protection under those conventions. . . .

JUSTICE SCALIA: We don't—we don't intervene on habeas corpus when somebody says that the panel is improperly constituted. We wait until the proceeding's terminated, normally.

GENERAL CLEMENT: That's exactly right, Justice Scalia. And this Court made clear that it doesn't intervene—

JUSTICE KENNEDY: Well . . . is that true? If a group of people decide they're going to try somebody, we wait until that group of people finishes the trial before the Court—before habeas intervenes to determine the authority of the tribunal to hold and to try?

GENERAL CLEMENT: Well, with respect, Justice Kennedy, this isn't a "group of people." This is the President invoking an authority that he's exercised in virtually every war that we've had. It's something that was recognized in the Civil War, something in World War II that this Court approved.

JUSTICE KENNEDY: I had thought that the historic function of habeas is to . . . test the jurisdiction and the legitimacy of a court.

GENERAL CLEMENT: Well, but—habeas corpus generally doesn't give a right to a pre-enforcement challenge. . . .

JUSTICE SCALIA: To a forum that is prima facie properly constituted. I mean . . . this is not a—you know, a necktie party. Where it parades as a court, and it's been constituted as a court, we normally wait until the proceeding's completed.

GENERAL CLEMENT: Well, that's exactly right, Justice Scalia. . . .

JUSTICE STEVENS: But, Mr. Clement . . . if you assume that the laws of war apply, and perhaps the treaty applies, isn't the issue whether this is a "group of people," on the one hand, or a "regularly constituted court," on the other?

GENERAL CLEMENT: Well, I mean, I don't really think there's any serious dispute about which it is. I mean, this is something that is—

JUSTICE STEVENS: Well, they argue very strenuously that this is really just a "group of people" . . . because it's not a "regularly constituted court" within the meaning of the treaty.

GENERAL CLEMENT: Let me try to hit a couple of highlights. . . . I think the events of 9/11 speak to the fact that this is a war where the laws of war are involved.

As to whether or not the law of war encompasses the crime of conspiracy to violate the laws of war, we think that is clearly established. That is something that the United States treated as a valid war crime in the Civil War. That is something that the United States treated as a valid war crime in World War II. . . . The most prominent examples are the Lincoln conspirators and a conspiracy at Andersonville Prison to deny POWs their lawful rights. Clearly, those are classic war crimes. . . .

GENERAL CLEMENT: . . . Now, I take it that the thrust of the question, though, is: Don't these Geneva Conventions . . . form the background of some sort of customary international law that influences what—how we should interpret the word "law of war" in the statute? And I would say, at a minimum, if there is some role for customary international law here, it has to . . . take into account and give due weight to a controlling executive act.

Here, the President has determined, for example, that conspiracy is an actionable violation of the law of war that can be tried in front of these commissions. He's made that clear. . . .

JUSTICE BREYER: Is it the President, and not Congress, defining the content of the law, the criminal law, under which a person will be tried? Isn't there a "separation of powers" problem there?

GENERAL CLEMENT: I sure hope not, Justice Breyer, because that's been the tradition for over 200 years. And Article 21 itself makes this clear, because what does it say can be tried by military commission? It says anything that's made a violation of statute or law of war.

JUSTICE STEVENS: But I don't . . . think, Mr. Clement, the 200 years have approved of his adding additional crimes under the law of war. I mean, he has never—I don't think we have ever held that the President can make something a crime which was not already a crime under the law of war.

GENERAL CLEMENT: I think that may be true, Justice Stevens. . . . But there's no innovation in trying conspiracy as a violation of the law of war. . . .

JUSTICE STEVENS: . . . [[Have]] you read the footnote that the—Mr. Clement relies on very heavily?

MR. KATYAL: With respect to conspiracy? Yes, I have. And I do believe the text says that they're referring to domestic [[U.S.]] offenses. It's certainly the case that conspiracy has been tried as a violation of the laws of war at some point in the Civil War. But that has been entirely eclipsed by the modern laws of war, which have rejected it everywhere.

And if you adopt the Government's reading, Justice Stevens, that the laws of war are frozen into time in 1916, then I believe there goes the Government's case entirely, because the thrust of the Government's case is the laws of war have to adapt to this stateless, territoryless organization known as al Qaeda. If we're playing by 1916 rules, there is no way that this commission would have been accepted in 1916. . . .

IV. THE DECISION

While the Supreme Court considered the contested issues of *Hamdan* during the spring of 2006, the public's perception of GBNB continued its downward spiral, especially at the international level. Even Tony Blair, the prime minister of Great Britain and the United States's closest ally in the war on terrorism, called GBNB an "anomaly." In May, Blair's colleague, Lord Goldsmith, Britain's attorney general, demanded that GBNB be closed and denounced the military commissions as "unfair." Even President Bush's opinion regarding military commissions and GBNB seemed ambivalent. Interviewed by a German television correspondent, Bush said, "I very much would like to end Guantanamo; I very much would like to get people to a court. And we're waiting for our Supreme Court to give us a decision as to whether the people need to have a fair trial in a civilian court or in a military court."[28] A few weeks later, soon after the death of Abu Musab al-Zarqawi, the leader of al Qaeda in Iraq, Bush announced that he wanted "to end Guantanamo" and that, in his view, the detainees "ought to be tried in courts here in the United States." He added, "We will file such court claims once the Supreme Court makes its decision as to . . . as to the proper venue for these trials."[29] His comments left the impression that GBNB might be soon closed and the system of military commissions dismantled.

The June 10 announcement that three detainees had committed suicide by hanging themselves with bed sheets darkened GBNB's already bleak image. Although Rear Admiral Harry Harris, commander of GBNB, claimed that what had happened was "not an act of desperation," but rather "an act of asymmetric warfare waged against us," critics of GBNB charged that the suicides were the product of the kind of depression and despair that would naturally accompany long-term detention without any opportunity of a fair trial.[30] Reacting to the three suicides, which were the first deaths of detainees at GBNB, the military suspended all military commissions at the detention facility. At a press conference on June 14, President Bush again expressed his desire to close GBNB, but he also said that some of the detainees were dangerous and should be tried by military courts. He added, "And that's why we're waiting on the Supreme Court to make a decision."[31]

Two weeks later the Supreme Court handed down a 5–3 decision that denied that the DTA eliminated the Court's jurisdiction and invalidated President Bush's system of military commissions. Justice Stevens wrote the majority opinion; Justices Kennedy and Breyer wrote concurring opinions; and Justices Scalia, Thomas, and Alito wrote dissenting opinions. The decision was a fractured one, even more so than the number of concurring and dissenting opinions might suggest. Justice Kennedy refused to join two parts of Justices Stevens's majority opinion (which meant that these two parts only had the support of a plurality of the justices) and Justices Souter, Ginsburg, and Breyer did not agree with all aspects of Kennedy's concurrence. Justices Thomas and Scalia joined each other's dissent and Justice Alito's, but Alito refused to join certain parts of Justice Thomas's. The Court's decision in *Hamdan* is therefore a complicated one. A tally of which justices refused to join what parts of what opinions will be included in the excerpts that follow. Chief Justice Roberts, of course, took no part in the decision.

According to Justice Stevens's opinion, since the exclusive-review provisions of the DTA—the ones that granted the D.C. Circuit jurisdiction to hear all appeals from military commissions and CSRTs—were explicitly applied to "pending cases," the lack of such an explicit reference in the jurisdiction-stripping provisions meant that the federal courts yet had jurisdiction over all pending habeas cases from GBNB detainees. Regarding the merits, which the excerpts below will focus on, Stevens refused to answer the question whether the president had the unilateral constitutional authority to establish military commissions. It was unnecessary to answer this question, in his opinion, because Congress through Article 21 of the UCMJ had granted the president a *limited* authority to establish commissions. A commission established under Article 21 had to conform to both the common law and the "law of war." The military commission that was about to try Hamdan, however, conformed to neither because it was convened outside a "theatre of war," the offense charged was not committed during the war, the charge of conspiracy was not a proper offense, and there was no clear military necessity for the commission. In addition, the procedures of Hamdan's commission violated the "uniformity" principle of the UCMJ and the CA3 of the Geneva Conventions. Congress had granted the president the authority to establish military commissions only in conformity with the "law of war," which rendered CA3 judicially enforceable.

In their two concurrences, Justices Breyer and Kennedy emphasized that President Bush was free to go to Congress and ask for additional authority regarding military commissions. Although Justice Kennedy agreed with Justice Stevens, and the other three justices, who together constituted a majority of the Court, that the UCMJ implemented CA3 of the Geneva Conventions, he refused to join those parts of the majority opinion that went beyond the conclusion that military commissions were not "regularly constituted" if they unjustifiably deviated from courts-martial. Accordingly, he refused to decide whether a "regularly constituted" commission had to recognize a defendant's right to be present, whether Article 75 of Protocol I was binding on all commissions, whether conspiracy was a valid offense under the "law of war," or whether common law imposed additional limitations on military commissions. Kennedy thereby refused to inject limitations on military commissions into the UCMJ above and beyond the UCMJ's "uniformity" principle," which implemented CA3 by requiring all military commissions to be like courts-martial "so far as practicable."

The three dissenters in *Hamdan* all agreed that the DTA deprived the Court of jurisdiction. Justice Scalia focused on this issue, arguing that the majority had ignored a "venerable rule" that statutes eliminating jurisdiction apply to pending cases unless the jurisdiction over pending cases was explicitly reserved. Since his dissent is confined to the question of jurisdiction, no excerpts from it will be included below. In contrast, Justice Thomas's dissent attacked Justice Steven's arguments that Hamdan's commission was unauthorized because it was held outside a "theatre of war," because the charged offense took place before the war began, and because conspiracy did not constitute a violation of the law of war. In his view, Stevens's claim that Hamdan's military commission was not authorized for these reasons did not rest on history or authority, but rather on an evaluation that the commissions were not a "military necessity," a judgment outside the judiciary's competence. The procedures of a military commission, according to Thomas, did not have to be "uniform" to those of a court-martial. Moreover, President Bush had determined at the time he established the commissions that court-martial procedures would "hamper our war effort" and were "impracticable" for that reason. The judiciary has no right to second-guess that determination. Lastly, the Court's attempt to make CA3 judicially enforceable failed because the UCMJ did not make any part of the law of war judicially enforceable that was not so beforehand. Consequently, Hamdan's claims under CA3 were "foreclosed by *Johnson v. Eisentrager*," were without merit because the conflict with al Qaeda was of "an international character," or were unpersuasive since the president's understanding of CA3's requirements was "entitled to great weight."

Justice Alito agreed with Justice Thomas that conspiracy could be a valid charge, but he refused to support Thomas's conclusion that membership in a group, by itself, could be a violation of the law of war. In addition, Alito endorsed Thomas's view that the Geneva Conventions were not judicially enforceable, but he refused to accept Thomas's position that CA3 was inapplicable to the conflict with al Qaeda. Accordingly, for Alito, President Bush had an obligation under international law to try Hamdan before "a regularly constituted court," but the obligation was not one that Hamdan could judicially enforce. The majority, however, had mistakenly concluded that "a regularly constituted court" could not diverge from a court-martial unless there was an "evident practical need" for the divergence. In Alito's view, tribunals that vary widely in structure and procedure could yet be "regularly" or "properly" constituted. Moreover, even if some of the procedures of Hamdan's commission improperly diverged from those of a court-martial, the proper remedy was to invalidate the improper procedures, "not to outlaw the commissions."

EXCERPTS FROM THE OPINIONS

JUSTICE STEVENS announced the judgment of the Court and delivered the opinion of the Court with respect to Parts I through IV, Parts VI through VI-D-iii, Part VI-D-v, and Part VII and an opinion with respect to Parts V and VI-D-iv, in which *Justice Souter, Justice Ginsburg,* and *Justice Breyer join....*

[[1. President's Authority to Establish Commissions.]] The military commission, a tribunal neither mentioned in the Constitution nor created by statute, was born of military necessity. ...

Exigency alone, of course, will not justify the establishment and use of penal tribunals not contemplated by Article I, Section 8 and Article III, Section 1 of the Constitution unless some other part of that document authorizes a response to a felt need. And that authority, if it exists, can derive only from the powers granted jointly to the President and Congress in time of war. ...

Whether . . . the President may constitutionally convene military commissions "without the sanction of Congress" in cases of "controlling necessity" is a question this Court has not answered definitively, and need not answer today. . . .

. . . Contrary to the Government's assertion, . . . *Quirin* did not view the authorization as a sweeping mandate for the President to "invoke military commissions when he deems them necessary." Rather, the *Quirin* Court recognized that Congress had simply preserved what power, under the Constitution and the common law of war, the President had had before 1916 to convene military commissions—with the express condition that the President and those under his command comply with the law of war. That much is evidenced by the Court's inquiry, *following* its conclusion that Congress had authorized military commissions, into whether the law of war had indeed been complied with in that case.

The Government would have us dispense with the inquiry that the *Quirin* Court undertook and find in either the AUMF or the DTA specific, overriding authorization for the very commission that has been convened to try Hamdan. Neither of these congressional Acts, however, expands the President's authority to convene military commissions. First, while we assume that the AUMF activated the President's war powers, and that those powers include the authority to convene military commissions in appropriate circumstances, there is nothing in the text or legislative history of the AUMF even hinting that Congress intended to expand or alter the authorization set forth in Article 21 of the UCMJ. . . .

Together, the UCMJ, the AUMF, and the DTA at most acknowledge a general Presidential authority to convene military commissions in circumstances where justified under the "Constitution and laws," including the law of war. Absent a more specific congressional authorization, the task of this Court is, as it was in *Quirin*, to decide whether Hamdan's military commission is so justified. It is to that inquiry we now turn.

[[2. Lawfulness of Conspiracy Charge: Justice Kennedy does not join this part of Justice Steven's opinion.]] The classic treatise penned by Colonel William Winthrop, whom we have called "the 'Blackstone of Military Law,'" describes at least four preconditions for exercise of jurisdiction by a tribunal of the type convened to try Hamdan [[a commission to try a violation of the law of war]]. First, "[a] military commission, (except where otherwise authorized by statute), can legally assume jurisdiction only of offenses committed within the field of the command of the convening commander." The "field of command" in these circumstances means the "theatre of war." Second, the offense charged "must have been committed within the period of the war." No jurisdiction exists to try offenses "committed either before or after the war."

Third, a military commission not established pursuant to martial law or an occupation may try only "[i]ndividuals of the enemy's army who have been
guilty of illegitimate warfare or other offences in violation of the laws of war"
and members of one's own army "who, in time of war, become chargeable
with crimes or offences not cognizable, or triable, by the criminal courts or
under the Articles of war." Finally, a law-of-war commission has jurisdiction
to try only two kinds of offense: "Violations of the laws and usages of war
cognizable by military tribunals only," and "[b]reaches of military orders or
regulations for which offenders are not legally triable by court-martial under
the Articles of war." . . .

The charge against Hamdan . . . alleges a conspiracy extending over a number of years, from 1996 to November 2001. All but two months of that more
than five-year-long period preceded the attacks of September 11, 2001, and
the enactment of the AUMF—the Act of Congress on which the Government
relies for exercise of its war powers and thus for its authority to convene military commissions. Neither the agreement with Osama bin Laden and others
to commit war crimes, nor a single overt act, is alleged to have occurred in a
theater of war or on any specified date after September 11, 2001. None of the
overt acts that Hamdan is alleged to have committed violates the law of war.

These facts alone cast doubt on the legality of the charge and, hence, the
commission; as Winthrop makes plain, the offense alleged must have been
committed both in a theater of war and *during*, not before, the relevant conflict. But the deficiencies in the time and place allegations also underscore—
indeed are symptomatic of—the most serious defect of this charge: The offense it alleges is not triable by law-of-war military commission.

There is no suggestion that Congress has, in exercise of its constitutional
authority to "define and punish . . . Offences against the Law of Nations" pos-
itively identified "conspiracy" as a war crime. As we explained in *Quirin* that
is not necessarily fatal to the Government's claim of authority to try the alleged offense by military commission; Congress, through Article 21 of the
UCMJ, has "incorporated by reference" the common law of war, which may
render triable by military commission certain offenses not defined by statute.
When, however, neither the elements of the offense nor the range of permissible punishments is defined by statute or treaty, the precedent must be plain
and unambiguous. To demand any less would be to risk concentrating in military hands a degree of adjudicative and punitive power in excess of that contemplated either by statute or by the Constitution. . . .

At a minimum, the Government must make a substantial showing that the
crime for which it seeks to try a defendant by military commission is acknowledged to be an offense against the law of war. That burden is far from
satisfied here. The crime of "conspiracy" has rarely if ever been tried as such

in this country by any law-of-war military commission not exercising some other form of jurisdiction, and does not appear in either the Geneva Conventions or the Hague Conventions—the major treaties on the law of war. . . .

The Government . . . points out that the Nazi saboteurs in *Quirin* were charged with conspiracy. . . .

That the defendants in *Quirin* were charged with conspiracy is not persuasive, since the Court declined to address whether the offense actually qualified as a violation of the law of war—let alone one triable by military commission. . . .

The charge's shortcomings are not merely formal, but are indicative of a broader inability on the Executive's part here to satisfy the most basic precondition—at least in the absence of specific congressional authorization—for establishment of military commissions: military necessity. Hamdan's tribunal was appointed not by a military commander in the field of battle, but by a retired major general stationed away from any active hostilities. Hamdan is charged not with an overt act for which he was caught red-handed in a theater of war and which military efficiency demands be tried expeditiously, but with an *agreement* the inception of which long predated the attacks of September 11, 2001 and the AUMF. That may well be a crime, but it is not an offense that "by the law of war may be tried by military commissio[n]." None of the overt acts alleged to have been committed in furtherance of the agreement is itself a war crime, or even necessarily occurred during time of, or in a theater of, war. Any urgent need for imposition or execution of judgment is utterly belied by the record; Hamdan was arrested in November 2001 and he was not charged until mid-2004. These simply are not the circumstances in which, by any stretch of the historical evidence or this Court's precedents, a military commission established by Executive Order under the authority of Article 21 of the UCMJ may lawfully try a person and subject him to punishment.

[[3. Procedures of Hamdan's Commission: Justice Kennedy rejoins Justice Stevens's opinion.]] . . . Article 36 [[see p. 257 above]] places two restrictions on the President's power to promulgate rules of procedure for courts-martial and military commissions alike. First, no procedural rule he adopts may be "contrary to or inconsistent with" the UCMJ—however practical it may seem. Second, the rules adopted must be "uniform insofar as practicable." That is, the rules applied to military commissions must be the same as those applied to courts-martial unless such uniformity proves impracticable.

Hamdan argues that Commission Order No. 1 violates both of these restrictions; he maintains that the procedures described in the Commission Order are inconsistent with the UCMJ and that the Government has offered no explanation for their deviation from the procedures governing courts-martial, which are set forth in the Manual for Courts-Martial. . . .

. . . Without reaching the question whether any provision of Commission Order No. 1 is strictly "contrary to or inconsistent with" other provisions of the UCMJ, we conclude that the "practicability" determination the President has made is insufficient to justify variances from the procedures governing courts-martial. Subsection (b) of Article 36 was added after World War II, and requires a different showing of impracticability from the one required by subsection (a). Subsection (a) requires that the rules the President promulgates for courts-martial, provost courts, and military commissions alike conform to those that govern procedures in *Article III courts*, "so far as *he considers* practicable." Subsection (b), by contrast, demands that the rules applied in courts-martial, provost courts, and military commissions—whether or not they conform with the Federal Rules of Evidence—be "uniform *insofar as practicable*." Under the latter provision, then, the rules set forth in the Manual for Courts-Martial must apply to military commissions unless impracticable. . . .

The absence of any showing of impracticability is particularly disturbing when considered in light of the clear and admitted failure to apply one of the most fundamental protections afforded not just by the Manual for Courts-Martial but also by the UCMJ itself: the right to be present. Whether or not that departure technically is "contrary to or inconsistent with" the terms of the UCMJ, the jettisoning of so basic a right cannot lightly be excused as "practicable."

Under the circumstances, then, the rules applicable in courts-martial must apply. Since it is undisputed that Commission Order No. 1 deviates in many significant respects from those rules, it necessarily violates Article 36(b). . . .

[[5. Procedures Violate CA3.]] [[We need not consider the argument that the Geneva Conventions are inapplicable to the conflict with al Qaeda]] . . . because there is at least one provision of the Geneva Conventions that applies here even if the relevant conflict is not one between signatories. Article 3, often referred to as Common Article 3 because, like Article 2, it appears in all four Geneva Conventions, provides that in a "conflict not of an international character occurring in the territory of one of the High Contracting Parties, each Party to the conflict shall be bound to apply, as a minimum," certain provisions protecting "[p]ersons taking no active part in the hostilities, including members of armed forces who have laid down their arms and those placed *hors de combat* by . . . detention." One such provision prohibits "the passing of sentences and the carrying out of executions without previous judgment pronounced by a regularly constituted court affording all the judicial guarantees which are recognized as indispensable by civilized peoples."

The Court of Appeals thought, and the Government asserts, that Common Article 3 does not apply to Hamdan because the conflict with al Qaeda, being "'international in scope,'" does not qualify as a "'conflict not of an international character.'" That reasoning is erroneous. The term "conflict not of an international character" is used here in contradistinction to a conflict between nations. . . . Common Article 3 . . . affords some minimal protection, falling short of full protection under the Conventions, to individuals associated with neither a signatory nor even a nonsignatory "Power" who are involved in a conflict "in the territory of" a signatory. The latter kind of conflict is distinguishable from the conflict described in Common Article 2 chiefly because it does not involve a clash between nations (whether signatories or not). In context, then, the phrase "not of an international character" bears its literal meaning. . . .

Common Article 3, then, is applicable here and, as indicated above, requires that Hamdan be tried by a "regularly constituted court affording all the judicial guarantees which are recognized as indispensable by civilized peoples. . . ."

. . . At a minimum, a military commission "can be 'regularly constituted' by the standards of our military justice system only if some practical need explains deviations from court-martial practice." As we have explained, no such need has been demonstrated here.

[[6. Article 75 of Protocol I: Justice Kennedy does not join this part of Justice Stevens's opinion.]] Inextricably intertwined with the question of regular constitution is the evaluation of the procedures governing the tribunal and whether they afford "all the judicial guarantees which are recognized as indispensable by civilized peoples." Like the phrase "regularly constituted court," this phrase is not defined in the text of the Geneva Conventions. But it must be understood to incorporate at least the barest of those trial protections that have been recognized by customary international law. Many of these are described in Article 75 of Protocol I to the Geneva Conventions of 1949, adopted in 1977 (Protocol I). Although the United States declined to ratify Protocol I, its objections were not to Article 75 thereof. Indeed, it appears that the Government "regard[s] the provisions of Article 75 as an articulation of safeguards to which all persons in the hands of an enemy are entitled." Among the rights set forth in Article 75 is the "right to be tried in [one's] presence."

We agree with Justice Kennedy that the procedures adopted to try Hamdan deviate from those governing courts-martial in ways not justified by an "evident practical need," and for that reason, at least, fail to afford the requisite guarantees. We add only that various provisions of Commission Order No. 1 dispense with the principles, articulated in Article 75 and indisputably part of the customary international law, that an accused must, absent disruptive conduct or consent, be present for his trial and must be privy to the evidence against him. . . .

[[7. Conclusion: Justice Kennedy rejoins Justice Stevens's opinion.]] Common Article 3 obviously tolerates a great degree of flexibility in trying individuals captured during armed conflict; its requirements are general ones, crafted to accommodate a wide variety of legal systems. But *requirements* they are nonetheless. The commission that the President has convened to try Hamdan does not meet those requirements.

We have assumed, as we must, that the allegations made in the Government's charge against Hamdan are true. We have assumed, moreover, the truth of the message implicit in that charge—viz., that Hamdan is a dangerous individual whose beliefs, if acted upon, would cause great harm and even death to innocent civilians, and who would act upon those beliefs if given the opportunity. It bears emphasizing that Hamdan does not challenge, and we do not today address, the Government's power to detain him for the duration of active hostilities in order to prevent such harm. But in undertaking to try Hamdan and subject him to criminal punishment, the Executive is bound to comply with the Rule of Law that prevails in this jurisdiction. . . .

Justice Breyer, with whom *Justice Kennedy, Justice Souter, and Justice Ginsburg* join, concurring.

. . . The Court's conclusion ultimately rests upon a single ground: Congress has not issued the Executive a "blank check." Indeed, Congress has denied the President the legislative authority to create military commissions of the kind at issue here. Nothing prevents the President from returning to Congress to seek the authority he believes necessary.

Where, as here, no emergency prevents consultation with Congress, judicial insistence upon that consultation does not weaken our Nation's ability to deal with danger. To the contrary, that insistence strengthens the Nation's ability to determine—through democratic means—how best to do so. The Constitution places its faith in those democratic means. Our Court today simply does the same.

Justice Kennedy, with whom *Justice Souter, Justice Ginsburg, and Justice Breyer* join as to Parts 1 and II, concurring in part.

[[1. Military Commissions Not Authorized.]] Military Commission Order No. 1, which governs the military commission established to try petitioner Salim Hamdan for war crimes, exceeds limits that certain statutes, duly enacted by Congress, have placed on the President's authority to convene military courts. This is not a case, then, where the Executive can assert some unilateral authority to fill a void left by congressional inaction. It is a case where Congress, in the proper exercise of its powers as an independent branch of government, and as part of a long tradition of legislative involvement in matters of military justice, has considered the subject of military tribunals and set limits on the President's authority. . . .

[[Accordingly,]] domestic statutes control this case. If Congress, after due consideration, deems it appropriate to change the controlling statutes, in conformance with the Constitution and other laws, it has the power and prerogative to do so. . . .

At a minimum a military commission like the one at issue—a commission specially convened by the President to try specific persons without express congressional authorization—can be "regularly constituted" by the standards of our military justice system only if some practical need explains deviations from court-martial practice. . . .

Against this background, the Court is correct to conclude that the military commission the President has convened to try Hamdan is unauthorized. . . .

[[For example, the Military Commission Order]] . . . imposes just one evidentiary rule: "Evidence shall be admitted if . . . the evidence would have probative value to a reasonable person." . . .

The rule here could permit admission of multiple hearsay and other forms of evidence generally prohibited on grounds of unreliability. Indeed, the commission regulations specifically contemplate admission of unsworn written statements; and they make no provision for exclusion of coerced declarations save those "established to have been made as a result of torture." Besides, even if evidence is deemed nonprobative by the presiding officer at Hamdan's trial, the military-commission members still may view it. In another departure from court-martial practice the military commission members may object to the presiding officer's evidence rulings and determine themselves, by majority vote, whether to admit the evidence. . . .

In sum, as presently structured, Hamdan's military commission exceeds the bounds Congress has placed on the President's authority in Sections 836 and 821 of the UCMJ. Because Congress has prescribed these limits, Congress can change them, requiring a new analysis consistent with the Constitution and other governing laws. At this time, however, we must apply the standards Congress has provided. By those standards the military commission is deficient.

[[2. Issues that Need Not be Considered: Justices Breyer, Souter, and Ginsburg do not join this section of Justice Kennedy's concurring opinion.]] In light of the conclusion that the military commission here is unauthorized under the UCMJ, I see no need to consider several further issues addressed in the plurality opinion by JUSTICE STEVENS and the dissent by JUSTICE THOMAS.

First, I would not decide whether Common Article 3's standard—a "regularly constituted court affording all the judicial guarantees which are recognized as indispensable by civilized peoples"—necessarily requires that the accused have the right to be present at all stages of a criminal trial. As JUSTICE

STEVENS explains, Military Commission Order No. 1 authorizes exclusion of the accused from the proceedings if the presiding officer determines that, among other things, protection of classified information so requires. JUSTICE STEVENS observes that these regulations create the possibility of a conviction and sentence based on evidence Hamdan has not seen or heard—a possibility the plurality is correct to consider troubling.

As the dissent by JUSTICE THOMAS points out, however, the regulations bar the presiding officer from admitting secret evidence if doing so would deprive the accused of a "full and fair trial." This fairness determination, moreover, is unambiguously subject to judicial review under the DTA. The evidentiary proceedings at Hamdan's trial have yet to commence, and it remains to be seen whether he will suffer any prejudicial exclusion.

There should be reluctance, furthermore, to reach unnecessarily the question whether, as the plurality seems to conclude, Article 75 of Protocol I to the Geneva Conventions is binding law notwithstanding the earlier decision by our Government not to accede to the Protocol. For all these reasons, and without detracting from the importance of the right of presence, I would rely on other deficiencies noted here and in the opinion by the Court—deficiencies that relate to the structure and procedure of the commission and that inevitably will affect the proceedings—as the basis for finding the military commissions lack authorization under 10 U. S. C. Section 836 and fail to be regularly constituted under Common Article 3 and Section 821.

I likewise see no need to address the validity of the conspiracy charge against Hamdan. . . . In light of the conclusion that the military commissions at issue are unauthorized Congress may choose to provide further guidance in this area. Congress, not the Court, is the branch in the better position to undertake the "sensitive task of establishing a principle not inconsistent with the national interest or international justice."

Finally, for the same reason, I express no view on the merits of other limitations on military commissions described as elements of the common law of war in Part V of JUSTICE STEVENS'S opinion. . . .

Justice Thomas, with whom *Justice Scalia* joins, and with whom *Justice Alito* joins in all but Parts I, II-C-1, and III-B-2, dissenting. . . .
[[1. Proper Scope of Commissions.]] . . . [[T]]he plurality concludes that the legality of the charge against Hamdan is doubtful because "Hamdan is charged not with an overt act for which he was caught red-handed in a theater of war . . . but with an *agreement* the inception of which long predated . . . the [relevant armed conflict]." The plurality's willingness to second-guess the Executive's judgments in this context, based upon little more than its unsupported assertions, constitutes an unprecedented departure from the traditionally limited role of the courts with respect to war and an unwarranted

intrusion on executive authority. And even if such second-guessing were appropriate, the plurality's attempt to do so is unpersuasive.

As an initial matter, the plurality relies upon the date of the AUMF's enactment to determine the beginning point for the "period of the war," thereby suggesting that petitioner's commission does not have jurisdiction to try him for offenses committed prior to the AUMF's enactment. But this suggestion betrays the plurality's unfamiliarity with the realities of warfare and its willful blindness to our precedents. The starting point of the present conflict (or indeed any conflict) is not determined by congressional enactment, but rather by the initiation of hostilities. . . . Moreover, while the President's "war powers" may not have been activated until the AUMF was passed, the date of such activation has never been used to determine the scope of a military commission's jurisdiction. Instead, the traditional rule is that "[o]ffenses committed before a formal declaration of war or before the declaration of martial law may be tried by military commission." Consistent with this principle, on facts virtually identical to those here, a military commission tried Julius Otto Kuehn for conspiring with Japanese officials to betray the United States Fleet to the Imperial Japanese Government prior to its attack on Pearl Harbor. . . .

The third consideration identified by Winthrop's treatise for the exercise of military commission jurisdiction pertains to the persons triable before such a commission. Law-of-war military commissions have jurisdiction over "'individuals of the enemy's army who have been guilty of illegitimate warfare or other offences in violation of the laws of war.'" . . . This consideration is easily satisfied here, as Hamdan is an unlawful combatant charged with joining and conspiring with a terrorist network dedicated to flouting the laws of war.

The fourth consideration relevant to the jurisdiction of law-of-war military commissions relates to the nature of the offense charged. As relevant here, such commissions have jurisdiction to try "'[v]iolations of the laws and usages of war cognizable by military tribunals only.'". . .

[[2. Membership in al Qaeda is a Valid Charge: Justice Alito does not join this part of Justice Thomas's dissenting opinion.]] For well over a century it has been established that "to unite with banditti, jayhawkers, guerillas, or any other unauthorized marauders is a high offence against the laws of war; *the offence is complete when the band is organized or joined. The atrocities committed by such a band do not constitute the offence, but make the reasons, and sufficient reasons they are, why such banditti are denounced by the laws of war.*" In other words, unlawful combatants, such as Hamdan, violate the law of war merely by joining an organization, such as al Qaeda, whose principal purpose is the "killing [and] disabling . . . of peaceable citizens or soldiers." This conclusion is unsurprising, as it is a "cardinal principle of the law of war . . . that the civilian population must enjoy complete immunity." . . .

[[3. Conspiracy is a Valid Charge: Justice Alito rejoins Justice Thomas's dissenting opinion.]] "[T]he experience of our wars" is rife with evidence that establishes beyond any doubt that conspiracy to violate the laws of war is itself an offense cognizable before a law-of-war military commission. World War II provides the most recent examples of the use of American military commissions to try offenses pertaining to violations of the laws of war. In that conflict, the orders establishing the jurisdiction of military commissions in various theaters of operation provided that conspiracy to violate the laws of war was a cognizable offense. . . .

The Civil War experience provides further support for the President's conclusion that conspiracy to violate the laws of war is an offense cognizable before law-of-war military commissions. Indeed, in the highest profile case to be tried before a military commission relating to that war, namely, the trial of the men involved in the assassination of President Lincoln, the charge provided that those men had "combin[ed], confederat[ed], and conspir[ed] . . . to kill and murder" President Lincoln. . . .

Ultimately, the plurality's determination that Hamdan has not been charged with an offense triable before a military commission rests not upon any historical example or authority, but upon the plurality's raw judgment of the "inability on the Executive's part here to satisfy the most basic precondition . . . for establishment of military commissions: military necessity." This judgment starkly confirms that the plurality has appointed itself the ultimate arbiter of what is quintessentially a policy and military judgment, namely, the appropriate military measures to take against those who "aided the terrorist attacks that occurred on September 11, 2001." . . .

Today a plurality of this Court would hold that conspiracy to massacre innocent civilians does not violate the laws of war. This determination is unsustainable. The judgment of the political branches that Hamdan, and others like him, must be held accountable before military commissions for their involvement with and membership in an unlawful organization dedicated to inflicting massive civilian casualties is supported by virtually every relevant authority, including all of the authorities invoked by the plurality today. It is also supported by the nature of the present conflict. We are not engaged in a traditional battle with a nation-state, but with a worldwide, hydra-headed enemy, who lurks in the shadows conspiring to reproduce the atrocities of September 11, 2001, and who has boasted of sending suicide bombers into civilian gatherings, has proudly distributed videotapes of beheadings of civilian workers, and has tortured and dismembered captured American soldiers. But according to the plurality, when our Armed Forces capture those who are plotting terrorist atrocities like the bombing of the Khobar Towers, the bombing of the USS *Cole,* and the attacks of September 11—even if their plots are advanced to the very brink of fulfillment—our military cannot charge those criminals with any offense against the laws of war. Instead, our troops must catch the terrorists "red-handed," in the midst of *the attack itself*, in order to bring them to justice. Not only is this conclusion fundamentally inconsistent with the cardinal principal of the law of war, namely protecting noncombatants, but it would sorely hamper the President's ability to confront and defeat a new and deadly enemy. . . .

[[4. Procedures of Commission.]] Nothing in the text of Article 36(b) supports the Court's sweeping conclusion that it represents an unprecedented congressional effort to change the nature of military commissions from common-law war courts to tribunals that must presumptively function like courts-martial. And such an interpretation would be strange indeed. The vision of uniformity that motivated the adoption of the UCMJ, embodied specifically in Article 36(b), is nothing more than uniformity across the separate branches of the armed services. There is no indication that the UCMJ was intended to require uniformity in procedure between courts-martial and military commissions, tribunals that the UCMJ itself recognizes are different. To the contrary, the UCMJ expressly recognizes that different tribunals will be constituted in different manners and employ different procedures. . . .

Even if Article 36(b) could be construed to require procedural uniformity among the various tribunals contemplated by the UCMJ, Hamdan would not be entitled to relief. . . . On the same day that the President issued Military Commission Order No. 1, the Secretary of Defense explained that "the president decided to establish military commissions because he wanted the option of a process that is different from those processes which we already have, namely the federal court system . . . and the military court system" and that "[t]he commissions are intended to be different . . . because the [P]resident recognized that there had to be differences to deal with the unusual situation we face and that a different approach was needed." . . . The Court provides no explanation why the President's determination that employing court-martial procedures in the military commissions established pursuant to Military Commission Order No. 1 would hamper our war effort is in any way inadequate to satisfy its newly minted "practicability" requirement. On the contrary, this determination is precisely the kind for which the "Judiciary has neither aptitude, facilities nor responsibility and which has long been held to belong in the domain of political power not subject to judicial intrusion or inquiry.'" . . .

[[5. Geneva Conventions Not Judicially Enforceable.]] . . . [[T]]he Court concludes that petitioner may seek judicial enforcement of the provisions of the Geneva Conventions because "they are . . . part of the law of war. And compliance with the law of war is the condition upon which the authority set forth in Article 21 is granted." But Article 21 authorizes the use of military commissions; it does not purport to render judicially enforceable aspects of the law of war that are not so enforceable of their own accord. The Court cannot escape *Eisentrager*'s holding merely by observing that Article 21 mentions the law of war; indeed, though *Eisentrager* did not specifically consider the Court's novel interpretation of Article 21, *Eisentrager* involved a challenge to the legality of a World War II military commission, which, like all such commissions, found its authorization in Article 15 of the Articles of War, the predecessor to Article 21 of the UCMJ. Thus, the Court's interpretation of Article 21 is foreclosed by *Eisentrager*.

In any event, the Court's argument is too clever by half. The judicial nonenforceability of the Geneva Conventions derives from the fact that those Conventions have exclusive enforcement mechanisms, and this, too, is part of the law of war. The Court's position thus rests on the assumption that Article 21's reference to the "laws of war" selectively incorporates only those aspects of the Geneva Conventions that the Court finds convenient, namely, the substantive requirements of Common Article 3, and not those aspects of the Conventions that the Court, for whatever reason, disfavors, namely the Conventions' exclusive diplomatic enforcement scheme. The Court provides no account of why the *partial* incorporation of the Geneva Conventions should extend only so far—and no further—because none is available beyond its evident preference to adjudicate those matters that the law of war, through the Geneva Conventions, consigns exclusively to the political branches. . . .

[[6. Common Article 3 Does Not Apply: Justice Alito does not join this part of Justice Thomas's dissenting opinion.]] In addition to being foreclosed by *Eisentrager*, Hamdan's claim under Common Article 3 of the Geneva Conventions is meritless. Common Article 3 applies to "armed conflict not of an international character occurring in the territory of one of the High Contracting Parties." "Pursuant to [his] authority as Commander in Chief and Chief Executive of the United States," the President has "accept[ed] the legal conclusion of the Department of Justice . . . that Common Article 3 of Geneva does not apply to . . . al Qaeda . . . detainees, because, among other reasons, the relevant conflicts are international in scope and common Article 3 applies only to 'armed conflict not of an international character.'" . . .

The President's interpretation of Common Article 3 is reasonable and should be sustained. The conflict with al Qaeda is international in character in the sense that it is occurring in various nations around the globe. Thus, it is also "occurring in the territory of" more than "one of the High Contracting Parties." The . . . Court, without acknowledging its duty to defer to the President, adopts its own, admittedly plausible, reading of Common Article 3. But where, as here, an ambiguous treaty provision ("not of an international character") is susceptible of two plausible, and reasonable, interpretations, our precedents require us to defer to the Executive's interpretation. . . .

[[7. Requirements of Common Article 3: Justice Alito rejoins Justice Thomas's dissenting opinion.]] The Court concludes Hamdan's commission fails to satisfy the requirements of Common Article 3 not because it differs from the practice of previous military commissions but because it "deviate[s] from [the procedures] governing courts-martial." But there is neither a statutory nor historical requirement that military commissions conform to the structure and practice of courts-martial. A military commission is a different tribunal, serving a different function, and thus operates pursuant to different procedures. The 150-year pedigree of the military commission is itself sufficient to establish that such tribunals are "regularly constituted court[s]."

Similarly, the procedures to be employed by Hamdan's commission afford "all the judicial guarantees which are recognized as indispensable by civilized peoples." . . . [[T]]he plurality concludes that Hamdan's commission is unlawful because of the possibility that Hamdan will be barred from proceedings and denied access to evidence that may be used to convict him. But, under the commissions' rules, the Government may not impose such bar or denial on Hamdan if it would render his trial unfair, a question that is clearly within the scope of the appellate review contemplated by regulation and statute. . . .

In these circumstances, "civilized peoples" would take into account the context of military commission trials against unlawful combatants in the war on terrorism, including the need to keep certain information secret in the interest of preventing future attacks on our Nation and its foreign installations so long as it did not deprive the accused of a fair trial. Accordingly, the President's understanding of the requirements of Common Article 3 is entitled to "great weight." . . .

Justice Alito, with whom *Justices Scalia* and *Thomas* join in Parts I–III, dissenting. . . .

[[1. Common Article 3.]] I see no basis for the Court's holding that a military commission cannot be regarded as "a regularly constituted court" unless it is similar in structure and composition to a regular military court or unless there is an "evident practical need" for the divergence. There is no reason why a court that differs in structure or composition from an ordinary military court must be viewed as having been improperly constituted. Tribunals that vary significantly in structure, composition, and procedures may all be "regularly" or "properly" constituted. Consider, for example, a municipal court, a state trial court of general jurisdiction, an Article I federal trial court, a federal district court, and an international court, such as the International Criminal Tribunal for the Former Yugoslavia. Although these courts are "differently constituted" and differ substantially in many other respects, they are all "regularly constituted."

If Common Article 3 had been meant to require trial before a country's military courts or courts that are similar in structure and composition, the drafters almost certainly would have used language that expresses that thought more directly. . . .

I also disagree with the Court's conclusion that petitioner's military commission is "illegal" because its procedures allegedly do not comply with 10 U.S.C. Section 836. . . . [[If]] some of the procedures that may be used in military commission proceedings are improper, the appropriate remedy is to proscribe the use of those particular procedures, not to outlaw the commissions. I see no justification for striking down the entire commission structure simply because it is possible that petitioner's trial might involve the use of some procedure that is improper. . . .

In sum, I believe that Common Article 3 is satisfied here because the military commissions (1) qualify as courts, (2) that were appointed and established in accordance with domestic law, and (3) any procedural improprieties that might occur in particular cases can be reviewed in those cases. . . .

V. POSTSCRIPT

The Supreme Court's decision in *Hamdan* held that the Bush administration's system of military commission violated both the UCMJ and CA3 of the Geneva Convention. Since CA3 not only required "regularly constituted courts," but also prohibited "violence to life and person, in particular murder of all kinds, mutilation, *cruel treatment and torture*" and "*outrages upon personal dignity, in particular, humiliating and degrading treatment*" (emphasis added; see box 5.2 above), the Court's ruling had implications beyond the legality of military commissions, especially since a 1996 criminal statute defined any violation of CA3 as a possible "war crime."[32] In effect, *Hamdan* raised the possibility that interrogators could be prosecuted for war crimes if they had engaged in coercive techniques that violated CA3. The War Crimes Statute authorized punishments up to a life sentence and, if the victim died as a result of the abuse, the death penalty was a possibility.

In August 2005, British authorities disrupted a major bomb plot targeting multiple airplanes flying from Heathrow Airport to locations inside the United States. A month later, the Bush administration transferred fourteen detainees who had previously been held in secret CIA facilities to GBNB (including Khalid Sheik Muhammad, Abu Zubaydah, and Ramzi bin al-Shibh) for trial by military commission and sent to Congress a proposed Military Commission Act of 2006 (MCA). The latter development suggested that the Bush administration, by seeking from Congress what the Supreme Court had ruled it did not have in *Hamdan*, was following the advice that Justices Breyer and Kennedy had offered in their concurrences. Of course, the transfer of the al Qaeda leaders buttressed the rationale for the proposed legislation. The MCA would provide an explicit statutory foundation for a system of military commissions that significantly diverged from the procedures of the UCMJ and the Manual for Courts Martial.

The Bush administration's proposed MCA included several provisions related to CA3. Section Six stated that if detainees were treated in accordance with the "shock-the-conscience" standard, then CA3 would not be violated, which arguably "watered down" CA3 to the level of the DTA. The same provision added: "No person in any habeas action or any other action may invoke the Geneva Conventions . . . as a source of rights . . . for any purpose in any court in the United States," which precluded any federal court from enforcing CA3. Section Seven amended the War Crimes Act by creating a list of specific offenses. The list included "cruel or inhuman treatment," which the law defined in terms nearly identical to that of "torture," but there was no inclusion of any of the other language contained in CA3. Accordingly, "Outrages upon personal dignity, in particular humiliating and degrading treatment," would no longer constitute a war crime. Lastly, the proposed MCA deprived federal courts of jurisdiction of all habeas claims from unlawful enemy combatants, not just those detained at GBNB, and explicitly applied this jurisdiction-stripping provision to all pending cases.[33]

Bush's proposed legislation placed Democrats in a dilemma: if they supported the measure, it would transfer a significant amount of power to President Bush; if they opposed it, they would be labeled soft on terrorism during the upcoming midterm elections, more worried about protecting the rights of terrorists than prosecuting the high-level al Qaeda operatives now detained at GBNB. However, three Republican senators who had been the primary sponsors of the DTA—John Warner (R-VA), John McCain (R-AZ), and Lindsey Graham (R-SC)—opposed Bush administration's efforts to deflate the meaning of CA3 and objected to the policy of convicting terrorists on the basis of secret evidence. Bush claimed that the three Republicans were undermining national security because, if CA3's language triggered a possible violation of the War Crimes Act, then he would have no choice but to end the special CIA interrogation program. The "professionals" in the CIA would not be willing to use their "alternative set of procedures" if CA3's vague language could be the basis for incurring criminal liability. Press reports speculated that the controversy was about the use of sleep deprivation, isolation, and stress positions during interrogations. Such techniques arguably did not shock the conscience, but would likely be considered outrages on personal dignity. It was assumed that the Bush administration had already abandoned the practice of "waterboarding," which arguably violated the shock-the-conscience standard of the DTA. Waterboarding consisted of immobilizing a detainee on a board with his head lower than his feet while pouring water over a cloth covering his face. The technique apparently gave the detainee the false but real impression that he was drowning.[34]

Holding to their position that it would be a disastrous precedent for the United States to water down the Geneva Conventions or convict someone of a crime on the basis of secret evidence, the three Republican senators, joined by former secretary of state Colin Powell, stood their ground in the face of considerable White House pressure. In the end, a compromise was reached on September 21. The language indicating that compliance with the DTA fully satisfied all the requirements of CA3 was dropped, but criminal liability under the War Crimes Act was limited to a list of "grave breaches" of CA3. The list included "torture" and "cruel and inhuman treatment," but not "outrages upon personal dignity." The implication was that a CIA interrogator who engaged in the latter type of conduct might violate international law, but he would not be guilty of a war crime. In this sense, CA3 remained fully binding on the United States, which is what the three Republican senators wanted, but the exposure of CIA interrogators to criminal liability was significantly reduced, which was presumably President Bush's objective. To insure that international views of what constituted "cruel and inhuman treatment" would not influence the meaning of the War Crimes Act, Congress prohibited the use of any foreign or international sources of law as "a basis for a rule of decision in the courts of the United States" in all cases involving war crimes.[35] Congress retroactively applied the MCA revisions of the War Crimes Act to November 26, 1997, the date the initial War Crimes Act had gone into effect.

Congress also revised the initial proposal's provisions that dealt with military commissions. Bush's major concession was that he gave up the option of convicting terrorists on the basis of secret evidence. According to the final version of the MCA, a judge could redact the classified information or craft a substitution that summarized the evidence in question, but the defendant would see all the evidence against him and he could not be excluded from the trial unless he engaged in misconduct.[36] Coerced testimony, so long as it did not involve torture, could be used depending on whether the coerced statement was made prior to the enactment of the DTA. If it was made prior to its enactment, then it could be used if a judge found it to be "reliable" and if "the interests of justice would best be served by admission of the statement into evidence." If, on the other hand, the statement was made after the DTA's enactment, the judge had to also find, in addition to the above two criteria, that the interrogation methods used to obtain the statement did "not amount to cruel, inhuman, or degrading treatment."[37] Moreover, the prosecution could introduce hearsay evidence only if the defense was given advance notice and could not demonstrate that it was "unreliable" or "lacking in probative value."[38]

The MCA also included a broader jurisdiction-stripping provision than the one that the Supreme Court had sidestepped in *Hamdan*.[39] All federal courts were deprived of jurisdiction to review any habeas petition from any unlawful enemy combatant, not just those detained at GBNB, and there was unambiguous language indicating that the provision applied to pending cases.[40] Moreover, the MCA significantly expanded the definition of unlawful enemy combatant to include anyone "who has purposefully and materially supported hostilities against the United States or its cobelligerents" or who has or will be "determined to be an unlawful enemy combatant by a Combatant Status Review Tribunal (CSRT) or another competent authority established under the President or the Secretary of Defense."[41] Congress also reaffirmed the provision of the DTA that granted the D.C. Circuit exclusive jurisdiction to review all CSRT designations of unlawful enemy combatants and final decisions by military commissions.[42]

The MCA is no doubt the most important piece of legislation regarding the war on terrorism that Congress has enacted since the 9/11 attacks. In effect, it gave President Bush several tools to circumvent the central holding of *Hamdan* that five justices had supported: the holding that CA3 applied to the war on terrorism. Accordingly, although President Bush had to make some trade-offs in negotiating with Congress over the terms of the MCA, it would appear, all in all, that he came out of the legislative process in late September stronger than he had been in the aftermath of the Supreme Court's *Hamdan* decision in June. However, the American electorate repudiated Bush's Iraq policy at the midterm elections in November, giving both houses of Congress to the Democrats. Bush's support for a new "surge" that would increase the number of American troops in Iraq by approximately 21,500 during the first five months of 2007 further undermined his political support. In January 2007, his overall approval rating fell to 28 percent, only four points above Nixon's all-time low.[43]

The passage of the MCA increases the likelihood that momentous issues of constitutional law involving the war on terrorism will eventually arrive at the Supreme Court. One such issue is whether the jurisdiction-stripping provision of the MCA is a *de facto* suspension of the writ of habeas corpus, and, if it is, whether Congress can suspend the writ on the ground that the 9/11 attacks constituted an invasion. Regarding this question, Judge Robertson, who had decided in Hamdan's favor in 2004 on the merits, dismissed Hamdan's habeas petition in late 2006 on the ground that the MCA had deprived him of jurisdiction following the Supreme Court's remand of the case to the district court.[44] In a similar vein, on February 20, 2007, a panel of the D.C. Circuit held in *Boumediene v. Bush* and *Al Odah v. United States* that the GBNB detainees had no rights under the U.S. Constitution and therefore the jurisdiction-stripping provision of the MCA did not violate the Suspension Clause.[45] On April 2, 2007, the Supreme Court, with three justices dissenting, declined to hear *Boumediene* and *Al Odah*, presumably on the ground that the jurisdiction-stripping provisions of the MCA could not be properly reviewed under the Suspension Clause until the D.C. Circuit decided what kind of review of CSRT designations was required under the DTA.[46] If the D.C. Circuit decided that the review of the designations had to be thorough and rigorous, then perhaps the jurisdiction-stripping provision of the MCA was constitutional since the detainees had been given an adequate alternative remedy to habeas review. A different panel of the D.C. Circuit was considering this question in *Bismullah v. Gates* when the Supreme Court declined to hear *Boumediene*.[47]

Following Judge Robertson's ruling, Hamdan's attorneys asked the Supreme Court to retake the case before the D.C. Circuit ruled on how the MCA's jurisdiction-stripping provision applied to his situation, but the Court turned down his request in late April. Hamdan then appealed to the D.C. Circuit, claiming that his circumstances were unlike those of other GBNB detainees because he was facing a trial in front of a military commission. As a defendant, he argued, the jurisdiction-stripping provision could not take away his habeas rights without violating the Suspension Clause. However, in a surprising development, the military judge presiding over Hamdan's trial, Captain Keith J. Allred, dismissed all pending charges against Hamdan in early June. Allred reasoned that the commission lacked jurisdiction to try Hamdan because the CSRT that had reviewed Hamdan's status had only designated him an "enemy combatant," not an "unlawful enemy combatant." Since the MCA purportedly limited the jurisdiction of military commissions created under it to "unlawful enemy combatants," a new CSRT would first have to designate Hamdan as an "unlawful enemy combatant" before any trial before a military commission could proceed.[48] The government had no choice but to appeal Allred's decision to the Court of Military Commission Review, an appellate military tribunal authorized by the MCA, but one that had not yet been created or staffed.

On June 29, there was a second surprising development. The Supreme Court changed its mind and scheduled *Bounediene* for oral argument during the fall of 2007. Since it took five, rather than four, votes for the Court to reverse its earlier decision not to hear the case, at least two justices switched sides. Speculation arose as to why this very unusual switch had occurred. Attention quickly centered on an affidavit by Lieutenant Colonel Stephen Abraham, which had been appended to one of the briefs filed by the GBNB detainees' lawyers in support of its petition for a rehearing. In this affidavit, Abraham explained that he had served as an agency liaison at the Office for the Administrative Review of the Detention of Enemy Combatants from September 11, 2004 to March 9, 2005. In that capacity, he had worked with other government agencies to gather and validate information relating to the detainees for use in the CSRTs. Regarding the CSRT process itself, Abraham claimed that the individuals who compiled the information and documents for combatant status determinations "did not have access to numerous information sources generally available within the intelligence community;" that he personally was not permitted to confirm the absence of exculpatory information regarding a particular detainee by reviewing all available information; that information used to support enemy combatant designations was often "generic," "arbitrary," and "non-credible" in character; that members of a CSRT panel who did not find a detainee to be an enemy combatant had to "explain their finding" to military superiors; that such panels were ordered to reopen hearings to allow additional evidence to be entered against the detainee; that he himself was not assigned to another CSRT panel after he served on a panel that declined to designate a detainee an enemy combatant. The accompanying brief insisted that Abraham's affidavit established that "in every phase" the CSRT process "was infected with command influence" and that it was "an illusion" and "a sham process" that could not be cured by any form of judicial review.[49]

It is not known whether or not Abraham's affidavit was the primary reason why the Supreme Court decided to hear *Boumediene* and *Al Odah*, but Colonel Abraham, a forty-six year old decorated reserve Army intelligence officer, was the first "military insider" to criticize the CSRT process under oath. The Supreme Court reversed course a week after his affidavit was filed at the Court. In the order granting the motion for rehearing, the Supreme Court indicated that supplemental briefing would be scheduled if and when the D.C. Circuit decided *Bismullah v. Gates*, the case dealing with the nature of the judicial review of CSRT decisions required by the DTA.[50] D.C. Circuit handed down *Bismullah* on July 20. In a definite setback for the Bush Administration, it ruled that the DTA required a broad review of all "reasonably available" information pertaining to each CSRT designation, not just the evidence the government had used to support the designation. The court could not determine whether the DTA's "preponderance of the evidence" standard was met "without seeing all the evidthe authorityence, any more than one can tell whether a fraction is more or less than one half by looking only at the numerator and not at the denominator." In addition, the defense counsel for the detainee, though not the detainee himself, must also have access to the above information so that he or she could "aid the court" in making its judgment concerning the relative weight of the evidence.[51]

The D.C. Circuit's *Bismullah* decision will undoubtedly be a factor in how the Supreme Court, during the upcoming term, will evaluate whether the MCA, in conjunction with the DTA, is or is not an unconstitutional suspension of the writ of habeas corpus in *Boumediene*. Unless there is another surprise, it therefore seems likely that the American people will soon have an answer to this question. Other important constitutional questions will probably not be resolved during the Supreme Court's upcoming term, yet they are visible on the horizon. Do the Geneva Conventions confer rights to individuals or limit the authority of executive authorities in ways that are judicially enforceable? Does the MCA's broad definition of "unlawful enemy combatant" and its expanded list of offenses triable by military commission constitute an unconstitutional intrusion by the political branches into the judicial branch in violation of Article III of the Constitution? Finally, can the MCA limit the parameters of judicial decision-making, precluding references to international treaties and foreign sources of law? The number of constitutional controversies ignited by the war on terrorism has therefore not declined with the passage of time since the 9/11 attacks. For this reason, almost six years after the 9/11 attacks, it is more imperative than ever that the American people consider the nature of the threats we face in the war on terrorism and the means by which we can protect ourselves from attack without abandoning our constitutional traditions and principles.

NOTES

1. The UCMJ is Title 10 of the United States Code, which is available at findlaw.com. The Manual for Courts Martial is available at the website of the Institute for Military Justice at www.apd.army.mil/pdffiles/mcm.pdf.

2. *Military Order of Nov. 13, 2001: Detention, Treatment, and Trial of Certain Non-Citizens in the War Against Terrorism,* 3 C.F. R. 918, available at www.whitehouse .gov/news/releases/2001/11/20011113-27.html.

3. See Military Commission Order, Aug. 31, 2005, 6 D (5) (b), available at www .defenselink.mil/news/Sep2005/d20050902order.pdf. This order was the last of a series of orders that are available at www.defenselink.mil/news/Aug2004/commissions _orders.html.

4. For a more comprehensive discussion of the early history of military commissions, see Louis Fisher, *Military Tribunals & Presidential Power: American Revolution to the War on Terrorism* (Lawrence: University of Kansas Press, 2005), chapters 1–3.

5. Mark E. Neely, *The Fate of Liberty: Abraham Lincoln and Civil Liberties* (New York: Oxford University Press, 1991), p. 168–69.

6. Government Court Martial Order No. 707, reprinted in H.R. Doc. No. 314, at 785.

7. *Ex Parte Milligan,* 71 U.S. 2 (1866).

8. Fisher, *Military Tribunal & Presidential Power,* pp. 65–70; William H. Rehnquist, *All the Laws But One: Civil Liberties in Wartime* (New York: Alfred A. Knopf, 1998), chapters 11–13. The quotes from Judge Boyton's 1868 opinion are on pp. 167–168. Over a hundred years later, Mudd's descendants tried to clear his name, but ultimately a federal district court concluded that the military had jurisdiction to try him for violations of the laws of war. See *Mudd v. Caldera,* 134 F.Supp.2d 138 (D.D.C. 2001).

9. Ibid., chapter 5.

10. See generally, *Ex Parte Quirin,* 317 U.S. 1 (1942). During World War II, the political and military authorities of the Territory of Hawaii also declared martial law, suspended the writ of habeas corpus, and established military courts to try all of-

fenses, including those committed by civilians. Since these courts tried regular criminal offenses, like embezzlement and murder, they were not the type of law-of-war commissions that the Supreme Court upheld in *Quirin*. The Supreme Court eventually reviewed the legality of the Hawaiian military tribunals in *Duncan v. Kahanamoku*, 327 U.S. 304 (1946), holding that the Organic Act of Hawaii, which Congress had enacted in 1900, did not authorize them. The Court refused to believe that Congress would permit such powers to be delegated to the military and rejected the notion that the residents of Hawaii had fewer constitutional rights than the residents of the forty-eight states. See Fisher, *Military Tribunals & Presidential Power*, pp. 130–39.

11. *In re Yamashita*, 327 U.S. 1 (1946). Also see Fisher, *Military Tribunals and Presidential Power*, pp. 143–50. There were numerous allied military commissions in the Far East that tried top Japanese military commanders and politicians. In *Hirota v. MacArthur*, 338 U.S. 197, the Supreme Court held that U.S. civilian courts had no jurisdiction to review the lawfulness of these tribunals because they were not created by the United States, but by the Allied Powers.

12. See 10 U.S.C. 821.

13. See 10 U.S.C. 836.

14. For example, see Eric Mshmitt and Kate Zernike, "U.S. Charges an Australian with Fighting for Taliban," *The New York Times*, June 11, 2004, available at http://nytimes.com.

15. Military Commission Order No. 1, Provision 6. B. (3), August 31, 2005 version of this order available at www.defenselink.mil/news/Sep2005/d20050902order.pdf.

16. *Hamdan v. Rumsfeld*, 344 F. Supp. 2d 152, 158-166 (D.C.D. 2004).

17. Id. at 166–73.

18. *Hamdan v. Rumsfeld*, 415 F.3d 33 (D.C. Cir. 2005). Judge Williams concurred in all aspects of the majority opinion except the conclusion that Common Article 3 did not apply to the conflict with al Qaeda. In William's opinion, the phrase "not of an international character" in Common Article 3 meant any conflict that was not between nations, which would include the conflict with al Qaeda, despite the fact it is being fought around the world. However, even if Common Article 3 was applicable, that did not change the fact that all provisions of the Geneva Conventions were not judicially enforceable. Accordingly, enforcing Common Article 3 was the responsibility of the political branches.

19. Stephen Gillers, David J. Luban, and Steven Lubet, "Improper Advances: Talking Dream Jobs with the Judge out of Court," *Slate Magazine*, August 17, 2005, available at www.slate.com/id/2124603/.

20. See James Risen and Eric Lichtblau, "Bush Lets U.S. Spy on Callers Without Courts," *The New York Times*, December 16, 2005, available at http://nytimes.com.

21. Detainee Treatment Act of 2005, Sections 1002 and 1003, available at http://jurist.law.pitt.edu/gazette/2005/12/detainee-treatment-act-of-2005-white.php.

22. President's Statement on Signing of H.R. 2863, the "Department of Defense, Emergency Supplemental Appropriations to Address Hurricanes in the Gulf of Mexico, and Pandemic Influenza Act, 2006," December 30, 2005, available at www.whitehouse.gov/news/releases/2005/12/20051230-8.html. The DTA was included in this appropriations bill.

23. Charlie Savage, "3 GOP Senators Blast Bush bid to Bypass Torture Ban," *The Boston Globe*, January 5, 2006.

24. Tim Golden, "Tough U.S. Steps in Hunger Strike at Camp in Cuba," *The New York Times*, February 9, 2006.

25. Corine Hegland, "Detained and Dangerous?" *National Journal*, February 4, 2006.

26. Drew Brown, "FBI Memos Reveal Allegations of Abusive Interrogation Techniques," Knight/Ridder Tribune News Service, February 23, 2006, available through LexisNexis.

27. Memorandum for Inspector General, Department of the Navy from Alberto J. Moro, Office of General Counsel, June 18, 2004, available at www.newyorker.com /images/pdfs/moramemo.pdf. Jane Meyer first reported the Mora memo in February. See her "The Memo: How an Internal Effort to Ban the Abuse and Torture of Detainees was Thwarted," *The New Yorker,* February 27, 2007.

28. Interview of the president by Sabine Christiansen of ARD German television, May 4, 2006, available at www.whitehouse.gov/news/releases/2006/05/print /20060507-3.html.

29. "President Bush and Prime Minister Rasmussen of Denmark Participate in Joint Press Availability," June 9, 2006, available at www.whitehouse.gov/news/releases /2006/06/20060609-2.html. Later that month, at a press conference, Bush again expressed a willingness to try the GBNB detainees in civilian courts. See "President Bush Participates in Press Availability at 2006 U.S.-EU Summit," June 21, 2006, available at www.whitehouse.gov/news/releases/2006/06/20060621-6.html.

30. Charlie Savage, "Criticism of Guantanamo Rises; Pentagon IDs 3 who Killed Selves," *The Boston Globe*, June 12, 2006.

31. Press conference of the president, June 14, 2006, available at www.whitehouse .gov/news/releases/2006/06/20060614.html.

32. 18 U.S.C. 2441.

33. The jurisdiction-stripping provisions are found in Section 5. The entire bill is available at www.law.georgetown.edu/faculty/nkk/documents/MilitaryCommissions .pdf.

34. See Jim Rutenberg and Sheryl Gay Stolberg, "Bush Says G.O.P. Rebels are Putting Nation at Risk," *The New York Times*, September 16, 2006, available at nytimes.com and R. Jeffrey Smith, "Behind the Debate, Controversial CIA Techniques," *Washington Post*, September 16, 2006, available at www.washingtonpost.com.

35. Ibid., 5(a). Section 6(a)(3) of the MCA also recognized the President's authority to interpret the Geneva Conventions and "to promulgate higher standards and administrative regulations for violations of treaty obligations which are not grave breaches of the Geneva Convention." Pursuant to this section of the MCA, President Bush issued an Executive Order on July 20, 2007 claiming that the US was in full compliance with CA3 if it avoided torture, various criminal acts, "cruel, inhuman, or degrading treatment," and "willful and outrageous acts of personal abuse done for the purpose of humiliating or degrading the individual in a manner so serious that any reasonable person, considering the circumstances, would deem the acts to be beyond the bounds of human decency" (Section 3(b)(i)(E)). Accordingly, "outrages upon personal

dignity" that were not beyond the "bounds of human decency" or, for that matter, that were engaged in for the purpose of obtaining information from detainees, rather than for the purpose of degrading them, arguably were neither violations of international law nor war crimes. See "Executive Order: Interpretaion of the Geneva Conventions Common Article 3 as Applied to a Program of Detention and Interrogation Operated by the Central Intelligence Agency," July 20, 2007, available at http://www.whitehouse .gov/news/releases/2007/07/20070720-4.html. It is unclear whether the Executive Order is consistent with the spirit of the MCA.

36. Ibid., 3, IV, 949d, (f).

37. Ibid., 3, III, 948r, (c) and (d).

38. Ibid., 3, IV, 949a, (b)(2)(E).

39. Ibid., 7(a)(e)(1).

40. Ibid., 7(b).

41. Ibid., 3, 948a, (1) (i) and (ii).

42. Ibid., 7(a)(2).

43. CBA News Poll, "Poll: Bush Approval Rating at New Low," January 22, 2007, available at www.cbsnews.com/stories/2007/01/22/opinion/polls/main2384943.shtml

44. *Hamdan v. Rumsfeld*, 464 F. Supp. 2d 9 (2006).

45. 476 F.3d 981 (D.C. Cir. February 20, 2007). *Al Odah v. United States was* the companion case argued before the Supreme Court with *Rasul v. Bush*, the case discussed in Chapter 2. In *Rasul*, the Supreme Court ruled that the federal judiciary had jurisdiction to consider petitions for writs of habeas corpus from GBNB detainees based, at a minimum, on the federal habeas statute. In *Boumediene*, the D.C. Circuit held that the MCA had withdrawn this form of statutory jurisdiction and that the detainees had no constitutionally-rooted right to habeas relief.

46. 127 S. Ct. 1478 (2007).

47. (No. 06-1197). A companion case is *Parhat v. Gates* (06-1397).

48. *United States v. Hamdan,* Decision and Motion, June 4, 2007, available at http:// nimj.com/display.aspx?base=MilitaryCommissions&ID=183. On the same day, a different military judge, Colonel Peter E. Brownback, III, dismissed another military-commission case on nearly identical grounds to those relied on by Allred. See *United States v. Khadr*, Order on Jurisdiction, June 4, 2007, available at http://nimj.com/display .aspx?base=MilitaryCommissions&ID=181.

49. "Reply to Opposition to Petition for Rehearing," in *Al Odah v. United States*, June 22, 2007, p. 4, available at http://www.scotusblog.com/movabletype/archives /Al%20Odah%20reply%206-22-07.pdf. See also Lyle Denniston, "Final Push for Rehearing for Detainees," SCOTUSBLOG, June 22, 2007, available at http://www.sco-tusblog.com/movabletype/archives/2007/06/final_push_for.html and William Glaberson, "Unlikely Adversary Arises to Criticize Detainee Hearings," *The New York Times*, July 23, 2007, available at nytimes.com.

50. *Boumediene v. Bush*, 2007 U.S. Lexis 8757; 75 U.S.L.W. 3707 (2007).

51. *Bismullah v. Gates,* 2007 U. S. App. 17255, 19. The D.C. Circuit did except "certain highly sensitive information" from the rule that "all reasonably available information" must be disclosed to attorneys for the GBNB detainees.

Index

313

About the Author

H. L. Pohlman is the A. Lee Fritschler Professor of Public Policy. Previously he was a Distinguished Fulbright Lecturer in the United Kingdom, a Judicial Fellow at the Supreme Court of the United States, a Reporter of an Ad Hoc Committee of the Judicial Conference of the United States, and a director of the K. Robert Nilsson Center for European Studies in Bologna, Italy. He has received a number of awards, grants, and fellowships. He has published widely in the fields of legal theory and American constitutional law.